$5-

THE FBI STORY

THE FBI STORY

A Report to the People

By Don Whitehead

Foreword by J. Edgar Hoover

 RANDOM HOUSE · NEW YORK

TO MY WIFE

MARIE

Preface

MORE than two years ago I set out to find the answers to questions which intrigued me as a newspaperman. I wanted to know how it was that J. Edgar Hoover had survived as Director of the FBI for thirty years in a city of politics where the casualty rate runs high among Bureau heads. I wanted to know why and how the FBI operates as it does. And I wanted to know whether there was any basis of truth to insinuations I had heard that the FBI represented a shadowy menace to civil rights.

In short, I wanted to learn the facts so that I could report the inside story of the FBI—a story which, curiously enough, had never been told in its entirety.

When Director Hoover agreed to permit a look behind the scenes, a tremendous amount of unpublished material was made available to me. In addition to this information, I had gathered almost everything of any importance which already had been published. I found, too, that the FBI was willing at all times—within the bounds of national security and protecting individuals from needless embarrassment—to provide the answers to any questions which were asked.

As I dug into the record, a story began to emerge which was far more exciting to me and far bigger in scope than I had realized it would be. The "mystery" of the FBI was no longer a mystery. The shadows disappeared. I found in the FBI story a stirring American adventure of pioneering on the frontiers of law enforcement and national security.

But the most important thing of all in this pioneering was the struggle to achieve incorruptible enforcement of the law by professionals trained to protect civil rights.

In telling this story, I have selected the case histories and the information which I believe give a clear picture of the FBI's activities and the motives of the men who run the organization.

The selection of material has been difficult because there was so much from which to choose. A number of important cases had to be pushed aside reluctantly and many important activities of the Bureau had to be touched on lightly because of space limitations.

However, I hope that in this record the reader will be able to arrive at a just judgment of the FBI and the work it is doing. As for myself, I have found satisfactory answers to the questions which were in my own mind more than two years ago.

DW

Arlington, Va., September 8, 1956

Contents

The New FBI

Roosevelt and the FBI

World War II

War's Aftermath

The Cold War

A Look at the Record

List of United States Attorneys General and Heads of the Federal Bureau of Investigation

ATTORNEYS GENERAL

Charles J. Bonaparte	1906–1909
George W. Wickersham	1909–1913
James C. McReynolds	1913–1914
Thomas W. Gregory	1914–1919
A. Mitchell Palmer	1919–1921
Harry M. Daugherty	1921–1924
Harlan F. Stone	1924–1925
John G. Sargent	1925–1929
William D. Mitchell	1929–1933
Homer S. Cummings	1933–1939
Frank Murphy	1939–1940
Robert H. Jackson	1940–1941
Francis Biddle	1941–1945
Tom C. Clark	1945–1949
J. Howard McGrath	1949–1952
James P. McGranery	1952–1953
Herbert Brownell, Jr.	1953–

HEADS OF THE FEDERAL BUREAU OF INVESTIGATION

Stanley W. Finch	1908–1912
A. Bruce Bielaski	1912–1919
William J. Flynn	1919–1921
William J. Burns	1921–1924
J. Edgar Hoover	1924–

Foreword

THE FBI is a closely knit, cooperative organization of more than 14,000 men and women. It is an organization which functions as a team. I like to speak of it as a "we organization." Each member of its staff has clearly defined duties and personal and individual responsibility for the performance of those duties. No one case is solved through the efforts of any one person. Our achievements have come through the combined efforts of the organization.

No one person has built the FBI to the organization it is today. It was built by the loyal, sacrificial efforts of the thousands of men and women who have served in its ranks over the years. I tell my associates repeatedly that one man did not build the reputation of the FBI —but one man can pull it down.

To carry the credentials of the FBI is a trust. It always has been and it must remain so through all the years to come. The FBI must always be conscious of its trust. A part of that trust is confidence. Without confidence we cannot possibly fulfill our responsibilities.

One of the greatest satisfactions I have is the manner in which law-abiding people extend their cooperation to our agents.

The fact that some 7,000 young people, their parents and other visitors call at our headquarters each week throughout the year is a source of pride to us; but also our visitors are a constant reminder that we must live up to their confidence and expectations.

When an agent arrests a wrongdoer or uncovers crookedness, corruption or dishonesty, it is not a pleasant experience. It's a duty that must be done. When acts of treason and subversion come to our attention we cannot be impassive—we are outraged as every American should be outraged. We feel, too, the keen disappointments that come from indifference and an utter lack of consciousness of the destructive forces which manifest themselves from time to time. In short, the FBI is a very human organization. It is never very far from the crossroads of America, either spiritually or physically. Our agents are always as close to you, the reader, as your telephone. You can depend on them day or night, week end or holiday, should emergencies arise.

At this point, I wish to state emphatically that the FBI is not and never can be a national police organization as long as its development continues to be on cooperative lines. The most lasting contributions made by the FBI have been those which encourage cooperation with local, county and state law enforcement agencies. Through the FBI National Academy, which has now been in operation for over twenty-one years, more than 3,200 select representatives of the country's law enforcement agencies have been graduated. Today, more than a fourth of the graduates head their law enforcement agencies. Better police training and administration, with a growing recognition of civil rights, have been the result. There is never any doubt within the FBI that the home-town law enforcement agency must ever be in the forefront of crime control.

An organization such as the FBI attains its highest degree of effectiveness when it is tightly knit, tightly controlled and highly mobile and hard-hitting. For my part, I have never wanted to see the FBI expanded to the point where it would be unwieldy and decentralized. I will welcome the day when conditions make it possible not to have added duties assigned to us.

We are not a policy-making organization. The FBI is a service organization which is subordinate to the Department of Justice. And that is as it should be. The FBI should never be permitted to become an independent agency, operating without the checks and controls under which it now operates.

The FBI is an action agency in securing facts, apprehending violators of federal laws within its jurisdiction, and servicing law enforcement agencies. Once we gather the facts, apprehend the violator and provide our services to other agencies, our duty is fulfilled. We submit the results of our investigations to other officials of government. We neither evaluate the results of our investigations nor make recommendations. We do not inject ourselves into the administrative operations of other agencies of government by saying who is loyal and who is not loyal or who is a security risk or who is suitable for service in the federal government. We merely report the facts.

Another strength of the FBI arises from the fact that our organization is a career service, in which appointments and promotions are made on the basis of ability, merit and competence. Each of the eleven attorneys general under whom I have served as director has been unswerving in his support of the Bureau as a career service. And each has supported the Bureau against any move to inject the element of political favoritism into its operation.

The policy of making promotions from within the Bureau, which I established in 1924 under the late Chief Justice Harlan Fiske Stone, when he was Attorney General, has proven its value. Every person serving today in an executive or supervisory capacity in the field or in

Washington has come up the line from the staff; it is to be hoped that it will always be so.

It is not easy to develop good executives. And the fine executives who have been developed within the FBI have developed through experience and having added responsibilities placed upon them as they demonstrate their capabilities. The energy and devotion they have given the Bureau could not be bought. Each could double and triple his salary in private industry. If money alone were the prime consideration in these men's lives, then I would not have the caliber of executive ability around me that I do.

From its earliest days the FBI has reflected the tempo of the times. Its work when carefully observed is like a barometer foretelling the stormy and bright days which lie immediately ahead.

On the crime front, we should soon be emerging from the moral chaos and breakdown which follow all wars. There are hopeful signs. There is a greater public awareness of the problem of crime than ever before. An outraged public opinion is forcing a more dutiful discharge of parental responsibility. Community resources are being mobilized and there is a growing recognition that law and order can become a reality if there is a determination to make it a reality.

The acts of the subversive, particularly the "dyed-in-the-wool" Communist, call for increased vigilance. The security of our country has suffered because too many of our people were "hoodwinked" by the propaganda which claimed that the Communist Party was a political party like the Democratic or Republican Party. Likewise, too many of our people have fallen for the line that spies, subversives, agents of foreign governments and Communists who have been convicted and sent to prison are "political prisoners." "Political prisoners" do not exist in the United States. Those who are prisoners violated the laws of the United States, were indicted by federal grand juries and convicted in federal courts. I do not think they deserve the special treatment, with special rights and privileges, which is sought for them by their sympathizers.

In the United States, the subversive is a lawbreaker when he violates the law of the land, not because he disagrees with the party in power. And anyone who violates the law commits a criminal act even if the motives of the lawbreaker are self-servingly claimed to be political. If we ever permit political motives to justify lawbreaking, we shall develop political tyrannies in this country as similar instances have developed tyrannies in other countries.

For more than thirty years, as the FBI's director, I have watched the story of the Bureau being reported on a day-to-day basis by the press, radio and, now, television. Our organization has been scrutinized by committees of Congress, by the Budget Bureau and by the courts. In magazine articles and books, many phases of the Bureau's work have been recorded. Some of those accounts were correct, others were distorted and some were figments of the imagination.

Through these past years, no one could find in a single volume the real story recounting the FBI's birth, development and struggles. Frankly, the fact that this information was not available in book form to the public has been the subject of frequent inquiry from people interested in learning about the FBI. It seemed to me that far too many people had no real understanding of the FBI's work. It was too much of a "mystery." It was a mystery because of its scattered record occasioned by its wide-spread operations, and to learn of its many activities would require research which few people have time to conduct.

In the summer of 1955, Don Whitehead revived a request he had previously made to do a book which would span the entire history of the Bureau. Mr. Whitehead was well known on the Washington scene. He had won two Pulitzer Prizes for distinguished reporting on domestic and foreign affairs. He was generally regarded as one of the top war correspondents in World War II and in the Korean war. He had written stories on the Bureau and we had complete confidence in his integrity, ability and objectivity.

To do the job properly, the author had to have access to the record, within the bounds of security and policy considerations. There will always be areas of the Bureau's work wherein security considerations, common decency and operating policy do not permit disclosures. Mr. Whitehead had to have the facts if there was to be a worth-while objective result, and full facts were given him so long as they did not violate security.

The author was free to ask questions and we felt it was our duty to provide him with full facts so that he could form his own independent judgment on our policies, procedures and performance. In extending our cooperation to the author it was with the full approval of the Attorney General of the United States, the Honorable Herbert Brownell, Jr.

This volume, then, is Mr. Whitehead's report. He has selected the material which has been used, and the facts reported are supported by the Bureau's record. My one regret has been that the author did not have the space to call the full roll of the loyal men and women who have contributed so much to the achievements of the FBI. There have been many of them.

In recent years, a campaign of falsehood and vilification has been directed against the FBI by some ignorant and some subversive elements. In the world-wide struggle of free peoples, the truth is still one of our most potent weapons. And the record of the FBI speaks for it-self. It is the best answer to the falsehoods, half-truths and rumors spread by Communists, their stooges and defenders.

The FBI story has been a happy and worth-while experience. In retrospect, its achievements have been possible because the American people wanted it that way. The three branches of government, the legislative, the judiciary and the executive, have given it a measure of support which is heart-warming and which insures its future service to all the people.

My associates and I are deeply grateful for the painstaking care of the author, Don Whitehead, in his accurate portrayal of the record of the FBI, and for the interest of Mr. Bennett Cerf in its publication.

J. Edgar Hoover

September 8, 1956.

The FBI

1: *The FBI in Action*

A COLORADO beet farmer had milked the cows and finished up his chores for the day. He closed the barn door and turned toward the house, where supper was waiting. He noticed the blinking lights of United Air Lines Flight Number 629, eleven minutes out of Denver and heading for Portland, Oregon, with thirty-nine passengers and five crew members. The dark shadow up there was death hurtling through the heavens and winking at those some 5,700 feet below.

Then the shadow was ripped apart by a terrible explosion. A ball of fire hung in the sky and streamers of flaming gasoline trailed down the curtain of night. A flare ignited and drifted down to illumine the scene with ghostly light. The wreckage of the shattered DC-6B and the bodies of those aboard were strewn over two square miles. It was 7:03 P.M., November 1, 1955. The farmer standing in his barnyard had witnessed one of the most shocking mass murders in the annals of American crime.

When news of the tragic crash reached Denver and was flashed across the nation, only one man knew that murder had been done that night. Only one man knew that a time bomb had been ticking in a battered old suitcase when it was stowed aboard the plane. That man was sullen-eyed, husky (six feet, one inch, a hundred and ninety pounds) Jack Gilbert Graham, aged twenty-three, who had once told a neighbor, "I'd do anything for money."

Jack Graham had driven his mother, Mrs. Daisie King, to the Denver airport to put her aboard Flight 629, the beginning of a long-planned journey to visit a daughter in Alaska. He had carried her brief case, a small traveling case and her battered old suitcase from the automobile to the ticket counter to be weighed. The luggage was thirty-seven pounds over the sixty-six-pound limit.

An airline ticket agent suggested to Mrs. King that she might save $27 by lightening her luggage and mailing part of her clothing. She still had time to open the bags and take out anything she wished.

Mrs. King turned to her son. "Do you think I'll need all this?"

"Yes, Mother," he said. "I'm sure you will need it."

Mrs. King hesitated a moment and then shrugged. While she was paying the overweight charge, her son fumbled with a machine which dispensed life insurance policies—$6,250 worth for each quarter dropped into the coin slot. His fumbling ruined one policy for $18,750 and another for $43,750 before he steadied himself.

Then he filled out two policies for $37,500 each, writing his own name as beneficiary. On two others, for $6,250 each, he wrote the names of an aunt in Missouri and a half-sister in Alaska as beneficiaries. Mrs. King signed three of the policies but for some reason Jack didn't get her signature on one for $37,500. Perhaps the ticking of the time bomb was beginning to pound in his brain and he was becoming panicky. His mother's plane was behind schedule and time was running out.

Other passengers were buying insurance heavily that evening. Perhaps there was some dark, subconscious premonition of death which none of them recognized. At any rate, Flight 629 became one of the most heavily insured flights ever to leave Denver. Eighteen of the passengers were insured by flight policies totaling $752,200 and not including whatever personal life insurance they carried.

Flight 629 arrived eleven minutes late. Mrs. King gave good-by kisses to her son and his wife, Gloria, and their twenty-two-month-old son, Allen. She hurried aboard the plane.

For Jack Graham, there were twelve more agonizing minutes while the plane sat waiting for a tardy passenger. At last the door of the plane slammed behind the late passenger, and at 6:52 P.M. the big ship roared from the runway.

The Grahams went into the airport coffee shop for a bite to eat. Jack suddenly became ill and went into a rest room to vomit. He seemed to feel better when he came out.

The Grahams heard the rumor of a plane crash as they were leaving the airport to return home. Gloria said later, "We finally heard his mother's name on the radio and Jack just collapsed completely."

Roy Moore, Assistant Special Agent in Charge in the Denver FBI office, was sitting at home watching television when news of the disaster was announced about 7:25 P.M. As usual in such tragedies, the United Air Lines (UAL) was advised immediately that the FBI was ready to help in identifying the victims and in establishing the cause of the crash if help were needed. Then Moore notified FBI Headquarters in Washington.

Later that evening, the UAL flight surgeon asked the FBI's aid in identifying the bodies, and the Civil Aeronautics Board (CAB), which has the responsibility for investigating the cause of plane crashes, requested that an FBI Laboratory expert be sent to the crash scene to help examine the wreckage. These agents arrived in Denver from Washington the next day.

The Colorado crash inquiry was a remarkable study in the vast strides made in the FBI's investigative techniques, efficiency and cooperative effort from the day in 1924 when J. Edgar Hoover took over command of an inept and politics-riddled Bureau. This is how a murderer was tracked down by modern, scientific methods and the cooperation of government agencies, aviation engineers and private citizens.

The bodies of the crash victims were taken to a temporary morgue set up in the National Guard Armory at Greeley, Colorado, and nine of them were quickly identified by relatives and friends or by their personal effects. The FBI agents fingerprinted the other thirty-five and were able to identify twenty-one of them from prints which were on file in the FBI Identification Division.

A husband and wife from Canada were identified by the fingerprints taken when they applied for U. S. citizenship in 1954. Five passengers were identified by fingerprints taken during their service in the armed forces. One victim had had his fingerprints filed for personal identification. Others were found to have been fingerprinted as government workers or as employees in wartime defense plants.

The FBI Laboratory agent joined the team of investigators from the United Air Lines, the Douglas Aircraft Company and the Civil Aeronautics Board. Their job was to discover, if possible, whether the crash came about because of a mechanical failure, human error or sabotage. And sabotage was the least likely cause.

First, a surveyor marked a line through the center of the crash area in the direction of the plane's flight. At 1,000-foot intervals, the base line was bisected by 1,000-foot lines to form a grid of squares which were numbered. Teams of men went over the grid picking up pieces of metal, luggage and anything else that came from the ship. Each piece was marked and its location on the grid squares carefully measured in relation to the other pieces.

The tail assembly was virtually intact and looked as though it had been sliced from the plane with a huge knife. The tail was a mile and a half from the point where the nose of the plane and engines had torn into the earth.

These parts were taken to a Denver warehouse and placed on a scaled-down grid in the relative spots at which they had been found at the crash scene. The pieces were then carefully wired to a wooden mock-up of the DC-6B. Slowly the fuselage was reassembled. The big ship's shell became reasonably complete—except at one point. No pieces could be found to fit a jagged hole on the right side of the plane near the tail. This was the location of Number 4 cargo pit.

Engineers found that the metal at this point had been bent outward by some force more violent than a crash. They found shattered pieces of fuselage, clean on one side but burned on the other and discolored by a gray-and-white substance. Bits of metal had been driven through the soles and heels of shoes. Brass fittings from a suitcase had been driven deep into a stainless-steel container. No ordinary crash could hurl slugs of metal with such terrific force.

Experts of the FBI, CAB, Douglas Aircraft Company and United Air Lines added up the evidence. It was clear that a violent explosion had occurred in cargo pit Number 4. There were no gasoline lines or tanks in this part of the plane, therefore the tragedy had been caused either by an accidental explosion of illegal cargo or by deliberate sabotage.

On November 7, the CAB asked the FBI to begin a sabotage investigation. Within twenty-four hours some one hundred agents in twenty cities were digging into the backgrounds of the plane's crew and passengers seeking a motive for murder, and checking manifests of air freight to determine whether there had been any illegal shipments of materials which might have exploded accidentally.

Information poured into the FBI office at Denver about the lives and backgrounds of the passengers and the cargo that was carried. There was no evidence of any illegal shipments. Agents studied the mass of information seeking someone—a relative, a friend, a business enemy—who might have had a motive for murder and who could have caused the crash.

The face of Jack Graham began to emerge in dim outline.

The first small suspicion of Graham came when agents were unable to find Mrs. Daisie King's luggage except for a piece here and there. They did find a handbag which Mrs. King had carried aboard the plane. And in the personal effects in this bag was a 1951 newspaper clipping which said Graham was being hunted by police for forgery.

Gradually the FBI began to center its attention on Graham while other possible suspects were eliminated one by one.

Jack Graham had been born in Denver in 1932. His father, Mrs. King's second husband, died when he was almost five years old. The mother, left penniless, farmed Jack out to an orphanage for six years. But they were reunited in 1943, when the mother married a well-to-do rancher, John Earl King.

Young Graham had better-than-average grades in school, but he was a restless, brooding boy with a vile temper. He left home at sixteen and joined the Coast Guard by lying about his age. He was in the Coast Guard for nine months, during which he was AWOL for sixty-three days. He was discharged as a minor.

As they dug into his past, agents saw in Graham's background the familiar pattern of a juvenile delinquent from a broken home who defied discipline and whose excesses were forgiven by a too-indulgent mother. In the forgery case, Jack had gone to work for a Denver manufacturer in 1951 as a payroll clerk. His $200-a-month wage wasn't enough. Jack stole some of the company's checks, forged the name of a company official and managed to cash $4,200 worth of them. He bought a flashy $2,000 convertible and put the dust of Denver behind him in a five-state spree.

In Lubbock, Texas, young Graham was arrested for bootlegging but only after he had crashed his car through a police roadblock in a hail of bullets. He served sixty days in the county jail and was released to Denver authorities to answer the forgery charges. Daisie King, like most mothers, couldn't bear to see her son in jail. She arranged to pay $2,500 of the stolen $4,200 and to have her son put on probation with the understanding he would repay the balance. For a time it appeared that Jack Graham was going straight. He worked hard. In 1953 he married Gloria Elson, a Denver girl, and they had two children.

When Mrs. King's third husband died in 1954, he left her in good financial condition. She invested $35,000 in a drive-in restaurant in West Denver and Jack managed it. She also bought a home for her son and his family and, while in Denver, lived with them. When Jack wasn't busy at the restaurant, he worked in a Hertz Drive-Ur-Self garage. Gradually he reduced the forgery debt to $105.34. Outwardly, at least, it appeared he had become a responsible citizen.

But in their investigations, FBI agents heard reports that Graham had stalled a pick-up truck in front of a railroad train to collect insurance. There had been a gas explosion in the restaurant, too, which had caused $1,200 damage and looked like another deliberate effort to collect insurance. And while Daisie King indulged her son, the two of them sometimes fought "like cats and dogs" over his management of the drive-in.

Agents questioned Jack Graham on November 10. They got around to asking about Mrs. King's luggage.

"I don't know what she put in her luggage," Graham said. "Mother liked to pack things herself and she never let anyone help her. I do know she took some shotgun shells and rifle ammunition with her. She was planning on doing some hunting in Alaska."

No, Jack said, he hadn't put anything in the luggage himself.

The young man answered questions readily and with apparent frankness. Next day agents talked to Mrs. Graham, who verified her husband's story that Mrs. King liked to do her own packing. But Gloria said her husband had taken a gift-wrapped package to the basement just before they drove Mrs. King to the airport. The gift, she thought, was a set of drills, files and cutting tools which Jack had bought for his mother to use in her hobby of making costume jewelry and knickknacks from sea shells. She estimated that the package was about eighteen inches long, fourteen inches wide and about three inches deep. She supposed her husband had given the package to his mother just before they drove to the airport.

The agents were intrigued by the story of the Christmas gift. Graham had said nothing about a tool kit. But again it was mentioned by one of Graham's neighbors who had heard Jack talk about it. She told agents, "I heard Jack say he had searched the town to find the kind of kit he wanted, and he had gift-wrapped it and placed it in his mother's luggage as a surprise for her when she reached Alaska."

Only two stores in Denver sold tool kits of the type that could be used for cutting sea shells. A check at the stores disclosed that no one had bought such a kit during October. The flaws in the suspect's story had to be explained.

The second interview with Jack Graham took place when he came with his wife to the FBI office on Sunday afternoon, November 13, to identify fragments of leather believed to be all that was left of Mrs. King's luggage. Gloria stayed for a few minutes and then returned home to the children while Jack retraced with agents the story of his life. He went out with the agents for a late lunch and then returned to answer more questions. He consistently denied knowing anything about a Christmas gift package.

Late in the afternoon, Agent Roy Moore called the FBI Laboratory in Washington to ask about the results of the analysis of the burned pieces of metal found at the crash scene. The report was: "There is positive evidence of a dynamite explosion." The Laboratory had found that the metal showed traces of sodium carbonate, sodium nitrite and sulphur-bearing compounds—the residue left by an explosion of dynamite.

Moore said later, "When I got this laboratory report, I knew we were on the right track."

At 6:40 P.M., Moore walked into the room where Graham was being questioned.

"I want you to know you have certain rights," Moore said. "The door there is open. You can walk out any time you wish. There is a telephone. You can call your wife or an attorney if you wish. You don't have to tell us anything—and if you do it can be used against you in a court of law. There will be no threats and no promises made while we talk with you.

"Jack," he said, "we have gone over what you told us. You blew up that plane to kill your mother, didn't you?"

"No, I didn't," Graham protested.

"Then do you mind if we search your home?"

"No, I don't mind."

Graham signed a waiver which gave agents his permission for them to search his home without appealing to a court for a search warrant. Moore dispatched agents to the Graham home, where they began a methodical search.

An agent called in to the office to say: "Mrs. Graham says Jack told her not to tell about the Christmas present. She signed a statement." A bit later the agents found the shotgun shells and ammunition which Graham had claimed his mother had packed in her luggage.

These discrepancies in his story were ticked off by the agents. "What about it?" the youth was asked.

Graham finally admitted that he had bought a present for his mother, an X-Acto tool set, from "some guy" unknown to him. He said he paid $10 for it and two of his buddies over at the Hertz garage were there at the time. He drew a picture of the box and the tools in it and said he had slipped the box into his mother's suitcase. He had bound it with Scotch tape and put what was left of the tape in the glove compartment of his car.

Agents at the Graham house found no Scotch tape in the car, but they did find a small roll of wire in one of his shirt pockets, wire of the type used for detonating dynamite.

At 10:15 P.M. the searchers found a $37,500 insurance policy signed by Daisie King payable to Jack. The policy was hidden in a cedar chest in Jack's bedroom. This was the first time the FBI knew young Graham had had a policy on his mother's life in that amount. The insurance companies had provided copies of the insurance bought by passengers on Flight 629—but somehow the policies signed by Mrs.

King had been overlooked by the company and hadn't reached the FBI with the other policies.

The agents found something else of interest, too—stockings and a cosmetic bag, and some gifts which Mrs. King had intended for her daughter in Alaska, things she might have been expected to take with her.

"Why didn't your mother take these things with her?" Graham was asked.

"I told her not to take them because her baggage was overweight," he replied.

At 12:01 A.M., agents reported that the two men who worked at the Hertz garage couldn't recall Graham's buying a tool kit. If anybody had come into the garage they were sure they would have seen him. Graham was confronted with this report and with the report that the FBI Laboratory tests proved the crash was caused by a dynamite explosion.

At 12:05 A.M., Graham asked, "Can I have a glass of water?"

An agent handed him the water and he took a long, gulping drink.

He looked around sullenly and then said: "Okay, where do you want me to start?"

"Wherever you want to."

"Well, it all started about six months ago. Mother was raising hell because the drive-in wasn't making any money . . ."

Without a trace of emotion he told of making the time bomb with twenty-five sticks of dynamite, two electric primer caps, a timer and a six-volt battery. He had worked at an electric shop for ten days at $1.50 an hour to learn more about electricity before buying the dynamite and timer. He had taken some things out of his mother's suitcase and slipped the bomb in their places.

Graham talked for twenty minutes and then a stenographer was called in to take his confession.

At 1:42 A.M., a doctor arrived. Graham was given a thorough physical examination so there would be medical evidence that he had not been forced to confess by third-degree methods, and so there could be medical testimony that he was in sound mental condition and capable of freely and voluntarily giving a confession. He told the doctor he had not been mistreated. He signed the confession.

At 3:42 A.M., Jack Graham was arrested for sabotage. Later he was turned over to Colorado state officials to be tried for murder.

Curiously, in this case the confession came first and the evidence of guilt came later. The places where Graham bought the dynamite and the timing device were located and Graham was identified as the purchaser.

While he was in jail awaiting trial, Graham told a guard: "You can send my mail to Canon City [Prison] until next month. After that, you can send it to hell."

During the trial, Graham repudiated his confession although he admitted signing it. The evidence enmeshed him so tightly, however, that the jury required only seventy-two minutes in which to decide that he was guilty of murder in the first degree. His case was appealed to the Colorado Supreme Court on August 8, 1956.

The case of Jack Graham is another baffling crime solved by the FBI. But it is more than that. It is also a window that provides a glimpse into the progress made by the FBI toward the goal of scientific law enforcement by professionals trained to serve justice—and yet preserve civil liberties in carrying out their tasks.

The FBI is almost half a century old. Its name is known to millions as a symbol of integrity and efficiency. But it remains a mystery organization to a great many Americans even though its activities are interwoven with the protection of civil rights and the security of the nation.

Few know how the FBI operates. Few realize that in the protection of the country the FBI also maintains a rigid around-the-clock system of checks and controls over its own agents and their activities. Hoover can and does pick up his telephone and within a matter of minutes learn where an agent is at any given time, the case on which he is working and the progress being made.

The control system works in this fashion. The special agents in charge of the FBI's fifty-two field divisions are considered to be Hoover's personal representatives. They are responsible directly to him for the work within the geographic area of their assignments. Each special agent in charge has an assistant—a position regarded as a training ground for the development of future FBI executives.

FBI offices, such as in New York, Chicago and Los Angeles, have field supervisors who direct the work of agents and are responsible to the special agent in charge and his assistant. The field offices are located as near the geographic centers of the work load as possible. In the smaller cities surrounding the field offices, the FBI has stationed some 1,200 resident agents who are responsible for the work in given subsections of the division. This distribution of agents in strategic centers gives the FBI a well-deployed force which can move quickly to any given place, saving time and money.

At the main headquarters in Washington, the operation is highly integrated and centralized. For example, all bank robbery reports come to one desk, where supervisors have the responsibility for tying together the investigative efforts in two, three or perhaps a half-dozen cities. Perhaps the thieves' operating method in robbing a Chicago bank is recognized by a supervisor as the identical method used a few days earlier in Los Angeles. There may be some piece of information known at Headquarters which ties a suspect to a crime. This same operating procedure is used in espionage cases to tie together widely separated operations and to coordinate the agents' work.

The agents are required to telephone their home office at intervals throughout the day and report their movements. Periodic reports are made on the progress of each investigation, and the progress is reflected on the agents' assignment cards.

Through more than thirty years, Hoover has insisted on discipline in the ranks of the FBI. This discipline is sternest, of course, in the special agent force of some 6,200 men. But it is also maintained among the other 8,000 employees. Obedience to official regulations is demanded to a degree that is astonishing to an outsider.

The reason for this obedience is always clear to anyone who knows anything of the undisciplined operations which almost destroyed the Bureau in the pre-Hoover days.

Over and over, Hoover has stressed the point that there must never be a scandal in the operations of the FBI. "One man didn't build the FBI," he says, "but one man can tear it down."

The life of a special agent isn't an easy one. He knows he may be dismissed summarily from the service if he violates certain rules. For example:

1. He cannot drink intoxicants while on duty. Even off duty excessive use of intoxicants is banned, since the agent is subject to call at any time.

2. He cannot use a government automobile for any purpose except official business.

3. He is forbidden to use brutality or duress in dealing with persons under investigation.

He can be disciplined for a number of other things. Among the "shall nots" are these:

1. He cannot disclose information to any unauthorized person, not even his wife.

2. He cannot accept rewards or gratuities in any form.

3. He cannot fail to pay his taxes or to meet other financial obligations.

4. He must not lose official property issued to him.

And the list goes on and on.

The newly appointed agent begins to learn discipline from the day he reports into Headquarters to begin an intensive training course which lasts for eighteen weeks. The course is divided into two parts. There is the classroom study of investigative techniques, FBI responsibilities under the law and administrative work; and there is the rugged training in self-defense and the use of firearms given at the FBI Academy on the Marine base at Quantico, Virginia.

Each agent, including the scientists and engineers who work in the Laboratory, must know how to take care of himself in a gun battle. He learns the "quick draw," in which a pistol is whipped from a holster with split-second precision in a stance which gives the steadiest position for firing accurately. "Never shoot while running" is an FBI axiom.

He is taught to use his weapons from standing, kneeling, sitting and prone positions, shooting at stationary and moving targets. He learns to shoot with either hand while firing from behind barricades, and how to take cover under fire.

In addition to the pistol, he must learn to handle a thirty-caliber rifle, a repeating shotgun and a submachine gun.

The agent is instructed in jujitsu and other tricks of taking care of himself in a rough-and-tumble fight. The roll of eighteen agents killed in line of duty is a reminder that the battle against criminals is a dangerous one.

The FBI's training system produced such sound results that even prior to World War II the Marine Corps arranged to have agents train the Marines in hand-to-hand defensive and disarming tactics. Lieutenant General Alexander A. Vandegrift, Marine Commandant, advised the FBI during the war: "I can assure you those tactics have been put to good use."

But the FBI traveled a long road to reach this point. It had its beginning in 1908 when President Theodore Roosevelt demanded an investigative agency in his crusade against the "land thieves" in the West and the big-business "trusts" in the East. For many years the agency was known as the Bureau of Investigation. It wasn't named the Federal Bureau of Investigation until 1935 although we shall refer to the Bureau as the FBI prior to that date.

Here, in summary, is how the FBI developed through the years:

1908–1924

In its beginning, the Bureau was a disorganized and loosely directed agency without character or discipline. Washington held little control over the agents in the field. There were no fixed standards of training or personal conduct. Political endorsements carried more weight than experience or character in the selection of agents.

The small and inept force of 219 agents which existed in 1915 failed in its first great mission. It was totally unequipped to deal with the clever espionage and sabotage ring of World War I which was organized by German Ambassador Johann von Bernstorff. Saboteurs were left free to bring about such outrages as the infamous "Black Tom" explosion in New York Harbor, which destroyed the United States' greatest arsenal with a mighty roar heard for more than a hundred miles. They destroyed defense plants with explosives and fired wheat fields in the West.

These were years of violent social unrest, when men preached anarchy, when mysterious bomb explosions spread terror, and when the Communist Party was first formed in America to advocate the overthrow of the government by force and violence. In combating violence, the Bureau's agents were not trained to protect civil liberties in such affairs as the "Palmer Red Raids" of 1919, when alien extremists were rounded up for deportation. Vigilante groups took the law into their hands in many cases.

These also were the years when corruption spread through the country and into the government in Washington. And the time came at last when the Bureau itself was threatened with destruction by the indignant public reaction to dishonesty.

1924–1933

Attorney General Harlan Fiske Stone took the advice of President-to-be Herbert Hoover and named young J. Edgar Hoover (no relation) to do a housecleaning job in the Bureau of Investigation. Hoover's first move was to fix high standards of personal conduct for his agents. Then he began to get rid of the political appointees who couldn't measure up to these standards. They were replaced by young men with training as lawyers and accountants.

Hoover brought the agents under strict supervision. Procedures were set up for checking on their conduct and performance. Uniform operating procedures were adopted. A school was established for training new agents. The FBI became an organization with character and with a firmly fixed purpose—to make law enforcement an honorable profession for trained career men.

1933–1939

The times demanded an aggressive, hard-hitting campaign against gangsters who were running wild across the country in the aftermath of Prohibition. The clean-up job was given to the FBI.

Agents were trained by Marine and Army experts to shoot fast and shoot straight. Congress gave them the authority to carry weapons and to make arrests. A series of crime bills extended the FBI's jurisdiction to deal with kidnapings, bank robberies, extortions and other crimes.

During these years, Hoover and his men emerged as the "G-Men" (the nickname coined by George "Machine Gun" Kelly, short for government men), who couldn't be corrupted by all the millions of gangland. These were the slam-bang, rough-and-tough years of blazing gun battles with the John Dillinger gang, the Barker-Karpis gang and other hoodlum combinations who were terrorizing the Middle West.

The FBI was hardened as a mobile crime-fighting organization. Hoover brought science into the fight against criminals with the establishment of the FBI Laboratory. The FBI National Academy was organized to train local police officers in the latest crime-fighting techniques and to encourage federal-local cooperation in law enforcement as the means of avoiding the national police force which was being demanded at that time.

1939–1945

During these war years, the FBI's operations assumed a new dimension. President Roosevelt made the Bureau responsible with the Army and the Navy for guarding against espionage, sabotage and subversion. The FBI became not only a crime-fighting organization, but also an intelligence agency.

In startling contrast to the Bureau's fumbling in World War I, the FBI was alert to Nazi espionage, and spy rings were broken up long before the United States entered the war. There was not a single case of foreign-directed sabotage throughout the war—no "Black Tom" explosions and no saboteurs' fires sweeping through chemical plants. And the huge war job was carried out with meticulous regard for civil rights. There were no mass raids and no vigilantes.

In a super-secret operation, FBI agents went into Central and South America to help friendly governments break up Nazi spy rings and search out hidden radios pouring intelligence information into Germany.

In contrast to intelligence work in the past, which had been limited to specific, short-term assignments, President Roosevelt made the FBI's responsibility a continuing one, involving a broad new front.

1945–1956

During the Cold War years, the FBI concentrated largely on the fight against communism in addition to the upsurge in crime. In 1936 President Roosevelt had given the FBI a secret directive through Secretary of

State Cordell Hull to investigate Communist activities throughout the
country, and agents had kept close watch on the Communist Party.

Now the investigations began to uncover evidence of the Communist subversion which Hoover had warned against for years. The
stories of Fuchs and Harry Gold and the Rosenbergs began to unfold,
along with contemporary evidence that the Communist Party leaders
were conspiring to overthrow the United States Government by force
and violence. This was the period when the FBI literally went to war
against the Communist Party. But the war against crime continued as
well and led FBI agents down strange trails in the pursuit of criminals
such as those involved in the kidnaping of little Peter Weinberger on
Long Island and the acid attack which blinded labor columnist Victor
Riesel.

Despite the strict discipline, long hours and hard work, relatively
few agents leave the FBI for easier, higher-paying jobs. There is
something in the FBI which holds them, an intangible spirit akin to the
pride developed in the Marine Corps. In 1955, for example, the
turnover among agents was less than one-half of one percent.

Who are these men called FBI agents?

They are a cross-section of American life. They are men trained in
law, accounting, science and engineering. But adaptability and versa-
tility are as important as academic training in investigative work, and
the FBI looks for young men whose interests are wide and varied.

Some agents were once commercial artists. Some studied medicine
and then decided they preferred the life of an agent. Some worked as
musicians, pharmacists, bookdealers, social workers, salesmen, archi-
tects, newspapermen, teachers, auditors, brokers, cashiers, farmers
and factory workers, among other pursuits. Among them, they speak
or read thirty different languages and dialects and their hobbies vary
from art to sports.[1]

These men form the FBI. They are professionals highly trained for
their work and guided by the principle that establishing innocence is
just as important as establishing guilt in their investigations.

The early years of struggle were bitter ones. But there can be no
understanding of the FBI without looking into the forces which helped
in the past to shape its future.

2 : *The Story Begins*

THE crusade in which the Federal Bureau of Investigation had its beginning on July 26, 1908, was President Theodore Roosevelt's fight to curb the "public be damned" greed of big business combines and to halt the outrageous thievery of public lands in the western states.

From the time he entered the White House in September, 1901, Roosevelt was roaring against political and business corruption and demanding stronger federal controls over the excesses of the rich and the powerful. He was thumping heads with his "big stick," and he sometimes included heads in Congress.

There was ample reason for the Rooseveltian roars. There was, in truth, a "mess in America." There was a mess in which the industrial combines, the "trusts," were flouting the Sherman Antitrust Act and in effect thumbing their noses at the federal government and the people.

There was a mess, too, in which men of high repute were conniving with federal officials to rob the government of valuable land in the West, where almost 40,000,000 acres had been set aside by previous administrations as forest reserves. This green and tempting treasure was supposedly being watched over by a government agency, the General Land Office, which was more interested in selling land for private use than it was in Roosevelt's policy of conservation. The thieves were busily dipping into this treasury even as Roosevelt took office after the assassination of President McKinley.

Roosevelt was determined to halt the thievery and the antitrust violations. But in the midst of his fight Congress suddenly balked at the Department of Justice's use of "detectives" in its investigations and passed an amendment to the Sundry Civil Appropriation Act, which left the Department without an investigative arm with which to collect evidence for prosecutions.

Roosevelt was furious. But his fury could be understood only against the background of what had happened in the past.

After the Civil War, Congress had passed several laws encouraging homesteading and making it possible for families and individuals to buy land and settle in the West. One of these laws was the Timber and Stone Act of 1878, which provided for the sale of lands in California, Oregon, Nevada and the Washington Territory. The lands were considered unfit for cultivation, but they were covered with virgin forests worth millions.

Enforcement of the land law was lax. People fenced public lands— sometimes innocently—for their own use. Others bought huge acreages through fraudulent schemes to turn a quick and easy profit in resales to lumber companies.

Roosevelt had been in office only a few months when the Secretary of the Interior, Ethan A. Hitchcock of Missouri, had reason to suspect that his own department was involved in the land frauds. He detected a bad odor in the General Land Office, and he began an inquiry. He arranged for an agent to resign from the Treasury's Secret Service and take a quiet look behind the scenes in the West. His suspicions were confirmed when the agent reported that some of the General Land Office's own detectives were so deeply involved in land manipulations that they were actually tools of the land thieves. Afraid to trust his own people, Hitchcock decided the frauds should be investigated by the Department of Justice. The Attorney General arranged to "borrow" agents from the Treasury's Secret Service to make the investigation. Among the outstanding Secret Service agents lent to the Department of Justice was Lawrence Richey, who was later to become Secretary to President Herbert Hoover.

The roundup in the land-fraud drive was a sensation. Scores of people were indicted and convicted on charges of "conspiracy to defraud the United States out of public lands." Tens of thousands of acres of public lands were recovered which had been fenced illegally or bought by fraudulent representations.

The shocker came when U. S. Senator John H. Mitchell and Representative John N. Williamson, both of Oregon, were charged with conspiracy to defraud. They were indicted in 1905 and convicted, Williamson on his third trial. It was learned years later that some of the prosecutions were so corrupt and politically tainted that the agents of justice appeared without doubt to be guilty of actions far worse than the crimes charged to the prosecuted.

Here is the story of what happened, according to the investigation made in 1911 by President William Howard Taft's Attorney General, George W. Wickersham. In preparing his prosecution of land-fraud cases in the federal court in Oregon, U. S. Attorney Francis J. Heney had the assistance of William J. Burns, a detective, to investigate prospective jurors. Burns and his men then arranged in some manner to have the jury box filled with Democrats, Populists, Socialists and Republicans who were political enemies of the Mitchell faction of the Republican Party.

The detectives' reports on prospective jurors went like this: "Convictor from the word go" . . . "Socialist. Anti-Mitchell" . . . "Good reliable man" . . . "Would convict Christ" . . . "He is apt to wish Mitchell hung." Some notations were found to be in Burns's own handwriting.

Wickersham reported that there was no doubt Burns had managed the selection of the jury as Heney's agent. There were affidavits that Burns had compelled witnesses by threats and intimidation to give perjured testimony to a grand jury and to petit jurors.

Neither Roosevelt nor Congress was aware of the Burns-Heney episode at the time. But the fact that members of Congress had been investigated, accused and convicted was enough to increase tensions between Congress and the White House. Other defendants in this case were U. S. Commissioner Marion R. Biggs and a man named Van Gesner, who was a business partner of Representative Williamson. The chief prosecutor in the case was to have been U. S. District Attorney John H. Hall, until it was discovered that Hall himself was involved in the illegal fencing of public lands. Hall was thrown out of office, indicted, convicted and later pardoned because of the jury box manipulations. Gesner and Biggs each paid a fine and served a jail sentence. Senator Mitchell appealed his conviction but his death came before the higher courts had ruled on his guilt. Williamson appealed his conviction and won a reversal in the Supreme Court, which led to the subsequent dismissal of the charges.

The Roosevelt Administration's use of Secret Service agents in the clean-up campaign came under attack. Stories were circulated that the President was using detectives to spy into the private lives of members of Congress and to collect information to be held as a political club. The rumors were never substantiated, either before or after Roosevelt's death, but they helped to cast a shadow over the investigative methods used in the land-fraud and antitrust cases.

The "spy" stories created an atmosphere of hostility when Attorney General Charles J. Bonaparte called Congress' attention in 1907 to the lack of an investigative organization in the Department of Justice.

Bonaparte said: "The attention of the Congress should be, I think, called to the anomaly that the Department of Justice has no executive force, and, more particularly, no permanent detective force under its immediate control . . . it seems obvious that the Department on which not only the President, but the courts of the United States must call first to secure the enforcement of the laws, ought to have the means of such enforcement subject to its own call; a Department of Justice with no force of permanent police in any form under its control is assuredly not fully equipped for its work."

Congress pointedly ignored Bonaparte's plea, although the need for investigative work within the Justice Department had been recognized as early as 1871. At that time, an appropriation of $50,000 had been made for "the detection and prosecution of crimes against the United States," and the Attorney General had appointed the Department's first "special agent" to handle investigations.

As the years passed, the Justice Department (and other government departments) adopted the practice of "borrowing" agents from the Treasury Department's Secret Service. The Secret Service had been organized after the Civil War primarily to combat a wave of counterfeiting of U. S. currency and securities. These agents-on-loan, although working for the Department of Justice, continued to make reports to the Chief of the Secret Service. They regarded the Secret Service Chief, not the Attorney General, as the man to whom they were responsible.

Under this arrangement, no government official had any real check or control over the agents' activities. Most of them were hired on a part-time basis from a list of private detectives "approved" by the Secret Service; some were suspected of being ex-criminals, and they were called "Secret Service" men even though they were not regular Secret Service agents.

This makeshift system continued until May 27, 1908, when Congress forbade the Department of Justice—and all other executive departments—to use Secret Service agents in investigating law violations. The ban was accomplished by an amendment to the Sundry Civil Appropriation Act.

The action was a crippling blow to federal law enforcement, and Roosevelt—a former police commissioner of New York City [1]—was keenly aware of the fact. He knew that if the laws of the land were to be enforced, then there had to be investigators to gather the evidence of wrongdoing. The law was in fact a roadblock in the path of Roosevelt's clean-up campaign.

The President had tried to sidetrack the amendment. A few weeks before the House voted, he wrote House Speaker Joseph G. Cannon and said: "The provision about the employment of the secret service men will work very great damage to the Government in its endeavor to prevent and punish crime. There is no more foolish outcry than this against 'spies'; only criminals need fear our detectives."

The New York *Times,* in an editorial titled "Tools of Thieves," said: "It was the combination of 'land sharks,' according to report, that persuaded the Appropriations Committee to approve, and the House to pass, the Amendment to the Sundry Civil bill which undoes the deterrent and detective labors of the Secret Service . . . The Representatives have, however unwittingly, become the tools of thieves. The Senators are duly warned."

There was, briefly, some hope the amendment could be killed in the Senate. From New York City, U. S. Attorney Henry L. Stimson (who was later to serve in the cabinets of Presidents Taft, Hoover and Franklin D. Roosevelt) wrote to Attorney General Bonaparte: "I should feel as if the fighting power of my office were almost crippled by such a statute. Is there no way in which the Bill can be stopped in the Senate?"

But Congress was in no mood to listen.

After the restrictive amendment was approved, word spread through the Department of Justice that President Roosevelt had called Attorney General Bonaparte to the White House and directed him to organize an investigative service.

A memorandum in the FBI files written by old-time Agent James G. Findlay says it was known at the time that "President Roosevelt directed Bonaparte to create an investigative service within the Department of Justice subject to no other department or bureau, which would report to no one except the Attorney General." And on July 26, 1908, Bonaparte issued the order creating an investigative agency within his Department—the order which was the beginning of the FBI.

The angry debate between Congress and the White House served a purpose. It produced general agreement that the Department of Justice needed, and should have, an investigative arm, but that no single agency should be permitted to develop into a terroristic "spy system" such as those which despots had used in Europe.

Twelve days after President William Howard Taft succeeded Roosevelt in the White House on March 4, 1909, the new Attorney General, George W. Wickersham, gave the Department's investigative service a secure place and the dignity of a title—the Bureau of Investigation.

This was the start of the story which would send Bureau agents on strange missions across the country and around the world as Congress gradually expanded the Bureau's responsibilities for curbing the evils of interstate crime.

One of these manhunts sent Agent Jim Trent [2] deep into the Cumberlands of Tennessee. He left his automobile on the main road and trudged up a mountain trail leading to a little gray cabin huddled against the hill in the late-afternoon shadows.

At last Trent paused on the path. He saw the cabin in the clearing ahead and he wondered if the man he was after would be there. . . .

Bill Howard was his man. Young, hot-blooded Bill Howard, fugitive from justice and probably as good a sharpshooter as Sergeant Alvin York, the most decorated hero of World War I, who lived only a few miles across the ridges. Jim Trent was after Bill Howard because a federal grand jury at Nashville had indicted Howard on charges of violating the White Slave Traffic Act, commonly known as the Mann Act. Howard allegedly had forced a Jamestown, Tennessee, schoolgirl to accompany him on a trip across the state line into Kentucky, where he had abused her before allowing her to return home.

But Bill Howard was a hard man to find in the hills, particularly by a stranger who asked too many questions.

Trent walked on up the path, past a little cemetery and onto the cabin porch. He knocked, and when the door opened he stepped inside. First he saw the high-powered rifles leaning against the wall. And then he saw the four men and the woman watching him, their gaze as chill as the wind outside.

Trent singled out a grizzled, elderly man as most probably Bill Howard's father, and he was correct. He identified himself and then told the father why he was there.

"If your son's here, Mr. Howard," he said, "I've got to take him with me."

The old man said in a flat voice, "I ain't so sure you will." And then he told Trent what he thought about "the law" in general, revenuers in particular, and Trent himself.

When the burst of angry words stopped, Trent said, "I don't blame you for your feelings, Mr. Howard. If you say your son isn't here, I'll take your word for it. But if he is, I've got to take him into custody."

The old man growled, "He's not here and you fellers couldn't find him in a thousand years."

"All right. If you say he's not here, I'll take your word and I'll be going."

Trent started for the door. But a quiet voice stopped him. The voice said, "You ain't leaving this house, mister!"

Trent turned slowly and looked at the faces in the room—faces as hard and unyielding as the tombstones in the graveyard he had passed. He shrugged and sat down on the cane-bottom chair near the fireplace. Silence settled in the room as though these people were waiting for the shadows to grow deeper outside.

Trent sensed the ridiculous overtones in this tobacco road farce being played in a hillbilly cabin on a lonely mountainside. But there was nothing ridiculous about those rifles or about the hardness of the faces in front of him. And so he sat. The woman left the room but the men didn't move except to pass a jug of corn whiskey to each other occasionally and to light an oil lamp hanging in the corner.

And then Trent saw the violin. It was on the ledge above the fireplace. He reached up and took the instrument in his hands and brought it into tune, waiting for someone to snatch it from his hands. But no one did. He began to play, softly at first, melodies like "Carry Me Back to Old Virginny" and "The Rosary." And after a while he sensed an easing of the tension in the room. He kept playing, remembering old tunes from the days he had played in his high-school orchestra.

By midnight, Agent Trent was sawing away at "She'll Be Comin' Round the Mountain," with requests coming from the shadows in the room, and a little foot-stomping to help.

At last Trent put the violin back on the shelf. It was now or never. He said, "Well, Mr. Howard, if you have an extra bed, I'd like to spend the night." And then he waited for the decision.

The old man looked at him for a long moment. Finally he nodded and held out his hand, almost in a gesture of resignation. "Just send the papers to Louisville," he said. "I'll have the boy turn hisself in there."

Trent left the cabin the next morning after a friendly breakfast. His hosts walked down the mountain with him. And within a few days Bill Howard surrendered to the government. He pleaded guilty and was fined $200.

This years-old incident in the hills of Tennessee may seem to have little or no significance in the story of the FBI—but historically it had a great significance.

The White Slave Traffic Act, passed by Congress in 1910, was aimed against the transportation of women and girls in interstate or foreign commerce for immoral purposes. The principle this legislation established in law gave the federal government enlarged jurisdiction over interstate crime. This was the law which opened the way for the FBI to become a national crime-fighting organization.

By 1902, the "trade in white women" (*traite des blanches,* as the French called it) had become such an international scandal that representatives of thirteen European nations met in Paris to discuss the problem. Out of the conference came an agreement for a concerted effort to stop the vice traffic. The United States Government formally adhered to the pact by proclamation of President Theodore Roosevelt, June 15, 1908.

A public clamor grew for police action, not only against the importation of alien women for purposes of prostitution, but against the prostitution rings which were shuttling women from city to city in the United States. Stories in the daily press and magazines gave their shocked (and sometimes avid) readers a look into a world where sex was for sale and big profits were reaped by the vice syndicates.

One of the sensations of the day came when the U. S. Attorney in Chicago seized correspondence and books disclosing the operations of a vice syndicate headed by Alphonse Dufaur and his wife, Eva. The records revealed that over a ten-year period the syndicate's procurers had imported some 20,000 women and girls into the United States, passing them through customs as their wives or sisters. In the twelve months prior to their arrest, the Dufaurs' books showed an income of $102,000.[8]

Amid such developments as these, Representative James Robert Mann of Illinois introduced the White Slave Traffic Act in the House. It was designed not only to break up commercial traffic in women between countries and between the states, but also to control the interstate transportation of women for immoral purposes.

The measure carried tremendous popular and emotional appeal. But the debate in Congress, for the most part, held to the constitutional aspects of the measure, with its opponents arguing that the attack on vice was an invasion of the states' police powers. The supporters of the bill argued that in Article One of the Constitution the Congress shall have the power ". . . to regulate Commerce with foreign Nations, and among the several States." Congress adopted the bill by unanimous consent in the summer of 1910. The Supreme Court was unanimous in holding the White Slave Traffic Act to be constitutional.[4]

It was apparent from the first that Congress had enacted a controversial law in the Mann Act. While it was called the White Slave Traffic Act, the law forbade the interstate transportation of a woman for immoral purposes whether she was a "slave" or not. And the Supreme Court ruled that the woman wasn't necessarily the innocent victim in vice cases—she might even be guilty herself of a conspiracy to violate the law.[5]

Yellowed records in the Department of Justice show that when Congress passed the Mann Act, Attorney General Wickersham foresaw the difficulties ahead. He was fully aware of the need for prudence in enforcing the White Slave law. He cautioned that federal courts should be careful to avoid "being turned into ordinary courts of quarter sessions to deal with . . . violations of the police regulations of the community which should be dealt with by the local tribunals."

And at that time he advised U. S. Attorneys: "As to specific cases, the Department must rely upon the discretion of the district attorneys who have first-hand knowledge of the facts, and opportunity for personal interviews with the witnesses, and who will thus be able to ascertain what circumstances of aggravation, if any, attend the offense; the age and relative interest of the parties; the motives of those urging prosecution; and what reasons, if any, exist for thinking the ends of justice will be better served by a prosecution under federal law than under the laws of the state having jurisdiction."

Thus Wickersham established the basic policy for handling Mann Act violations, a policy continued unchanged through the years.[6]

In those early years, the Bureau chiefs had no real authority. They could transfer agents from one city to another, but even in this they often ran head-on into opposition from politicians looking after their friends.

But gradually the Bureau's responsibilities were increasing.[7] These responsibilities called for the investigation of every alleged violation of federal laws except those specifically assigned to another governmental investigative agency.[8]

Then the storm clouds gathered in Europe. And the Bureau was far from being prepared for the test.

The Years of Unrest

3: *Espionage and Sabotage, Unlimited*

THE Imperial German Army was marching across Belgium through the flames of World War I when a transatlantic liner steamed into New York Harbor in August, 1914. Among the passengers who disembarked from the liner were two urbane and impeccably dressed gentlemen deeply concerned with America's neutrality.

The two men were Count Johann von Bernstorff, German Ambassador to the United States, and Dr. Heinrich Albert, the German Commercial Attaché. The courtesies of diplomatic immunity spared them the delay of opening their luggage for Customs inspection; and soon they were hurrying on their way—von Bernstorff to the Embassy in Washington, and Dr. Albert to his offices in the Hamburg-American Building in New York.

In this casual manner, Ambassador von Bernstorff carried into the United States $150,000,000 in German treasury notes to finance the first foreign espionage and sabotage apparatus to be organized in this country.

Conditions were favorable for von Bernstorff and his aides. America was the unsuspecting innocent, magnificently isolated, and unschooled in the plotting and counterplotting of the European powers. Americans were more interested in their own aches and pains than in the affairs of Europe. There was the trouble south of the Rio Grande and along the Mexican border, where revolution had boiled for three years. There was the unrest in industry, where young unions were fighting for recognition by management. Industrial disputes were often erupting into terrible, bloody conflicts, such as the pitched battle between four hundred striking miners and two hundred state militia in Colorado—a battle which one editor said "lasted longer and was more fiercely fought than most of the battles of the Mexican revolution." Twenty-five were killed, including fourteen children and two women.

In this ferment, a small group of men and women were preaching the doctrine of workers' control over production and encouraging violence. They were rallying workers to join the Industrial Workers of the World (IWW) and other extremist groups, whose membership included many who were to become the outriders of the Communist Party in America.

At the time of the Ambassador's arrival, the United States Government's intelligence work was handled for the most part by five small organizations. The Department of Justice had the poorly organized, six-year-old Bureau of Investigation, charged with policing violations against the federal statutes. The Secret Service was responsible for the protection of the President, the prevention of counterfeiting and a few other duties. The State Department had an intelligence section of its own. The Army's intelligence section assembled in full force totaled two officers and two clerks. The Navy had only a few officers assigned to Naval Intelligence. Each of these units operated on its own, without coordination.

Von Bernstorff quickly went to work. His staff was small but efficient and well departmentalized: Dr. Albert handled the money and directed complex business manipulations; Captain Karl Boy-Ed, the Naval Attaché, was responsible for the sabotage of ships carrying arms to the Allies; and Captain Franz von Papen,[1] the Military Attaché, supervised other espionage and sabotage throughout the United States and Canada.

Five months after von Bernstorff and Albert landed in New York, the Imperial Embassy at 1435–1439 Massachusetts Avenue, N. W., in Washington, received a secret message from the German General Staff, routed via Stockholm, saying:

> For Military Attaché: People fit for sabotage in United States and Canada can be ascertained from following persons: [three names listed] . . . In United States sabotage can reach to all kinds of factories for war deliveries; railroads, dams, bridges must not be touched there. Under no circumstances compromise Embassy, and equally Irish-German propaganda.

In the months that followed, mysterious explosions blew up ammunition dumps, powder plants, guncotton storehouses and chemical plants.

War plants were gutted by fires. American ships en route to England, France and Russia, loaded with munitions and other supplies, caught fire at sea and many sank.

In the dark morning hours of July 30, 1916, frightful blasts from 2,000,000 pounds of dynamite jarred Manhattan and Jersey City, N. J. The explosions were on Black Tom Island in New York Harbor, a major transfer point for supplies shipped to Europe. The thunderous noise was heard a hundred miles away. The concussion shattered almost every window in Jersey City, and heavy plate-glass windows crashed to the sidewalks in Manhattan and Brooklyn. Black Tom Island's usefulness was destroyed. Three men and a child were killed.

A similar explosion rocked Kingsland, N. J., in January, 1917, when a shell assembly plant went up in flames, showering shells around the plant area. Fortunately, the shells were not equipped with detonating fuses—and didn't explode. The damage was estimated at about $17,000,000.[2]

In one sabotage case, a former German soldier, Werner Horn, dynamited the international bridge linking the United States and Canada at Vanceboro, Maine. German agents gave him a suitcase filled with dynamite to do the job, and paid him $700 expense money.

Horn placed the dynamite on the bridge, lit the fuse, pinned a tiny German flag on the outside of his overcoat sleeve, and walked away to be arrested a few hours later. Horn claimed that because he was wearing the flag, he should be treated as a prisoner of war. He was convicted, not for sabotage—because there was no federal law covering sabotage—but for transporting dynamite on an interstate passenger train.

British Intelligence had advance warning of the German sabotage campaign in America. The German General Staff's message to von Bernstorff was intercepted by the intelligence department of the British Admiralty and passed on to the American State Department officials in London. But no record has been found in Department of Justice files indicating that the information ever reached the Bureau of Investigation.

Early in 1915, Berlin sent another message to von Bernstorff: "Inform Rintelen who arrives today . . . about Papen's proposals."

And the next day: "Inform Boy-Ed as to Papen's proposals for transmission to Rintelen."

The new arrival from Germany, who came by way of Norway with a forged Swiss passport, was Franz von Rintelen. He was an officer in the German Navy and as daring and resourceful a saboteur as ever set foot on American soil. Within a matter of days, he had $500,000 at his disposal.

Von Rintelen moved fast. He knew the United States well from previous visits, when he had studied banking. He spoke fluent English. He was persuasive, attractive and chameleon-like in his ability to change his protective coloring to fit a given situation.

Von Rintelen organized E. V. Gibbons, Inc., a New York firm specializing in the export of war supplies to Europe. The supplies handled by E. V. Gibbons, Inc., went aboard ships which were sabotaged at von Rintelen's convenience. His associates formed a marine insurance company as a handy means of obtaining sailing schedules and cargo manifests.

The elusive von Rintelen conceived the idea of organizing "Labor's National Peace Council," a union which would pay remarkably generous benefits to members who struck at war plants or along the water front. Von Rintelen conceded later that even he regarded the idea as utterly fantastic. But the more he thought of it, the less fantastic it became.

Von Rintelen enlisted the aid of anyone he could find, and this included two members of Congress, Representatives Frank Buchanan and H. Robert Fowler of Illinois. In his memoirs, von Rintelen recalled:

> The first thing I did was to hire a large hall and organize a meeting, at which well-known men thundered against the export of munitions. Messrs. Buchanan and Fowler, members of Congress; Mr. Hannis Taylor, the former American Ambassador in Madrid . . . together with a number of University professors, theologians and Labour leaders appeared and raised their voices. I sat unobtrusively in a corner and watched my plans fructifying. None of the speakers had the faintest suspicion that he was in the "service" of a German officer sitting among the audience.

But Samuel Gompers, President of the American Federation of Labor, recognized the union as a German front. He protested, "The American labor movement as a body is loyal to America . . . It has nothing to do with those anti-American, pro-Kaiserist activities of which the People's Council is the promoter, and is, in fact, exactly in opposition to them."

All of von Rintelen's plans seemed to flourish. He discovered that Dr. Walter T. Scheele, a brilliant German-born chemist who had lived in the United States for twenty-five years, had invented a clever and diabolical little fire bomb which could be timed to explode within minutes or days—as the need might be. Dr. Scheele was eager to help, and had already been active in the von Bernstorff conspiracy. He had made a substantial contribution to the German cause when he found a means to ship oil as a solid, disguised as fertilizer.

Von Rintelen put Dr. Scheele to work manufacturing the bombs aboard a German ship interned at Hoboken. He was able to turn out from thirty-five to fifty a day while von Rintelen found men on the water front willing to carry the devices aboard outgoing ships loaded with supplies for the Allies. Von Rintelen is believed responsible for destroying or damaging cargoes in some thirty-six ships, valued at $10,000,000.[3]

While von Rintelen, von Papen and Boy-Ed were busy with their sabotage—and there were no federal statutes at the time providing punishment for either espionage or sabotage—Dr. Heinrich Albert was deeply involved in cornering scarce war materials, and obtaining control of a part of America's munitions production.

Dr. Albert's boldest venture was in organizing the Bridgeport Projectile Co., which negotiated contracts that blocked off badly needed supplies from the Allies for more than a year. He even wangled from the United States Government a $1,210,000 order for shells, and another $1,387,000 order for 146 5-inch naval guns—with no intention of ever making delivery.

The Bureau of Investigation picked up von Rintelen's trail when, using an assumed name, he tried to buy 300,000 rifles from the government. And then a Secret Service agent snatched Dr. Albert's brief case from the seat of an elevated car in New York when the doctor absent-mindedly left it unguarded for a moment. The contents of the brief case spilled out some of the secrets of the von Bernstorff apparatus and exposed the first details of the operation to government officials.

The full story of the German intrigues was uncovered after the United States entered the war. The Bureau of Investigation learned that the Germans had left a storeroom full of documents at the Swiss Consulate, on the ninth floor of the building at 11 Broadway in New York, and Division Superintendent Charles DeWoody assigned agents to the job of obtaining these papers. After the Swiss consular employees had left the Broadway office one afternoon in April, the agents tunneled through a wall into the consulate. There they found boxes and trunks bound with yards of tape and sealed with wax bearing the imprint of the Imperial German Seal.

Working swiftly, the agents carefully removed the seals and tape. They emptied the trunks and boxes of perhaps a ton of papers, ledgers, code books, letters and records. When they left, the room appeared to be just as they had found it, including the yards of tape around the boxes and trunks. The seals were unbroken.

DeWoody reported:

These records disclosed methods by which the enemy was enabled to secure information for delivering war materials and supplies by enemy ships under neutral flags. These papers also furnished the United States Government with information as to the identity [of] methods of codes and enemy intelligence system activities in this country from the beginning of the War.

American opinion slowly turned against Germany throughout 1916. On January 31, 1917, Germany resumed unrestricted submarine warfare, sinking American shipping without warning. On April 6, Congress declared war against Germany. President Woodrow Wilson gave the Bureau of Investigation the task of enforcing his proclamation governing the conduct of enemy aliens.

The Bureau had only 300 agents to police the activities of more than 1,000,000 males required to register as enemy aliens; and in addition the Bureau had its regular duties to perform. In England, all Germans had been interned for the duration, but the Wilson Administration believed such a plan was impractical and unwise in this country. The vast majority of the so-called enemy aliens were expected to be loyal and they were.

Twenty-four hours after war was declared, 63 enemy aliens had been arrested; and, in the first month of the war, the number increased to 125. During the entire war period, about 6,300 enemy aliens were arrested under presidential warrant, but only 2,300 were interned in the Army's custody. Most of those arrested were released on parole.

Congress passed a selective service act, and men between the ages of twenty-one and thirty, inclusive, were ordered to register in the first draft on June 5. The day passed quietly.

But a rising note of hysteria was beginning to creep through America. The nation was experiencing its first great spy scare. The New York *Tribune* said spies were "everywhere." Anger mounted against the IWW and anarchist groups whose leaders were opposing the war and the draft at the same time that President Wilson was appealing to the nation's patriotism for support in the conflict.

The resentment against the IWW was fed by IWW declarations such as: ". . . we openly declare ourselves determined opponents of all nationalistic sectionalism or patriotism, and the militarism preached and supported by our enemy, the Capitalist Class." And stickers appeared bearing the name of the IWW leader, W. D. Haywood: "Sabotage—sabotage means to push back; pull out or break off the fangs of capitalism."

There was wide suspicion that the IWW was being financed by enemy money and that its members were responsible for acts of sabotage from Chicago westward.

In the Justice Department, Assistant to the Attorney General Charles Warren favored courts-martial to deal with civilians obstructing the war effort. Finally he carried his proposals to members of Congress. But President Wilson and his Attorney General, Thomas W. Gregory, quashed this effort. Gregory termed the proposal "subversive of fundamental principles of justice." Gregory wanted laws to deal with espionage, sabotage and disloyal utterances and acts, even to talking and writing in a manner that would support the cause of the enemy. And Congress passed the statutes.

The Amendment to the Espionage Act covering "seditious utterances" was recognized as one open to abuse. The Department of Justice instructed U. S. attorneys:

> It should not be permitted to become the medium whereby efforts are made to suppress honest, legitimate criticism of the administration or discussion of Government policies; nor should it be permitted to become a medium for personal feuds or persecution.

But volunteer citizens organizations sprang up across the country as the judges of disloyal acts and utterances. In Henry County, Missouri, the Council of Defense, headed by the Reverend A. N. Lindsay, devised its own means of dealing with anyone considered by the Council to be "speaking or acting in a disloyal way."

First the suspect received a white card warning:

> You have been reported to the Committee on Patriots and Patriotism as in your attitude and utterances dangerous and disloyal. We recommend CAUTION and a complete change of attitude. (Signed) Committee of Patriots

When the suspect's attitude didn't change to the committee's satisfaction within a week of careful scrutiny, he received a blue card:

> The White Card meant CAUTION; the Blue WARNING.
>
> Every flag in our Country waves to protect you—your life and property. Your duty is to defend your Country's Flag with your life. (Signed) Committee of Patriots

In case the blue card wasn't convincing, there was the final red card:

> If unjustly reported, or if you desire to avoid Summary Action, report at once your change of front to the Postmaster. No harm will come to you if you continue loyal in your devotion to your country in its hour of need. FINAL. (Signed) Committee of Patriots

It is possible to relate that no one in Henry County, Missouri, ever received the red card, and only a few required prodding with the blue. The Henry County Council's white-blue-red-card warning system was recommended by the Reverend Lindsay to the Department of Justice, but it was rejected.

While councils such as the Henry County Committee of Patriots were going to one extreme, there were others working at the opposite pole. In New York, Alexander Berkman and Emma Goldman, long-time anarchists, formed the No-Conscription League, with promises of help to those who refused to register and be drafted.

In Texas, a group of men decided they and their sons would resist conscription. They went to Dallas, bought Winchester rifles, pistols and ammunition, and, with their friends, were prepared to make a stand in the woods against the federal officers. In Oklahoma, about 2,500 young men, allegedly influenced by the IWW, joined in the "Roasting Ear Rebellion." They took up arms and deployed into the cornfields to fight against conscription by the "moneyed class." Alleged attempts at sabotage were reported by the thousands.

It was in this atmosphere of tension that Americans learned of the revolution in Russia, the abdication of the Czar, and finally the collapse of the Russian Army in mutiny and revolt. For a time there was hope that the Kerensky provisional government would lead the Russians to a democratic form of government, but the Bolsheviki counterrevolution in November, 1917, swept Kerensky aside. A man named Nikolai Lenin exulted:

> Now we have a revolution. The peasants and workmen control the Government. This is only a preliminary step toward a similar revolution everywhere.

4: *The Vigilantes*

WITH the call to arms in World War I, the Bureau of Investigation was swamped with work. The agent force was increased immediately from 300 men to a total of 400. But this was a puny squad for policing more than 1,000,000 enemy aliens, protecting harbors and war-industry zones barred to enemy aliens, aiding draft boards and the Army in locating draft dodgers and deserters, and carrying on the regular duties of investigating federal law violations.

Bureau Chief A. Bruce Bielaski had realized the enormous job that would have to be done when it became apparent that war was near. For this reason, he was interested in a letter he received in March, 1917, from a Chicago advertising executive, A. M. Briggs. Briggs suggested the formation of a volunteer organization of loyal Americans who would give their time and service to the government to help the Bureau of Investigation in work involving national defense. The citizens would bear all the expenses of the operation.

The idea appealed to Bielaski, and to Attorney General Gregory. Briggs was encouraged to go ahead. Four days after receiving this Department of Justice and Bureau blessing, Briggs had formed the American Protective League, with national headquarters in Chicago.

The organization snowballed. Within three months it had nearly 100,000 members. The number swelled to 250,000. APL divisions were formed in every major city in the country. The rush for membership was so great that enlistments had to be suspended temporarily until headquarters could catch its breath and get a fresh batch of the seventy-five-cent badges bearing the legend: "American Protective League, Secret Service Division." The badges were to be worn concealed; and badges and credentials were to be shown only in emergencies. The members were cautioned that they were not representatives of the government and had no power of arrest, but such details soon were forgotten by many APL members in their zeal to nail a spy.

Three months after the APL was formed, Secretary of the Treasury McAdoo protested to Attorney General Gregory against the APL's use of the words "Secret Service" in its literature and on its badges. He said the APL was being falsely identified with the Treasury's official Secret Service, and causing the Treasury embarrassment. "You will recall," McAdoo wrote, "that during the American Revolution a voluntary organization . . . was formed under the title of 'Sons of Liberty.' It committed grave abuses and injustices. This 'Secret Service' division of the American Protective League contains the same evil potentialities. . . ."

Gregory defended the American Protective League and its patriotic purpose, but he promised that the words "Secret Service" would be eliminated from literature and badges in the future. The new badges would read: "American Protective League, Auxiliary to the U. S. Department of Justice."

McAdoo's warning was prophetic. The good work which many responsible and sober citizens performed, with full regard for the law, was buried beneath the violations of civil rights perpetrated by the army of amateur sleuths. APL operatives made illegal arrests and searches, and in many cases they encouraged the impression that they were federal officers. Labor leaders protested bitterly that the League, in some cities, was being used as a tool of employers to intimidate strikers.

The regular Bureau of Investigation agents were inclined to jeer at the "greenhorns" and "voluntary detectives," until warned by their superiors that any insulting or slurring remarks directed at APL members might cost them their jobs.

Although the APL membership eventually climbed to 250,000, most of the members were "inactives" and were content with their badges. In the Chicago area, for example, there were some 7,500 members with only about 300 active. But the Department of Justice and the Bureau of Investigation were to learn to their sorrow that even the ratio of 300 active APL members to 7,200 inactives was too great, because the evils would overshadow the good that was done.

A growing impatience with the due process of law encouraged a spirit of vigilantism across the country. Violent crimes were committed in the name of patriotism. In Butte, Montana, six masked men entered a boarding house and seized Frank Little, a member of the Executive Committee of the IWW. They dragged him into the night and hanged him from a railroad trestle for what they judged to be treasonable actions and utterances.

A congressman asked on the floor of the House whether those who professed no allegiance to the United States "have any right to 'squeal' when citizens of this country hang one of them occasionally?" A western newspaper said Butte had "disgraced itself like a gentleman." The situation was such that President Wilson felt constrained to speak out against "the great danger of citizens taking the law into their own hands."

But the President did believe, as did Attorney General Gregory, that the government should take action against the IWW. They discussed the problem and Gregory had the Bureau of Investigation and U. S. attorneys begin a quiet check on IWW activities and the source of its money. Gregory strongly suspected that the Germans were financing the IWW.

On September 5, 1917, Bureau agents raided IWW headquarters in Chicago and on the West Coast. They seized records, files, papers and propaganda material. The Socialist headquarters in Chicago was also raided. IWW leader W. D. Haywood was arrested along with others.

A federal grand jury in the Northern District of Illinois found that the IWW was trying to destroy the capitalistic class, "not by political action" but by force and violence, with the ultimate aim of "the forcible revolutionary overthrow of all existing governmental authority in the United States . . ." In the government's fight to convict the IWW leaders, President Wilson supported his Attorney General and advised

Gregory that the Industrial Workers of the World "certainly are worthy of being suppressed." Haywood and 98 other defendants were convicted.

Late in 1917, war work in the Department of Justice became so heavy that shortly after the IWW raids Gregory named John Lord O'Brian, a Republican from Buffalo, N. Y., as Special Assistant to the Attorney General for War Work. Among O'Brian's many aides was a twenty-two-year-old lawyer named J. Edgar Hoover who had joined the Department on July 26, 1917. O'Brian put young Hoover in charge of a unit in the enemy alien registration section.[1]

The war brought new and heavy burdens to the Department of Justice and the Attorney General improvised ways to meet them as best he could. But he would have shuddered had he foreseen the storm that was about to break against the Department, the Bureau of Investigation and the American Protective League in the summer of 1918.

The first small cloud was in the form of a letter dated August 5, 1918, from Secretary of War Baker, informing Gregory that: "The record of desertion under the first and second drafts discloses the fact that on June 10, 1918, there existed a known desertion from both drafts of 308,489 . . ."

Here, roughly, was the equivalent of some twenty-five divisions of men who were evading military service, if the Secretary of War's figures were accurate. The letter was passed on to Bureau Chief Bielaski, whose own agents—and those of the APL—had been cooperating with the Army and draft boards in helping run down the "slackers," those who failed to register or report to their boards, and the deserters, those who failed to answer the call to service after registering.

Bielaski went to work to help the Army on a far larger scale than before. He had experimented with a slacker roundup in Pittsburgh, using local police and APL operatives, and it had seemed to work well. Bielaski reported to Gregory: "Especially successful canvasses of this kind were recently had in Chicago and Boston where 500 and 800 men, respectively, were found to be deserters and inducted into the draft service."

Now he decided to comb the draft dodgers out of New York, Brooklyn, Jersey City and Newark. The operation was to be in charge of Division Superintendent DeWoody. The dates first chosen were August 29–30–31, but the difficulties of organizing such a huge undertaking forced a postponement to September 3–4–5.

Newspapers were requested to carry notices cautioning all men between the ages of twenty-one and thirty-one to carry their draft classification cards with them at all times as required by law—and those outside this age group should have some "properly attested evidence of the date of their birth." But no warning was given to the public that a roundup was to take place.

Regimental armories were designated as detention points for the evaders who would be picked up. A fleet of automobiles was provided for transporting the suspects. Draft board members and APL volunteers were alerted to be prepared to check on the military eligibility of those brought in.

When zero hour arrived, DeWoody had his task force organized for the sweep: 35 special agents from the Bureau of Investigation; 2,000 operatives from the APL; 1,350 soldiers and National Guardsmen; 1,000 sailors; and several hundred policemen. The largest part of the force, of course, was concentrated in New York and Brooklyn.

The roundup began at 7:00 A.M., Tuesday, September 3. At the close of the three-day raid, some 50,000 men had been hustled from theaters, restaurants, street cars, railway stations, pool halls and street corners, sometimes to the jeers of street crowds. Soldiers, with bayonets fixed on their rifles, halted men on the streets and demanded proof of registration. APL operatives "arrested" suspects. Out-of-town visitors who had forgotten their cards were hauled off to the roped arenas which became known as the "bull pens." Worried wives came searching for lost husbands. Workers were seized when they left their jobs. Men were forced to stand for hours, without food, unable to telephone for help in establishing their innocence.

One New York newspaper described this scene at a railroad station:

As fast as groups of 50 or 100 had been collected . . . they were told by a sergeant to fall in. Here they got their first taste of discipline.

If they had suitcases a porter did not carry them; the prisoners did that work. And they marched with military briskness from the stations to the Sixty-ninth Regiment Armory.

Behind each group was a sergeant, and if one of the captives showed signs of faltering or letting down his bags he heard a sharp "Hold up there! Hold up there! Hip, hip, hip!"

The New York *World* called the slacker raids "this monstrous invasion of human rights" and a "shameful abuse of power."

On the Senate floor, Senator Hiram Johnson of California told his colleagues "to humiliate 40,000 citizens, to shove them along with bayonets, to subject them to prison and summary military force, merely because they are 'suspects,' is a spectacle never before presented in the Republic."

Some Senators spoke in defense of the raids. Senator Miles Poindexter of Washington argued that citizens should be willing to be inconvenienced "in order to help and to facilitate the discovery and the arrest of deserters and slackers. . . ." A final report on the raid by Bielaski showed that an estimated 1,505 men had been inducted into military service, while 15,000 were tabbed as delinquents and referred to their draft boards.

The weight of opinion was against the manner in which the slacker raids had been handled and President Wilson asked Gregory for a report. Gregory told the President, "I take full and entire responsibility"; he deplored the use of extra-legal methods, but said that unless otherwise instructed he would continue to make use of the dragnet method to round up slackers. The war ended November 11, 1918, and canceled any need for such action. The American Protective League was officially disbanded on February 1, 1919.

Out of the slacker raid fiasco there did emerge some good—a realization within the Department of Justice and the Bureau of Investigation that vigilantism and amateur sleuths have no place in law enforcement, even in the stress of great emergencies.

5 : *The New Enemy—Communism*

THE hour was nearing midnight in the nation's capital. The star-filled night was soft, warm and peaceful. The lights winked out, one by one, in the fashionable homes on R Street, Northwest. A car drove through the tree-lined streets and then swung into a garage at No. 2131 R Street. Assistant Secretary of the Navy Franklin D. Roosevelt stepped out and entered his home. Across the street, the new Attorney General, A. Mitchell Palmer, and his wife had switched off the lights in their first-floor library, and had gone upstairs. They were preparing to retire.

It was 11:15 P.M., June 2, 1919.

The Palmers were startled by a thump downstairs which sounded as though something heavy had been thrown against their front door. Then the house was shaken by a mighty explosion. The blast blew in the front of the house, shattered the library, cracked the ceiling, broke windows and knocked pictures from the wall. The front windows were blown out in the Roosevelt residence and the house next door was badly damaged. Windows were shattered in the home of Senator Claude A. Swanson, two doors from the Roosevelts, and houses two blocks away were damaged.

In the wreckage were bits of the bodies and clothing of two men, apparently the dynamiters, destroyed by their own infernal machine. A fragment of one body fell on the Roosevelt doorstep. Another fragment of flesh was hurled through the window of the residence of the Norwegian Minister, a few doors from the Roosevelt home.

The blast on R Street was echoed by eight other explosions that June night—in Philadelphia, Pittsburgh, New York, Boston, Cleveland, Newtonville, Mass., and Paterson, N. J.

At the scene of almost every bombing police picked up handbills reading:

Plain Words

The powers that be make no secret of their will to stop here in America the worldwide spread of revolution. The powers that be must reckon that they will have to accept the fight they have provoked. A time has come when the social question's solution can be delayed no longer; class war is on, and cannot cease but with a complete victory for the international proletariat. . . .

A wave of fear and indignation swept the country, which had been shocked a month earlier when bombs were sent through the mails to twenty-nine prominent persons. One of the earlier bombs had exploded, injuring a servant of Senator and Mrs. Thomas W. Hardwick of Georgia. No other persons were injured by the bombs.

These thirty-eight incidents, involving bombs either intercepted or exploded, had as their intended victims three members of the President's Cabinet, a Supreme Court justice, four United States senators, two members of the House of Representatives, a U. S. district judge, and two governors. Others were John D. Rockefeller and J. P. Morgan, the symbols of private wealth.[1]

The New York *World* said: "Murder is being preached in the United States openly and defiantly . . . There has been no suppression of murderous speech except as it interfered with war." The Philadelphia *Record* saw in the bombings the work of "a few individuals obsessed with Bolshevistic or radical designs" and the New York *Times* called them "plainly of Bolshevik or I.W.W. origin." The general opinion was that the conspirators probably would be found among the country's 9,000,000 aliens. The Buffalo *Evening News* said the time had come to teach "Americanism" to these aliens and the *Times* agreed that something had to be done "to shut off the ceaseless flow of falsehood and to teach truth."

Attorney General Palmer decided on a course of action. He named Francis P. Garvan of New York as Assistant Attorney General in charge of all investigations and prosecutions dealing with the problem. He appointed William J. Flynn, former Chief of the Secret Service, as Director of the Bureau of Investigation to succeed A. Bruce Bielaski, who had resigned the post earlier in the year.

As part of Garvan's administrative staff, Palmer created a General Intelligence Division under command of the twenty-four-year-old Special Assistant to the Attorney General, J. Edgar Hoover. Young Hoover was instructed to make a study of subversive activities in the United States to determine their scope and what action could be taken in the field of prosecution.[2] Operational control over the Bureau of Investigation remained with Flynn, whose agents sent the GID copies of all reports dealing with Communists and anarchists, and with syndicalist groups such as the IWW.[3]

When Hoover began his study, the extremists on the left were divided, roughly, into three groups—Communists, anarchists and the IWW. The IWW believed in an industrialized government—a state controlled by workers—and its members advocated violence to achieve their ends. The anarchists believed in no government whatever, and advocated the overthrow of all government as an oppressor of men's freedom.

As Hoover dug through the background of the Communists, he saw something which seemed clearly to him to be a conspiracy, centered in Moscow, and aimed at the overthrow by force and violence of all non-Communist governments throughout the world—including the government of the United States.

The reason Hoover arrived at his conclusion was this: he saw in the writings of Karl Marx, Friedrich Engels, Leon Trotsky, Nikolai Lenin and their followers a blueprint for action in communizing the world—not by free elections and free choices, but by violence and subversion. He saw in the actions of the Communist Party the carrying out of this conspiracy.

Once the Communist Party's teachings and announced aims were accepted literally, then communism was not a political movement in the ordinary political sense. Neither was it an idealistic theory of government. It was a conspiracy so vast, so daring, that few people at first could even grasp the sweep of the Communist vision. It was a conspiracy against history itself. It was a conspiracy to destroy totally and completely the religion, governments, institutions and thinking of the Judaic-Christian world, the Buddhist world, the Moslemic world and all religious beliefs.

The creators of communism saw a new society rising from the ashes of the old society, which had been built by centuries of struggle toward

human dignity and freedom. It would be a world of, for and by the
"scientific" minds of the Communist Party elite, minds "free" from
such chains as a belief in God, patriotism, nationalism—free from all
the cloying, outmoded things which the Party faithfully regarded as
having polluted man's thought processes from the beginning of time,
and which, according to Marxist doctrine, had been used by the re-
ligionists and the imperialists for the oppression of the masses. Communism, these creators said, was the logic of history, the inevitable
end of the class struggle, the hope of the world—not a conspiracy, but
an idealistic social movement in which Soviet Russia was the pioneer,
the "fatherland," the teacher.

Once the masses had been encouraged to destroy existing governments, they promised the new reign—a benign reign inspired only by
the most unselfish, the purest motives. This world dictatorship would
be good, they said: this dictatorship would lead the way to the better
world on earth even if it had to kill several millions who didn't want
to be led. It would be called a "dictatorship of the proletariat," thus
identifying the Communist intelligentsia with the masses, mingling them
as one and the same. The dictatorship would be clothed from head to
foot in the garments of a workers' struggle against oppression and for
freedom. It would be given the appearance of a righteous directorate of
true liberalism, dedicated to correcting the old economic and political
evils of a reactionary past. It would, in outward form, be a rule of
"people's democracies." But, in actuality, it would prove to be nothing
more than a dictatorship of the Communist social scientists, the Party
elite who could not trust the people with a freedom of choice. But they
would hold out the promise that on some glorious, unspecified day the
scientifically managed world would not need a state and the state would
wither away.

The Communist Party platform adopted by the Third International
under the guiding hand of Lenin, the intellectual genius, gives the
promise. And the key to understanding lies in the realization that whenever the platform refers to "proletariat" in a governing sense, the word
really means "Communist Party elite." The platform reads:

> Just as every state, so the proletarian [Communist Party elite] state repre-
> sents an apparatus of compulsion, and this apparatus of compulsion is
> now directed against the enemy of the working class . . . On the other
> hand the dictatorship of the proletariat [Communist Party elite] which will
> place this class officially in a position of the dominant class in society,
> represents a transition state. In measure as the opposition of the bourgeoi-
> sie is broken, the latter will be expropriated and gradually converted into
> a working class of society and the dictatorship will disappear and the
> state and the dividing of society into classes will die out.

Once the masses had been led to rebel against the old society, capitalism and all its forms would be smashed, they said, and racial lines would be dissolved. National boundaries would disappear. The world's workers, they said, would control the state, own the property and reap all the profits from their labors. Philosophy, science, music, law, education and government would be given new frontiers to conquer, unchained by the past.

Thus the door of communism was opened to all the world's discontented, troubled millions. The lure was a new beginning for everyone, from the poor, oppressed peasants to the most brilliant intellects who had not found peace within themselves. But the reins of control had to remain in the hands of those "scientifically" equipped to say what was best for the people; and these were the leaders of the Communist Party, the Party which must be obeyed in all things because the Party knew best what was good for humanity.

Here was the most evil, monstrous conspiracy against man since time began—the conspiracy to shape the future of the world and to control the masses on the basis of cold, "scientific" social formulas conceived in the brain of a few Communists. These formulas could be "proved," so they claimed, in the Communist laboratory of dialectical materialism just as problems in physics are proved by mathematical equations. Thus the Communist Party's elite would rule supreme. The blackboard of history would be wiped clean—and there would be the new, "scientific" history.

But the Communist ruling clique in Moscow couldn't realize this goal until existing governments everywhere were destroyed by infiltration, subversion or conquest. The workers had to be made the pawns of the Communist elite, or the "pure" realm of "scientific" social thinking and planning could not be achieved. There could be no questioning of authority in this new order. It was, in fact, the new "religion" of materialism. It demanded unswerving loyalty by the truly faithful, because, the new teachers said, communism was loyalty to humanity itself. It was bigger than home. It was bigger than country. It was so big, in fact, that only the Kremlin's masters could be trusted with its direction.

The breadth and depth of communism were not easily grasped because the Communists were daring to tear history itself from its moorings. Twice, in 1864 and 1889, the early Communists and Socialists had tried to form an international association to weld their groups into a militant force. These were their First and Second Internationals. But in each case internal dissension over tactics and an incomplete grasp of Marxism broke them up. The old Socialists, too many of them, were thinking in terms of "reforms" such as better hours, wages and working conditions, with public ownership of property—not in terms of uprooting the whole of the old society.

The Socialist Party of America was organized in 1901 and it was beset with internal strife from the start, just like all the Socialist groups before it. In the main, the divisions were over using parliamentary methods to gain control of the government—or using violence.

In 1916 left-wing Socialists formed the Socialist Propaganda League, which advocated the Russian Bolshevik program for American Socialists even before the Bolshevik revolution in November, 1917. Early in 1919, Socialist dissidents began working in earnest to capture the Socialist Party. One group, in its newspaper, *The Revolutionary Age,* demanded an emergency national convention for reorganization of the Party's policies and tactics. If the left-wingers couldn't capture the Socialist Party, they intended to wreck it.

The American pro-Bolshevists were elated when the Third International was organized. At Moscow, the delegates met and rubber-stamped the program already formulated by Lenin. The Third International's Manifesto said in part:

> We, communists, representatives of the revolutionary proletariat of the different countries of Europe, America, and Asia, assembled in Soviet Moscow, feel and consider ourselves followers and fulfillers of the cause . . . It is our task now to . . . hasten the victory of the communist revolution in the whole world.

In the famous "21 points" adopted by the International, Point Number 16 said:

> All the resolutions of the congresses of the Communist International, as well as the resolutions of the Executive Committee are binding for all parties joining the Communist International.

American left-wing Socialists embraced the Third International's program. The right and left wings of the Socialist Party squared off for a fight. Morris Hillquit on the right issued a call to "Clear the Decks," and the left wing took up the challenge. The National Executive Committee of the Socialist Party expelled some 40,000 members in organizations considered to be disruptive forces in the cause of socialism.

The left-wing Socialists were split into two groups by an internal fight over tactics. One group wanted to form an American Communist Party immediately. The majority favored capturing the Socialist Party. Despite their split, the left-wingers emerged victorious in the Socialist Party's election of national officers in the spring of 1919, but when an emergency national convention was held in Chicago late in August, the regular executive committee refused to yield its seats to the left-wingers.

The Socialist leftists met in two separate conventions. One group organized the Communist Labor Party of America on August 31, 1919, while the other formed the Communist Party of America on September 1, 1919. Actually, except on minor points, there was little difference in the character of the two.[4]

Years later, Hillquit would say bitterly that the Soviet government was "the greatest disaster and calamity that has ever occurred to the Socialist movement."

The Communists' meetings were held one month after Hoover began his study of the ultra-radical forces then operating in America. A man whose activities drew particular attention was Ludwig C. A. K. Martens, who had arrived in New York in March—soon after the meeting of the Third International—with advance ballyhoo as the official trade representative of Soviet Russia, although the United States Government had not given diplomatic recognition to the Soviets. He was purported to have $200,000,000 in gold to be used in reopening trade relations between the two countries.

Martens set up shop at 299 Broadway in an office occupied by Santerri Nuorteva, who was in charge of Bolshevist propaganda in the United States. The Russian Bolshevik Federation in America hailed Martens' arrival in its daily paper in this fashion:

> The great significance of the appointment here of a Soviet representative consists precisely in that this appointment opens now before the American proletariat new perspectives and new opportunities; an opportunity of revolutionary activity in direct contact and cooperation with the Russian proletariat and Soviet Government of Russia.

Martens immediately became active in affairs of the left-wing Socialists. He was the center of Communist propaganda activities and, as Moscow's representative, was wined and dined and regarded as an authority on communism.

Soon Martens became involved in a fight within the Party. The suspicion gained currency that Comrade Louis C. Fraina was an undercover agent for the Department of Justice. Martens' office colleague, Nuorteva, filed formal charges with the Party against Fraina, and arrangements were made for a trial. Fraina was first given a Party trial in New York City by American Communists, and judged not guilty. Then his case was investigated by the executive committee of the Third International in Moscow, and again he was found not guilty—a proceeding which, incidentally, revealed the true chain of command in the Communist Party. As Bureau agents observed Martens' activities and associates, they began to realize that the real brains behind Martens was his secretary, Nuorteva, a light-haired, blue-eyed German, who was known to have contacted Scandinavian seamen from time to time. On July 22, 1920, a Swedish sailor who had arrived on the *S.S. Stockholm* was caught smuggling diamonds into the country. The courier carried a packet of letters to persons in this country, propaganda material and Communist directives. One envelope was addressed to Martens and contained 231 diamonds appraised at $50,000. When Martens' residence was searched, correspondence was found which referred to the shipment of diamonds. It was in this manner that the Soviets financed their early propaganda campaign in the United States.

Martens' activities also drew the attention of the New York State Legislature's Lusk Committee, which had been named to look into "seditious activities" of American citizens and aliens. The committee was an early and controversial forerunner of the House Committee on Un-American Activities. Called before the Lusk group, Martens testified that he was a member of the Russian Communist Party and that "the Revolution has been my life."

But when four months passed without any visible results in solving the June bomb plots, Senator Miles Poindexter of Washington introduced a resolution in the Senate demanding an explanation "for the failure" of the Department of Justice to take legal action leading to the punishment of American citizens, and the deportation of aliens, who advocated the overthrow of the government by force and violence.

6: *Palmer's "Red Raids"*

IT WAS 12:01 P.M., September 16, 1920—New York City.

A horse and wagon stopped near Broad Street, in front of the United States Assay Office, opposite the J. P. Morgan building. It was lunch hour and the street began to fill with secretaries, clerks and businessmen pouring from the buildings of finance. But no one paid any attention to the man slouched in the driver's seat or the object, hidden by a covering, carried in the wagon. After a few minutes the driver secured the reins and stepped down from the wagon. He walked away unnoticed.

And then the object in the old wagon exploded. It was a bomb made of dynamite and cast-iron window weights. The metal rods were hurled like shrapnel through the narrow street. Men and women were mowed down in bloody, screaming heaps. Thirty were killed and three hundred injured. The House of Morgan was damaged and one employee inside the building killed. Other financial houses were badly damaged.

The specter of terrorism was seen again in America.

The Wall Street bombing—never solved—was like a massive, thunderous taunt to those who sought to suppress the violence of the times. It was an echo of the terrorists' bombings of the year before.

After the 1919 bombings, the United States Senate had given a virtual ultimatum to Attorney General Palmer to do something—and do it quickly.

Palmer had attempted in several test cases to determine whether the wartime espionage act was applicable to the peacetime activities of anarchist groups believed responsible for the bomb terror. A test case against the El Ariete Society of Buffalo, N. Y., a Spanish anarchist association, was based on the Society's manifesto, which said in part: "Proclaim yourself openly an anarchist. Let the revolution come. Hail to the immaculate and redeeming anarchy."

Federal Judge John Raymond Hazel held that the government had failed to prove that such language constituted a conspiracy to overthrow the government. He said: "The manifesto in evidence contains many objectionable phrases—phrases of disloyalty, phrases which are seditious—but . . . which are not in violation of any statute to which my attention has been called."

Palmer was convinced that the espionage laws could not be applied to "the present radical activities," but he decided that he had authority to act under a statute providing "that any alien who, at any time after entering the United States, is found to have been at the time of entry, or to have become thereafter, a member of any one of the classes of aliens [advocating violent overthrow of the government] shall . . . be taken into custody and deported. . . ." [1]

One of Palmer's first targets was the Federation of the Union of Russian Workers, which was composed primarily of aliens who had taken no steps, after five years' residence in this country, to obtain American citizenship. The Secretary of Labor ruled that these aliens were subject to deportation on the ground that the Federation advocated violent overthrow of the United States Government.[2] The Labor Department itself had not acted in this field because Congress had refused to appropriate money for enforcement of the deportation laws. However, the Labor Department issued warrants by which agents of the Bureau of Investigation and the Immigration Bureau rounded up more than 250 Federation officers and members in twelve different cities. This was the first of the so-called "Palmer Red Raids."

The final roundup included Emma Goldman and Alexander Berkman, two admitted anarchists who had been convicted during the war of a conspiracy to persuade men not to register for the draft. In this trial, the two of them argued that their speeches and writings were individual acts and their own expressions against war—not a conspiracy. But the Supreme Court affirmed their conviction, which carried a penalty for each of them of two years in prison and fines of $10,000.

Goldman and Berkman had been anarchists for years. The government alleged that it was Emma Goldman's inflammatory speeches and writings which influenced Leon Czolgosz to kill President McKinley. As for Berkman, he had walked into the office of steel magnate Henry C. Frick during the 1892 Homestead Steel strike, and shot him. Berkman regarded Frick as a tyrant. He later wrote in his book, *Prison Memoirs of an Anarchist:* "The removal of a tyrant is not merely justifiable; it is the highest duty of every true revolutionist. Human life is, indeed, sacred and inviolate. But the killing of a tyrant, of an enemy of the people, is in no way to be considered as the taking of a life."

Goldman and Berkman were given deportation hearings at Ellis Island and the government's cases were presented by young J. Edgar Hoover. Both anarchists were ordered deported and the Supreme Court affirmed the decision.[3]

The U. S. Army solved the problem of how these revolutionaries would be deported to Russia. A transport, the *Buford,* was provided and 249 aliens were put aboard the ship, which the press promptly labeled the "Soviet Ark."

Several congressmen went from Washington to New York to observe the ship's sailing. When Emma Goldman left the transfer boat and prepared to board the ship, one of the congressmen said: "Merry Christmas, Emma." She returned the greeting by thumbing her nose at him.

Berkman was wearing high Russian boots, khaki pants and coat and a sombrero hat. He was issuing orders as the boss man of the group. And then he saw Bureau Chief Flynn and some of his agents. Berkman shook his fist at them.

"We'll come back," Berkman shouted. "And when we do, we'll get you ————!"[4]

The New York *Herald* reported: "Chief Flynn was so much impressed by the threat that he offered Berkman a cigar. He is so used to threats against his life that the outburst of the anarchist seemed to make him feel at home."

All the deportees seemed to have been supplied with plenty of money. One man asked Hoover to cash a $3,000 check. Hoover suggested he send it to his friends and have them cash it.

"I wouldn't trust you people to give it to my friends," the man said.

"All right," Hoover replied, "take it to Russia and trust the bolsheviki."

The "Soviet Ark" sailed on December 21, 1919, for Russia.

Eight days later, Hoover submitted to Attorney General Palmer a legal document titled:

MEMORANDUM BRIEF
prepared upon the status of
LUDWIG CHRISTIAN ALEXANDER KASLOVITCH MARTENS [5]
Under the Act of Congress, approved October 16, 1918

This was one of the first legal briefs drawn against the Communist Party from the viewpoint that it was a conspiracy aimed against non-Communist governments the world over. But for its application to Martens' particular case, the argument was confined to the proposition that the Party was engaged in a conspiracy to overthrow by force the government of the United States, and thus, as a member of this Party, Martens was subject to deportation.

In its essentials, Hoover's argument was that the Soviet Government was controlled by the same men who controlled the Russian Communist Party, and this Party advocated the overthrow of the United States Government by force and violence. The Russian Communists, as well as the American Communists and all others, adhered to the principles and tactics adopted by the Third International; the Third International was in reality a creature of the Russian Communists.

"Having established the above points," Hoover said, "the conclusion necessarily follows that if Ludwig C. A. K. Martens is a member of the Communist Party of Russia and if that party advocates the overthrow of the government of the United States by force and violence, Martens falls within that class of persons subject to deportation under the Act of Congress, approved October 16, 1918."

Here was an effort, within the narrow confines of a single statute, to reduce to legal language the vast political-social conspiracy of the Communist dictatorship. Hoover prepared similar briefs on the Communist Party of America and the Communist Labor Party. And Palmer chose these two organizations as his next targets.

Orders went out to Bureau of Investigation agents, signed by Director Flynn's assistant, Frank Burke, calling for raids on the Communist meeting places on the evening of Friday, January 2, 1920. Agents were supplied with copies of Hoover's briefs. They were instructed by Burke to send reports of the raids to Hoover in the GID, where the names and activities of the extremists were being catalogued.

Burke's order said in part:

All literature, books, papers, and anything hanging on the walls should be gathered up; the ceilings and partitions should be sounded for hiding places . . . Violence towards any aliens should be scrupulously avoided . . . If found in groups . . . they should be lined up against the wall and there searched . . . I leave it entirely to your discretion as to the method by which you should gain access to such places. If . . . it is absolutely necessary for you to obtain a search warrant for the premises, you should communicate with the local authorities . . . grounds for deportation in these cases will be based solely upon membership in the Communist Party of America or the Communist Labor Party. . . .

At the appointed time, agents in thirty-three cities, armed with some 3,000 warrants issued by the Bureau of Immigration, rounded up approximately 2,500 aliens for deportation hearings. A total of 446 were deported in the fiscal year ending June 30, 1921.

The outcry against injustices in these raids was to be heard for years. Complaints rolled in not only from Communists and other extremists, but from lawyers, labor leaders and newspapers, who protested that Bureau agents had invaded private homes and meeting places without search warrants; aliens and citizens had been arrested and held without warrants; and prisoners had been denied the right of counsel. It was alleged, too, that agents were guilty of assault, forgery and perjury.

Before the House Rules Committee, Palmer tangled with Assistant Secretary of Labor Louis F. Post in a row over Post's refusal to approve many deportations. Post said that the nation's press had created a "great terroristic scare in the country." Post's lawyer charged that Palmer had acted in "absolute ignorance of American principles" and accused the Department of Justice of organizing Communist branches, enlisting members and then reporting their names for deportation.

Palmer angrily denounced these statements as "outrageously false." He defended the raids and accused Post of leaning "toward protection and tolerance for the anarchists." He implied that Post had unconsciously become a victim of Bolshevik propaganda and had refused to approve deportations when the evidence was overwhelming.

A committee of twelve lawyers representing the National Popular Government League kept the controversy boiling with a "Report upon the Illegal Practices of the United States Department of Justice." Then a subcommittee of the Senate Judiciary Committee was formed to investigate, and Palmer was again called on to explain the actions of his agents. The Attorney General once more defended his department and accepted responsibility for the policy that had been followed. He recalled that the Senate, by resolution, had virtually hounded him to do something about the bomb plots of June 2, 1919.

Palmer said:

I say that I was shouted at from every editorial sanctum in America from sea to sea. I was preached upon from every pulpit; I was urged—I could feel it dinned into my ears—throughout the country to do something and do it now, and do it quick, and do it in a way that would bring results to stop this sort of thing in the United States . . . I accept responsibility for everything they [my agents] did. If one or two of them, overzealous or perhaps outraged as patriotic American citizens—and all of them were —by the conduct of these aliens, stepped over the bounds and treated them a little roughly, or too roughly, I forgive them. I do not defend it, but I am not going to raise any row about it.

But Palmer's unyielding defense could not justify the abuses in the raids. Dean Harlan Fiske Stone of the Columbia University School of Law gave as his judgment: "It appears by the public admissions of the Attorney General and otherwise that he has proceeded on the theory that such aliens are not entitled to the constitutional guaranty of due process of law." Stone urged legislation to give aliens better protection from "arbitrary exercise of power."

During the Palmer raids controversy, Secretary of Labor Wilson had ruled that alien members of the Communist Party of America were deportable, the organization having an objective of violent overthrow of the government. But he held that the Communist Labor Party, in its program, had left the door open to political change by parliamentary means—and thus its members did not fall into the same class as those of the Communist Party. Hoover's argument in these cases was that the two parties had the same aims and principles, and were twinlike in their beliefs, a view supported later by Communist leader William Z. Foster, who saw only matters of "sectarianism" dividing them. But the Secretary of Labor's decision on the Communist Labor Party was final.

In deportation cases reaching the federal courts, the legal dispute revolved around the Bureau of Investigation agents' disregard of civil rights, and the ruling by Secretary Wilson that the Communist Party of America advocated the violent overthrow of the United States Government. The opinions handed down in two cases were startling in their clash of logic. It was as though these judges were not talking about the same subject.

Judge George W. Anderson, in the U. S. District Court of Massachusetts, saw in the Communist Party a pacifist organization,

. . . like that of a fraternal society constituted on the lodge system . . . Its whole scheme is for propaganda by words, not by deeds. No weapons of the cutting or exploding kind, with which . . . revolutions are carried on, were found in this raid. There is therefore not a scintilla of evidence warranting a finding that the Communists are committed to the "overthrow of the Government of the United States" by violence . . . The conclusion is irresistible that the only force worth discussion, believed in or advocated by this party, is the general strike; otherwise, its methods are those of ordinary political and social propaganda. It is true that in the Manifesto and Platform . . . are found . . . some stock phrases concerning . . . "conquest of the power of the state" . . . But it is notorious that political platforms generally adopt the language of exaggeration . . . Here in the Occident, freedom, and a saving sense of humor and of proportion, have, until recently, saved us from being frightened by crusaders' rhetoric . . . Institutions grounded on liberty and justice under law are too well rooted to warrant us in being terrorized by criticisms and mooted changes. The whole Communist Party is negligible.[6]

Judge John C. Knox, in the Federal Court, Southern District of New York, saw the Communists in this light:

. . . I am of opinion that the manifesto and program of the Communist Party, together with other exhibits in the case, are of such character as to easily lead a reasonable man to conclude that the purpose of the Communist Party is to accomplish its end, namely, the capture and destruction of the State as now constituted by force and violence . . . It is suggested by counsel for the relator that communism, an abstract human idealism, is on trial in this proceeding. With such statement I can not agree . . . I am unable to perceive how the expropriation of private property can be accomplished without the employment of forbidden instrumentalities . . . Should such a transfer [of property] be demanded and refused, could it for a moment be supposed that the communists, if they considered their strength sufficient, would hesitate and seek peaceful means of persuasion? It seems to me that they would unquestionably exert whatever coercion and employ whatever force and violence was necessary to the achievement of their success . . . I am free to say . . . such possibility is not of the immediate future . . . the question here is not one of degrees of imminence of overthrow by force and violence, but, rather, whether that is the ultimate purpose of the organization.[7]

These opposite views—voiced in 1920—drew the lines in America's battle over communism. On the one side were those who saw communism as a force of idealism and the Communist Party as merely another political group. On the other were those who saw communism as a conspiracy leading to the denial of true freedom, and the Party as the tool for achieving this end by violence—when enough power was in its hands.

The Palmer raids drove the Communist Party underground and reduced its membership from an estimated 60,000 members to a hard core of 10,000. The raids came at a time of violent labor unrest and industrial adjustment in the postwar period. After the war ended there were the great steel strike, the Boston police strike, a general strike in Seattle and others. Most employers were fighting hard against union demands for recognition and improved working conditions—and the Communists and IWW were active in the strikes. The Department of Justice and the Bureau of Investigation were accused of siding with employers against labor, and using the "Red scare" as a strike-breaking weapon.

Throughout the months of unrest, young Hoover had continued to receive information on the activities of the Communists. In August, 1922, he noted in a memorandum: "The Communist Party of America is holding a convention at Bridgman, Berrien County, Michigan. Three agents of the Chicago office are at Bridgman under cover, having under surveillance certain persons attending the convention."

These "certain persons" were three representatives from the Third International who had gathered with U. S. Communist leaders in a woodland hideaway on Lake Michigan. They were meeting to decide whether to maintain the Communist underground or to abolish it and work through a united front. Moscow decreed that the basic principles of Marxism-Leninism called for both an open and an underground organization. For three days the delegates bickered over details in caucuses, while Bureau agents watched them from the forest. These leaders had not yet learned all the lessons of strict conformity to the Party line —but they were learning.

The Bridgman meeting was thrown into high confusion when William Z. Foster, while strolling in the woods, stumbled onto two Bureau agents. The alarm was spread and the delegates fled. Some were arrested by Michigan police officers and charged with violating the state's syndicalist laws.

The Bridgman meeting showed the grim determination of the Communists to seek new ways to attack American life. A few months later, in April, 1923, the underground Communist Party consolidated with the above-ground Workers Party, which had been formed by the Communists in late 1921. Actually, they were one and the same.

But when the Communists fled from the Bridgman meeting, they left behind them a detailed history of underground communism, including a list of all those who had been at the meeting. This list was a "Who's Who" of early American communism—found buried in the woods in two potato barrels.

Washington Turmoil

7: *A National Disgrace*

BLUFF, handsome Warren G. Harding became the twenty-ninth President of the United States on March 4, 1921. He drew around him the friends from Ohio whom he had known as a small-town newspaper editor and politician. They had been his poker-playing pals and his political board of strategy. They had helped chart his victorious campaigns leading to the White House.

It was hardly surprising that Harding named his old Ohio friend, Harry M. Daugherty, to the Cabinet post of Attorney General. But the next three years were to be packed with surprises. These surprises would almost wreck the Bureau of Investigation, and would leave the country disillusioned with men in high places who had betrayed the people's trust.

Before the Harding inauguration, Department of Justice employees had been playing the old government game of guessing who would be missing in the new administration's personnel shake-down. The Democrats had controlled federal patronage for eight years. Now the Republicans, by right of political conquest, had their turn.

In this fog of uncertainty, William J. Flynn tried to dispel the doubts about his own future as Director of the Bureau of Investigation. Letters praising Flynn and recommending him for retention came to Daugherty not only from members of Congress but also from four federal court judges.

Flynn had reason to be uneasy about his job. Reports were being circulated that the next Director of the Bureau of Investigation would be "the famous international sleuth, William J. Burns." Burns was seen around town with Daugherty and others who had easy access to the White House. He and Daugherty had been boyhood friends in Ohio, and he had become well known as the president of the William J. Burns International Detective Agency.

Burns's business clients gave him their support. The vice president of a Chicago bank wrote the White House that "no man in his line in the United States has a stronger following among the bankers of the country than Wm. J. Burns . . ."

The reports began to picture Burns's future role in government as one of giant proportions. He wasn't to be merely the Director of the Bureau of Investigation, but a super-chief of all the investigative agencies throughout the entire government. The *Chicago Banker* newsletter said:

> There is joy all along the [Pennsylvania] avenue on a report that President Harding is to make William J. Burns "commander-in-chief" of all the detective and secret service departments of the government. Attorney General Daugherty, who has known Burns for years and employed him on special occasions, is the sponsor for the detective. Large business interests, especially those controlled by certain New York banking houses, also are working for Burns . . . Labor is "ferninst" [against] Burns, but everybody not in the "Union" is for him.

Labor certainly was against Burns. The Central Trades and Labor Council of Greater New York wrote President Harding and urged him to find a man for the job "about whom no odium has ever been cast . . ." A Canadian newspaper exposé charged that the William J. Burns International Detective Agency of Canada, Ltd., had been sending letters to manufacturers offering, for a price, to spy on workers in plants or union conventions and then report "when, where and how labor troubles will break out." His agents were accused of deliberately fomenting labor discord.

One letter to the President recalled the 1912 scandal in which Burns and his men had been accused by former Attorney General George W. Wickersham of rigging a jury box with "convictors." The Wickersham report on this case was attached to the letter. Perhaps Harding never saw the damning report. It was routed by Harding's secretary, along with other protests, to Daugherty in the Department of Justice.

The protests were useless. Daugherty fired Flynn with a curt telegram, dated August 18. Burns was notified of his appointment on the same day and he wired Daugherty: "I cannot find words to fully express my appreciation of the confidence reposed in me by you in this appointment . . ." Flynn protested that he was fired unjustly and not given a reason for his dismissal.

In the Daugherty shake-up of the Department of Justice, twenty-six-year-old J. Edgar Hoover found himself transferred from his post as Special Assistant to the Attorney General into the position of Assistant Director of the Bureau of Investigation on August 22, 1921. Hoover went on the Bureau's payroll at an annual salary of $4,000.

The Bureau's old records reflect the strong political influences at work in the Harding Administration. One memorandum to Burns, reportedly from a senator, gave a breakdown on the party affiliations of the Bureau's Chicago agents. The Republicans were listed without comment, but after the names of the Democrats were such comments as: "Son-in-law of Democratic State Senator; maintains active affiliation with Democratic organization." "Placed by Congressman A." "Democrat and active as such." "Let out some two years ago but was later reinstated and it is understood through the efforts of Senator B."

Into this state of affairs strode the notorious detective, Gaston B. Means, to become an agent of the Bureau of Investigation on October 28, 1921, by Burns's appointment. He quickly established the fact that he was Burns's favorite investigator and close friend. But Means and Hoover clashed almost immediately. Hoover asked Burns to order Means to stay out of his office. Hoover didn't like the man's spending habits or his morals.

One of Means's hangouts in the Department of Justice was the private office occupied by a "mystery man" with the ordinary name of Jess Smith. Means and Smith got along well and seemed to understand each other perfectly—Means knew Smith was no ordinary fellow.

Jess Smith was Harry Daugherty's closest friend and he lived with the Daughertys in their Wardman Park Hotel apartment. Although he had no official position in the government, the word soon got around Washington that Jess Smith was a man with influence in high places. He was known to be a personal friend of President and Mrs. Harding and he was often among the invited guests at exclusive White House social affairs. He carried on a voluminous personal and semiofficial correspondence from his Justice Department office. It was said that he used Means for confidential investigations of people and matters of interest to Daugherty.

The New York *Sun* later took this notice of Means:

Means has been in the papers a long time . . . He was an agent of Germany (in 1916) paid to embarrass British commerce. In 1917 he was accused of the murder of a rich widow, Mrs. Maude A. King, who was killed by a pistol bullet while in North Carolina with . . . Means. He was acquitted of the killing, only to be denounced in another court for filing a forged will which would have put the King estate practically at his disposal. Next we find this fellow an investigator in the Department of Justice. . . .

For years, Means had been battling spies, crooks and international thieves, all of whom seemed to be banded together to thwart his honest aims, as Means told the story. Once he recovered trunkloads of documents vital to America's defense only to have them "stolen" by foreign agents just before delivery to Army Intelligence. The flaw in this story was that the trunks weighed the same when delivered without the documents as they did when supposedly crammed with secret papers. Means didn't get the letter of recommendation from the Army which was the purpose of that scheme.

But Burns stoutly defended his old friend against his detractors. Soon after Means came to the Bureau, an attorney who had helped prosecute Means for Mrs. King's death protested to Attorney General Daugherty and Burns that Means had threatened him, using "foul and indecent language." Burns wrote the attorney that he had "done Mr. Means a very great injustice," inasmuch as Means's own "official diary" showed he couldn't possibly have made the alleged call.

But too many people were asking embarrassing questions about Means, and Daugherty and Burns solved the problem in this fashion: the Attorney General suspended Means as a Bureau agent on February 9, 1922, "until further notice," then Burns put Means on the Bureau's payroll as an informant, where he continued business as usual.

The country itself was sick, and running a high fever in the postwar adjustment. Jobless men were walking the streets by the millions. Within a few months Harding's "Back to Normalcy" campaign slogan was being jeered at by the Democrats. The *Nation* taunted Harding on his legislative record and his support of higher tariffs, saying: "He is now slowly and painfully finding out what should have been patent . . . that you cannot turn back the hands of time . . . to McKinley-ize America, to treat it as if nothing had changed since 1896. . . ."

On the labor front, trouble had been brewing for months on the railroads. The Government's Railroad Labor Board had decreed a 12-percent wage cut for almost all railroad employees in 1921, and then averted a strike with assurances that no further wage reductions would be considered for some time to come.

But as revenues continued to fall, the railroads demanded relief in the form of further wage cuts. The Railroad Labor Board on June 6, 1922, announced that railroad shopmen would have to take another 12-percent cut. On July 1, 400,000 shopmen walked out on strike. The "Big Four" Railroad Brotherhood unions—the trainmen—didn't strike.

The railroads' management took the position that those who struck would have no seniority rights when they returned to their jobs. President Harding tried to halt the strike by mediation, but his effort collapsed on the issue of guaranteed seniority rights—the issue which had come to overshadow the original wage issue.

There was violence. Nonstrikers were beaten. Strikers were attacked by railroad guards. Men were killed. Bridges were dynamited and engines sabotaged. The movement of trains was slowed and strangulation of the nation's economy was feared.

On July 20, Burns sent a message to Bureau agents:

> Department [of Justice] advised that disorders are prevalent in the several districts due to refusal or inability of State and municipal authorities to enforce [the] law. In localities where United States Marshals and deputies need assistance on account of disorder, the Attorney General directs that all special agents shall cooperate with U. S. Marshals in seeing that the commerce and mails . . . are moved and not obstructed. You will use your sound judgment in assigning agents to such cooperation. . . .

A complaint was received, too, that U. S. deputy marshals were acting as employment agents and hiring strikebreakers for the Chicago, Milwaukee and St. Paul Railway. Daugherty asked Burns to make "a confidential investigation . . . and let me have a memorandum on the results obtained."

President Harding met with his Cabinet. The decision was made to obtain an injunction against the strikers. Daugherty appeared in the Federal District Court in Chicago on September 1, and obtained what was to be called "the most sweeping injunction ever issued." The Attorney General declared he would use the powers of the federal government to prevent labor unions "from destroying the open shop."

Under the Daugherty restraining order, any act or word which interfered with the railroads' operations could be a violation of the injunction under a literal interpretation of the language.

So it was that a decision by the Harding Cabinet, carried out by Attorney General Daugherty, involved the Bureau of Investigation in the railroad fight along with the U. S. marshals, U. S. attorneys, and all the law enforcement machinery of the federal government.

Fortunately, union leaders and officials representing a number of the nation's railroads came to an agreement two months after the strike began. The workers retained their seniority rights and their union claimed a victory of principle. But the wage cut stood. The strike continued on some roads for a full year, and when Daugherty's temporary injunction was made permanent the New York *World* commented: "In effect, a law has been created by a Federal court at Mr. Daugherty's request [to prohibit strikes affecting interstate commerce], a law at variance with American traditions, in conflict with majority opinion and utterly impossible to enforce."

More evidence of the sickness of the times was reflected in the mushroom growth of a secret "fraternity" which promised in its own manifesto:

> . . . to protect the weak, the innocent, and the defenseless from the indignities, wrongs and outrages of the lawless, the violent, and the brutal; to relieve the injured and the oppressed; to succor the suffering and the unfortunate . . .

By any humane standard, this was a noble purpose. But these particular protectors of the oppressed were the Knights of the Ku Klux Klan.

The first Klan was born in the bleak, terrible days of the South's Reconstruction after the Civil War. Some historians say it started in Pulaski, Tennessee, merely as a harmless secret society whose members were seeking amusement. But amusement soon turned to terror. Hooded men used the Klan to frighten Negroes and to maintain the ascendancy of the white natives over Negroes and carpetbaggers. In time the movement died out.

But in 1915, Colonel William S. Simmons of Atlanta, Georgia ("They call me Colonel largely out of respect"), had revived a Klan which was anti-Negro, anti-Catholic and anti-Jew. The Klan made slow progress until 1920, when Colonel Simmons joined forces with Edward Young Clarke, whose Southern Publicity Association had managed World War I membership drives for the Red Cross, YMCA and other worthy causes. Clarke and the Colonel agreed on a contract. Clarke became an Imperial Kleagle and sent his salesmen—or kleagles —across the land. Out of each $10 initiation fee paid by a klansman, Clarke and his organization received $8. The other $2 went to Colonel Simmons, the Klan's Imperial Wizard. In addition, of course, there was the income from the bed-sheet robes and masks which probably cost all of $1.25 wholesale and were sold to the klansmen for $6.50 each.

In an incredibly short time, fiery crosses were blazing in the night from New England to California. Grown men, many of them leading citizens of their communities, gathered solemnly at night and peered from behind their bed sheets to watch initiation ceremonies. They joined by the tens of thousands, and the Klan spread to virtually every state in the Union. The Klan for a time was said to hold the balance of political power in Indiana. It was strong in New England. At one time it reportedly dominated the Texas legislature. In a good many states, candidates for public office could not hope to win election without Klan support.

In some communities the Klan was no more than a harmless fraternal lodge. In other places its interests were purely political. But hooded men began to terrorize families. Then communities. Then entire states. The old pattern of Reconstruction days was repeating itself.

For more than a year, the Bureau of Investigation checked on Klan activities without finding any federal law violations. But one day in September, 1922, J. Edgar Hoover sat in his office at the Bureau and listened to a fantastic tale brought to him by Paul Wooton, Washington correspondent for the New Orleans *Times-Picayune,* who had been working on an exposé of the Ku Klux Klan.

"Do you mean to say the Governor of Louisiana can't even use the telephone, telegraph, or the United States mails because of the Klan?" Hoover exclaimed.

"That's just what the Governor told me personally when he sent for me to come to Louisiana," Wooton replied. He handed Hoover a letter from Governor John M. Parker of Louisiana. "I brought you this letter because Governor Parker can't trust the mails. His mail is watched by the Klan and his telephone is tapped by klansmen. He needs help."

The letter delivered by Wooton was addressed to Attorney General Daugherty. Fantastic it might sound—but it was true. Governor Parker was asking help to break the hold of the Klan over northern Louisiana, where two men were believed to have been kidnaped, tortured and murdered by klansmen.

Hoover conferred with Attorney General A. V. Coco of Louisiana. It was decided that Governor Parker should direct his appeal for help directly to President Harding. And this the Governor did in a letter to the President dated October 2, 1922. The letter said in part:

> Due to the activities of an organized body reputed to be the Ku Klux Klan . . . not only have the laws been violated, but men taken out, beaten and whipped. Two men have been brutally murdered without trial or charges . . . my information tonight is that six more citizens have been ordered to leave their homes (in Morehouse Parish) under penalty of death. These conditions are beyond the control of the Governor of this State . . . a number of law officers and others charged with the enforcement of law in this State are publicly recognized as members of this Ku Klux Klan.

Parker asked the President to direct the Department of Justice to take action in accordance with Section 4, Article 4, of the Constitution of the United States, which guarantees to the state federal protection against domestic violence—on application by either a state legislature or a state's chief executive.

The final decision by the Department was that Bureau agents would be sent to aid Governor Parker, but that the state itself would handle any prosecutions. The decision was regarded as a precedent that would affect future police relationships between the states and the federal government. The agents began working under cover, themselves hunted by klansmen at times. But slowly they pieced together the story.

The Klan controlled the whole of northern Louisiana by terror. The Klan's membership included law enforcement officers and leading townspeople. Persons considered undesirable by the Klan were ordered out of their communities. Women and men were flogged or jailed on orders of the Klan leaders, who made their own rules for judging morality.

One night Dr. B. M. McKoin, a klansman and a former mayor of Mer Rouge, reported that his car had been fired on by would-be assassins. Some cynical citizens suggested that McKoin fired the shots himself for a self-serving purpose. Klansmen seized Watt Daniels and T. F. Richards for questioning about the McKoin case, but each had an alibi and they were released with a warning not to talk.

Daniels and Richards told friends they recognized some of their kidnapers and the word got around. A week later, hooded, armed men halted the automobiles of Mer Rouge townspeople as they returned home from a barbecue and baseball game. Women screamed and fainted. Their unarmed menfolk were helpless. The raiders seized Daniels and Richards. No one saw them alive again.

Professional divers, guarded by state militiamen, searched the waters of Lake La Fourche, where a gasoline fire had blazed on the bank the night of the kidnaping. On December 22, 1922, the lake yielded the headless, mutilated bodies. Almost every bone in the bodies was broken. Old wagon wheels had been used as torture racks. The autopsy indicated that the mutilations had been performed by someone skilled in surgery.

Murder charges were filed against Dr. McKoin and a deputy sheriff. But no indictments were returned. The *Times-Picayune* reported one explanation—a majority of the grand jurors were klansmen.

Despite the lack of convictions, this fight helped turn public sentiment against the Klan, but the change came slowly. After Colonel Simmons formed his alliance with the super-salesman Clarke, the Klan grew to almost one million members in forty-six states. In 1925, the Klan, in a giant show of political strength, paraded 50,000 sheeted men down Pennsylvania Avenue in Washington.

The power of the Klan was gradually broken by the FBI and local law enforcement officers with the aid and support aroused by crusading newspapers. Although the Klan upheld the purity of womanhood, one of the FBI's earliest encounters with the Klan involved the arrest of Imperial Kleagle Clarke in New Orleans, Louisiana, and his indictment in Houston, Texas, on White Slave Traffic Act charges. Clarke pleaded guilty on March 10, 1924, in Federal Court and was fined $5,000.

For years the Bureau's agents had been used by the Department of Justice in the protection of civil rights, particularly in an effort to stamp out peonage, which had existed in various forms throughout the country even after the abolition of slavery.

Peonage became a federal problem because some states had laws which invited corrupt and immoral practices. It was possible for an employer to swear out a warrant against a poor and ignorant laborer, arrange his release on bail or as surety, and then force the man to work on his farm or plantation through threats of imprisonment. In other cases, the law permitted an employer to pay a prisoner's fine and then bind the prisoner by contract to work out the debt.

One of the worst peonage cases on record came under the Bureau's investigation in 1921 in Georgia, when reports were received that John S. Williams "bought" Negro prisoners from county and state road gangs and jails and then forced them to work out the "purchase price" on his farm. They were in fact Williams' slaves. When Williams learned that the Bureau of Investigation was investigating him, he allegedly killed more than twelve Negroes—thus removing them as potential witnesses. He was convicted of murder and given a life sentence.

Public sentiment was so aroused against these practices that peonage became a charge rarely heard in courts of law.

Ironically, while Bureau agents were being used to protect civil rights in Louisiana and other places, William J. Burns and Jess Smith were sending men to spy on members of Congress who were then demanding investigations of reported corruption in the Harding Administration—corruption that had included the infamous "Teapot Dome" scandal.

Soon after taking office, President Harding had turned over to the Interior Department the administration of naval oil reserves in California and Wyoming, the latter known as the Teapot Dome oil field. Secretary of the Interior Albert B. Fall signed a contract with private interests headed by Harry F. Sinclair and Edward L. Doheny, permitting them to pump and store the oil from naval reserves on a royalty basis. The transaction was defended on the grounds that Teapot Dome oil reserves were being drained off by nearby private wells, and that the new arrangement would protect the government's interests.

But soon after the agreement was announced, Fall's neighbors in New Mexico noted sudden signs of prosperity at the Fall ranch, where expensive improvements were being made. Later Sinclair and Doheny explained that they had "loaned" Fall more than $135,000. Doheny said his $100,000 share of the loan was merely "an accommodation to an old friend."

These explanations didn't satisfy Congress. Questions were being asked, too, about the handling of the Veterans' Administration and the Alien Property Custodian's Office, and the Department of Justice's failure to prosecute alleged frauds in World War I contracts.

Just as the storm was breaking over the Harding Administration, the mysterious Jess Smith killed himself, on May 30, 1923, leaving an estate valued at some $500,000. President Harding became ill on a trip to Alaska, and died on August 2, 1923. Calvin Coolidge became President of the United States, inheriting a truly great mess.

Reports of corruption snowballed. An outcry was raised in Congress for Daugherty's resignation. At first there were no charges that the Attorney General himself was involved in wrongdoing. The *Literary Digest* commented that Daugherty's resignation was being demanded because Congress and the people had lost confidence in him, "not because of anything he has done, but because of what he has failed to do."

Senator Burton K. Wheeler of Montana was one of the outspoken leaders in the fight against Daugherty. The Republicans blocked several investigation efforts in Congress, but on March 1, 1924, on a resolution sponsored by Wheeler, the Senate voted to look into Daugherty's conduct in office. The only dissenting vote was cast by Senator Davis Elkins of West Virginia.

While the Senate was conducting its sensational investigation of the Attorney General, Wheeler himself was indicted by a Great Falls, Montana, grand jury. He was charged with taking money from a syndicate of oil prospectors with the understanding he would persuade the Department of the Interior to give the syndicate exclusive oil and gas prospecting leases. Wheeler immediately charged that he was the victim of a "frame-up" by the Department of Justice. The Raleigh, North Carolina, *News and Observer* called his indictment a concoction of William J. Burns, Harry Daugherty and the Republican National Committee.

Developments gave strong support to the newspaper's theory. A Senate committee and then a Montana jury found Wheeler innocent. The Philadelphia *Record* said the trial was "one of the most contemptible and vindictive political persecutions ever known in this country." Burns admitted in the Daugherty investigation that he sent three Bureau of Investigation accountants into Montana to help work on the Wheeler case. These accountants, Department of Justice records show, were on the payroll of the Bureau of Investigation, but they were assigned to John S. Pratt, Special Assistant to the Attorney General, and they reported exclusively to Pratt.[1]

The Daugherty investigation would never have been complete without Burns's old friend, Gaston B. Means—and Means made his appearance a spectacular one, testifying to espionage directed against the senators themselves. Means said he had arranged to have agents sneak into senators' offices, open their mail, search their files and spy on them in an effort to find something damaging which could be used to stop their attacks on Daugherty. Means said he delivered his reports to Jess Smith. He indicated that he never dealt with anyone below the Daugherty-Smith-Burns level of authority.

At one point, Senator Wheeler said: "Senator Moses [of New Hampshire] suggests to me that I can save time by asking you what Senators you have not investigated?"

Means: "Oh, there are lots of them I haven't. They are a pretty clean body. You don't find much on them, either. You don't find very much."

Means explained to the senators how a "detective" operates: "Oh, search . . . [for] all the mail that comes in, all the papers, anything that he has got lying around. Find out in his home. Just like you . . . pursue, Senator, when you make a criminal investigation . . . report what you find . . . if it is damaging, why of course it is used. If it is fine, why you cannot use it. It does no damage."

Whether this testimony was truth, fiction or a combination of both, no one but Means would ever know. But his testimony blended well with the general picture of corruption of which he had been a part. As historian Samuel Hopkins Adams said later, the Department of Justice had "reached its lowest ebb in morale, morals, and efficiency, and this in spite of many able sub-executives. The blight of the Daugherty-Jess Smith-Burns system was over it all."

On March 28, 1924, President Coolidge demanded, and received, Daugherty's resignation as Attorney General. At last the time had arrived for the big housecleaning in government.

8: *Hoover's Housecleaning*

PRESIDENT CALVIN COOLIDGE welcomed into his White House office one day in March, 1924, a big New Englander with the plodding, deliberate gait of a countryman. The visitor was Harlan Fiske

Stone, New Hampshire-born Republican, New York attorney and former Dean of the Columbia University School of Law.

The President talked to Stone for a long time. Here was the man Coolidge hoped would become his Attorney General, and whose rock-like integrity he believed could restore public confidence in the Department of Justice, which was being called, with reason, the "Department of Easy Virtue." When Stone left the White House that bleak March day he had agreed to take on the job of reorganizing the Department, particularly its Bureau of Investigation.

Coolidge announced on April 2 that Stone, his old schoolmate at Amherst College, would succeed Harry Daugherty as Attorney General. With a few exceptions, congressional reaction to Stone's appointment was one of approval. There was considerable talk recalling that Stone had criticized the Palmer "Red Raids" in 1919 and that he had lifted his voice in unpopular defense of conscientious objectors during World War I. Later, Senator Tom Heflin of Alabama called Stone "a hireling of the Morgan bank" because he had once been associated in the practice of law with a son-in-law of the financier J. P. Morgan. He was pictured in the dual role of a liberal and a reactionary. But the Senate overwhelmingly confirmed Coolidge's appointment of Stone on April 6. Stone was launched on the public career in which he became Chief Justice of the United States and won lasting recognition for his indestructible honesty and moral courage.

Stone moved into the Department of Justice driver's seat and then looked around cautiously before making any moves toward reorganization. He was not a man to make snap judgments, and without doubt he wanted to be sure he was choosing the right men for the right jobs. But first there had to be a housecleaning. As the Pittsburgh *Gazette Times* said, "[Stone] will find a degree of demoralization in the Department of Justice that will have to be eliminated before he can get down to the real business of the office."

One month and seven days after his appointment, Stone accepted the resignation of William J. Burns as Director of the Bureau of Investigation. The old era had ended for the Bureau.

Stone had been looking around for the right man to put in charge of the Bureau of Investigation. He mentioned his problem at a Cabinet meeting attended by Herbert Hoover, who was then Secretary of Commerce. When Hoover went back to his office he told his assistant, Larry Richey, that Stone was looking for an intelligent young man to put in charge of the Bureau.

Richey replied, "Why should they look around when they have the man they need right over there now—a young, well-educated lawyer named Hoover."

"You think he can do the job?" the Secretary asked.

"I know he can," Richey replied. "He's a good friend of mine."

A few days later, Herbert Hoover told Richey he had talked to Stone and the Attorney General was going to "try young Hoover out."

The day after Burns resigned, twenty-nine-year-old J. Edgar Hoover was summoned to Stone's office. It was May 10, 1924. The news had already circulated through the Bureau that Burns was leaving. Hoover wasn't sure whether he would be next or not. Stone was known to be gruff and tough, and heads were falling.

Hoover entered Stone's office and saw the big man seated behind his desk. Stone was over six feet tall and weighed more than two hundred pounds. He looked to Hoover at that moment as if he'd been carved out of solid stone.

"Sit down," Stone said, scowling as usual. The scowl was a habit.

Hoover took a seat. Stone peered at him over his glasses and the two men looked at each other across the desk. Then Stone said abruptly, "Young man, I want you to be Acting Director of the Bureau of Investigation."

Hoover realized the magnitude of the compliment. He knew in that instant that Attorney General Stone had rejected the arguments that he was too young for the job. Far more important, he knew that Stone did not hold him responsible for the policies, mistakes and corrupt actions of those who had directed the Department of Justice and the Bureau of Investigation in the past.

Finally Hoover said, "I'll take the job, Mr. Stone, on certain conditions."

"What are they?"

"The Bureau must be divorced from politics and not be a catch-all for political hacks. Appointments must be based on merit. Second, promotions will be made on proved ability and the Bureau will be responsible only to the Attorney General."

The Attorney General scowled and said, "I wouldn't give it to you under any other conditions. That's all. Good day."

Thus it was, under the guidance of Harlan Fiske Stone, that Hoover took over the command of the Bureau of Investigation, first as Acting Director, and then, seven months later, as Director.

In those first months, Hoover leaned heavily on Stone for support. And he received it. The Bureau was in disrepute. Demands were being heard across the country that the Bureau be disbanded and its work distributed throughout the other departments and agencies of government.

But Hoover believed strongly that the Department of Justice should have lawyers and accountants trained in collecting evidence. He recognized that the government's cases too often were not presented properly because the evidence was gathered in a haphazard fashion by untrained agents. Yet the collection of evidence was the basis for proving innocence or guilt.

Stone and Hoover had no difficulty agreeing on basic policies for the Bureau. Three days after Hoover's appointment, it was agreed:

1. The Bureau would be a fact-gathering organization, and its activities would be limited strictly to investigations of violations of federal laws.

2. Investigations would be made at and under the direction of the Attorney General.

3. The personnel of the Bureau would be reduced as far ". . . as is consistent with the proper performance of its duties."

4. The incompetents and the unreliables would be discharged as quickly as possible.

5. All the "dollar-a-year" men, "honorary" agents and others not regularly employed would be cut from the rolls.

6. No new appointments would be made without the Attorney General's approval—and preference would be given to men of good character and ability who had some legal training.

This agreement, in the form of a memorandum of instructions, gave Hoover elbow room in which to work. He began issuing a rapid-fire series of orders to agents, who were startled by the sudden and unexpected burst of attention from Washington. The Bureau records indicate that many agents dismissed the whole thing as a passing flurry —they were confident that if they sat around long enough, it would go away, and that if it didn't, they could always write their senator or congressman. Other agents expressed delight, because they glimpsed the hope of an organization of which they could be proud.

One of Hoover's first acts was to see that Gaston B. Means was fired, officially and finally. Means had remained in the status of a "temporarily suspended" agent all during the months he had worked for Burns and Jess Smith as an undercover man. Hoover sent a memorandum to Stone suggesting that Means's name be erased from the rolls. Stone's reaction was: "Please do this."

Six days after taking command, Hoover sent a note to Stone, saying:

I have . . . instructed the heads of the respective Divisions of the Bureau that the activities of the Bureau are to be limited strictly to investigations of violations of the federal statutes under your direction . . .

I have already commenced an examination of the personnel files of each of the employees of the Bureau and have already recommended a number of Special Agents whose services may be discontinued for the best interests of the service. I shall continue to submit these recommendations to you . . . as rapidly as I can examine the personnel files.

Every effort will be made by the employees of the Bureau to strengthen the morale . . . and to carry out to the letter your policies.

The slow, difficult job of reorganization was under way. It was a two-pronged campaign. On one side was the fight to weed out the patronage hacks, to enforce the new code of conduct and to weld the organization into an efficient force. On the other side was the battle to convince members of Congress and political leaders of both parties that the Bureau was no longer a dumping ground for patronage appointments.

Again and again, in letters and instructions to special agents, Hoover hammered on a central theme: "This Bureau is to operate solely upon the basis of efficiency. Influence, political or otherwise, will not be tolerated and any Agent or employee of this Bureau resorting to same will be disciplined."

One of Hoover's first moves was to give the special agents in charge at the field offices greater authority over the special agents assigned to them. The old system in which the agents sent individual administrative reports directly to Washington was discontinued. The agents reported to the special agent in charge and he made his reports to Washington. Thus a chain of command was established which had not existed before. Agents were reclassified on a basis of efficiency, and Hoover saw to it that the best men received the highest pay. Paper work was reduced. Authority was strengthened.

Hoover notified special agents in charge in a letter dated July 1, 1924:

I look to you as the Special Agent in Charge as my representative and I consider it your duty and function to see that the Special Agents and other employees assigned to your office are engaged at all times upon government business . . . you are to exercise even closer supervision over the work of the Agents under you . . .

A field inspection system was established in which inspectors visited each office and checked on the agents' efficiency, character, and industry.[1] Office routine was systematized and standardized so that agents going from one office to another would find precisely the same methods and rules of operation. Agents were expected to put in an honest day's work—and not to close shop in midafternoon as many had been doing.

Hoover demanded that special agents in charge stop the practice of "passing the buck" to Washington when an agent had to be notified that his work wasn't satisfactory. Too often when Hoover told agents that their agents in charge had made adverse reports about their work, the agents complained that this was the first they had heard of it.

Hoover notified the agents in charge:

> I do not desire to be embarrassed as I have been in the past by [such] incidents . . . I desire that absolute frankness be maintained in all dealings with agents by Agents in Charge. The same frankness will continue to be observed by the Bureau in its dealings with all Bureau employees.

There can be no understanding of the modern FBI without an understanding of Hoover's views on discipline. His code of conduct became a way of life for those who wished to stay in the Bureau. Hoover and his men were called "college-trained flat feet" and jeered at as "Boy Scouts" in the field of law enforcement. He was called a bureaucrat who was unreasonable in his demands on the people who worked in the Bureau. He forbade his agents to drink whiskey either publicly or privately. (When the prohibition era ended, the FBI regulations were modified.) His men had to be neat in dress and discreet in their habits. He regarded them as representatives of the Bureau whether they were at work or enjoying a social evening with friends. And even the clerks and stenographers and other Bureau employees had to measure up to strict standards. Employees had to pay their debts. And there was continuous inspection by home-office inspectors and continuous self-criticism within the Bureau.

In a personal and confidential letter written in May, 1925, to all special agents in charge, Hoover explained why he felt so strongly about agents conducting themselves with circumspection. He said:

> I want to bring to your personal attention certain conditions existing in the Bureau in the past and which I do not intend shall continue in the future . . . I do know that some years past the forces of the Bureau of Investigation did not enjoy the best reputation . . . I am strongly of the opinion that the only way whereby we can again gain public respect and support is through proper conduct upon our part. . . .

> I am determined to summarily dismiss from this Bureau any employee whom I find indulging in the use of intoxicants to any degree or extent upon any occasion. This, I can appreciate, is a very drastic attitude and I shall probably be looked upon by some elements as a fanatic. I am not, however, one of those who may be classed as a "white ribbon" advocate, but I do believe that when a man becomes a part of this Bureau he must so conduct himself, both officially and unofficially, as to eliminate the slightest possibility of criticism as to his conduct or actions . . . I, myself, am refraining from the use of intoxicants . . . and I am not, therefore, expecting any more of the field employees than I am of myself.

This Bureau cannot afford to have a public scandal visited upon it in view of the all too numerous attacks made . . . during the past few years. I do not want this Bureau to be referred to in terms I have frequently heard used against other governmental agencies. . . .

What I am trying to do is to protect the force of the Bureau of Investigation from outside criticism and from bringing the Bureau of Investigation into disrepute because of isolated circumstances of misconduct upon the part of employees who are too strongly addicted to their own personal desires and tastes to properly keep in mind at all times and upon all occasions the honor and integrity of the service of which they are a part.

It was clear to Hoover that if the Bureau ever hoped to move from under the shadows of the past, the employees would have to submit to a stern code of conduct even in their private lives.

The new rules began to reflect results almost immediately. In one case, a special assistant to the attorney general in a southwestern state requested that an agent investigate the activities of a U. S. senator's son. In the past, such an investigation would have been made without question by the agent—but this time the agent refused unless he received specific instructions from Washington.

Hoover notified the agent: ". . . the action taken by you in this matter is approved . . . This Bureau cannot be used for partisan purposes."

After seven months of watching Hoover's work, Attorney General Stone removed the word "Acting" from his title and appointed him Director of the Bureau of Investigation on December 10, 1924. In a later letter to Dean Young B. Smith of the Columbia University Law School, Stone said:

. . . I took the responsibility of appointing Mr. Hoover as head of the Bureau of Investigation, although many people thought that Mr. Hoover was too young a man, and had been in too close contact with the Burns regime to be given the post. I thought I knew my man, and the event has proved that I was right. I found him responsive to the ideas I held, that efficient police work could be done by men who were not crooks and who did not resort to crooked methods. Mr. Hoover has steadily built up the Bureau. . . .

When Hoover heard a rumor that ex-agents were being given access to Bureau information, he wrote all employees on February 27, 1925, saying:

Rumors . . . have come to my attention, that former employees and officials of the Bureau may be able to obtain information of the Bureau's work and activities and may be shown special consideration in their dealings with the Bureau. Such a report, I trust, is without foundation, but I want to make certain that all employees of the Bureau understand fully that there is to be no special consideration shown to anyone whether or not he has been previously connected with the Bureau . . . and, further, that the files, records and activities of this Bureau . . . are not to be discussed with or disclosed to anyone not officially connected with the Bureau or Department.

While this reorganization and re-education of the Bureau was under way,[2] Hoover was trying to make good his word that politics would not enter into the selection or the promotion of an agent. An early test came when he transferred an agent to the Southwest who had been too active in politics. Within a few days, a senator with considerable influence called on Hoover and demanded to know why the agent had been transferred. The senator needed the agent to work in his coming campaign for reelection.

"I'm very sorry," Hoover told the senator, "but I think it will be best for the agent and best for the Bureau if he gets away from his political ties. This will give him a new chance."

"I'll take this up with the Attorney General," the senator snorted.

Fifteen minutes later Hoover was summoned to Stone's office.

Stone peered over his glasses. "Hoover, what are the facts in this case?"

Hoover explained the situation.

"I think you are not on entirely sound grounds," Stone said.

Hoover later recalled that he braced himself and the thought flashed through his head: "Well, here's where you resign."

Stone added: "I'm surprised you didn't fire the fellow at once."

There was the case of Agent B., who was a holdover from the Burns regime. He was sponsored by a midwestern senator and sent to work in Arkansas in 1922. The U. S. attorney at Little Rock complained that Agent B. was so inept that he was useless—so Agent B. was transferred to his home state of Minnesota.

But he no sooner landed in Minneapolis than the special agent in charge found that Agent B. had once been convicted in Minnesota of highway robbery and had served a prison sentence. Even if innocent, as he claimed, he was worthless as a witness in government prosecutions. The special agent in charge asked for Agent B.'s transfer.

At this point a congressman wrote Hoover that, although he realized the handicap involved, he thought Mr. B. should be retained. Hoover, who had now fired the agent, explained the entire situation in detail and added ". . . you will see that it will be impossible to effect Mr. B.'s reinstatement . . ."

This ended the matter, or so Hoover thought. But a year later another congressman wrote Hoover, saying: "The writer has known Mr. B. for a number of years and has no hesitancy in commending him to you in every way . . . He is a hard-working man and I have always found him dependable . . ."

Again the long explanation of why Mr. B. couldn't be reinstated and the tag line, "I sincerely regret that I am unable, therefore, to accede to your interest in Mr. B."

Another case involved an agent who didn't want to leave New York to accept assignments. When Hoover notified him he was to be dropped from the service, he appealed to his representative in Congress. The representative wrote Hoover. And the old merry-go-round began to turn again.

Hoover wrote a memorandum to one of Stone's assistants, saying:

> One of the greatest difficulties with this service has been the general impression that Agents can, through influence, have orders and instructions changed. If L. is reappointed and placed at New York there will be no doubt but that other Agents of the New York Office will claim that he was able to bring this arrangement about through his Congressional influence. . . .

Nevertheless, Hoover was inclined, for the first time, to give the agent another chance. He wrote him to come to Washington for a personal interview, in which the situation could perhaps be ironed out. But L. replied with a bitter attack on the special agent in charge in New York, implying that he gave Catholics preferred treatment over Protestants. L. agreed to return to work if Hoover would transfer the special agent in charge.

Hoover sent a curt reply saying that the special agent in charge had never shown anything but fairness and impartiality in his administration and that the charge of religious bigotry was unfounded and unfair. "In view of your attitude," Hoover wrote, "it is unnecessary for you to arrange your affairs for a conference with me at Washington as I shall consider your case closed."

To the special agent in charge, Hoover confided in a letter, ". . . it convinces me all the more that once we let a man out, we should never effect his reinstatement unless we are absolutely certain that an injustice has been done."

It took Hoover roughly three years to shake down the Bureau of Investigation and to perfect the basic organization which was to become renowned for its efficiency. Through all the formative years, Hoover maintained a close friendship with Harlan Fiske Stone, who remained in the Department of Justice for eleven months and then was appointed to the Supreme Court.

Frequently Stone would plod into the Bureau to keep an eye on how things were going, and to say, "Edgar, I came by to inquire into your stewardship."

On January 2, 1932, Stone wrote Hoover:

> I often look back to the days when I first made your acquaintance in the Department of Justice, and it is always a comfort to me to see how completely you have confirmed my judgment when I decided to place you at the head of the Bureau of Investigation. The Government can now take pride in the Bureau instead of feeling obliged to apologize for it.

And so the wheel had turned.

9: *The FBI Cracks Down*

A WEALTHY German financier, Richard T. Merton, arrived in Washington on March 10, 1921, to find the city in a gay mood and still celebrating the inauguration of President Warren G. Harding.

Merton wasn't particularly interested in the intangibles of gaiety. He had come from Germany to lay claim to a tangible $6,968,929.97 held in trust by the Alien Property Custodian. The German visitor had no difficulty in finding his way around town and meeting the right people. He sized up the situation carefully and then decided to do business with John T. King, a Republican National Committeeman from Connecticut who had friends in the inner circles of the new administration.

Merton approached King with this proposition: he would pay King a $50,000 retainer fee to act as his agent and he would pay another $391,000 if King succeeded in obtaining the release of the impounded millions. King agreed and received the first payment of $50,000.

The millions these men were after had an interesting background. After the United States declared war on Germany, the U. S. Government had seized enemy-owned property which included 34,644 German-owned shares of American Metal Company stock. This property was held in trust by the Alien Property Custodian. Late in 1919, the stock was sold at public auction in New York City for $166 a share, or a total of $5,750,904. The accrued dividends and interest added slightly more than $700,000 to the sales price.

Shortly after Merton made his bargain with King, he was introduced to the mysterious Jess Smith, the close friend of Attorney General Daugherty. In turn, Smith arranged for Merton to meet Colonel Thomas W. Miller, the Alien Property Custodian. Smith and Miller were such old and good friends that Miller had deposited $50,000 of alien property funds in a bank at Washington Courthouse, Ohio, that was owned by Mal Daugherty, a brother of the Attorney General.

Through these introductions, Merton had at last reached the men who could talk business. He informed Colonel Miller that before the United States went to war against Germany, the German stockholders had transferred their stock by oral agreement to a Swiss company. This oral transfer meant, Merton explained carefully, that the money impounded in the stock sale was not German money at all, but Swiss money being held unjustly. Merton produced documents which allegedly supported the oral-transfer claim.

This was the first time anybody involved in the American Metal Company situation had ever heard of Swiss ownership of the stock. Officials of the company themselves had never questioned the German ownership. Even after the war began, discussions about the stock had been with the German owners of record.

But on September 23, 1921, a mere six months after his arrival, Merton's claim to the stock was approved by Colonel Miller and by Department of Justice subordinates acting at the direction of Attorney General Daugherty. The Department attorneys who approved the release of funds were not given one important batch of documents relating to the German ownership of the stock. These documents were not in the file jacket when it came from the Alien Property Custodian —although they later were returned to their proper place among the records.

A few days after the money was released to Merton, champagne corks were popping in a suite at the Ritz-Carlton Hotel in New York City. Voices were raised in hilarious celebration of Merton's extraordinary achievement. In the midst of this merriment, Colonel Miller handed Merton two checks drawn on the U. S. Treasury and totaling $6,453,979.97. In addition, the government had released to Merton $514,950 worth of Liberty Bonds and mailed them to the National City Bank in New York City in payment of accrued dividends and interest.

Merton kept his part of the bargain with John T. King. He turned over to him $391,000 of the Liberty Bonds. And then Merton returned to Germany in triumph.

The whole strange affair lay unnoticed under the accumulated dust of almost three years until Attorney General Stone asked the FBI to trace the coupons from the Liberty Bonds which had been in Merton's hands. Agents traced coupons from bank to bank and traced transfers of money from bank account to bank account. Coupons were traced to Harry Daugherty, Jess Smith, John T. King and Colonel Miller. The evidence indicated that King had received $112,000 of the bonds, Miller $50,000 and Smith $90,000. The unsolved puzzle was: what had happened to the remaining $139,000 worth of bonds?

The mystery of the bonds was never to be entirely solved. The trails led to too many blank walls. Jess Smith had killed himself in 1923, leaving an estate of some $500,000 of which 25 percent was willed to Harry Daugherty. Certain records in Mal Daugherty's bank at Washington Courthouse, Ohio, were missing and Mal told agents his brother had taken them away and burned them. King admitted receiving $50,-000 to represent Merton, but he said it was a legitimate fee and the money he gave to the others was in repayment of political campaign debts. Before the inquiry ended, King died and his records vanished.

Colonel Miller was convicted of a conspiracy to defraud the United States, sentenced to eighteen months' imprisonment and fined $5,000. On February 1, 1933, Miller was given a presidential pardon with a restoration of his civil rights. The jury failed to reach a decision on former Attorney General Daugherty.

While one group of agents dug into the alien property–bond deal, another group was sifting through the accumulated filth left in the Veterans' Bureau by Colonel Charles R. Forbes, the first administrator of veterans' affairs, whose flagrant dishonesty had already been aired by Senate investigators.

Forbes, in his youth, had served a two-year hitch with the Marines and then joined the Army at the age of twenty-two. He deserted at Fort Myer, Virginia. The Army caught him four years later and he was jailed at Fort Strong, Massachusetts. He had signed his enlistment papers as a single man, but the Army received complaints from a Mrs. Forbes that he had left her and their two children, and had refused them further support. "He has been sending through the Department of Public Charities of New York a small amount," she wrote. "They now notify me he will send me no more."

Forbes claimed he had divorced his wife and the Army decided it had no authority to force such payments. He was forgiven his desertion on his promise to serve out his enlistment and conduct himself as a good soldier. He was sent to the Philippines and rose to the rank of sergeant. His buddies called him "Willie off-the-Pickle Boat"—he was remembered by enlisted men and officers alike as the life of the barrack room. A good many soldiers hated to see Forbes quit the Army and go back to civilian life.

Forbes picked up some experience in the construction business as foreman of a cement gang in the Northwest, where he was active in ward politics. By this time he was developing into an effective orator and a man with considerable rough charm and wit.

Before World War I, Forbes drifted to Honolulu. He entered Hawaii politics and before long he became Commissioner of Public Works, a job which placed him among the welcoming party when Senator Warren G. Harding arrived on an official visit. Beautiful island girls, according to custom, draped fragrant leis of ginger and pikaki about the Senator's neck and there were *luaus* (feasts) under the stars. By the time Harding left, he and Forbes had reached a back-slapping "Warren" and "Charlie" relationship—and Charlie had an invitation to visit Harding at Marion, Ohio, at any time.

Then came the war. Forbes applied for a commission as major in the Army Signal Corps and received it. Apparently no one bothered to check his old Army record of desertion. But to his credit, he saw front-line action in France, won a Distinguished Service Medal and a French Croix de Guerre, and rose to the rank of lieutenant colonel.

Then Charlie Forbes came home. He went into the construction business in Seattle and there he was in 1920, when Harding's political star shot above the horizon.

Forbes was an opportunist. He was among the first visitors to show up at Marion after the presidential election. One report at the time was that Forbes asked to be put in charge of the Shipping Board, but that Harding finally said, in substance, "Charlie, they say you won't do for the Shipping Board. But I have something just as good for you. We're going to lump this whole business of caring for ex-soldiers into one bureau. With your army record, you'll do fine there. It's yours if you want it."

Naturally, Forbes wanted it. As the director of the most expensive agency in government, spending more than $450,000,000 a year, Forbes became an important man about town. One reporter recalled later:

> He had no visible means of support except his salary of $10,000 a year, [yet] he lived expensively, gave "parties" which this generation of Washington will always remember for lavish hospitality, maintained his family in Europe.

> While others waited in line to see the President, Forbes just walked in. They were still "Warren" and "Charlie." In his rough wit, his bubbling high spirits, his back-slapping good-fellowship, the President got relief from the burdens of a position which weighed heavily on his own kindly

spirit. All the insiders of Washington knew that; and Forbes, quite naturally, used this reputation for his own ends.

Forbes was so confident Congress would approve a $17,000,000 veterans' hospital building program that he urged a friend to become the agent for as many hospital equipment suppliers and contractors as possible and his friend quickly made a 35-percent-of-profits deal with a construction contractor. Long before the hospital sites were announced, it was later testified, Forbes had tipped off the contractor to their locations.

There was one joy-filled junket through the western states by Forbes and his friends on an "inspection" of hospital sites. There were reports of Forbes and a lady friend jumping into a swimming pool fully clothed, and of $5,000 being handed to Forbes casually during a poker game— money that was never repaid. There was an alleged deal to divide a $450,000 profit on hospital construction so that Forbes would receive $150,000. There were secret bids and deals in which not only Forbes was involved—but also the Veterans' Bureau legal counselor, Charles F. Cramer.

In November, 1922, Forbes signed a contract for the disposal of war-surplus hospital supplies stored at Perryville, Maryland.

Mrs. Cramer sent a telegram to her husband on the West Coast which said: ". . . Think it necessary you return at once; think Colonel is a traitor. Has ordered Perryville cleaned out this week . . ."

When FBI agents moved into action, they found evidence to confirm the sordid scandal first uncovered by Senate investigators. In one two-month period, 155 carloads of surplus property had been moved out of Perryville, including 98,995 pairs of pajamas contributed by American women to the Red Cross during the war. The official inventory of surplus supplies approved for sale listed 2,000 bed sheets— but more than 83,000 good-as-new sheets were found to have been shipped to the buyers. The sheets were sold for 27 cents each, and at the same time the government was buying sheets at $1.03 each.

Outraged officials of the Public Health Service watched supplies which they needed badly, and were entitled to have, leaving Perryville. Finally they managed to get their protests to President Harding through General Charles E. Sawyer, resident White House physician. Twice Harding ordered a halt to the Perryville shipments—and twice his orders were ignored.

At last, just as the scandal was breaking, Harding called Forbes to the White House. Reports at the time said Harding grabbed Forbes and shook him "as a terrier shakes a rat," crying, "You yellow-belly! You've double-crossed me again!" Forbes was fired. He walked out of the White House pale and shaken, his world in collapse.

Methodically the FBI traced surplus supplies from depot to depot. They checked records of the War and Navy Departments, the Public Health Service and the Veterans' Bureau to determine the origin and cost of supplies. They reported: "The total amount criminally involved was over $400,000."

Forbes was sent to prison for two years and fined $10,000. Charles F. Cramer killed himself.

While these cases were developing, Attorney General Stone was disturbed by persistent reports of mismanagement and misconduct in the federal prison at Atlanta. Stone called Hoover to his office and they discussed the reports.

"I think you had better look into it," Stone said. "These reports seem to be based on more than rumor." Hoover agreed.

Hoover ordered agents to investigate conditions in the Atlanta prison on October 1, 1924, and within two days it was evident to agents that Warden A. E. Sartain was operating more on country club lines than by approved prison rules.

The first reports went like this:

Prisoners seen walking around the yard outside the Penitentiary, unguarded, as late as 10 o'clock at night . . . Prisoners wearing the uniform of the Penitentiary permitted to spend time in City of Atlanta without guards . . . Prisoners seen sitting on front porches of residences of Atlanta . . . Seven prisoners observed lying around in the yard of the Warden's home . . . Mail room of the prison is in charge of Grady Webb, who is serving 25 years for robbing the mails, and all of his assistants in the mail room are prisoners who have been convicted for violation of postal laws.

As the FBI agents went deeper into the prison's operations, they uncovered a conspiracy in which well-heeled convicts were paying prison officials from $1,500 to $5,000 for "soft jobs" and prison privileges such as the right to gather over the Warden's garage and play $50-a-card poker. But most shocking of all was the fact that the prison's chaplain was deeply involved in the bribery.

Warden Sartain and other prison officials tried to block the inquiry. Witnesses were intimidated and efforts were made to induce prisoners to repudiate the information they had given to the agents. But despite the opposition, the agents developed the inside story.

The chaplain broke down and confessed. He told agents that on one occasion he went to an Atlanta hotel and met representatives of a gang of Savannah rumrunners who had been convicted of violating the Prohibition laws. They agreed to pay $10,500 after the chaplain's assurances that seven of the convicted men would be given special treatment when they entered the prison. Later, the chaplain said, he went to Savannah with one of Warden Sartain's friends, Laurence Riehl, who collected the money and then gave him $2,100 as his share.

George Remus of Cincinnati, known as "King of the Bootleggers," and Emanuel Kessler of New York, tagged "The Millionaire Bootlegger," told agents they paid prison officials from $2,000 to $5,000 for special food, special sleeping quarters and preferred treatment. Two big-time bootleggers said they paid $2,500 each for the privilege of having their meals served in the chaplain's quarters.

One convict told in an affidavit of acting as a go-between in a deal by which Warden Sartain gave a chauffeur's job to Chesley Tuten, one of the Savannah rumrunners. The convict's affidavit reads like a page written by Damon Runyon:

> . . . after the conversation with Warden, I got in touch with Tuten and told Tuten . . . that if he felt like he wanted the job that I would get it for a consideration . . . Tuten said: "I'm on . . . I would like the job. How much will it cost?"
>
> At that time, I could not tell him, but I told him I would let him know later . . . I came back and talked to the Warden . . . He said: "What do you think we could get?" . . .
>
> I said: "I do not know. I have not spoken to Tuten about it because I have merely carried out your instructions because you told me that you needed some money." I knew that Tuten was frail and delicate and wanted to get outside . . .
>
> And then [Sartain] says: "What do you think about $2,000 or $2,500?"
>
> I went over to Chesley Tuten, and we talked about it, and Chesley refused to pay more than $2,000 and I said: "That is all right."
>
> I communicated the message to Warden Sartain, saying that I had delivered his message and had talked personally with Tuten, and Tuten said he would not give $2,500 for the job, but would give $2,000, and Sartain said that he could make the necessary arrangements. The job was chauffeur for the doctor. It was about three weeks after that before Chesley got the job. The money was turned over by me to the Warden . . . he took the money and put it in his pocket . . .

Warden Sartain and his friend, Laurence Riehl, were convicted of a conspiracy to accept bribes from prisoners. Riehl was sentenced to a year and a day in prison and Sartain to eighteen months. The former Warden became prisoner No. 24207 among the convicts whose money he had accepted for special favors. There was a mistrial in the case of the chaplain, who was removed from his prison post by his bishop.

After their investigation, FBI agents recommended sweeping reforms at the Atlanta prison—and the Attorney General later told Congress:

"Their report was the basis of instituting extensive reforms in the operation and management of the Atlanta Penitentiary."

During this period, the government exercised only loose control over banks and financial houses dealing with stocks and bonds. Bogus securities were being sold to the gullible at the annual rate of tens of millions of dollars, and President E. H. H. Simmons of the New York Stock Exchange was moved to protest: "It is literally true that it is much more dangerous to be caught pilfering a ten-cent loaf of bread than selling a million dollars' worth of fraudulent stock."

This was a golden age for the swindler, and the FBI was thrown into the fight time after time to match wits with the crooks and to build a case against them. In one case in Georgia, an FBI agent played the role of a "madman" in order to bring to trial a crooked banker who was feigning insanity.

This case had its beginning when W. D. Manley, a native of Georgia and a bright young financier, became the president of the newly organized Bankers Trust Company of Atlanta in 1911. The new corporation grew out of a well-established banking house and in time became the fiscal agent for some 185 banking associations located in Georgia and Florida. They were known as the Manley Chain.

The Bankers Trust Company went into the hands of receivers on July 13, 1926, and, like dominoes falling, eighty-six banks in Georgia and Florida closed their doors within sixty days. These member banks were loaded with $18,000,000 worth of notes sold to them by the parent Bankers Trust Company—about half of the paper representing obligations of the Bankers Trust Company and its subsidiary corporations. In the final count, the losses amounted to about $10,000,000. At least six people killed themselves as a result of the crash.

FBI agents and post office inspectors developed a mail-fraud case against the top officers of the corporation. The agents waded methodically through tons of bank records, analyzing financial operations over a period of more than twenty years. At last the evidence was spread before a jury, and four of the bank's officials were convicted and sent to prison.

But President W. D. Manley wasn't among them. He had escaped trial with claims that he was too ill. And then, in 1929, he had entered an "invalids' home" at Milledgeville, Georgia—one of those genteel private places where "unfortunates" are put away by relatives who thereafter speak of them in hushed tones. It was reported that Manley was mentally unbalanced and both physically and mentally unable to stand trial.

Soon after Manley's commitment, a young man listed as Charles

Seymour was admitted to the home by sorrowing relatives. His medical chart showed that he was suffering from melancholia. At first he kept to himself, but then he began to wander about the place and the doctor was pleased with the spark of interest he was showing in his surroundings.

Seymour became friendly with Manley. They visited in each other's rooms and discussed books and financing and affairs of the day. Seymour liked to doodle as he talked to Manley—although his doodles looked remarkably like shorthand symbols. Soon Seymour was recovered sufficiently to leave the home.

A sanity hearing was ordered for Manley, and "Charles Seymour" —FBI agent—produced his shorthand doodles in the form of a daily diary of Manley's activities in the invalids' home. The court held that while Manley might possibly be sick, he was mentally and physically able to stand trial. He was tried, convicted and sentenced to serve seven years in prison and to pay a fine of $10,000.

All the big-time wheeling and dealing in the Teapot Dome scandal, the Veterans' Bureau scandal, the Alien Property Custodian scandal and the banker Manley scandal were merely manifestations of a moral collapse in which crime was breeding at an alarming rate throughout the nation. Gangsterism was on the rise. City, state and federal agencies had become polluted.

And so it fell to the FBI to take over the leadership in the drive against the gangsters.

The Roaring Twenties

10: *The Gangsters Rise to Power*

THE gangsters shot and bribed their way into places of power in the Roaring Twenties and the FBI was virtually powerless to deal with such hoodlums as Alphonse "Scarface" Capone, who rose from an errand boy in a bawdyhouse to become the overlord of Chicago's underworld.

These were the years in which the gangsters created their own invisible empires through unholy alliances with crooked politicians, crooked lawyers, crooked doctors and crooked police. The gangsters' revenues from bootleg whiskey, beer, alcohol, robberies, prostitution, gambling, narcotics and "protection" rackets ran to uncounted hundreds of millions of dollars. The income of Chicago gangs alone was estimated variously as from $100,000,000 to more than $300,000,000 at the peak of their power.

Curiously, the FBI was powerless to move against these underworld empires unless and until the gangs violated a federal law, such as the Antitrust Act, which forbids restraint of interstate commerce.

Capone was only in his mid-twenties when he took over full command of the Chicago underworld. Even when he "retired" to a plush estate on Palm Island, near Miami, Florida, in 1927, he ruled the mob by remote control and remained a symbol of evil and terror. When he issued a command—men died.

Capone was virtually untouchable for years. But finally he made a slip and the FBI went after him. In 1929 he pleaded illness as an excuse for failing to answer a subpoena to appear as a witness in a federal Prohibition case in Chicago. Claiming he had been bed-ridden for six weeks while suffering with broncho-pneumonia, he produced a doctor's sworn statement as proof that he was in no condition to travel.

FBI agents checked into Capone's story. They found that during the time he was supposedly ill and in bed, he had gone to the horse races, taken a boat trip, flown to the Bahama Islands, and visited public places with a glow of health on his cheeks.

As a result of this investigation, Capone was cited for contempt of court and ordered before a federal grand jury in Chicago. He was arrested in Florida and released on $5,000 bond on March 27, 1929. Two months later, Capone was arrested in Pennsylvania and convicted of carrying a concealed weapon. When his one-year sentence expired, he was prosecuted on the contempt of court charge and given six months in jail. While Capone was serving this sentence, Internal Revenue Bureau agents took a close look at Capone's financial affairs. He was charged with income tax evasion. The one-time bawdyhouse courier couldn't beat this rap. He was sent to prison for ten years.

The reason for the rise of gangsterism in the 1920's is still disputed —but there is no dispute that its beginning coincided with the nation's letdown after the war and with the arrival of national Prohibition.

The country went "dry," officially, on January 16, 1920. At Norfolk, Virginia, Evangelist Billy Sunday preached the funeral of John Barleycorn. A span of horses drew a hearse to the tabernacle. A twenty-foot coffin was lifted from the hearse and carried into the meeting, trailed by a dispirited devil. Billy Sunday shouted, ". . . Goodbye, John! You were God's worst enemy. You were Hell's best friend. I hate you with a perfect hatred. . . ."

But John Barleycorn refused to be buried. Millions of Americans didn't want Prohibition, and the bootlegger stepped in to supply the demand for spirits. Foreign ships brought cargoes of whiskey from England, France, Bermuda and other points. They anchored in international waters outside the three-mile limit, and transferred their cargoes to the high-powered boats of rumrunners. These boats often sneaked quietly through the Coast Guard defenses at night, but sometimes they tried to fight their way through with machine guns blazing. The risk was great but so were the profits. A case of whiskey bought for $15 at wholesale could be retailed for $70 to $80. A barrel of beer which wholesaled for $3 brought $60 on the retail market. At one time the ships on "Rum Row" outside New York Harbor were loaded with whiskey estimated to be worth $225,000,000. And whiskey, beer and alcohol were literally poured across the Canadian border.

Congress gave the Treasury Department responsibility for enforcing

Prohibition, and soon a small army of some 4,000 agents was deployed from 105 offices.

With their huge treasuries, the gangsters corrupted city officials, police and federal agents. A $44-a-week Prohibition agent or policeman could earn hundreds of dollars a week merely by looking the other way at the right time. In New Jersey, a federal Prohibition administrator protested that all the agents in his office, except three, were accepting bribes and that he couldn't "lead an army into battle" when most of his soldiers were in the pay of the enemy. A group of forty U. S. attorneys in 1925 recommended that the entire force of Prohibition agents be fired and replaced by carefully selected men. Assistant Secretary of the Treasury Seymour Lowman charged in 1927 that ". . . Bribery is rampant . . . Some days my arm gets tired signing orders dismissing crooks and incompetents." Another Prohibition official reported that a brewery combine had offered a bribe of $300,000 a week if an agent wouldn't interfere with their operations. The honest agent and public official became bogged in a morass of greed in many cities.

The truth was that the public, generally, was apathetic about crime, even though homicides in 1926 had reached the staggering rate of 12,000 a year. Gangland massacres were commonplace. In the Chicago area alone during thirty months of 1924–1926, there were ninety-two gangland murders and 90 percent of them were unsolved. The crime bill mounted to billions of dollars. The nation's stream of politics was polluted because political machines across the country were allied with the underworld. The government could act only in crimes where federal laws were violated, so the cleanup job was primarily one for the cities themselves—but the indignation of the people against corrupt and lax law enforcement was slow to develop.

Early in 1925, the FBI received complaints that Cincinnati was a graft-ridden city in which the police were deeply involved in a conspiracy with the underworld. Saloons were operating openly within two blocks of the Federal Building, and narcotics reportedly were being peddled at an alarming rate. Conditions had become so bad that city officials had finally appealed to the Department of Justice for help.

Hoover discussed the situation with Attorney General Stone and, with Stone's approval, ordered a special squad of investigators into Cincinnati. Within two days, the agents found indications of a graft ring in the city's police department which involved violations of federal laws. Methodically they began to interview hundreds of witnesses, and to collect affidavits. One narcotics peddler confessed he had grossed $455,056 over a thirty-month period and paid out $18,000 in protection money. A saloon keeper grossing $3,500 a day in liquor sales admitted he had paid about $200,000 to the police over a three-year period.

In villages near Cincinnati, the FBI men found that so-called "dry agents" were operating an extortion racket out of justice of the peace courts, which were known as "liquor courts" but were actually local racket centers. These officers were paid on the basis of the number of arrests made and the amount of the fines assessed.

In less than three months' time, the FBI agents were ready to act. A special federal grand jury was called and sealed indictments were brought against forty-eight Cincinnati police and twenty-three village "dry agents" charging conspiracies in violation of federal Prohibition and narcotics laws. Some of the accused men fled. They were trailed by the FBI as far as Miami, Los Angeles and Syracuse, N. Y., and brought back for trial. Of the seventy-one indicted, seventy were tried and sixty-two convicted. One man escaped to Montreal, Canada.

This investigation opened the way for a reform movement in Cincinnati which swept the old city hall gang out of office along with the crooked police, who, according to the evidence, had received some $348,000 in graft over a three-year period.

Soon after this cleanup, Hoover received the shocking report that FBI Special Agent Edward B. Shanahan had been shot and killed by a professional automobile thief named Martin James Durkin. For the first time an FBI agent had been killed in line of duty.

Hoover called in an aide. "We've got to get Durkin," he said. "If one man from the Bureau is killed, and the killer is permitted to get away, our agents will never be safe. We can't let him get away with it."

Durkin had been sought by the FBI for an automobile theft and Shanahan had gotten on his trail. But when the agent finally found his man and started toward him to make an arrest, Durkin had swept an automatic pistol from the seat beside him and shot Shanahan through the breast.

The hunt for Durkin began.

Durkin killed a policeman and wounded another in Chicago. The FBI traced him to California and then picked up his trail when a Cadillac was stolen from the display room of a San Diego sales agency. The job had all the earmarks of a Durkin theft and a salesman identified Durkin's picture. The trail led through California, Arizona, New Mexico and into Texas. It was picked up, lost, and then picked up again. Interstate cooperation between police, and police cooperation with the FBI, were in an early stage of development—and this made it easier for Durkin.

At Pecos, Texas, Durkin had a close call. A suspicious sheriff checked on a Cadillac parked on the street and saw a pistol lying on the seat of the car beside the driver. The young man at the wheel told a plausible tale. He was a deputy sheriff from California on vacation and that was why he had the gun. He would prove it, too, if the sheriff would only permit him to go to his hotel room and get his identification papers. The sheriff agreed. Durkin roared off into the desert with the Cadillac, a woman companion by his side.

The sheriff at Pecos notified the FBI at El Paso of the incident in a letter which gave a description fitting Durkin. "I figured you just might have something on this bird," the sheriff wrote.

Now the trail was hot. FBI agents scoured the desert country. They found the Cadillac, wrecked and abandoned in a clump of mesquite. The car was identified as the one stolen at San Diego. A nearby rancher recalled that a man and woman had come to his door and asked to be driven to the nearest railway station. "I hauled them over to Girvin," the rancher said. "They were talking about going from Girvin to Alpine to catch a train."

Alpine was near the Mexican border. The FBI agents figured Durkin would never head into Mexico or into the desert. He was too fond of cities and night life. They checked with the ticket agent at Alpine, describing Durkin and his companion.

"Come to think of it," the agent said, "a young fellow and a woman —he said she was his wife—got aboard No. 110 night before last. He bought tickets for San Antonio."

Through conductors, ticket agents and porters, the agents learned on the morning of January 20, 1926, that Durkin and his girl friend had boarded the M. K. & T. "Texas Special," due to arrive in St. Louis at eleven o'clock that same morning. Hurried calls were made to the FBI office at St. Louis, and agents were given the number of the car and the compartment in which Durkin would be found.

Special agents in the St. Louis office got in touch with St. Louis detectives and explained the situation. Oddly enough, the government couldn't prosecute Durkin for the murder of Shanahan because killing a federal officer was not then a violation of federal laws. He could be prosecuted for murder only in the courts of the state in which the crime occurred.

With city detectives cooperating, arrangements were made with railroad officials to have the "Texas Special" stopped at a small town outside St. Louis. Then if Durkin tried to escape, he would have to run across open plowed fields and there would be no danger to bystanders in a gun battle. When the "Texas Special" came to a halt, the FBI agents and detectives boarded the train and hurried through rows of startled passengers. They rushed into Durkin's compartment before he could reach for the pistols in his overcoat. He was taken from the train in manacles.

Martin Durkin, killer and thief, was captured a little more than three months after his gun felled Special Agent Shanahan. He admitted the killing. He was twenty-five years old when the book was closed on his criminal career. State and federal courts sentenced Durkin to a total of fifty years in prison—thirty-five for slaying Shanahan and fifteen for a long series of automobile thefts. Durkin entered prison facing the chilling possibility that he would not be a free man again—if he lived that long—until he was seventy-five years old. However, he spent only twenty-eight years in prison and was released in 1954.[1]

One of the FBI's strangest cases in this era had nothing to do with graft or corruption. It involved the capture of an army, including the general staff, the infantry, armor, artillery, ammunition and air force.

It happened in 1926. A warning reached the FBI that Major General Enrique Estrada, one-time Secretary of War under Mexico's President Obregon, was recruiting and training on American soil a revolutionary army to be used for an invasion of a friendly nation, namely, Mexico. The General had fled from Mexico to California in 1924 after an abortive effort to overthrow the Obregon government. A number of the bad guessers in that revolt had found sanctuary in Los Angeles, a city of remarkable tolerance even in those days.

These exiles gathered at times to plot ways and means of returning to Mexico with a conquering army and seizing power. In the spring of 1926 plans began to take form. General Estrada depended not on the great munitions makers to supply the necessary arms—but on a local hardware company.

The hardware which General Estrada first ordered included 400 Springfield rifles and 150,000 rounds of thirty-caliber ammunition. Then the General and his friends purchased two Marlin machine guns, 5,000 rounds of machine-gun ammunition, 300 pounds of dynamite, and pipe fittings and sheet iron suitable for make-it-yourself aerial bombs. When they had spent about $62,400, General Estrada and his staff had on order an air force of four Ryan monoplanes complete with three aviators; an armored task force of two two-and-a-half ton armored trucks; and a supply train of five used trucks.

Estrada's recruiting officers—there were four who ranked as Generals in addition to Estrada—went into the Los Angeles Mexican colony to recruit the infantry.

"Come with us," the recruiters said in effect. "You will be paid generously. You will advance quickly in rank from private. And when the revolution succeeds, you will be given land and good jobs in Lower California."

The arms, ammunition and planes arrived and all went well, it seemed. The advance echelon of the invasion army rolled out of Los Angeles on Saturday afternoon, August 14, composed of two trucks loaded with arms and ammunition, and an automobile. Unnoticed in the traffic behind them were three automobiles carrying FBI agents, four officers from the Los Angeles police force, and two agents of the Pacific Coast Auto Underwriters. This convoy stopped for the night in Santa Ana.

Next day, Estrada's main army assembled in Los Angeles. The troops, numbering some 115, were issued canteens, tobacco and cigarettes. They were loaded into the remaining trucks and into automobiles loaned by relatives, or owned by the drivers, and off went the convoy toward the rendezvous point near the Mexican border while FBI Special Agents James G. Findlay and A. A. Hopkins [2] kept watch.

The plan was to invade Mexico near Engineer Springs, and, just after dark, storm the Mexican garrison at Tecate. Then, they reasoned, the revolution would gain support and followers and swell into a mighty force that would march on Mexico City. But FBI agents in San Diego had alerted the U. S. Border Patrol and the San Diego County sheriff's office. Now the counterforces were on the march, too.

The ammunition train reached the rendezvous point on schedule and waited for the arrival of the General Staff and the troops. But the "enemy," infiltrating and attacking from the rear, overran the entire train without a shot fired. In the busy hours that followed, FBI agents, Border Patrol officers, San Diego County sheriff's deputies and Los Angeles police captured General Estrada's ground forces, his armor and his air force, picking them off piecemeal, as military men say. Estrada himself was arrested by Agents Findlay and Hopkins.

The dejected generals and their troops were lodged for safekeeping at the Marine Base at San Diego. General Estrada, wearing civilian clothes over his military uniform, did not cut a dashing figure. His army's brass, for organizing a military expedition on American soil, were sentenced to prison terms ranging from twelve to twenty-one months and were fined from $1,000 to $10,000. The infantry had it better—most of them were released. And so ended a dream of revolution.

This was an amusing interlude, but there was nothing amusing about the seriousness of the crime situation confronting the nation.

President Herbert Hoover had become so concerned with crime conditions by 1929 that he named a National Commission on Law Observance and Enforcement to study the situation and report its findings. Congress made $250,000 available to the Commission for "the purpose of a thorough inquiry into the problem of enforcement of Prohibition . . . (and) the enforcement of other laws."

The study group became known as the Wickersham Commission because it was headed by former Attorney General George W. Wickersham. For two years it probed into the problems of law enforcement, covering a field far broader than enforcement of Prohibition. President Hoover said the work was the first official effort to envisage our crime problem as a national problem.

When the Commission issued its report, the findings were, in effect, a shillelagh which belabored police, politicians, Congress, crooks and the public for the crime conditions which existed and the lack of proper enforcement. It stirred a controversy across the land—but the report did succeed in centering greater attention on law enforcement and crime. The *Michigan Law Review* said of the report: "Its true significance lies in its usefulness as a focus for continuing discussion of the problems of criminal law enforcement."

Indirectly, the Wickersham report played an important part in shaping the future of the FBI because it emphasized the national character of crime. And when the people's revulsion against crime and gangsterism finally boiled over, it was the FBI to which Congress turned for the cleanup.

But before the FBI reached this point, rumors were circulated that the FBI would be abolished, and also that it would be merged with the Prohibition Enforcement Bureau. The rumors coincided with President Franklin D. Roosevelt's launching of his New Deal Administration in 1933. The outgoing President heard of the reports, and while riding with Roosevelt from the 1933 inaugural ceremonies, Herbert Hoover pointed out to Roosevelt that the Bureau had been reorganized and operated on a nonpartisan basis and said that he hoped it would continue under young Hoover's management. Roosevelt said he would look into the situation and see what he could do.[3]

A Washington gossip column reported that J. Edgar Hoover was going to be dismissed as FBI Director and transferred to an undesignated field office; in effect, he was to be exiled to some Siberia in the vast reaches outside Washington.

This story said in part:

> The Prohibition Bureau and the . . . Bureau of Investigation are about to vanish from public life . . . The Bureau of Investigation, a little known department to the general public, will be abolished, and in its place will be set up a small, compact and efficient organization charged with making all investigations for the various government departments. Instead of the 800 investigators now serving under J. Edgar Hoover, bureau chief, it is probable the investigatory personnel will be no larger than 350 or 400 . . .

At this time, the FBI actually had only 266 special agents and 60 accountants, or a total of 326 investigators. The investigative force had remained at about this level during the first nine years of J. Edgar Hoover's administration.

The gossip in June proved to be wrong in July. President Roosevelt, instead of casting Hoover into outer darkness, decided not only that he should remain in charge of the FBI, but also that he should take over command of Prohibition enforcement. The Prohibition Enforcement Unit had been shifted to the Justice Department from the Treasury Department in 1930, but its operations had remained entirely separate from those of the FBI and outside Hoover's responsibility.

By an executive order dated June 10, 1933, President Roosevelt ordered the Prohibition Bureau and the Bureau of Investigation consolidated in a Division of Investigation within the Department of Justice.

Hoover was appalled by the idea of any consolidation which would mean a literal merger of the two units. The Prohibition Bureau was a sprawling organization with a record which reeked of graft, corrupt practices and inefficiency. On the other hand, Hoover had worked for nine years to overhaul the FBI's management practices, to train agents in scientific crime detection and to keep the organization free from scandal. He was convinced that if the FBI's 326 agents were mingled with the 1,200 Prohibition agents, the character and identity of the FBI would be lost—and his years of labor would have been worthless.

Hoover carried his problem to President Roosevelt's Attorney General, Homer S. Cummings. He poured out his fears and suggested that the FBI should remain entirely separated from the Prohibition Bureau, without any merging of investigative work, offices, personnel or files. He argued that this separation could be maintained even though the two were placed under a single administrative head.

In a memorandum to Cummings, Hoover made this argument also:

. . . the Bureau of Prohibition, by reason of forthcoming repeal of the Eighteenth Amendment, will necessarily recede in size and diminish in importance . . . and with . . . repeal there should be no necessity for the maintenance of an investigative force such as has been maintained by the Bureau of Prohibition.

Hoover recommended that the Prohibition Bureau's field offices be reduced immediately from 105 to 23 and that the Bureau be placed in charge of a chief Prohibition agent who would be responsible for operations and personnel.

Hoover won his argument, perhaps the most important one since he had taken on the job in 1924. Attorney General Cummings approved his plan of organization and operation to keep the FBI a separate entity. Hoover notified his agents of the decision, and told them to refer all Prohibition enforcement matters to the Prohibition agents. He made it clear he wanted the separation of units to be both physical and spiritual.

This time—the early 1930's—was as turbulent for the FBI as it was for the whole country, which was mired in the Depression.

11: *Rebellion against Crime*

A KIDNAP-MURDER in New Jersey, a gang massacre in Missouri and a kidnaping in Oklahoma were the crimes of 1932–1933 which shocked the nation and, by their chain reaction, sent the FBI into a strange kind of guerrilla warfare against the armed forces of the underworld.

During the twenties most of the country had watched the growth of crime and gangsterism with a so-what attitude. Those fellows in the gangs, many people felt, were no worse than the thieves in dinner jackets who had been corrupting federal, state and local governments; about the only difference was that one group used guns and the other didn't. But this tolerance gave way to angry demands that something be done about the menace of the gangsters and racketeers. And the beginning of the change in attitude can be pinpointed as to time and place.

It began on March 1, 1932, near the little town of Hopewell, N. J., sometime between the hours of 8:00 P.M. and 10:00 P.M. That was when a kidnaper stole through the darkness to the home of Colonel and Mrs. Charles A. Lindbergh, a secluded place in the foothills of the Sourland Mountains.

Quietly the invader placed a homemade ladder against the house. He climbed to the window of the second-floor nursery where twenty-month-old Charles A. Lindbergh, Jr., had been tucked in bed by his nurse. The man slipped into the nursery, lifted the blond, blue-eyed child from his crib and carried him down the ladder. Kidnaper and child disappeared into the night.

On the nursery window sill, Lindbergh found a note which said:

Dear Sir

Have 50000$ ready 25000$ in 20$ bills 15000$ in 10$ bills and 10000$ in 5$ bills. After 2–4 days we will inform you were to deliver the mony. We warn you for making anyding public or for notify the police. The child is in gut care. Instruction for the letters are singnature.

The "singnature" was a symbol of two interlocking circles in which three holes had been punched.

In the days that followed, Dr. John F. Condon, a retired school principal, became the intermediary for the Lindberghs and established contact with the kidnaper as the result of an offer to act as go-between which was published in the Bronx, N. Y., *Home News.*

Condon became "Jafsie" in the negotiations, the kidnaper "John." On April 2, in St. Raymond's Cemetery in the Bronx, Condon turned over $50,000 in cash to a man who identified himself as "John." Condon received a receipt for the money and instructions that the missing boy would be found on a boat named "Nellie" near Martha's Vineyard, Massachusetts.

Even as this scene was being enacted in the cemetery, the Lindbergh child lay dead in a shallow grave only four and a half miles from the nursery from which he had been kidnaped. The body was found on May 12, 1932, quite by accident, by a truck driver's helper. Apparently the boy had been killed soon after he was taken from his crib. A blow had crushed his skull.

The brutal kidnap-murder aroused the country to anger as no crime had done in years, not even the mass murders of the underworld. Three months after the kidnaping, Congress passed an act known as the Lindbergh Kidnap Law, which, as later amended, provided the death penalty for transporting a kidnaped person across a state line.

The investigation of the Lindbergh case was directed by the New Jersey State Police, who had primary responsibility. But it developed into a cooperative effort between the New Jersey State Police, the New York City Police and the FBI. The big break finally came on September 15, 1934—two years, six months and fourteen days after the kidnaping—when a motorist bought five gallons of gasoline at a filling station on the fringe of the Bronx and handed the attendant a ten-dollar gold certificate.

After giving the driver his change, the attendant wrote on the bill the license number of the car—4U-13-41. He didn't connect the driver with the Lindbergh kidnaping, but he was suspicious of the gold certificate because these notes had been called in by President Roosevelt in April, 1933, when the United States went off the gold standard.

Three days later, a teller at the Corn Exchange Bank and Trust Company spotted the bill as a Lindbergh ransom note. The FBI was notified and the bill was given to one of the FBI-State-City investigative teams organized to concentrate on the kidnaping. A check with the State Motor Vehicle License Bureau disclosed that the license number had been issued to a Bruno Richard Hauptmann, of 1279 East 222nd Street, the Bronx.

Hauptmann was arrested. A twenty-dollar gold ransom note was found in his pocket. Another $13,000 of the ransom money was discovered in his garage. Dr. Condon identified Hauptmann as the "John" to whom he paid the $50,000. Evidence piled up against the accused man. He was convicted after a sensational trial, and on April 3, 1936, Hauptmann was electrocuted for the murder of Charles A. Lindbergh, Jr.

In a curious sideline development of the Lindbergh case, the FBI once again got onto the trail of that extraordinary man, Gaston B. Means. By any normal standards, Means had been so thoroughly discredited by 1932 that it seemed unlikely anyone would believe his stories. Perhaps he was surprised himself when wealthy Mrs. Evalyn Walsh McLean, of Washington, D. C., sent for him three days after the Lindbergh kidnaping.

Mrs. McLean knew Means was a crook. But for that very reason she wondered if he might not have underworld contacts who could arrange the safe return of the Lindbergh baby. She put the question to Means. As far as the record shows, Means didn't bat an eye or quiver a muscle to give warning of the larceny he was hatching at that very moment. This kind of situation was his meat and potatoes. Solemnly he confided to Mrs. McLean that her call to him was in fact a very strange coincidence. It just so happened that a few days before the kidnaping he had been in a New York speakeasy where he met an old pal he had known in the Atlanta Penitentiary. This convict had urged him to join in a big kidnaping job, but of course he had refused.

When he read of the Lindbergh child being stolen, Means said, he knew this was the "big job" discussed by his friend. In fact, he had checked and confirmed his suspicions. This man was a member of the gang which was holding the child—and he was certain he could locate them. By the time Means finished his story, Mrs. McLean was under the extraordinary illusion that she had discovered the great secret of the kidnaping.

Means had no trouble "making contact" with the kidnapers. He returned to Mrs. McLean and told her the baby was well and the gang was demanding $100,000 ransom. Six days after the kidnaping, Mrs.

McLean gave Means the money. He promised, without the trace of a smile, not to pay the kidnapers unless and until the baby was safely in Mrs. McLean's hands. He devised an elaborate secret code. The baby was "The Book." Means was "Number 27." Mrs. McLean became "Number 11." And the gang leader was "Number 19," or "The Fox."

The weeks that followed were a cruel nightmare for the woman who had trusted Means. Mysterious telephone calls came from Means and "The Fox." Once "The Fox" turned up at Mrs. McLean's cottage at Aiken, S. C., to discuss details of how the baby should be delivered. He wore gray suede gloves and carefully wiped off all polished surfaces that he touched, as though a fingerprint might have shown through the fingers of his gloves. Always the gang was on the verge of "breaking through the police lines" and delivering the baby—but always something happened to prevent it. Mrs. McLean paid Means another $4,000. She was arranging to pawn her jewels to raise an additional $35,000 when her attorney discovered what was going on. He called a halt to the hoax, and at this point the FBI was called in.

The FBI's main problem was to find Means's confederate, "The Fox." Day by day, FBI special agents checked on long-distance telephone calls which had been made to Means and to Mrs. McLean. Most of them had been made from pay stations in North Carolina, South Carolina, Maryland, New Jersey and New York. But "The Fox" had made one slip in placing station-to-station calls from the same neighborhood to his own residence and to Means.

The caller in both instances had refused to give his name to the telephone operator and the two calls from the same area might have had no remote relationship to each other. But in running down the calls made to "The Fox's" residence, the name of Norman T. Whitaker emerged. A check of the Bureau's records in the Identification Division disclosed that Whitaker was an ex-convict and a disbarred attorney.

Whitaker was "The Fox." He was identified by Mrs. McLean and others in the McLean household. And so it was that Means and "The Fox" were convicted of a conspiracy to commit larceny and sentenced to serve fifteen years and eighteen months, respectively, in prison.

Hoover was in the courtroom when Means testified in his own defense, insisting he had made desperate efforts to find the baby. Finally, he stepped from the witness stand and sat beside Hoover.

"Well, Hoover," he said, "what did you think of that?"

"Every bit of it was a pack of lies," Hoover retorted.

Means blinked his eyes. "Well," he said, "you've got to admit that it made a whale of a good story."

But a "whale of a good story" to Means was a cruel story to most people. In the outcry raised by the Lindbergh kidnaping, the country and Congress came to the realization that the federal laws were woefully weak in combating interstate crime. Criminals were operating with high-speed automobiles, armored cars, high-powered rifles, machine guns and armaments which were better than those of the law enforcement agencies. Crime wasn't localized. One gang could, and frequently did, operate across the lines of a half-dozen states.

By 1933 bank robberies were occurring at the rate of almost two a day. Kidnapings had increased alarmingly despite the Lindbergh Kidnap Law. The Attorney General had urged people to report kidnapings to the FBI by calling the special "kidnap" number—NAtional 8-7117, Washington, D. C.

Many of the gang operations were not in violation of federal statutes and there were some curious inconsistencies in the laws. For example, a bank official who embezzled $50 or $50,000 from a federal bank in 1933 had violated a federal law. But a gang of bandits might rob a federal bank of $100,000, machine-gun the bank officials and escape into another state without violating a single federal statute. And the bandits could be reasonably sure that pursuit would end at the state line.

In 1933, also, FBI special agents could make arrests as any citizen could make an arrest—but agents did not have the full police authority given to city and state police. The result was that FBI men often had to enlist the aid of local police when searches and seizures were to be made, even at the risk of losing their man. In most cases, this cooperation was invaluable and police gave any help that was needed. But in some cities the FBI found that to confide their plans to local police was sometimes like putting water in a sieve. The plans were "leaked" even to criminals because the underworld had its friends on some police rolls.

Director Hoover explored the role of the federal government in the crime fight with President Roosevelt's Attorney General, Homer Cummings. Demands were being made that the nation's police be federalized and that the federal government appropriate funds for local police forces. But it was clear to Hoover that the federal government should not take over the nation's police work—and also that federal crime laws should be strengthened.

In a memorandum to Cummings following their discussion, Hoover noted the limitations under which the government worked in the effort to combat gangsters and racketeers. He had found that the most potent weapon available to the FBI against racketeers—those forming combines to extort money from legitimate businessmen—was the Antitrust Act. But Hoover pointed out that this was in fact a back-door approach to the crime problem, since the Antitrust Act was designed primarily for regulating big business and not for fighting criminals.

"The cry of the public," Hoover wrote, "is for Federal legislation and Federal prosecution of racketeers. It perhaps is not overlooked, but it is certainly under-emphasized, that the problem is a State one . . ."

He noted that the most effective federal laws for use against the underworld were the Prohibition and income tax laws—over which the Prohibition Bureau and the Internal Revenue Bureau had primary jurisdiction. But collecting evidence of Prohibition and income tax violations was a difficult job.

"The real leaders of the racket," Hoover said, "rarely place themselves in a position where they can be accused . . . and [they] are careful to leave as little record as possible of their income . . ."

The majesty of the law wasn't very majestic in too many places. And the insolence of gangsters toward law enforcement was never displayed more brazenly perhaps than it was in the "Kansas City Massacre" of June 17, 1933.

The day before this crime, FBI special agents had ended a long hunt by tracking down Frank Nash, an escaped convict and desperado who had eluded police and the FBI for three years. Nash was seized in Hot Springs, Arkansas, by two agents and Police Chief Otto Reed of McAlester, Oklahoma, one of the best known and most respected police officers in that part of the country. They spirited Nash to Fort Smith, Arkansas, to escape an expected ambush by gangsters who used Hot Springs as a watering place. And there they boarded a train for Kansas City, Missouri, en route to Leavenworth prison.

The news of Nash's arrest was flashed to Kansas City by the underworld, and a gunman named Vern Miller was told that the train carrying Nash would arrive at the Union Railway Station at 7:15 the next morning. Miller figured Nash would have to be transferred from the train to an automobile for the final ride to the prison. That night, as the FBI was to discover later, Miller enlisted Charles "Pretty Boy" Floyd and Adam Richetti, two of the most dangerous gunmen in the Middle West, in a plot to free Nash from the officers.

Nash and his guard arrived in Kansas City on schedule. They were met at the Union Station by two more FBI men and two Kansas City detectives, W. J. Grooms and Frank Hermanson. This group moved through the early morning travelers to the east end of the station, where FBI Special Agent Raymond Caffrey had parked his car across the street. Dozens of people were hurrying along the sidewalk, going to and from the station.

"Get into the front seat," Caffrey told Nash.

Chief Reed and two FBI agents climbed into the rear seat. The two city detectives and an FBI agent were standing beside the car while Caffrey walked around the automobile and reached for the door, preparing to slide under the wheel. All the officers were armed.

At this moment, the agents and police officers relaxed their guard. Suddenly three gunmen, two with machine guns and one with pistols, approached the car. A voice shouted: "Up! Up!" The officers looked up into the muzzles of the machine guns. Then the command came: "Let 'em have it."

The hoodlums opened fire. The attack was so sudden and devastating the officers didn't have time to swing their weapons into action. Detectives Grooms and Hermanson, Chief Reed and Agent Caffrey were killed in the first blast of fire. Two other FBI men were wounded—and one special agent escaped harm by some miracle. Within a few roaring seconds, four officers of the law were killed and two wounded. The killers leaped into a car and escaped.[1]

And Nash, the man these hoodlums were trying to free? He died with a bullet in his brain, a bullet from the gun of one of his "liberators." [2]

The "Kansas City Massacre" was a shocking defiance of the law, stirring demands for sterner law enforcement at local and federal levels. These protests had hardly subsided when gangsters again sneered at law enforcement with the kidnaping of a wealthy Oklahoma oil man. But at least the kidnaping proved that something could be done about the menace.

Shortly after midnight, Washington time, July 23, 1933, a light flashed on the FBI's switchboard, signaling a call on the special kidnap line. The operator switched the call to the home of Director Hoover.

The ringing of the telephone awakened Hoover. He picked up the receiver and Mrs. Charles F. Urschel of Oklahoma City spilled out to him the story that her husband and a friend, Walter R. Jarrett, had been kidnaped only a few minutes earlier.

She told Hoover that she and her husband were playing bridge with Mr. and Mrs. Jarrett on the Urschels' screened porch when two men, armed with a machine gun and a pistol, opened the screen door and stepped onto the porch.

"Which one of you is Mr. Urschel?" one of the gunmen asked.

When neither Urschel nor Jarrett replied, the kidnaper said, "Well, we'll take both of them." The gunmen warned the two women not to use the telephone. But when Mrs. Urschel heard the kidnapers' car drive away, she called the FBI.

Hoover immediately telephoned the Oklahoma City FBI office and ordered agents to the Urschel home. He told his men to be sure the

Oklahoma City police were alerted. Within an hour FBI special agents were converging on Oklahoma City from other points. They were under orders to cooperate with the family, and to do nothing that would jeopardize the safe return of the oil man. It was—and still is—the policy of the FBI not to advise a family whether ransom money should or should not be paid. Those were decisions for the family to make.

Jarrett returned to the Urschel home, disheveled and shaken, about two hours after the kidnaping. He said the kidnapers drove some ten or twelve miles northeast of the city, took $50 from him, put him out of the car and then headed south with Urschel.

Four days later, J. G. Catlett, of Tulsa, Oklahoma, a friend of the Urschels, received a package delivered by a Western Union messenger. The package contained four letters, one in Urschel's handwriting. Another was a typewritten letter addressed to E. E. Kirkpatrick of Oklahoma City, also a friend of the Urschels. This letter demanded $200,000 for the oil man's safe return. There were instructions to place an advertisement in the *Daily Oklahoman's* classified ad columns if the kidnapers' price was going to be met.

The innocent-looking ad appeared in the newspaper:

FOR SALE—160 Acres Land, good five room house, deep well. Also Cows, Tools, Tractor, Corn and Hay. $3750 for quick sale . . . TERMS . . . Box H-807.

Further instructions were received in a letter mailed from Joplin, Missouri, and Kirkpatrick left Oklahoma City carrying a handbag stuffed with $200,000 in twenty-dollar bank notes. The kidnapers' orders were followed to the letter, except that the FBI had a record of the serial numbers of the ransom bills.

Kirkpatrick registered at the Muehlebach Hotel in Kansas City, Missouri, on July 30. He waited in his room for the telephone call which finally came, giving him the rest of his instructions.

Late in the afternoon Kirkpatrick took a cab to the LaSalle Hotel. He stepped out, paid the driver and walked west. He had gone only a short distance when a stranger approached him and said, "Mr. Kincaid, I'll take that bag." Kirkpatrick protested that he had to have a message to take back to Mrs. Urschel. The stranger said, "The title deeds to the farm will be delivered within twelve hours." He took the bag from Kirkpatrick's hand and walked away with the money.

Urschel arrived home the next night, unharmed but exhausted. After he had rested, he gave FBI agents the story of his kidnaping in amazing detail. After his friend Jarrett was put out of the car, he was blindfolded with cotton, gauze and adhesive tape. About daylight, the kidnap car drove into a garage, or barn, and he was transferred to a larger car which he judged by its size to be a Buick or a Cadillac. He was placed in the back of the larger car on a pallet spread on the floor.

About three hours after changing automobiles their car stopped at a gasoline station, where a woman filled the tank without noticing anything unusual.

"How are crop conditions?" one of the kidnapers asked the woman.

"The crops around here are burned up," she said, "although we may make some broom corn."

Their next stop was another garage or barn and one of the kidnapers remarked that it was 2:30 P.M. Urschel was given a ham sandwich and a cup of coffee, and he remained in this place until nightfall. Then he was taken on foot to a house nearby where he spent the night. Next day he was taken to another house about twenty minutes' driving distance from the first one. He knew it was a farm or ranch house because he heard the familiar noises of chickens cackling, cows lowing and hogs grunting. He heard water being drawn by bucket from a well he judged to be northwest of the house. He drank from a tin cup without a handle and the water had a mineral taste. It was in this house that he wrote the letter to Catlett.

Handcuffed to a chain, Urschel managed to work his blindfold loose enough so that he could get a glimpse of his watch. He recalled that each morning about 9:45 and each evening about 5:45 he heard a plane pass over the house. But on Sunday, July 30, there was a downpour of rain and he didn't hear the morning plane. The next day he was driven to a point near Norman, Oklahoma, and released.

FBI special agents studied Urschel's recollections and decided that their best chance to locate the kidnapers' house was tied in with the account of the rainstorm and the failure of the plane to follow its usual flight course. The woman at the filling station had talked of a dry spell, so any area drenched by a recent rainfall was important. They began a systematic check of the airlines whose planes passed within six hundred miles of Oklahoma City. This check was coupled with a study of meteorological reports of the period during which Urschel was held captive.

They hit pay dirt. They found that on Sunday, July 30, an American Airways plane on the Fort Worth–Amarillo run had been forced to swing north from its usual course to avoid a rainstorm. The U. S. Weather Bureau records at Dallas disclosed that this general area had been suffering from a drought and the corn was beginning to burn until the July 30 rains came. A little calculation showed that the American Airways morning plane leaving Fort Worth and the afternoon plane leaving Amarillo would pass over a point near Paradise, Texas, at the approximate times recalled by Urschel.

They found the house described by Urschel. It was the ranch home of Mr. and Mrs. R. G. Shannon, who were the stepfather and mother of Kathryn Kelly. And Kathryn Kelly was the wife of the notorious "Machine Gun" Kelly, who reputedly could knock walnuts off a fence with his machine gun at twenty-five yards.

Urschel identified the Shannon home as the place where he was held. There was the well and the tin cup without a handle and the chain to which he had been handcuffed. He could never forget the mineral taste of that water.

The Shannons confessed that they had helped guard Urschel. And they admitted what the FBI special agents now suspected—the kidnapers were Kelly, Mrs. Shannon's son-in-law, and Albert L. Bates.

The FBI men tracked Bates to Denver, Colorado, where he was arrested. Kelly and his wife were traced to a house in Memphis, Tennessee, where Kelly once had been a "society" bootlegger. In the early hours of September 26, 1933, FBI special agents and Memphis police raided the Kelly hideaway. Caught without a machine gun in his hands, Kelly cringed before the officers and pleaded, "Don't shoot, G-Men! Don't shoot, G-Men!"

Kelly's nickname for the FBI's agents stuck with them for years. In newspapers, magazines and movies and over the radio they became "G-Men" in a wave of publicity that was to prove helpful—and embarrassing.

The interstate character of the gangster operations was underlined clearly in the Urschel case. The oil man was kidnaped in Oklahoma City, Oklahoma. He was held captive near Paradise, Texas. The ransom demand was mailed from Joplin, Missouri. The money was paid in Kansas City, Missouri. The "hot" money was circulated in St. Paul, Minnesota, and some of it was found in Oregon. Part of the money was dug up in a cotton patch in Texas. One of the kidnapers was caught in Denver, Colorado, and the other in Memphis, Tennessee.[3]

During this time, Hoover waded into another fight, this time against a proposed measure by Senator Royal S. Copeland of New York in which Hoover saw a threat to the FBI. Copeland favored expanding the FBI by having each governor of a state nominate men who would become FBI special agents by order of the Attorney General. The governors' appointees would be trained by the FBI and then given "roving commissions" within their own states to help enforce federal and state laws.

Hoover sent a strong memorandum of protest to Attorney General

Cummings, arguing that the Copeland plan would destroy the foundations of the FBI's success, which he listed as: nonpolitical selections of its agents, proper discipline and centralized administrative control.

"Such employees, designated by the Governors of the states," Hoover said, "would owe their positions, at least in part, to the Governors . . . tending to place the organization on a purely political basis."

The Copeland plan reflected the insistent demands being made at the time for drastic federal action against criminals. It was even suggested that martial law be declared and the Army sent into action to rid the country of crime. And there was a proposal to amend the Constitution and transfer all police power to the federal government.

Cummings agreed with Hoover's viewpoint that the primary responsibility for the suppression of crime rested with local law enforcement agencies. The Attorney General told Congress:

> . . . it is distinctly not the duty of the Federal Government generally to preserve peace and order in the various communities of our nation . . . we need expansion of the federal penal statutes to include control over the unlawful activities of those who deliberately take advantage of the protection presently afforded them by state lines in perpetrating their crimes.

Cummings laid before Congress nine major bills drafted for the purpose of giving the federal government greater leverage in the fight against crime. The St. Louis *Post-Dispatch* said of the program:

> The Attorney-General is ready to begin a powerful attack on the underworld. The nation has waited with the patience of a Job for this hour. In a determined Department of Justice backed by the resources of the national Government, gangsters face an invincible foe.

Congress quickly approved the crime bills and in May and June, 1934, President Roosevelt signed them into law.

These laws opened new avenues by which the FBI could move against the criminals. Now it was a federal crime to assault or kill a federal officer. Now it was a federal offense to rob a federal bank. Now it was unlawful to flee from one state to another to avoid prosecution or giving testimony in certain cases. Anyone carrying stolen property worth $5,000 or more across a state line was guilty of a federal offense. Using interstate communications such as the telephone and telegraph in extortions was illegal. And the kidnap law was amended so that interstate abductions became federal violations even though ransom or reward was not the motive.

On special occasions, the FBI special agents had been authorized to carry weapons. Congress passed laws giving the agents full powers of arrest and full legal authority to be armed in carrying out their duties.

And then it was that the FBI, literally, went to war against the underworld.

12: *The Roundup*

JOHN HERBERT DILLINGER led a kill-crazy gang which swept through the Midwest from September, 1933, until July, 1934, leaving a trail of ten men murdered, seven men wounded, four banks robbed, three police arsenals plundered and three jails from which prisoners were freed.[1]

But it wasn't the murders or the robberies or the jail deliveries which first sent the FBI after Dillinger, because none of these crimes was a federal law violation. He ran into trouble with the "G-Men" because he drove a stolen automobile across a state line.

Dillinger was wanted in Indiana for the murder of an East Chicago policeman and local police throughout the country were alerted to watch for him. He was recognized in Tucson, Arizona, and arrested with three members of his gang. The Tucson police found, among other odds and ends at the Dillinger hide-out, three Thompson submachine guns, two Winchester rifles mounted as machine guns, five bullet-proof vests and more than $25,000, part of which was identified as loot from an East Chicago bank.

Dillinger was returned to Indiana and placed in the County Jail at Crown Point—a so-called escape-proof jail—to await trial for the East Chicago murder. But he escaped on March 3, 1934. He always claimed he frightened the jail guards with a wooden gun which he had fashioned with a razor blade as he whiled away the time in his cell. The red-faced guards said Dillinger had a real forty-five which someone had slipped to him.

The fact remained that Dillinger did force a guard to open his cell door, then he grabbed two machine guns, locked up the guards, stole the sheriff's automobile and headed for Chicago. The instant he crossed the Indiana-Illinois state line, he violated a federal law—the National Motor Vehicle Theft Act, commonly known as the Dyer Act, which prohibits transportation of a stolen motor vehicle across a state line.

Until this escapade, Dillinger had violated only state and local laws. Now the FBI had the right and the duty to go after him as a violator of a federal law. And special agents began the hunt.

Dillinger jeered at "the law" after his jail break. He wrote his sister not to worry about him because that wouldn't help, "and besides I am having a lot of fun." Then he added:

> . . . [the reports] I had a real forty five Thats just a lot of hooey to cover up because they don't like to admit that I locked eight Deputys and and a dozen trustys up with my wooden gun before I got my hands on the two machine guns. I showed everyone the wooden gun after I got a hold of the machine guns and you should have seen *thire* faces. Ha! Ha! Ha! Pulling that off was worth ten years of my life. Ha! Ha!

As it happened, the escapade cost Dillinger a great deal more than just ten years of his life. He had only a few more weeks to live when he wrote the letter.

On two occasions, FBI agents thought they had Dillinger trapped. Each time he escaped in a barrage of machine-gun fire.[2] But the circle was tightening.

On the first day of June, two weeks after President Roosevelt had signed the new Crime Bills, Hoover called Special Agent Samuel P. Cowley [3] into his office to give him a special assignment. Cowley was a hefty, thirty-four-year-old Utah lawyer who had served as a missionary in the Mormon Church before he joined the FBI. He was to take charge of the Dillinger search.

As Cowley later recalled, Hoover told him: "Stay on Dillinger. Go anywhere the trail takes you. Take everyone who ever was remotely connected with the gang. Take him alive if you can but protect yourself."

Cowley's search led him to Chicago. Dillinger was reported to be in hiding somewhere in the city, recovering from a doctor's attempt to disguise the Dillinger features by plastic surgery. Cowley and Melvin Purvis, Special Agent in Charge of the Chicago office, worked closely with two East Chicago policemen, Captain Timothy O'Neill and Sergeant Martin Zarkovich, in running down the scores of rumors and tips from people who thought they had recognized Dillinger. O'Neill and Zarkovich exchanged information with FBI agents almost daily.

The break in the case came on the evening of July 21. O'Neill and Zarkovich brought a dark-haired, middle-aged woman to the FBI. She was Ana Cumpanas, who had come to the United States in 1914 from a small Romanian village. Now she was known as Mrs. Anna Sage.

Ana Cumpanas wanted to make a deal. She was in trouble. The

Immigration and Naturalization Service people wanted to have her deported as an undesirable alien because she was the madam of a bawdyhouse in Gary, Indiana. Her proposition was this: she would lead John Dillinger to the FBI—but she wanted a promise that she would receive a reward and also that something would be done to permit her to remain in the United States.

The reward was promised. Purvis told Ana Cumpanas he would do what he could do to help her; her cooperation would be called to the attention of the Department of Labor, since the Labor Department— and not the Justice Department—handled deportation matters at that time.

Ana Cumpanas disclosed that John Dillinger was planning to take her and his friend, Polly Hamilton, to a movie theater the next evening. She wasn't sure which theater, but possibly the Marbro in Chicago. She would let them know the next day. How would other FBI agents, who hadn't seen Ana Cumpanas, be able to identify her? Ana said she would be dressed in red.

Cowley and Purvis called in a squad of agents, along with East Chicago policemen, and the trap was planned for Dillinger.

Ana Cumpanas kept her word. She telephoned early in the evening of July 22. She still didn't know which theater. It might be either the Marbro or the Biograph. This meant that both places had to be covered.

These were the final instructions, as one agent recalled them in an after-action report:

> Gentlemen, you all know the character of John Dillinger. If . . . we locate him and he makes his escape it will be a disgrace to our Bureau. It may be that Dillinger will be at the picture show with his women companions unarmed—yet, he may appear there armed and with other members of his gang. There . . . will be an undetermined element of danger in taking Dillinger. It is hoped that he can be taken alive, if possible, and without injury to any agent . . . yet, gentlemen, this is the opportunity that we have all been waiting for and he must be taken. Do not unnecessarily endanger your own lives. If Dillinger offers any resistance each man will be for himself. It will be up to each of you to do whatever you think necessary to protect yourselves in taking Dillinger.

Dillinger decided to go to the Biograph, where Clark Gable was playing in *Manhattan Melodrama*. The FBI men and the policemen recognized Dillinger when he entered the theater that warm July evening with Polly Hamilton and Ana Cumpanas,[4] who was to become known as "The Woman in Red." Despite the plastic surgery, the outlaw was identified beyond doubt. Cowley called Hoover, who was pacing the library at his home in Washington. The decision was made to take Dillinger as he came out of the theater, rather than risk a gun battle inside the crowded show house.

When the trio emerged, by prearrangement Purvis lit a cigar. The trap began to close. Dillinger must have sensed that something was wrong. He glanced over his shoulder and saw an agent moving toward him. He darted toward an alley, clawing a pistol from his pants pocket. But before he could get his gun into action, three FBI agents fired five shots. Slugs tore into Dillinger's body and he pitched on his face. The chase was over.

The next day, Hoover wrote Cowley: "I wanted to write and to repeat to you my expressions of commendation and pleasure last evening upon the excellent results which you attained . . . Your persistence, patience and energy have made it possible . . . to attain this success, and I am proud of and grateful to you." As a reward, Hoover promoted Cowley to the full rank of inspector.

But Cowley didn't live long enough to receive the full measure of recognition from his new title. Four months after Dillinger's death, Cowley and Special Agent Herman E. Hollis unexpectedly ran onto two of Dillinger's old gang driving along a highway near Barrington, Illinois. They were John Paul Chase and "Baby Face" Nelson,[5] a killer who had been labeled by the press as "Public Enemy Number 1," despite his meek-sounding real name of Lester J. Gillis. Nelson's wife, Helen, was with him in the car. The FBI agents and the gangsters jumped from their cars, and in a gun battle Cowley [6] and Hollis were killed and Nelson wounded fatally. When Nelson died a few hours later, Mrs. Nelson and Chase laid his body in a ditch beside a highway.

In a curious revolt against reason, some people regarded Dillinger and Nelson as the heroes in these dramas, and the FBI men as the villains.

One Virginia newspaper editor assailed the FBI's killing of Dillinger as the work of cowards who were afraid to arrest him in the theater. "Any brave man," said the editorial, "would have walked down the aisle and arrested Dillinger . . . why were there so many cowards afraid of this one man? The answer is that the federal agents are mostly cowards."

A young girl wrote to a Chicago newspaper, "I certainly feel sorry for his [Dillinger's] old father, and if I were a man and a member of Dillinger's gang I'd certainly avenge his death."

Dillinger's girl friend, Evelyn Frechette,[7] came out of prison and joined a carnival side show. She told gaping crowds of her life with Dillinger. "He liked to dance and he liked to hunt," she said. "He—excuse me if you've heard this one—was a good shot . . . He liked music but he never sang. I think he liked gravy better than anything else. He liked bread and gravy." Audiences heard the bread-and-gravy revelation with open-mouthed wonder.

When two other gangsters were killed in gun battles, a Baltimore paper printed a letter saying:

> Those poor, dear boys . . . should have been detained and preached to. If the G-men had told them to go and sin no more, that would be true Christian example . . . We did not have any such scandals under the wise guidance of our God-fearing Mr. Harding, or Christian Mr. Coolidge or under our beloved Mr. [Herbert] Hoover. It remained for the vile Democrats to take sacred human life. (Signed) Mother.

One of the more mawkish of the stories was an interview with "Baby Face" Nelson's widow. The story said, in part: " 'Baby Face' Nelson died in the arms of his wife with a smile on his lips, but with tears in his eyes for his two young children.

"Those were the high-lights of a thrilling story told by Nelson's pretty widow, in which she gave a heart-broken account of his death at the hands of federal agents."

The widow was described by Nelson's sister as "one of the most devoted mothers I have ever known," despite the fact that she and Nelson had abandoned their children and that the children knew their mother only as an infrequent visitor called "Aunt Helen." A bare mention was made of the murdered Cowley and Hollis.

The vast weight of public opinion was on the side of Hoover and the FBI. Nevertheless, the sympathy poured out for the dead gangsters and the criticism of the FBI outraged J. Edgar Hoover's Presbyterian concept of right and wrong. He referred to criminals as "scum from the boiling pot of the underworld," "craven beasts," "public rats," "vermin" and "vultures." He took to the platforms of civic clubs, universities and conventions to hammer on the theme that criminals and those who knowingly associated with them were the real public enemies. He criticized "venal politicians" who were allies of the underworld, and lawyers who were the respectable fronts for gang operations. He spoke out against crooked police, and used such terms as "sob-sisters" and "sentimental yammerheads" to describe those who abused the states' parole systems by turning habitual criminals loose time after time to commit more crimes.

Behind Hoover's bitter assaults on lax and corrupt law enforcement was his knowledge of gang operations, such as those of the notorious Barker-Karpis gang, whose members killed ten persons, wounded four and obtained almost $1,000,000 in cash, securities and other property from 1931 to 1936. The worst members of this gang were paroled convicts and often the criminals of this gang and others found protection in cities where the police conveniently failed to recognize the faces of hunted men even when their photographs and wanted notices were posted at police headquarters.

In the parade of criminals, Alvin Karpis in time was labeled "Public Enemy Number 1"—wanted for the $100,000 extortion-kidnaping of William Hamm, Jr., of St. Paul, Minnesota, and on local charges of murder. He was known in the underworld as "Old Creepy." Hoover frequently referred to Karpis as a "rat," and finally this sneering barb riled Karpis. He sent word to Hoover that he intended to kill him just as FBI agents had killed Kate ("Ma") Barker and her son, Fred, in a 1935 machine-gun-and-rifle duel in Florida.[8]

Hoover issued instructions that when agents received any information on Karpis' whereabouts, he was to be notified so that he might take charge of the case. FBI agents mentally tagged Karpis as "the Boss's man."

Hoover thought his chance had come in March, 1936. He received word in New York that Karpis was hiding somewhere in Hot Springs, Arkansas. Hoover flew by special plane into Washington, where a squad of agents joined him at the airport. So many agents at Headquarters wanted to go along that Hoover finally had to order some of them back to their jobs. Hoover and his men waited in the plane at the airport for further word from Hot Springs. But the disappointing report came that Karpis had escaped—apparently tipped by local police that the G-Men were closing in.

Had Karpis been captured by Hoover in March, the FBI Director would have been spared at least part of the much-publicized grilling in April by Senator K. D. McKellar of Tennessee in a hearing before the Senate Appropriations Subcommittee.

McKellar questioned Hoover about his background and experience in the field of criminal investigations, and then placed emphasis on the fact that the Director had not himself made an arrest. The question was much the same as asking a commanding general why he wasn't down in a foxhole with a rifle rather than being at his command post.

The implications by the Senator were plain enough: the Director of the FBI wasn't much as a crime hunter because he'd never actually made an arrest.[9]

Hoover held his temper, although his face was flushed with anger. He said nothing to McKellar about the near arrest of Karpis the month before or the orders which had been given that he was to make the arrest. Hoover felt that his personal courage had been questioned publicly, with the implied accusation that he was asking his men to face dangers he would not face himself.

Hoover was in New York on the afternoon of April 30, when he received word that Karpis had been trailed from Hot Springs, Arkansas, to Corpus Christi, Texas, and then to New Orleans, where he was reported living in an apartment house on Canal Street. He flew to New Orleans with a squad of special agents. The local police weren't notified. No chances were taken on a "leak" flushing Karpis into flight.

As Hoover and his men approached the apartment building by automobile, Karpis and a companion unexpectedly walked out the door. For a few tense seconds the FBI cars were blocked by a man riding a white horse up the street, then the horse moved out of the way. Karpis climbed into his automobile. Hoover ran to the left side of the car and Assistant Director Earl Connelley to the right side. Hoover reached into the car and grabbed Karpis before he could reach for a rifle on the back seat.

"Put the handcuffs on him," Hoover ordered. But no one had remembered to bring handcuffs. An agent pulled off his necktie and tied Karpis' hands behind him. "Old Creepy," all the bravado gone and ashen with fear, was put aboard a special plane to be flown to St. Paul, Minnesota, to stand trial for the Hamm kidnaping.

The plane had been air-borne only a short time when Hoover noticed that Karpis' face was white.

"What's the matter? Are you airsick?" Hoover asked.

"Go ahead and do it!" Karpis blurted. "Get it over with."

"What are you talking about?"

Karpis looked at Hoover wildly. "I know what you're going to do. You guys are going to throw me out of this plane and then say it was an accident."

"Don't be a fool," Hoover snapped. "We don't do things like that. You're going to St. Paul and stand trial. Nobody's going to hurt you while you're with us."

Karpis had recognized Hoover when he first saw him.

"How did you know who I was?" Hoover asked.

Karpis replied: "I saw a picture of you after you caught a sail fish. Your luck is better than mine. I've been trying to catch one for three years."

It was a rough flight. When the plane stopped at Kansas City to refuel, the passengers got sandwiches and copies of the morning papers. One headline said: "Karpis Robs Bank in Michigan." Karpis laughed. "This is one time I've got a perfect alibi."

Karpis was given a life sentence for the Hamm kidnaping.

Thus the boss of the G-Men made his first arrest. Then he followed it up with others equally spectacular.

One of these was the arrest of the notorious Louis (Lepke) Buchalter whose gang forced the baking industry alone to pay them an estimated $1,000,000 for protection.

As the FBI closed in on Buchalter, Walter Winchell broadcast a radio appeal for the gang leader to surrender, with the promise that his civil rights would be respected by the FBI. Negotiations began immediately between intermediaries of Buchalter and Winchell and finally an agreement was reached.

On the night of August 24, 1939, Director Hoover walked alone through New York City's streets to the corner of 28th Street and Fifth Avenue. And there the hunted man, Buchalter, surrendered to him. The FBI got Buchalter, and Winchell got an exclusive story. Buchalter was turned over to state authorities and later was executed for murder.

The FBI developed what might be termed the scorched-earth policy in hunting criminals. Special agents not only went after the gangsters and kidnapers who committed the crimes, they also went after all the underworld fringe such as the crooked doctors, crooked lawyers, crooked police and those who knowingly gave criminals a hiding place.

The G-Men were glamorized by a wave of publicity comparable to the later "Davy Crockett" craze which swept the country. Hollywood turned from gangster films, in which the tough guy was the hero, to pictures of the G-Men who always got their man. Magazines and newspapers were on the bandwagon.[10] Anything Hoover did and said became news, even when he went to a night club, attended a boxing match or watched a horse race.

But while public opinion was on Hoover's side, he became a special target for attack, also. Once derided for not having made an arrest, he then was assailed as a headline hunter whose personal arrests were publicity stunts. One critic said:

It must be remembered that he never made an arrest and never went on the hot or cold spoor of a malefactor until after he had been subjected to senatorial inquisition on his record as a policeman. Then he flitted about the country by plane to be in at seizures to wipe off the tarnish on the crown of the No. 1 G-man and to forestall similar embarrassment in future visits to Capitol Hill.

Another critic sneered at the FBI's use of five, ten or even fifteen agents to seal off avenues of escape while arresting a dangerous criminal, saying Hoover was using "a sledgehammer to knock a fly off the baby's nose . . ."

One writer said: "We Americans no sooner set up a hero than we prepare to knock him down . . . It is working out that way with J. Edgar Hoover." And so it was.

At this same time, two Ku Klux Klan leaders approached a senator and lobbied for Hoover's removal. Also, a report gained wide circulation that "important New Dealers" were after Hoover's scalp, and that he might be ousted as FBI Director because "Liberals high in the Administration regard him and the vaunting power he has built up with strong misgivings."

A similar report had gained currency in 1933. Franklin D. Roosevelt had first chosen Senator Thomas Walsh to be his Attorney General—but Walsh died shortly before he was to take office. After Walsh's death a story went the rounds that he had planned to fire Hoover in one of his first official acts. But this report was scotched the same day it appeared in print by Walsh's nephew, John Wattawa, a Washington attorney, who wrote the Washington *Herald* that the story was "a gross inaccuracy." [11]

The 1936 attack on Hoover and the FBI reached a climax when the news broke that U. S. Secret Service agents were secretly investigating the two-year-old slaying of John Dillinger and one of his gang, Eddie Green, by FBI agents—an investigation widely interpreted in the press as an effort to discredit the G-Men as being trigger-happy amateurs. FBI agents had testified before a coroner's jury that Green was shot when he ran from a house in St. Paul, ignored a shouted command to halt, and then reached for his hip as though to pull a pistol. It was found that Green was unarmed, but the coroner's jury held that the agents had been justified in their actions.

During this time an unsuccessful effort was being made in Congress to consolidate all the Treasury's investigative agencies—Secret Service, Alcohol Tax Unit, Narcotics Bureau, Internal Revenue Intelligence Unit, Customs Agency Service, and Coast Guard—into a single agency which would overshadow the FBI.

Attorney General Cummings came to Hoover's defense. He announced publicly: "If there is anybody shooting at Hoover they're shooting at me. Hoover has my entire confidence and if anybody thinks they are going to get him out of his office they will have to get me first."

Secretary of the Treasury Morgenthau wrote a letter of apology to Cummings for the incident and ordered two Secret Service officials demoted, saying: "The irresponsible action taken by these men is one which I heartily disapprove and will not permit. . . ."

This was, indeed, a busy time for the FBI and its Director. Hoover was speaking out against abuses of the parole systems and "sob-sister wardens," prisons which are like "country clubs" and "convict-coddling."

The National Probation Association promptly tried to have Hoover "gagged." President Roosevelt and the Attorney General were asked to force Hoover to "refrain from issuing statements which are derogatory and destructive to the advancement of probation."

Hoover wrote the Attorney General: ". . . while it is a fact that from time to time in my public addresses I have taken occasion to criticize the administration of the parole and probation system, I have never criticized or denounced the theory or principle of parole or probation."

Hoover stuck to his guns. He told Cummings: "What I have talked about has been the administration of those systems by venal politicians and by inefficient and corrupt influences in some of our states, and I have not dozens, but literally hundreds and running into thousands of cases to prove my point. I cannot, I believe, be expected to remain silent in the face of this criticism which has been leveled at me . . ."

And Hoover had strong support. The International Association of Chiefs of Police condemned the "gag" effort as a move to curb "constructive criticism of the abuses in the parole system." The Oklahoma City *Times* stated the case as it was seen by many newspapers when it said: "A disgraceful, sentiment-guided clemency system that blankets the United States is responsible for a crime condition that challenges the people of America."

The FBI Director refused to be gagged—and neither President Roosevelt nor Attorney General Cummings ever made the effort. Hoover continued his fight for an improved parole system free from abuses.

The recurrent rumors that influential people close to the White House were going to oust Hoover always failed to note the fact that Hoover himself had friends in the Roosevelt inner circle. They were Roosevelt's Press Secretary, Steve Early; Major General Edwin M. ("Pa") Watson, Secretary to the President; and most influential of all, Franklin D. Roosevelt himself.

The attacks failed. Hoover was still solidly entrenched in his position as Director of the FBI, and in public popularity, when the assaults of the 1930's spent themselves.

13: *Murder by Proxy*

BANKER WILLIAM K. HALE returned from the annual Texas Fat Cattle Show to find his home town of Fairfax, Oklahoma, gripped by excitement . . . and fear.

As he walked up Main Street from the railway station, his friends stopped him to tell him the news. Their stories were confused, but he gathered that while he was in Fort Worth, an explosion had literally rocked the town. A few people who happened to be up and about at three o'clock that morning had seen a sheet of flames engulf the Bill Smith home—and then came the blast that ripped the big house apart.

". . . Killed Rita and the maid and Bill's dying . . . blew 'em to hell and gone . . . not much left of the house but a pile of kindlin' wood." Some people recalled hearing an automobile race through the town a few minutes before the explosion. No one could describe the car or driver.

Despite the confusion, Hale knew what it was. It was murder. The banker stopped to talk with his friend, the mayor, and discuss the terrible thing that had happened.

Hale left the mayor's office and walked on up the street, thinking of Bill Smith. He had known Bill and his wife, Rita, for years. They had lived out in the country until recently, when they decided to move into town. Rita's sister, Mollie, was married to one of Hale's nephews. So there really was a distant family relationship.

Banker Hale still had the Smith murders on his mind a few days later when he sent for Asa Kirby, who frequently did odd jobs for him. The two men talked for a while and then Kirby left the Hale house.

Later, Hale strolled downtown. He entered one of the Main Street stores and chatted confidentially with the proprietor. There was talk around town that the storekeeper had a valuable collection of diamonds in his safe.

That night the merchant didn't go home. He locked himself in the store and waited with a shotgun in his hands. It was about 2:30 A.M. when he heard the rear window of the store being pried open. And then a dark figure was framed in the window.

The shotgun roared, blasting "Ace" Kirby out of the window, mortally wounded. Dead men tell no tales—and Kirby would never be able to name the man who had paid him and a companion to blow up the home of Bill Smith.

That was Osage County, Oklahoma, in March, 1923, a dark and bloody hunting ground if ever there was one; and the craftiest hunter of them all in this oil-and-Indian kingdom was William K. Hale, banker, cattleman, merchant, politician and killer-by-proxy.

Throughout the Roaring Twenties there was no stranger case than that of Hale, who became known as "King of the Osage Hills."

For twenty years, Bill Hale was a power above the law in Osage County, growing rich from frauds and murders planned behind a front of respectability. He didn't kill with his own hands. He hired his killers. If anyone talked too much . . . well, there were ways to shut him up. Nobody had ever proved that Bill Hale had done anything wrong.

Before the turn of the century, Bill Hale had left his family's ranch near Greenville, Texas, and drifted into the "bandit hills" of Osage County. This was rough, broken country where outlaws hid in the ravines and caves, safe from pursuit until they were ready to ride again. Hale had no trouble making friends.

He lived in a tent for a time, scratching out a living by trading with the Indians. Curiously, when an Indian reported some of his cattle missing in one part of the county, Hale would turn up in another part with quantities of fresh meat for sale.

One day Hale went to collect a small bill from an Indian customer, only to find the man had just died. This wasn't misfortune for Hale— it was opportunity knocking for the first time.

Hale saw a lawyer and arranged to have a lien filed against almost everything the Indian had owned, including land, cattle and household possessions. It was sheer robbery, and the Indian's relatives prepared to fight the claim. But out of the badlands came Hale's friends to swear the Indian rightfully owed Hale the money. Yes, sir, they had heard Bill Hale plenty of times demanding payment from the Indian. Moreover, the Indian had acknowledged the debt. There wasn't a shred of documentary proof to support the claim, but Hale won his case.

After that it was easy. Rarely did an Indian die that there wasn't a claim of some kind against his property, filed either by Hale or by some other white man.

Then came the deluge of wealth for Osage County. Drillers struck oil and almost overnight the Osage Indians became the richest people per capita on earth. By reason of the "head rights" granted by the federal government to some 2,200 full-blooded Osage Indians, they were eligible to share the royalties paid on each gallon of oil pumped from their reservation. And there were the bonuses, too, from the lease sales. When an Osage died, his "head right" was passed on to his heirs. In this manner some Indians had more than one share in the tribe's pooled income.

Suddenly these Indians who had lived in poverty were fabulously wealthy. They bought huge houses and then spent most of their time in tents in the back yard. Grocery bills of more than $1,000 a month for one family were not uncommon. They vied with each other to see who could get the largest car. One Indian went to Oklahoma City and bought a new, shiny hearse with glass sides. He liked to ride through the countryside and admire the scenery from the depths of a comfortable rocking chair. The hearse was driven by a high-priced uniformed chauffeur.

The Osages were like children released in a vast new wonderland. But it was a wonderland that was to bring them misery, and even death.

The swindlers, gamblers, prostitutes, pimps and touts moved in to share the Osage wealth. White men married Indian women solely to get their hands on the oil money. Others developed a sudden "concern" for the Osages' welfare, and arranged to have themselves named legal guardians with control over their wards' money. Loan sharks charged exorbitant interest rates. Salesmen asked, and received, outrageous prices for their merchandise. Some Indians protested bitterly. But there were few to listen.

Bill Hale prospered as the Indians prospered. By 1920 the one-time cowpoke had moved from his tent in the badlands into control of a 50,000-acre ranch stocked with cattle and fine horses. He controlled a bank in Fairfax, and owned part interest in a mercantile store and an undertaking establishment. Whenever a full-blooded Osage died, Bill Hale prospered in some fashion.

The number of unsolved murders of Indians increased. They found Charlie Whitehorn with two bullet holes in his forehead. Joe Yellow Horse died frothing at the mouth and Bill Stetson, the great Osage roper, and Nina Smith, both full-bloods, died violently. Folks said it was poisoned whiskey.

Barney McBride, a white oil man, was enraged by the scandalous treatment of his Indian friends. The tribal chiefs appealed to him to help put a stop to the thievery and the murder and McBride set out for Washington to make a protest. His body, horribly mutilated, was found stuffed in a culvert near Meadows, Maryland. He died before filing the protest.

Joe (Gray Horse) Bates died, too, and Bill Hale produced a deed to his lands. When George Bigheart died, Hale allegedly had an argument at his deathbed over a deed which Hale claimed had been made to him. George Bigheart's lawyer was reported to have said the deed was fraudulent. The lawyer later fell—or was thrown—from a train. He was ground to death by the wheels.

Then the "King of the Osage Hills" got the most brilliant idea of his life. He must have wondered why the scheme hadn't occurred to him sooner. Oil was flowing faster and faster from the Osage wells, and the "head rights" were as good as a diamond mine in a man's back yard —that is, if a man could get control over a few of them.

There was old Lizzie Q. She was a full-blooded Osage worth maybe $330,000. Lord knows how much more she would be worth in another few years. That old squaw had three "head rights" herself; and her daughters held one and one-sixth "head rights" each.

Now, Hale mused, suppose old Lizzie Q. should die. And just suppose that two of her daughters, Anna Brown and Rita Smith, should die along with Rita's husband. Who would inherit all that money, maybe half a million dollars or more?

The answer was simple. The fortune—most of it, anyway—would go to the third daughter, Mollie. And Mollie was married to Hale's nephew, Ernest Burkhart. Then if Mollie should die, there would be no trouble handling Ernest. He was a weak-willed chucklehead anyway.

Hunters found Anna Brown's decomposed body in a ravine near Fairfax in May, 1921. She had been shot in the head. Her estate was worth $100,000. Old Lizzie Q. died two months later, apparently of natural causes; her estate was divided between Rita Smith and Mollie Burkhart. And just as the verse said, now there were only two little Indians.

Hale was a methodical man. He was in no hurry about rounding up Lizzie Q.'s family estate. Before any more moves in that direction, there was another murder job to be done.

Anna Brown had a cousin—a picturesque full-blooded Osage Indian named Henry Roan Horse who liked to wear his hair down his back in plaits. On February 6, 1923, Roan Horse's body was found outside Fairfax, slumped in the front seat of his car. Henry's brains had been blown out for reasons known best to Hale.

Two months later, while Hale was at the Texas Fat Cattle Show, Fairfax was shaken by the explosion which killed Bill and Rita Smith and their maid. After this, there remained only one little Indian— Mollie Burkhart.

But the blast that shook Fairfax also shook the Osage Tribal Council to action. In desperation, the Indians appealed to Washington. A lawyer composed their resolution, which said:

WHEREAS, several members of the Osage Tribe have been murdered . . . and many other crimes committed against members of the tribe . . . BE IT . . . RESOLVED that the Honorable Secretary of the Interior be requested to obtain the services of the Department of Justice in capturing and prosecuting the murderers of the members of the Osage Tribe. . . .

The appeal was relayed to the FBI and the order went out launching an investigation that was to last for three years and become one of the classic manhunts in FBI history.

FBI agents moved into Fairfax and found an almost impenetrable wall of fear. People were afraid to talk and witnesses who might have given information had long since disappeared. There were rumors which sent the agents off for days at a time on false leads. Someone, they knew, was deliberately "planting" stories to confuse their search. But the hunt continued.

No one in Fairfax paid any particular attention when four strangers drifted into town one by one, a cattle buyer, an insurance salesman, an oil prospector and an Indian herb doctor. They went about their business, minding their own affairs.

Weeks passed without a break in the case. But then a signal was passed and the four strangers met one night in the badlands to pool their information and plan their next moves. The "cattle buyer" was the oldest, and he was the FBI agent in charge for this special undercover detail.

After hearing the reports, he summed them up: "Here's where we stand: Anna Brown was killed on unrestricted [non-government] land and so were Bill and Rita Smith. We have no jurisdiction there. But Henry Roan Horse was killed on restricted [government] land—and that's our case. If we can break that case, I figure we'll find all the killers." The others agreed.

Months passed. The four strangers often met under the stars in the Osage hills to exchange information and each time they met they had a bit more information about the circumstances surrounding the murders. Gradually the picture was taking form. And the man in the picture was William K. Hale. Finally, the agent in charge told his men: "Hale is our man without a doubt. He had a $25,000 insurance policy on Henry Roan Horse's life. And it looks as if he was working to get the estates of Lizzie Q. and her daughters centered in the hands of that nephew of his. But we have to prove it."

Prove it they did. The wall against which they had pounded so long crumbled slowly but steadily. From the badlands came a tip that a certain convict in the Oklahoma State Penitentiary knew something about the murders. The agents found that the convict, who hated Hale, was ready to talk. He said, "Go see Ernest Burkhart. He can tell you everything you want to know."

This dovetailed with other information collected over the months. The agents confronted Burkhart with what they had, and what they suspected. Hale's nephew was the weak link. He broke and told the agents how Hale had dominated him all his life. He named the killers of Henry Roan Horse and the Smiths; and he said his uncle had plotted the murders.

One by one the killers confessed. In each case they pointed the finger at Hale. And the story unfolded of how "Ace" Kirby had been double-crossed after he blew up the Smith home.

But Hale fought back in one of the bitterest criminal trials ever held in the Southwest. He boasted when arrested that he could raise a million-dollar bond if necessary, and he must have spent a chunk of money. The courtroom battles were highlighted by charges of bribery, perjury and threats against witnesses.

Bill Hale's battery of lawyers almost succeeded in winning freedom for him. The Federal District Court held in his first trial that the government had no jurisdiction, but the U. S. Supreme Court reversed this decision. The second trial ended in a hung jury after a defense witness gave perjured testimony. The perjurer was convicted.

Hale was convicted on the third trial, but still the fight hadn't been won. The verdict was set aside on the ground that the trial had been held in the wrong district. On the fourth try Hale was convicted and sentenced to life imprisonment.[1] It was January 26, 1929.

In Osage County, the Indians' Tribal Council assembled again. And this time they adopted a resolution voicing "our sincere gratitude for the splendid work done in the matter of the investigating and bringing to justice the parties charged with the murders of . . . members of the Osage Tribe of Indians. . . ."

The bloody reign of the "King of the Osage Hills" had ended. The FBI had closed one of the most fantastic cases in its files.

The New FBI

14: *The Anonymous Nine*

DURING the gang-busting 1930's, J. Edgar Hoover became "Mr. FBI."

Through the years, the FBI was shaped in the image of this man's ideas and ideals. No other agency in the federal government bears the imprint of a single personality as clearly as the Federal Bureau of Investigation.

Hoover *is* the FBI. But his position of strength—and the strength of the FBI—isn't merely a matter of one man's personality. The real secret lies in the fact that Hoover has around him a group of top-flight executives who climbed from the ranks of the FBI's special agents. They came up the hard way, by merit and not as somebody's political pets. Hoover trusted them to make decisions. In turn, these men have repaid the trust with loyalty and fierce pride in the FBI. They accept without question the FBI policy of anonymity. Their names are not widely known beyond the doors of the FBI's Headquarters. And yet they hold in their hands much of the responsibility for the nation's safety.

This inner circle is composed of nine men of whom Hoover has said, "You can't buy the kind of energy and devotion they have given to the FBI."

Hoover's top lieutenants gather each Monday and Wednesday and if need be each weekday at 10:30 A.M. in what is known as "the FBI Executives Conference." The presiding officer is Clyde A. Tolson, who came to the Bureau on April 2, 1928.

Tolson is "the man who came to dinner" at the FBI. He intended to stay just long enough to get a little experience and enough money to start practicing law at Cedar Rapids, Iowa, where he had gone to business school. Tolson stated his short-term views on the FBI job in his application, causing a stir in the Chief Clerk's Office, which had grown accustomed to having applicants describe their ambitions for a lifelong career in the organization. The unusual letter found its way to Hoover.

"Hire him, if he measures up after the examination and investigation," Hoover said. "He will make us a good man." [1]

Several months after joining the FBI as a special agent, Tolson was brought to Headquarters as Chief Clerk, and then he moved up fast. He became an Assistant Director in 1931 and five years later he was named Assistant to the Director. In 1947, Hoover gave him the title of Associate Director—formal recognition that Tolson was the Number 2 G-Man.

Tolson, like Hoover, is a bachelor. The two men have become such close friends over the years that their intimates say they have even reached the point where they think alike. Tolson carries much of the administrative load which Hoover handled himself for many years, and serves in effect as Hoover's chief of staff.

The third man in the line of command is Louis B. Nichols, who handles a tremendous number of chores for the Director in addition to running the Records and Communications Division and representing the FBI in matters not handled personally by Hoover. Nichols is an Assistant to the Director, a title also held by the Number 4 man, Leland V. Boardman. [2]

Below Tolson, Nichols and Boardman, there are six assistant directors who are the operating chiefs of the Identification, Training and Inspection, Administrative, Domestic Intelligence, Investigative and Laboratory Divisions. [3]

These men did not reach their positions by being yes-men. They arrived by being willing to accept hard work, make decisions and take on responsibilities while submerging their own personalities in the FBI. They push themselves harder than they do their subordinates. It isn't unusual for them to work twelve or even fifteen hours a day. They do it because there is work to be done—and their work comes first.

In the conference room, each executive is expected to say what he thinks, whether the problem deals with his own work or the work of someone else. But he had better be ready to defend the position he takes, and have his reasons ready. These are strong-willed men and there are, at times, clashes of opinion. In questions of basic policy or in dealing with grave issues, the conference passes the decision on up to Hoover, but always with a recommendation as to what course should be followed. If there is disagreement, an alternative recommendation is also made. And then the decision is up to Hoover.

But when these men walk out of the conference room, they walk out as a team. The decisions have been made and each man knows where he is going and what he is to do. Their shoulder-to-shoulder teamwork is one of the keys to the FBI's reputation for unity and efficiency.

None of these men seems to see anything unusual in accepting anonymity as a part of the job. Any one, or all of them, could leave the organization and go into private industry at a large increase in salary. But they stick to the FBI.

Tolson once explained it this way: "I think most of them stay for the same reason I do. You get something out of working for the FBI that is more important than a pay check."

Another key to the FBI's efficiency is the exacting attention that is paid to small details. A typist who makes a mistake in a word or a number, and anyone else who overlooks the error, has done a sloppy job. Mistakes are never disregarded.

The effort to achieve accuracy in work details is time-consuming and might even be regarded in private industry as a waste of time and energy. But to the FBI, this effort is the essence of doing the job properly. Tolson said: "Precision is the cardinal virtue of an investigating agency. Many a criminal has been convicted, and many an innocent person absolved, because somebody took pains to be accurate about an 'unimportant little fact.'"

Employees would find fewer pressures and easier work if they left the FBI and took other jobs. But despite the strict discipline, constant supervision and demand for better-than-average performance, the FBI has an amazingly low turnover in personnel.[4] More than one fourth of the 14,000 employees have been with the Bureau ten years or longer. And more than one third of the special agents have been employed for at least ten years.

In this connection, a few statistics are interesting:

During 1955, the federal government as a whole had a monthly turnover of 1.8 percent and private industry reported a 3.3 percent turnover. Among FBI special agents, the monthly turnover was less than one-half of one percent, or approximately 27 out of a total of about 6,200 special agents. While 334 agents left the service (nine of them involuntarily), applications were received from seventy former agents asking to be reinstated. And there were 431 former clerical workers who applied for jobs.

Traditionally, Americans have not been regarded as a disciplined people. But the truth is that Americans accept discipline when they see the need for it—and when there is strong leadership to point out the road they are traveling and why discipline is necessary. That is why the FBI discipline is accepted.

What manner of men are these special agents of the FBI? Why do they stay with the FBI when they could find more money and an easier life in another career?

First, of course, there is no such thing as a "typical" FBI agent, just as there is no such creature as a "typical" American. Each is an individual, different from the others as all men differ from each other.

But certain traits of character and similarity in backgrounds do emerge from a sampling of the agents' biographies. And from the sampling comes the approximation, at least, of a so-called average agent whose name, let us say, is John J. Jones.

John Jones is thirty-four years old and he has a wife and two children. His father is a moderately well-to-do businessman, although not a rich one. Both his parents are a bit old-fashioned. They are the kind of people who bow their heads and say grace at mealtimes, and who teach their children to say their prayers at bedtime. John Jones and his brothers and sisters learned—sometimes in the woodshed—to have respect for authority when it is properly used. They were taught, too, that patriotism, honor and duty were interwoven in the achievements of America's great heroes, and that these were words whose meaning could not be debated away.

In high school, John had above-average grades. He was a good athlete and took part in debating and social affairs. He went to the State University and he worked at times during the summer to help pay his way. He was graduated with an A.B. degree and then entered law school.

John decided on an FBI career partly because it promised exciting and interesting work, and also because he felt he would be doing something worth while in an organization in which he could take personal pride. He passed the strict physical tests and the preliminary examinations.[5] He was investigated thoroughly as to his loyalty and personal integrity.

But these were preliminaries. John Jones, before becoming a special agent, had to survive eighteen tough weeks of training at the Bureau Headquarters and at the FBI's training center at Quantico, Virginia. He was taught how to write reports and how to go about making an investigation. He was drilled in the techniques and mechanics of law enforcement, fingerprint identification, crime detection, preservation of evidence at the scene of a crime, and a number of other essentials required to do a good job. He learned how to handle the four basic FBI weapons—pistol, submachine gun, shotgun, and rifle.

John Jones passed all the tests and requirements and became a special agent. He was assigned to his first office at a starting salary of $5,915 a year plus the $816 in overtime earned annually by most agents. As a rookie, he worked with an experienced agent for the first few weeks in the field. And then he was on his own, although he would find that his training would really never end as long as he stayed in the FBI; and his work would always be under the microscope of those above him.[6]

Each special agent signs a register, and jots down the time, whenever he enters or leaves his office, whether it's in New York City, Honolulu, Chicago or any other city. The system works the same way in all FBI offices. At three-hour intervals while on duty the agent must telephone to his office to check for any messages or any unexpected change of assignment. He tells the office where he is and where he is going, and a note is made of it. The special agent in charge can check the agent's register card in the communications section at any time and know where the agent is and the particular case on which he is working.

The assignment cards are reviewed each month and the agent is expected to make a formal, written report on each case on an average of every forty-five days. If he fails to make his reports on schedule, then he has become "delinquent" and he's called on the carpet. Naturally, the exciting and interesting work lies in getting out on investigations. And the dull job is making out the reports.

When the backlog begins to rise above a normal level in any office, the Washington Headquarters demands to know what is wrong. "They begin cracking the whip on us," one field official said, "and, of course, we begin cracking the whip on those who must turn out the reports."

It would seem entirely reasonable to expect an FBI agent to take a Bureau car home with him the night before he is to go on an investigation; then the car would be available for a quick start on the job next morning. But such is not the case. The agent doesn't take the car home. He leaves his house the next morning an hour earlier, if necessary, and comes to the central garage to pick up the car assigned to him. And he must return the car to the garage when he is finished with his work. Again, there is a reason for this rule. Hoover insists that his agents cannot have government vehicles parked outside their homes during off-duty hours because someone might say, "Look at that FBI man, keeping a government car for his personal use." Hoover has said, "We can't afford merely to be right. We must give every appearance of doing right to avoid criticism."

No FBI agent comes to the office in the morning wondering "What shall I do today?" He knows what he is going to do because he laid out his work schedule the night before. If it wasn't done the night before, then he must get to the office early and get it done. This advance planning is even carried into the agent's dictation of reports.

The day before an agent is going to make out reports, he must notify the supervisor in charge of the stenographic pool when he expects to begin his dictation and, roughly, how long it will take. He is expected to have his report organized in such a way that when the stenographer arrives, he is ready to begin dictation.

In this system, the FBI gives the stenographers what might be called the opportunity to become the critics of the boss. At periodic intervals, the stenographer is asked to note whether the agent had his work organized properly, whether his dictation was too fast or too slow, and what he might do to improve his dictation technique.

Once dictated, the agent's reports are checked, criticized and reviewed by a superior who then signs them and transmits them to the Headquarters in Washington.

There is no such thing as a 9:00 A.M. to 5:30 P.M. day in the life of an agent, because criminals and subversives work around the clock. No agent's life is ever quite his own, because he must be ready to go anywhere he is ordered, at any time. And his hours are long. During fiscal 1956, each special agent worked overtime a little more than two hours daily. The agents received more than $5,000,000 in overtime pay—but there was no pay for more than $6,000,000 worth of overtime, which, in effect, was a net saving to the taxpayer.

"One thing for sure," an FBI official said, "we intend to give the people value for their money. We expect an honest day's work and then just a little more."

This expectation of "just a little more" from employees has caused some criticism from time to time, but the FBI is convinced its personnel policies actually offer the workers more in security, entertainment, personal satisfaction and a sense of accomplishment than any other government agency.

There is no problem in recruiting either special agents or clerical help. From all parts of the country and from the territories comes a flow of applications from those who have read of the FBI or have been influenced by movies, television, radio or reports from friends. Many recruits are recommended by men and women already working for the FBI. Many fathers and sons, brothers and sisters, mothers and daughters are FBI employees—and now the grandsons of former employees are entering the service. One of the early agents in the FBI was Edward J. Brennan, who served with the Bureau from 1908 to 1925.

Brennan's son, John, came into the Bureau in 1919, and now young Edward J. Brennan, the third generation of the Brennans, is a special agent of the FBI.

Special agents visiting each town and city throughout the country are approached by high school and college students interested in a career with the FBI. And letters come by the hundreds from youths wanting to know what they should do to qualify for a job.

Some critics have called the FBI personnel policies an example of "paternalism" encouraging sweatshop methods. The FBI regards these same policies as being the most advanced and enlightened personnel practices of any government agency. The best thing, perhaps, is for the reader to judge from the hypothetical case of Mary Smith, who arrived in Washington to take an FBI job, slightly bewildered and just a little afraid. The case of Mary Smith is not unusual in any sense.

Mary had the FBI telephone number in her purse and she called the Personnel Section. She was immediately taken under the FBI's wing. A woman from the Housing Unit helped her find a room, in one of the approved homes, with another FBI girl who wanted someone to share expenses.

"If there is anything bothering you or anything we can do to help," Mary was told, "all you have to do is call. Somebody is there day and night just for that purpose."

On the following Monday, Mary reported for work and from that time on she was too busy to be either lonesome or scared. For the first two days she attended orientation lectures, where she learned about the FBI and its responsibilities in law enforcement and national security. She was told what was expected of her in her personal conduct and in her work; where she could find good food at reasonable prices; where to find a church in her neighborhood; where she would find good recreational facilities. Mary met the FBI Health Service nurse who explained to her the medical services to which she was entitled.

And then on the third day Mary was taken to an Assistant Director in charge of her division. She was later told the office rules about rest periods, working hours, lunch periods and how she must take care of property, supplies and security.

For the first few days, one of the girls who worked with Mary went to lunch with her and saw that she met other employees. Mary's name and home town were posted on the bulletin boards, and she began meeting other girls from her home state, who gave her advice. And then, at the end of ten days, Mary was called in for a personal interview with the supervisor, who told her she was doing very well.

At the end of sixty days, Mary was given a chance to see a written report which had been made on her work—a performance rating.

Mary was told how she could improve her work and, if she continued making progress, what her chances were for future promotions and greater responsibilities. She was told what her strong points were, and how to correct her weak points.

After that, Mary attended a divisional conference every six months, where she and the other employees were told what the division as a whole was doing and what the policies meant to them in their work. And there were letters from the Bureau to Mary's family, too, telling them of her progress and inviting them to visit the Bureau. When Mary was ill for a short time, the Bureau kept her family advised, and the Health Service checked every day to be certain she was all right and receiving good care.

Mary Smith is only one of some 8,000 non-agent employees in the FBI, but each one of them is given the same close personal supervision and help when they need it.

In its incentive awards program, the FBI has found a way to tap the reservoir of employee ideas for improving efficiency and saving money, and for rewarding meritorious service—such as the case in which a special agent braved a gunman's pistol fire to help a local policeman in the chase. His award was $500. During the 1956 fiscal year, 486 incentive awards worth $77,005 were given to FBI employees for their accomplishments. The FBI began its incentive awards program several years before the federal government adopted the program. Now the FBI program is part of the federal system, although it operates much as it always did.

A family-type magazine called *The Investigator* serves as a kind of small-town newspaper, reporting the doings of FBI folk in sports, social affairs, special activities, promotions and incentive awards. And the FBI Recreation Association (FBIRA) promotes outside activities such as dances, excursions, moonlight cruises, sports competition and camp shows. And there have been clubs for camera, drama, flying, writing and pistol enthusiasts. More than 13,000 FBI employees are members of the FBIRA and pay annual dues of $1.50 each.

One side of the FBI which few outsiders see is the kindness which runs through the organization when a member of the FBI family is in trouble. Not so long ago, a special agent—married and the father of two children—was stricken with bulbar polio and his condition was serious. FBI wives got together and arranged to help the agent's wife with the housework and the care of the children. A television set was sent to the agent's hospital room. Nurses from the FBI Health Service checked each day on his condition. An air conditioner was installed in his room by his friends.

An agent visited the hospital and returned to Headquarters with the report that the sick man had begun to worry about his job. Hoover went to see him and said, "We will always find a place for you. Don't worry about your work. Your job is to get well."

Finally the time came when the agent had used up all his vacation time and sick leave. His pay check stopped—and he was put on leave without pay. The agent's friends figured that if each special agent at Headquarters kicked in sixty cents each payday, the sick man's regular pay could be continued. The Executives Conference approved the plan, and collection boxes were placed in each section on payday. No records were kept of those who contributed and those who didn't. But the agent continued to receive his salary in full.[7]

This spirit is not new in the FBI. It has been going on for more than thirty years, and the files are filled with scores of such cases. When an agent has been killed or has died in service, then the agent's widow, if she can qualify, knows that she always will have a job with the FBI, or the children will be given a job. When Special Agent W. Carter Baum was killed by "Baby Face" Nelson back in 1934 at Spider Lake, Wisconsin, he was twenty-nine years old and the father of two children. Baum's widow accepted Hoover's offer of a job. And she stayed with the FBI until 1944, when her request to resign was accepted.

After Sam Cowley was fatally wounded in the gun battle with "Baby Face" Nelson, Mrs. Cowley was given a job. Mrs. Cowley stayed with the Bureau until 1948, when she asked to resign in order to spend more time with her two sons.

Despite the FBI's exacting physical standards, there are a good many handicapped persons who have found steady employment with the Bureau after showing a determination to overcome their handicaps.

Selected at random is the case of Jane X. When she was a child in Mississippi, Jane injured her left arm and it was amputated just below the elbow. The girl refused to let this tragedy ruin her life. In high school she became one of the best typists in her class. This girl's spirit so impressed a special agent that he suggested she stop by the FBI when her high school class came to Washington for a spring tour of the Capital. Jane came to the FBI and asked about a job. She threw her chin up and said, "I can do anything anyone else can do."

Jane got the job after she was graduated from high school. She won promotion after promotion, and even though she typed with only one hand, she was one of the most accurate and speediest typists in her section. This story had a happy ending, too. Jane found her man and they were married.

FBI employees are not under Civil Service, but they are entitled to the same benefits and privileges received by other government employees. But, here again, the FBI tries where possible to go a bit further.

For example, these are some of the privileges and benefits available to the FBI employees:

Sick Leave—Earned at the rate of thirteen working days a year. No ceiling on sick-leave accumulation, and some employees have built up as much as 1,000 hours, or about 125 days, to their credit.

Annual Leave—Those with fewer than three years of service are entitled to thirteen working days leave each year. Those with three years but less than fifteen years of service are entitled to twenty working days leave; and those with fifteen or more years in service are entitled to twenty-six.

Federal Employees Group Life Insurance—Employees have the option of obtaining term life insurance at a cost of $6.50 per year per $1,000 of coverage. A new agent earning $5,915 a year is entitled to $6,000 of insurance, and in all cases the insurance coverage is available in the amount of the nearest thousand dollars above the annual salary. The insurance provides double indemnity for any type of accidental death.

Special Agents' Insurance Fund—Available only to the FBI agents and operated by means of contributions made by the agents. It provides, in addition to the Federal Employees Group Life Insurance, an additional $10,000 payment in case of death from any cause. Premiums are in the form of voluntary contributions by agents who are members. They pay ten-dollar assessments whenever the reserve fund requires such payment. Since November, 1943, the assessment has averaged less than $15 a year.

Special Agents Mutual Benefit Association (SAMBA)—This again is a group-insurance program for agents,[8] providing $5,000 of term insurance, plus hospitalization, surgical and polio protection at a minimum monthly premium with no medical examination required for either the agent or any of his dependents if application is made within sixty days after the agent's appointment.

Compensation—All employees are covered by the Federal Employees' Compensation Act, which entitles them to medical, hospital and loss-of-pay benefits in case injuries are suffered in performance of official duties.

Retirement and Survivorship Benefits—An agent may retire at age fifty after twenty years of service as an agent, and he receives about 40 percent of the average annual salary he was paid during the top five consecutive years of his career. The maximum retirement pay is 80 percent at the end of 40 years of service.

There are survivor benefits for the widow and children under eighteen of an employee who has had at least five years of civilian service. The cost of all retirement benefits is 6½ percent of the employee's salary.

As an example of the benefits paid to the survivors of an agent, there is the case of the Special Agent M., who was killed in a gun battle by an ex-convict wanted for murder in California. The agent's widow received $23,905 in lump-sum benefits:

Special Agents' Insurance Fund	$10,000
Charles S. Ross Fund [9]	1,500
Special Agents Mutual Benefit Association	5,000
Accrued Annual Leave and Unpaid Salary	3,294
Funeral expenses paid by the Bureau of Employees' Compensation	400
Civil Service Retirement Refund	3,711
Total	$23,905

In addition, under the Federal Employees' Compensation Act, the widow and her three children will receive compensation payments of $6,300 a year.[10]

15 : *Fingerprints*

BACK in 1893, Mark Twain wrote the story of a remarkable lawyer in Missouri named David Wilson who pursued over the years a seemingly senseless hobby of collecting on glass the fingerprints of his friends and neighbors. He carefully identified the prints by name, noted the dates on which they were taken and filed them away. Everybody liked Wilson, but the townsfolk were agreed he wasn't the brightest fellow in Dawson's Landing and his hobby merely confirmed their judgment. That's why they called him "Pudd'nhead."

The town's estimate of Wilson's intelligence and his peculiar hobby was suddenly revised one day when "Pudd'nhead" proved with fingerprints in a dramatic courtroom scene, that (a) twins accused of murder were innocent; (b) the actual slayer was one who had never been suspected; and (c) the whole tragedy could be traced to the time when a nursemaid deliberately confused the identities of two children by switching them in their cribs.

Probably no better description of a fingerprint as an identification mark has been given, experts agree, than the one which Mark Twain had "Pudd'nhead" Wilson give to the jury:

Every human being carries with him from his cradle to his grave certain physical marks which do not change their character, and by which he can always be identified—and that without shade of doubt or question. These marks are his signature, his physiological autograph, so to speak, and this autograph cannot be counterfeited, nor can he disguise it or hide it away, nor can it become illegible by the wear and mutations of time . . . This autograph consists of the delicate lines or corrugations with which Nature marks the insides of the hands and the soles of the feet. If you will look at the balls of your fingers . . . you will observe that these dainty curving lines lie close together, like those that indicate the borders of oceans in maps, and that they form various clearly-defined patterns, such as arches, circles, long curves, whorls, etc., and that these patterns differ on the different fingers . . . One twin's patterns are never the same as his fellow-twin's patterns . . . You have often heard of twins who were so exactly alike that when dressed alike their own parents could not tell them apart. Yet there was never a twin born into this world that did not carry from birth to death a sure identifier in this mysterious and marvelous natal autograph.

Mark Twain's story of a crime solved by fingerprints was pure fiction. But it can be matched hundreds upon hundreds of times in whole or in part in the FBI Identification Division's records of crimes solved through fingerprints; in records of the capture of fugitives from justice, military deserters caught, lost persons found and families reunited; and in cases of men saved from suspicion, prison or perhaps death by fingerprint identification.

One of the strangest cases in identification began in 1928 when four men walked boldly into the First National Bank of Lamar, Colorado, on the morning of May 23, and suddenly drew pistols.

"Put up your hands! This is a stick-up!" snapped the leader.

Terrified customers and bank officials obeyed. The robbers scooped up some $219,000 in cash and bonds.

A. N. Parrish, the bank's elderly president, suddenly grabbed a gun from a desk drawer and fired in the face of one bandit. Blood spurted from the wound. The bandit's gun cracked and Parrish fell dead. The bank president's son rushed toward his fallen father. He was shot down, too.

The killers forced E. A. Lungren, bank teller, and Everett A. Kessinger, assistant cashier, into their waiting automobile as hostages and sped out of town with their loot. It was all over in a matter of minutes.

Sheriff Lloyd E. Alderman started in pursuit, armed only with a pistol. The bandits shoved Lungren out of their car—but kept Kessinger, using him as a shield in a gun battle with the sheriff. The bandits' rifle fire disabled the sheriff's car and he lost their trail.

A few hours after the Lamar robbery, a man came to the home of Dr. W. W. Weininger at Dighton, Kansas, 155 miles from Lamar. He told the doctor his friend had been injured in a tractor accident and needed medical aid. The visitor drove away with Dr. Weininger in the doctor's car.

A search party found Kessinger, the hostage. He had been riddled with bullets and his body dumped into an abandoned shack. They found Dr. Weininger lying dead in a ravine near his wrecked automobile. The doctor had obviously been lured from his home to treat the bandit wounded in the holdup and had then been murdered.

A fingerprint expert, R. S. Terwilliger of the Garden City, Kansas, Police Department, came to the death scene and carefully inspected the doctor's wrecked car in search of a fingerprint clue. It looked hopeless because the killers apparently had wiped the car clean of fingerprints with a damp cloth.

Terwilliger examined the car inch by inch. And then he found what he had been seeking—one fragmentary latent fingerprint on the upper, outside glass of the car's right rear door. He removed the glass and took it to Garden City to develop the print.

Two months later, the FBI Identification Division received enlarged photographs of the single, partial print. The Division's files are classified only on a ten-fingerprint system and it would have been a hopeless task to search through what were then two million files, attempting to match a single print. FBI fingerprint experts took the problem to Director Hoover and they discussed it.

Hoover finally said, "It's a long shot, but I want you to memorize the pattern of that print. Impress it on your memory, and it may be you will come across the print some day. I know it's unlikely, but it's the only thing we can do."

In the months that followed, four men were arrested and charged with the murders. Sixty Lamar citizens came forward and said they could identify the suspects as the bank robbers. But some officials felt there was a doubt as to their guilt, and the trials were delayed.

More than a year after the crimes, FBI Fingerprint Expert Albert B. Ground (now retired) sat at his desk in the Identification Division making a routine check to verify identifications made on a fingerprint card received that day. This card was from the Stockton, California, sheriff's office and carried the name of William Harrison Holden, arrested as a train holdup suspect. But in a search of the files Holden's fingerprints had been found to match those of a Jake Fleagle. Fleagle had been received at the Oklahoma State Penitentiary in 1916, to serve a one-year sentence for robbery.

Ground verified the identification and put the card aside. But then something, like a small warning bell deep in his memory, sounded an alarm. He picked up the card again and began to study it. That right index fingerprint seemed vaguely familiar. He should remember where he had seen it before.

Like a cartographer who glimpses a fragment of shoreline torn from a map—and then searches his memory for its proper geographical location—Ground tried to place the print. He went to the file cases seven times. But each time the print failed to match those he thought might be the mates. Then suddenly he remembered. The partial print in the Colorado and Kansas murders! He hurried to a cabinet, checked once more—and there it was. The print belonged to Jake Fleagle, alias William Harrison Holden.

At that time, it was not a federal offense to rob a national bank; the problem was one for the local authorities. Colorado and California authorities were notified by telegraph of the identification. Fleagle had been released at Stockton before the card had arrived at the Bureau. But now the police were on the right track.

The result: the four Lamar bank robbers were identified and there was a confession. Jake Fleagle died in a gun battle with officers, and his three confederates were hanged. The four innocent suspects were freed of murder charges.

The pattern of federal and local police cooperation in the Fleagle case became so commonplace that it was generally accepted as being merely routine. But behind this achievement of scientific criminal identification and police cooperation was a long and often bitter struggle. And like Twain's story of "Pudd'nhead" Wilson, it all revolved around the fingerprint, the "natal autograph."

Centuries ago, men recognized the distinctive patterns in fingerprints. In ancient China, a thumbprint in clay served as an identifying seal. Fingerprints were placed on early Chinese and Japanese legal documents. Kings and Oriental potentates used fingerprints as seals. A clay tablet in a British museum tells the story of a Babylonian officer ordered to seize property, make arrests and obtain the defendants' fingerprints.

Perhaps the first practical use of fingerprints in the United States was in 1882, when a geologist working in New Mexico placed his fingerprint on his orders and then signed his name across the print to guard against forgeries.

But the method of criminal identification which first came into popular use in Europe and the United States was the system devised in the 1880's by Alphonse Bertillon, a Frenchman. The Bertillon system was based on complex body measurements, such as the length and width of the head, the length of the left foot, left forearm, left little finger, and so on. Measurements were filed along with photographs of the subject. The scientific principle was that no two people would have the same appearance and physical measurements.

But the Bertillon system fell flat on its face one day in 1903 at the Federal Penitentiary at Leavenworth, Kansas, when a Negro named Will West was brought to the office of the record clerk to be photographed and measured.

"I've seen you before," the record clerk said. "Don't we already have your measurements?"

"No, sir," Will West said. "I've never been here before."

The clerk measured the incoming prisoner with his Bertillon instruments, and checked his files. He found the identification card of "William West." The measurements were virtually identical with those he had just taken. The face on the photograph looked to be an exact image of the man standing before him. Will West, so the photograph and measurements said, was William West.

"That looks like me, all right," Will West said, shaking his head. "But I've never been in this prison before."

Then the clerk realized that Will West was telling the truth—because William West was at that minute in a Leavenworth cell serving a life sentence for murder.

The Will West case spurred agitation in the United States for use of the fingerprint as the infallible means of criminal identification. England's Scotland Yard had abandoned the Bertillon system in favor of fingerprints in 1902, after Sir E. R. Henry had devised a method of classifying fingerprints.

During this early development of criminal identification, the International Association of Chiefs of Police (IACP) had recognized the need for a central bureau through which the nation's police could exchange information on crime and criminals. The IACP thought this work should be done by the Department of Justice, but its plan was rejected by Attorney General Judson Harmon. So the IACP voted in 1896 to establish its own National Bureau of Criminal Identification. It was located first in Chicago and then was moved to Washington, D. C.

The fingerprint system began to gain popularity. New York State adopted it for Sing Sing in 1903 and then for Napanoch, Auburn and Clinton prisons. In 1904 St. Louis became the first American city to switch from the Bertillon system to fingerprints. In the same year the Department of Justice authorized Warden R. W. McClaughry at Leavenworth to "expend a sum not to exceed $60" for installing the system.

In 1905 the Army began fingerprinting its enlisted and officer personnel, and the Navy and Marine Corps later followed suit. A fingerprint bureau was established in the Department of Justice for the benefit of federal and state penal institutions, but two years later the work was transferred to Leavenworth, where it could be done more cheaply with prison labor.

Year after year the IACP continued its campaign for a centralized bureau of identification which would serve all law enforcement agencies and institutions—federal, state and local. There was also dissatisfaction with the bureau at Leavenworth because convicts were handling the records and reportedly tampering with files.

The IACP finally received support from the American Bar Association's Special Committee on Law Enforcement, which in 1922 suggested "the establishment, under the control of the Department of Justice at Washington, of a Federal Bureau of Records and Statistics [in order that] fingerprints, etc., shall be immediately available to officers charged with enforcement of the criminal law . . . Without knowledge of the real situation, it will be impossible thoroughly to diagnose or properly deal with the problems of crime which confront us."

In November, 1921, Attorney General Daugherty had met with IACP representatives. He had agreed to establish an identification bureau in the Bureau of Investigation and to take over the IACP's records. With support from Daugherty and the American Bar Association, it appeared that the police chiefs were near the end of their long fight.

Then opposition came from an unexpected source. Police Commissioner R. E. Enright of New York City enlisted the support of New York congressmen for a bill to create a national bureau of identification in the Department of the Interior. Enright was head of the International Police Conference (IPC), which he had organized in 1920.

The IACP regarded Enright and his organization as johnny-come-latelies, trying to take over the plan which the IACP had sponsored since 1896. Chiefs of police from forty-seven states belonged to the IACP and they became a strong lobby in favor of centralizing identification within the Bureau of Investigation. The fight was carried to Congress when both sides introduced bills designed to achieve their purpose. The basic question was whether the service would be in the Department of Justice or the Department of the Interior.

In the midst of this argument, Attorney General Daugherty decided he had authority to act without waiting for legislation. As a result, the IACP's fingerprint and Bertillon records were accepted by the Department and the Leavenworth files were transferred to Washington. But then came another hitch. The Comptroller General of the United States refused to approve vouchers for setting up the identification service because Congress had not specifically authorized such expenditures.

And so it was for eight months that the nation's criminal identification system was bogged down for lack of funds.

When J. Edgar Hoover took over the FBI on May 10, 1924, the conditions were chaotic. Something had to be done to get an identification system operative again. About 800,000 fingerprint records were piled in storage, along with some 200,000 Bertillon files. Exasperated police in some cases were suggesting that it would be better to send the records back to Leavenworth. Even if the work was done by convicts under highly suspect conditions, that, they said, would be better than nothing.

Hoover went to work on the problem. He had the support of Attorney General Stone and, in Congress, strong backing from Representative William B. Oliver of Alabama and Representative Carl Hayden of Arizona (later a senator), who had been a sheriff himself and knew from experience the need for a central bureau of criminal identification.

Congress provided the money requested—$56,320—on July 1, and within sixty days the service was in operation again. Commissioner Enright continued his fight through 1925, when he lost his job in a change of administration in New York City. Congress decisively settled the dispute over the location of the service in June, 1930, with a law approving a permanent Division of Identification and Information within the FBI, which was intended to include fingerprints not only of criminals, but of law-abiding citizens as well.

Identification work increased rapidly. The number of law enforcement agencies cooperating in the program increased from 987 in 1924 to 4,712 in 1932 and then climbed to more than 12,000 in 1956. Hoover made the identification program international in scope through agreements with European police—thus giving police a check on crooks wanted in other countries.

Another valuable aid in the scientific fight against criminals was added in 1933, when a special section was set up to include the single fingerprints of the nation's top criminals. This section was manned by specialists concerned primarily with identifying latent single fingerprints—or parts of a fingerprint, palm print or footprint—left at the scene of a crime or found on an object used in a crime. Almost invisible prints left on a glass, a doorknob, a table or any smooth surface can be found when dusted with a special powder. Then the prints can be "lifted" onto adhesive tape. The powder clings to the adhesive and there reproduces the tiny skin ridges—a fingerprint which can be photographed.[1]

The FBI's identification files began to balloon in numbers in fiscal year 1933, when the Civil Service Commission turned over more than

140,000 fingerprints of government employees and job applicants. At this time Hoover set up a Civil Identification Section to handle personal identification prints. These prints were kept entirely separate from the criminal files.

The FBI encouraged citizens to have their prints filed away as a protective measure against frauds, loss of memory or the loss of identity resulting from a mutilating accident. Civil and business groups sponsored local campaigns to encourage fingerprinting, and to combat the impression that fingerprinting was for criminals only.

A few fingerprint enthusiasts throughout the years advocated compulsory fingerprinting of everyone in the United States, whether a criminal or a law-abiding citizen, and the idea of a national repository of personal identification fingerprints won increasing support as the years passed. But there were some who professed to see the voluntary fingerprinting program as a subtle plot by Hoover to lead the nation toward regimentation and suppression of civil rights.

One of the strongest attacks came in 1938, when a pamphlet entitled "Thumbs Down!" [2] assailed the FBI's voluntary fingerprinting program as "part of a general scheme for the compulsory regimentation of the entire population," saying that "as such it should be opposed."

The pamphlet continued, in part:

> Had the advocates of digital registration been cleverer in their early approach, they might have foisted drastic measures upon the nation, might have sharply curtailed civil liberties. Their efforts, however, were crude, haphazard, and decentralized. Until the advent of J. Edgar Hoover.

> Taking the campaign personally in hand, Hoover imparted to it a new and sinister impetus . . . he devised a whole new strategy . . . of "voluntary" fingerprinting . . . [which] is an early—and effective—move in the direction of general regimentation of the population.

There was another stormy round of protests a year later, when Colonel Brehon Somervell, Administrator of the Works Progress Administration (WPA) in New York City, ordered the fingerprinting of employees hired as teachers and guards as well as a variety of others. Somervell took the position that those employees who were to work with children, and in protecting property, should have their backgrounds checked for any criminal record.

Despite the protests, the fingerprinting program was carried out, and within two years 46,663 sets of WPA fingerprints had been checked through the FBI files. The result: 4,205 identifications of persons with a fingerprint record in the FBI criminal files, including 2,506 who had records of serious crimes. Of persons applying for jobs as watchmen or as workers in the child recreation program, some 50 had previous records of sex crimes.

While the FBI Identification Division became one of the strongest links in the chain of cooperation between federal and local law enforcement officers and a mighty force in fighting crime, it also proved to be a protector of civil rights in an astonishing volume of cases.

One of these cases involved John "The Bug" Stoppelli, a notorious narcotics peddler. "The Bug" was convicted on a narcotics charge in San Francisco in 1949. A so-called fingerprint expert claimed that a partial print on an envelope containing heroin matched one of Stoppelli's fingerprints.

Stoppelli's lawyer believed "The Bug" was telling the truth when he denied that he was guilty. The lawyer protested so persistently that finally the FBI was asked to check the fingerprint on the envelope against Stoppelli's prints. The FBI reported that the print on the envelope was not Stoppelli's print.

An official said: "No matter how low a man may be, he has civil rights. So we sent the FBI's report back to the U. S. Attorney in San Francisco." The result was that President Truman commuted Stoppelli's sentence.

In the early years, the FBI conducted a running fight against unethical practices in fingerprinting, ranging from "forged" fingerprints to false testimony by "experts" hired to do a job. Whenever there was any sign that fingerprints had been tampered with in any fashion, the FBI investigated. Those found guilty of such practices were denied the FBI's facilities and cooperation, and the guilty person's superiors were notified. Such practices became a rare thing.

In one case, the FBI received a letter from Tennessee in 1937 enclosing the photograph of what purported to be a latent fingerprint. In the same envelope were the fingerprints of a suspect. The FBI experts spotted the fraud. The alleged latent fingerprint was actually a photograph of the inked right ring finger impression on the suspect's fingerprint card. In other words, someone in that Tennessee police office had photographed one of the suspect's fingerprints on his card, and then tried to palm it off on the FBI as the fingerprint found at the scene of the crime. Had the trick succeeded, the FBI would have been in the position of linking the "suspect" with the crime.

There is a never-ending drama in the FBI's work of matching fingerprints with people. Each identification has its own little—or big—story. Here are a few samples:

In 1944 during World War II, a man's body was washed up on the beach five miles north of Bari, Italy. There were no identification papers on him. The Army sent his fingerprints to the FBI. He was identified as a seaman of British birth who had registered as an alien in New York City a few months earlier. There wasn't much doubt about what had happened—his ship had been sunk.

On March 12, 1956, a woman wandered into a police station in South Bend, Indiana. She had forgotten her name, her past and everything else that might have given a clue as to her identity. She was a victim of amnesia, lost in a world that suddenly had become a friendless, homeless place.

The South Bend police sent her fingerprints to the FBI. Her prints matched those of a woman who had been fingerprinted when she applied for jobs during World War II in Mishawaka, Indiana.

Through these fingerprints, the woman found again the world she knew.

In July, 1948, Hoover received a letter from a Wisconsin resident asking help in locating a brother whom he hadn't seen in thirty-three years. A search of the personal identification files yielded prints of a man who had once applied for a wartime job. His card gave an address in Milford, Connecticut, which was sent to the Wisconsin resident. Back came a letter: "I tried a long-distance telephone call at the address given. My brother answered the phone, the first time I had heard his voice for thirty-three years . . . you did more for me in one day than I have been able to do in years of inquiry and of following up leads that always led nowhere."

In 1948, a man applied for a job as assistant chief accountant with the Atomic Energy Commission. His application was impressive. His fingerprint record disclosed a long police record, including time in prison for robbery and attempted robbery. He didn't get the job.

On October 29, 1943, Miami Beach police sent the FBI finger impressions from a right hand which had been found in the stomach of a shark caught at Miami Beach, Florida. The fingerprints were compared with Navy Department records on gunners assigned to two tankers sunk off Florida. They were found to be identical with those of a young Texan who had enlisted in the United States Naval Reserve. The seaman's tanker had gone down off Florida with a loss of several lives.

But the cases are almost endless and each day brings new ones. In 1955, more than 13,600 fugitives from justice were identified from fingerprints. The doors of the Identification Division are never closed. The work goes on around the clock. When police need extraordinarily quick identification, they use a machine known as a Speedphoto Transceiver, by which prints may be transmitted to the Bureau just as pictures are transmitted by news services to newspapers. Within a matter of minutes, the FBI can supply photographs and prints.

By mid 1956, the FBI had a total of 141,231,773 fingerprints on file, of which 29,215,596 were in the criminal files section representing 11,336,712 persons. In the civil identification section there were 112,016,177 cards representing 60,753,062 persons. And one particularly interesting card in this latter file carries the classification:

$$\frac{15 \quad M \quad 9 \quad R \quad 000 \quad 18}{L \quad 19 \quad W \quad 000}$$

These are the symbols on President Eisenhower's fingerprint card.

16: *The FBI Laboratory*

THE United States Marshal at Nome, Alaska, had a problem in murder to be solved, and it came about in this manner.

In mid-March of 1936 a blizzard swept out of the North. The icy winds moaned across the Alaskan mountains and the flatlands, driving men and animals to shelter. And so it was that John Nilima, an old-time prospector and trader, retreated into his log cabin at a remote place called Old Buckland Village. Nilima's cabin was a combination home and trading post, where he bargained with the Eskimos for their furs, and it was his base of operations when he set out to grub for gold in the creeks and hills.

In the fury of the storm, a man stole to a sheltered side of the cabin and looked through a window at Nilima, who was sitting on a bunk. The man raised a rifle, took careful aim and shot John Nilima through the head. Quickly the killer opened the door and stepped inside. He looked at Nilima to be certain he was dead; then he found the trader's cashbox and hurried back into the blizzard. The snow soon covered his tracks.

When Nilima's body was found, the U. S. Marshal was notified. He searched the cabin but the only clue was the bullet from the rifle of the killer. The slug had gone through Nilima's head and embedded itself in a log. The Marshal pried the bullet loose.

In the days that followed, the Marshal found himself with two suspects. The first was an ex-convict, a known enemy of Nilima's who had once threatened to kill the trader because of an argument over prospecting. The Marshal noticed stains on his socks which looked to him like dried blood.

"Is that blood?" the officer asked.

"Yes," the ex-convict said. "I shot a reindeer and some of the blood dripped on my socks while I was dragging it home."

The Marshal searched for the reindeer carcass, but couldn't find it in the snow.

"Maybe the wolves dragged it off a ways," the suspect said.

The Marshal shrugged. He checked the ex-convict's thirty-caliber rifle. It had been fired and hadn't been cleaned. Despite the man's protests of innocence, the evidence seemed strong against him.

The Marshal knew the FBI had a laboratory in Washington, D. C., where evidence was examined by scientific means. It was a new development in law enforcement but worth trying out. Carefully he bundled up the ex-convict's rifle, the blood-stained socks and the bullet fired from the killer's gun. He mailed them to the FBI.

The Marshal's second suspect was a young Eskimo who had been spending more money than usual at a trading post near his village. He had been caught on a trail leading northeast, acting suspiciously like a fugitive. He, too, insisted he was innocent, and he stubbornly refused to account for the source of his money. The Marshal took the Eskimo's twenty-five-thirty-five-caliber rifle and mailed it to the FBI also. Then he waited for the answers.

In the Laboratory, the pieces of evidence were given to the men who had helped launch this project less than four years before. The stains on the ex-convict's socks were analyzed and the rifles and bullet were examined. The stains weren't human blood. And a ballistics expert found that the fatal bullet hadn't been fired from the thirty-caliber rifle. Both reports were negative—but they supported the ex-convict's claims.

Then a test shot was fired from the Eskimo's rifle into a cotton-filled box. The bullet was recovered and placed under a microscope beside the death bullet. Slowly the two bullets were revolved until the trained eye at the microscope saw that the grooves and lines etched on the bullets by the gun barrel matched perfectly.

No two gun barrels are alike in minute detail. The inside of each barrel has its own peculiar imperfections in the metal which leave tiny lines and grooves on the bullets fired through the barrel. It might be said that these bullet markings are the personal autographs of each gun barrel.

When the expert saw the same lines and grooves on both bullets, he knew the bullet that killed John Nilima could have come from one gun only—the gun owned by the Eskimo.

The ex-convict was freed. The Eskimo confessed to the murder and was sentenced to serve twenty years in a federal penitentiary, trapped by the scientific crime fighters through methods now accepted as routine.

In less than a quarter of a century, the FBI's scientific tools for use against crime and subversion have become more and more complex, and progressively more effective. The application of chemistry, physics, metallurgy, electronics and other specialized scientific and engineering knowledge in the FBI's work has grown beyond the bounds of public understanding since the day of John Nilima's murder.

For example, specks of dirt no larger than a pinhead, clinging to a man's shoe, may lead to his identification as a saboteur, a spy, or a criminal. Time after time the FBI experts have taken a few specks of dirt from the shoes or clothing of a suspect which have assisted in placing him at the scene of a crime.

This particular piece of detection work might be done in this way: the speck of dirt from a suspect's shoe and another piece of dirt taken from the scene of the crime are placed in one of the FBI-constructed twin furnaces. As the intense, controlled temperature rises in the furnaces, the two specks of dirt undergo certain measurable physical changes which are recorded automatically on a graph. If the graph lines are identical, it means the two specks of dirt underwent physical changes at precisely the same moments under the same degrees of temperature; and this precise sameness shows that the two specks of dirt were composed of similar mineral elements—and, therefore, could have come from the same place.

And there was the case in which a crack Navy test pilot climbed into a strange-looking aircraft and hurtled into the stratosphere. The sleek craft was an advanced jet fighter plane still in the secret stage of development and it had to be proved out in a hundred different ways before acceptance.

This was a plane so fast that it shattered one of the world's classic speed records as the pilot put it through its paces in the cold, thin atmosphere of upper space. Sensitive instruments built into the plane automatically recorded pressures, temperatures, speeds, and a vast amount of information vital to naval air supremacy over vast areas of the world which are ocean.

And then, suddenly, something went wrong! The aircraft went crazy in that crazy world beyond the sonic barrier, where pilots tell of forces which pitch and buffet a plane at times with maniacal fury. The pilot's voice came clearly to those listening in by radio. "Going to have to leave it!" he said. His words trailed off into a gibberish of sound. And then there was silence.

Searchers found bits and pieces of the plane and the pilot's body. But no one could unscramble the pilot's last words as the ship screamed toward the earth. And it was important to know. Each scrap of information, each spoken word from the cockpit of the plane, might be priceless.

The recording was finally sent to the FBI Laboratory, where specialists went to work on it. Their first steps were to prepare an exact working copy of the recording tape in order to preserve the original, and to determine the precise speed at which the original recording had been made.

Each word spoken by the pilot was intelligible up to the point where, obviously, the plane had run into uncontrollable trouble—but the final message was still a babble of sound, completely meaningless.

One of those who helped untangle the mystery recalled the highly technical laboratory work in these words:

We found an extremely high noise level in the background of the pilot's voice. I suppose it was due to the screaming dive of the plane. In a series of tests, we were able to filter out the noise frequencies above and below the normal voice frequencies—and at the same time amplify those frequencies of the human voice.

This improved the signal a great deal, but the pilot's words still were not intelligible. We tried another tack. We transferred the improved recording to a disk and in this way we could vary the speed at will.

You probably have slowed down a phonograph record and noticed that the pitch of the voice or music was lowered. But when the record was turned too fast you got a high, squeaky sound. In either case, the sound was distorted.

Our problem was to find the proper pitch—and, if we could do this, then perhaps the pilot's words would become understandable.

We used an instrument called a Sona-Stretcher which permitted us to speed up or slow down the record without changing the pitch. We were able to make the voice speak slower without changing pitch and this again improved the signal. But even though we knew we were getting close, the pilot's words still were not clear enough.

Then we began manipulating the speed during the actual transcription— that is, speeding it up and then slowing it down. This was the solution and finally we had the pilot's voice reproduced.

The excitement spread through the Laboratory, and technicians gathered to hear the completed recording—the voice, filtered out of all the strange sounds of a plane in its last dive, saying:

"Can't bail out . . . can't . . . bail . . . out!"

These were the last words of a brave naval pilot streaking toward his death. But those few terrible words provided a clue which led to the discovery of a defect in the plane—intelligence which meant that the lives of other brave men would be made safer.

The FBI Laboratory has found ways to adapt atomic energy as a tool in law enforcement. The first public hint that the atom had become a crime fighter came from Lewis L. Strauss, Chairman of the Atomic Energy Commission, who told the graduates from the FBI National Academy in November, 1954: "Some radioactive isotopes and the subatomic particles which even a few years ago were not known to science are now in use to make the work of the Bureau even more successful."

During World War II, the FBI Laboratory was given the job of making detailed technical inspections of heavy war materials, ranging from antisubmarine nets to heavily armored tank turrets. The FBI had to determine the truth of charges that faulty construction had resulted from fraud or sabotage. These inspections were made with radium whose gamma rays bored through the thick metals and "photographed" on film any hidden faults buried deep in the metals.

The use of radium became old-fashioned when nuclear reactors began turning out radioactive isotopes. The isotopes were tools whose characteristics could be engineered to fit the specific needs of the FBI. Money, gasoline and other things could be sensitized by isotopes and then later identified as infallibly as though they had been tagged. But the Laboratory found other procedures to be simpler and quite as good in marking things for later identification.

The FBI has its own nation-wide communications network which has made FBI special agents, without doubt, the most mobile crime-fighting organization in the world. Much of the equipment was designed and engineered by FBI Laboratory experts to fit the FBI's special needs.

In addition to telephone and teletype circuits, the FBI radio network links each of the 52 field offices, which in turn are linked with the Headquarters in Washington, D. C. Each office is like the hub of a wheel, with FM communications spokes fanning out in all directions to radio-equipped automobiles and to agents on foot carrying inconspicuous portable radios. The automobile radios have preset wave lengths so that agents may talk to the nearest office and then, by a flip of a switch, be in direct communication with other agents. Even when unseen by each other, the agents are able to work as a well-coordinated team.

These communications make it possible to save time and man power. Frequently an agent keeping a suspect under surveillance follows his man into a building which has, say, ten exits. Without inter-agent communication, ten agents would be required to cover the exits; but with radio communication, the agent inside the building can alert two or three outside agents when the suspect heads for an exit. And thus the surveillance continues without a break.

"Our problem," one Laboratory engineer said, "is trying to beat the criminal from a mobility standpoint. And we're doing it."

The FBI radio network was conceived by Director Hoover when German bombers were ripping savagely at England in the Battle of Britain. Intelligence reports showed that communications were one of the most critical problems for the British when bombs ripped up land lines and disrupted telephone and telegraph traffic.

Hoover discussed the British problem with some of his aides.

"We've got to face up to the problem," Hoover said. "Our own coastlines may become the targets for bombers and communications will be in danger. We can't afford to be immobilized in an emergency."

Radio stations with emergency power plants were installed in cities along the coastline. Automatic relay and repeater stations were erected at strategic points in the countryside—on a hilltop, a tall water tank or an aircraft hangar—to pick up the agents' broadcasts and increase their range of communications. When the Japanese attacked Pearl Harbor on December 7, 1941, the FBI's radio network was in operation due to this foresight. It became an asset of tremendous value during World War II.

Scientific aids to crime have developed largely from the needs of special agents in the field. And the FBI experts in the Laboratory know precisely what the field man is talking about when they get to-gether to discuss a problem, because all top-ranking personnel in the FBI Laboratory are special agents themselves. The titles are not a courtesy label. The chemist, the physicist or the electronics engineer has gone through the same training given to all special agents, and he has had actual field experience in investigative work.

The FBI's search for ways to improve investigative methods is never-ending. Sometimes a way is found that is simple but effective. On several occasions, special agents found themselves in a position where bloodshed and perhaps death could be avoided if a cornered criminal could only be told that he was surrounded and had no chance to escape. But they couldn't get close enough—without exposing them-selves dangerously to fire—to shout the message and be heard. This

problem was put to the FBI Laboratory, and the solution was a bat-
tery-powered, portable amplifier capable of amplifying a voice to a
roar which could be heard clearly for hundreds of yards.

The FBI's application of science to crime problems did not spring
forth in full blossom overnight. During the 1920's, little use was made
of science in American law enforcement. Some colleges and universities
offered courses relating to scientific law enforcement work, but, as a
whole, police agencies paid little attention to how science could help
solve daily investigative problems.

Most of the early experts worked in the field of handwriting identification. They demanded, and received, sizable fees whether working
for the prosecution or the defense. And each side usually came up with
its own experts.

One of the earliest records in the FBI files indicating an interest in
scientific examination of evidence is a letter dictated by Hoover in
1922 asking agents for the names of reliable handwriting experts. The
Special Agent in Charge at Baltimore named one man "whom I would
call dependable," and the New York office named two. Other FBI
offices throughout the country reported only a few names of men considered competent. In most areas, there was none.

Interest in relating science to crime investigations picked up mo-
mentum in 1929. In that year the FBI began assembling a library of
scientific books and papers dealing with subjects related to crime investigations, such as the testing of drugs, blood and hair. And, oddly
enough, a gangland massacre spurred the development in Chicago.
It was the so-called St. Valentine's Day Massacre.

This slaughter occurred on February 14, 1929. Members of the Al
Capone gang, disguised as police, cornered seven persons, one of whom
was believed to be "Bugs" Moran, in a garage. They stood their
victims against a wall and mowed them down with machine-gun fire.
During the coroner's jury investigation, some of the jurors asked what
purpose was served in keeping the bullets found at the garage.
Chicago police explained that ballistics experts could determine whether
the bullets had been fired from certain guns—but that the Chicago
Police Department had no laboratory in which to do such work.

The story told by the policemen interested two of the jurors particularly, Walter E. Olson, a rug manufacturer, and Burt A. Massee, a
soap company executive. Both were men of means, and they decided
to finance a laboratory at Northwestern University to serve Chicago
police needs. The laboratory became known as the Northwestern University Crime Laboratory.

While it was being established, Hoover sent one of his men on a survey
of universities throughout the country to see what they were doing in this

field, and special agents studied the operations of privately owned laboratories which examined evidence in criminal cases. Authorities in microscopy, photography, pathology, bacteriology and other fields of science, medicine and engineering were consulted.

With a borrowed microscope, ultraviolet light equipment, an instrument for examining the interior of a gun barrel and a few other odds and ends, the FBI's Laboratory was officially in operation on November 24, 1932.[1] Twenty-four years later, this million-dollar laboratory had become an institution in American law enforcement, with the services of its experts and equipment available to local law enforcement agencies without charge.[2] The FBI Laboratory development traveled a sometimes rocky road. Owners of private laboratories complained that the FBI's free service was cutting into their business with local law enforcement agencies. Hoover contended that the laboratory was merely repaying local police for help given to the FBI in other matters. He was also trying to eliminate the phony "expert" who turned up in criminal and civil cases.[3]

Over the years, the FBI has trained its scientists to take the mumbo jumbo out of scientific language and present their findings to a judge or jury by charts, photographs or other means which are admissible as evidence and easily understood.[4]

The FBI Laboratory is divided into a number of different sections and units. For example, the Physics and Chemistry Section has units which handle firearms, blood, toxicological, hairs and fibers, metallurgical, petrographic and spectrophotometric examinations; the Document Section handles handwriting, typewriting, forgeries, fraudulent checks, obliterated writing, extortion letters, inks, papers, charred documents and related examinations; and the Electronics Section is engaged in designing and developing new electronic equipment for use in the field and in setting up and maintaining a network of radio stations for use in the event of an emergency.

Among the important laboratory aids to crime fighting are the "reference files," which include photographic copies of forged checks and anonymous letters; type specimens from virtually every known make of American typewriter; animal hairs, including some from a wallaby and a wombat; rubber heels and tire prints; samples of the paints used by automobile manufacturers; and about 42,000 different records of watermarks in paper. Day after day, these files provide the clues which help to link a suspect with a crime.

In experimenting with X-ray emanations in the range of five kilovolts, so-called soft X-rays, the scientists found they could get clear radiographic images of watermarks which were obscured by handwriting, typewriting or other markings. This was a valuable tool in determining whether a watermark was genuine or a fraud.

Often an unknown substance such as a powder or a compound is found at the scene of a crime or on the person of a suspect—a substance such as a poison, a drug or some other compound important to the solution of a mystery. The magic of X-rays is used again. A narrow beam of X-rays bombards the substance and a motor-driven Geiger counter records the angles of the bending, or diffraction, of the rays. Since every crystalline substance bends these rays at known specific angles, the identification can be established without destroying or using up any of the material.

The FBI's scientists and technicians have done a tremendous amount of research on human hair—because hair is so frequently important in investigating crimes. The FBI Laboratory has contributed substantially to the knowledge in this field. Now it is possible to receive hair from an unknown source and to determine the person's race, indications of age and sex, how the hair was severed, whether bleached or dyed, whether a wave is natural or artificial, whether or not the hair was singed, and the part of the body from which it came. And the expert through his knowledge and experience determines whether or not two strands of hair could have come from the same person.

Another little-recognized result of the FBI Laboratory's work has been the sifting of the innocent from the guilty.

The FBI was able to rectify a miscarriage of justice which occurred in January, 1952, when Henry George Anderson was found guilty by a jury and sentenced to serve not more than ten years in the Minnesota State Penitentiary for allegedly forging a check for $93.80. Damaging testimony against Anderson was given by a so-called handwriting expert who testified for the state.

Anderson persisted in his denials of guilt and finally the FBI was asked to look at the check in question. FBI agents found that it had been written not by Anderson, but by George Lester Belew, a fraudulent check artist whose handiwork was on file in the Laboratory's Document Section and who was later to become one of the FBI's ten most wanted fugitives.[5] Minnesota state authorities were notified of the FBI's finding and on July 1, 1953, the Minnesota Board of Parole and Pardons granted a full pardon to Anderson.

Hardly a day passes in which the FBI Laboratory doesn't make a report saying in effect: "This bullet was not fired from this gun." This means in many, many cases that someone, somewhere, is no longer a suspect, since the negative report established innocence.

Circumstantial evidence can sometimes play tragic tricks. Such was the case on the night of February 13, 1950, when Mrs. Robert F. Parks ran from her home at Luray, Virginia, and pounded on the door of a neighbor. She was hysterical and near collapse. Her husband, she said, had been shot and she needed help. The police were called.

Luray police arrived within a few minutes. They found Parks, a former Army captain, lying dead in a bedroom which opened onto the dining room. A bullet had passed through his right arm, entered his body and smashed through his heart, lodging in his left side. In the dining room, police found an automatic pistol lying against the wall opposite the bedroom door. A cartridge case was jammed in the gun.

There were no powder burns and it was obvious, because of the direction from which the bullet entered Parks' body, that he couldn't possibly have held the weapon himself.

When Mrs. Parks was composed enough to talk, she was questioned by police. In brief, she told them: "I was in the kitchen when I heard the shot. I ran to the bedroom and Bob was standing there. He looked at me and said, 'Honey, the gun backfired.' And then he fell."

Police learned that the Parkses had had violent arguments at times. Witnesses said that two or three weeks before the shooting, Mrs. Parks had telephoned to San Francisco. They heard her ask someone to send her a bus ticket so that she could travel to San Francisco. The circumstantial evidence all was against Mrs. Parks. She was arrested and charged with murder.

But the investigation continued. On the third day, an alert policeman noticed that a metal grille over a hot-air duct in the doorway between the bedroom and the dining room had a bright dent in it. A bit of the brown paint had been knocked off by something. The police wondered if the dent could have been caused by the gun found in the dining room. There was brown paint on the rear of the gun slide. They decided to send the grille, gun, bullet and cartridge case found in the Parks home to the FBI Laboratory.

The gun picked up in the dining room was the death weapon. This was proved by an examination of the bullet taken from Parks' body. The brown paint on the grille was similar in color and texture to the paint on the gun slide. It was found that the gun could be fired when dropped on the rear part of the slide and the hammer.

The indentations in the grille matched marks made by the rear sight and knurling of the hammer. And when the rear sight and hammer were placed against the markings on the grille, it became evident the gun in this position would have been pointing in the direction of the bedroom where Parks stood.

In this cooperative effort between the Luray police and the FBI, the findings pointed to the strong possibility that Parks shot himself accidentally. Investigators reasoned that Parks, in a fit of temper, had thrown the gun against the grille; it had fired; the slide had jammed against the grille, preventing ejection of the cartridge; and the gun had skittered across the floor of the dining room. The murder charge against Mrs. Parks was dismissed.

As one FBI scientist said, "You never know in this business what will happen next. I guess that's one of the reasons I stay with it. There's a new, challenging problem every day."

17: *The West Point of Law Enforcement*

HAD J. Edgar Hoover ever dreamed of directing a huge federal police system enforcing the law for every city and hamlet in the country—such an objective might have been realized in the early 1930's.

This period was a nightmare in the history of crime in America. It was a nightmare in which an army of criminals had better weapons, faster automobiles, greater range of movement and far more political influence than the poverty-stricken local police.

This was the period when demands came for a national police force which would take over the job of the local police. One proposal was made that the local police and all federal investigative agencies, including the Army and Navy Intelligence units, be merged into one giant police force directed by a single chief. Another called for the Army to march against crime, as though criminals would array themselves in regiments and divisions for open combat.

In this tumult, Hoover fought for the principle that the enforcement of law in a democracy was primarily the responsibility of local law enforcement officers and not the federal government. He believed the answer to the crime problem lay in taking police work out of politics, and in giving all policemen scientific training in law enforcement.

At that time most rookie policemen received no training. They were given a badge and a gun and told to go to work. Few cities had any kind of training program for police officers, and generally there was an attitude that none was needed.

One chief of police commanding a force of more than a hundred men dismissed the idea of scientific police training with the curious comment: ". . . all that a policeman need know [is] the Ten Commandments." The mayor of a large midwestern city had a different notion about the qualifications of a policeman. Introducing his police chief to a convention of chiefs of police, he said, "I know that my man is going to be a good chief because he has been my tailor for 20 years. He knows how to make good clothes; he ought to be a good chief."

Time after time, Hoover argued—in letters, speeches, articles, and memoranda—that the basic responsibility for law enforcement in a democracy rested with the local police and should remain there. In a letter to the Topeka *Daily Capital,* in Kansas, Hoover said in 1936:

> The Federal Bureau of Investigation believes that the secret of crime eradication lies not in a national police force but in solidarity and the combined linking of all law enforcement agencies. It believes in a close-knit cooperation, each unit capable of handling its peculiar problems but capable also, when necessary, of mobilizing its efforts in a concerted drive against the criminal element of this country. . . .

He once stated his aims in this way:

> I want to see our field of activity become a real career, a profession, to which can be attracted the decent, honorable, respectable young men of the country who can go into it as a career and look forward to making something out of their life's work, rather than as a dumping ground, as all too frequently it has been, for some ward politician to use in repaying his obligations to his political party.

Hoover discussed his ideas with Attorney General Cummings, and together they carried a proposal for a police training school before the Attorney General's Crime Conference, which met in December, 1934. Hoover told the conference:

> The value of adequate training has already been proven in the training schools maintained by our Bureau for its personnel. . . . With but slight readjustment of operations, these training facilities already established could be extended to the local law enforcement agencies of the country.

The conference recommended that the school be established, and on July 29, 1935, the first class of twenty-three police officers gathered for twelve weeks of study.[1] This was the beginning of the FBI's now famous National Academy which was Hoover's answer to demands for a national police force.

In its first twenty-one years, the Academy gave instruction to more than 3,200 law enforcement officers. Out of this number, more than 28 percent climbed to positions as executive heads of their departments with such titles as chief of police, sheriff, and state police chief.

The number of graduates is small when compared with the total number of police officers in the United States—some 250,000. But each graduate has left the Academy qualified to organize police schools in his home town and to share the knowledge he has gained with the other members of his force. That was the basic purpose behind the formation of the Academy.

An Academy student is nominated by the head of his department. He must not be more than fifty years old and he must be in good physical condition. He must have the capacity to absorb a great amount of information in a short time and then pass this information on to others. He must be a man with a good reputation in his community, and a full-time officer employed by a city, county or state law enforcement agency. He must have had at least two years of prior experience in law enforcement.

Two twelve-week sessions are held each year—sessions in which some eighty students attend classes from nine to five, five days a week. After-dinner hours are taken up with the typing of notes and study.

It's a hard, grinding period in which no outside interests are allowed to interfere with work. The only excuses accepted for missing a class are sickness, illness in the family or complying with a court subpoena. Drinking while on duty is forbidden, and drunkenness at any time is cause for being shipped home. The student or his law enforcement agency pays all expenses for transportation, food and lodging during the session.

The Academy's regular instructors are experienced and well-trained FBI teachers. Other FBI special agents are available in the teaching of highly specialized courses. Lectures are given by educators, criminologists, lawyers and others. The subject matter ranges from the proper method of keeping police records to the lifting of a fingerprint from the scene of a crime, police photography and the calculation of an automobile's speed from skid marks.

There are elective courses dealing with police organization and administration, investigative methods and techniques, firearms training, traffic control and defensive tactics.

The Academy was a success from the beginning. Applications have poured in from law enforcement agencies at the ratio of about seven applications for each student admitted. Here is a typical letter from one of the Academy graduates to Hoover:

The intensive training program ranks as the greatest experience that I have ever been privileged to enjoy in my fourteen years of service in the law enforcement field. The example of competent personnel living a dedicated life of devoted and highminded public service taught lessons that could never be learned from books or lectures.

Some graduates have returned to their home towns to find fellow officers jealous, resentful and unwilling to cooperate in starting training schools. And there has been the deadening influence of politics and indifference. A Florida graduate wrote the Bureau:

> On my return from Washington, I found that the Administration of the City had changed. A new City Council and a new City Manager had been appointed. . . . This new group did not appear to have any interest in my training or in the training of the Department here. I tried to discuss it with some of them and pointed out why we should go ahead, but they could not see the necessity of spending money for such purposes . . . The Red Cross and some of the other Civic Organizations have offered cooperation and things looked fairly good until . . . the Chief was removed. Since that time every effort that I have made has been blocked.

In other cases, graduates found their fellow officers just as eager as they had been to learn new techniques. Despite lack of money and equipment, they managed to overcome obstacles and get training schools under way. Civic clubs, business firms, colleges and universities have helped.

Perhaps more than any other single program, the FBI's National Academy brought closer cooperation between the FBI and local police. The FBI agents and the students came to know each other and to have a better appreciation of the others' problems. FBI instructors went to the "grass roots" to set up schools of instruction designed to meet the specific needs of an area or a community. Cooperation between the FBI and local police became such a routine, everyday matter that it was lack of cooperation which drew attention.

Hoover laid down these ground rules on cooperation:

> The FBI is willing and ready to cooperate with all law enforcement agencies. The only exceptions are when officers of the law are corrupt and controlled by venal politicians; when they can't keep a confidence and be trusted; or when they are so incompetent that to cooperate with them would defeat our purposes.

Much of the improvement in cooperation can be traced to the FBI National Academy, which helped to break down at least some of the misunderstandings. Local officers saw the FBI men in an entirely different light—and the FBI's agents gained a new perspective by looking at the local men's problems.

There was, for example, a heavy-set officer from the sagebrush country who came to the Academy and immediately made himself appear aloof by refusing to associate in off hours with either the FBI instructors or the other students. He was overweight when he began training, and the pounds dropped off at an alarming rate. But he didn't complain. At mealtime, and at night, he went off by himself. He became the Academy "lone wolf."

At the close of the session, the "lone wolf" came to the office of the Assistant Director of the FBI in charge of training. He fiddled with his hat for a moment and then he blurted out his story: "I know you and the other fellows think I'm a pretty strange character, acting like I have. But I'd like for you to know the reason. I had to mortgage my house to get enough money to come up here and at the same time take care of my family back home along with some relatives who live with us. After I bought my railroad ticket and took out the money for the hotel, I only had 35 cents a day for food. I couldn't afford to eat with the others. That's why I went off by myself and why I lost so much weight."

The FBI man said, "But why didn't you tell me? We could have worked out something."

The police officer shrugged. "Pride, I reckon. I guess I was ashamed to say anything. But it's been worth it and I figure I'm a better man for what I've done." He shook hands and walked out.

This, of course, is a side of the policeman which the public seldom sees, or makes the effort to see. Hoover told a visitor of this incident and said: "I've seen this kind of thing so often it makes me sick at heart. They ask for law enforcement which will be honest, efficient and intelligent, protecting the people from criminals and at the same time protecting civil liberties. And then they offer a starting salary to a rookie policeman as low as $1,770 while a messenger gets a starting salary of $2,960 from the Federal Government. In one Eastern city, they give their policemen a starting salary of $3,725—and the starting pay for a garbage collector is $3,950. It's an outrageous insult."

But regardless of how grossly underpaid or how well paid law enforcement officers may be, all of them have the same practical problem of the best way to go about their job of enforcing the law. This work sometimes involves the use of confidential informants, a practice which, recurrently, has drawn heavy fire from some quarters even though it has long been sanctioned by law and court decisions.

The use of criminal informants might be termed the practice of having spies in the enemy's camp. In the fight against crime, the informant system is the intelligence service operating in the underworld. Criminal informants can hardly be gilded as paragons of virtue, but, basically, they do for law enforcement what the nation's secret agents do in the field of national security. The function in both cases is the same—to obtain information about the activities of an enemy.

Hoover once stated the FBI's position on the use of informants in this way: "The confidential informant is as old as man and is used in practically every walk of life . . . and is used as a means of establishing truth." He saw no basic difference between the FBI's use of confidential informants and the long-established use of confidential sources by newspapers to obtain news, by credit houses to establish credit reliability and by employers in sizing up job applicants.

Early English law gave legal recognition to the confidential, paid informant and this recognition first became a part of American law in 1789. During 1956, information given by criminal informants led to the arrest of 1,211 persons in Bureau cases and the recovery of 149 stolen automobiles. Information from these sources which was passed on to other agencies led to the arrest of 790 persons. More than $1,500,000 in stolen property was recovered.

One of the cardinal FBI rules in criminal cases is:

> No prosecutive action of any type can be taken solely on the basis of information furnished by informants; successful prosecution in criminal cases depends entirely on evidence and testimony of witnesses produced in court.

Statements of informants are used for lead purposes and the Bureau keeps a continuing check on the reliability of its sources of information.

Dispute has raged, too, around the use of wire tapping in law enforcement. During the FBI's early years under Hoover's direction, one of the Bureau's regulations was: "Wire tapping . . . will not be tolerated by the Bureau."

Hoover regarded wire tapping as a lazy man's way of obtaining information and he believed that its uncontrolled use was a handicap in the "development of ethical, scientific and sound investigative technique."

Even after the Supreme Court approved the use of wire tapping in 1928 and ruled that evidence obtained from a wire tap could be admitted as evidence in federal courts, Hoover held to the rule against taps.

But in January, 1931, Attorney General William D. Mitchell went before a House Committee and explained that while the FBI did not permit wire tapping, it was being permitted by the Prohibition Bureau, which was then a part of the Department of Justice. ". . . we cannot have one Bureau in which wire tapping is allowed," Mitchell said, "and another in which it is not permitted. The same regulations must apply to all . . ."

After giving this testimony, Mitchell ordered the FBI to change its wire-tap regulations to read: ". . . telephone or telegraph wires shall not be tapped unless prior authorization of the Director of the Bureau has been secured."

Even under these new instructions, Hoover did not authorize wire tapping until the wave of kidnaping broke out in 1932—and then it was limited to cases where it was believed that a life was in jeopardy or in which national security was involved.

Late in 1939, the Supreme Court banned in federal courts the admissibility of evidence obtained as a result of wire taps. The decision was based on the Federal Communications Act of 1934, which prohibited the interception and divulgence of a communication. The Department of Justice advised Hoover that the court decision did not affect the FBI's practices because the illegality of a wire tap was in the disclosure of the information and not in the interception.

At Hoover's insistence, the authorization for wire taps was placed in the hands of the Attorney General in 1940. Both the requests and the authorization for wire taps are in writing, so a record of responsibility is always available. In mid 1956, the Bureau had fewer than 90 wire taps. All of them involved national security.

Only a few people among some 14,000 FBI employees ever know when a tap is made—perhaps five or six in the field and a like number in the Headquarters at Washington.

President Roosevelt and succeeding administrations all gave their approval to the FBI's wire tapping. Beginning in 1933, eight successive attorneys general, three of whom went to the Supreme Court, ruled that the FBI was on sound legal grounds when making taps.

Roosevelt and the FBI

18: *The Enemy Within*

THE forces of fear and subversion were on the march in the summer of 1936. The one-time Austrian paper hanger, Adolf Hitler, had risen to power in Germany, and while he talked of peace he planned for war. The Japanese war lords stood astride Korea and Manchuria and, with bloody swords in their hands, threatened all of Asia. The Fascist chief, Mussolini, was carving out his new Roman empire in Africa. Spain was being torn cruelly by a civil war which pitted brother against brother, Fascist against Communist. In Soviet Russia, Stalin was continuing his blood purges, adding new victims to the list of millions already liquidated by guns and by deliberate starvation. And in the United States, nine million jobless walked the streets while the reactionary forces of fascism and communism were enlisting recruits to their causes.

This, in bare outline, was the gloomy state of the world on the morning of August 24. FBI Director J. Edgar Hoover left his headquarters to answer a summons to a White House conference—or rather, as it developed, the first of three conferences which would remain secret until this writing.*

Hoover was shown into President Franklin D. Roosevelt's office at 9:15. The President looked up from his work and smiled. "Sit down, Edgar." He pushed himself back from his oval desk and lit a cigarette.

* Author's note: This account of the 1936 conferences is based on memoranda written by Director Hoover immediately after the conferences, and on his recollection of the conversations that took place.

"I called you over," he said, "because I want you to do a job for me and it must be confidential."

Roosevelt went on to say he had become increasingly concerned about the activities of Communists and other subversive groups. He felt that he should have more information than he had been receiving. He wondered if there were some way by which he could obtain a broad intelligence picture of Communist and Fascist activities alike in relation to the economic and political life of the country.

"Mr. President," Hoover said, "there is no government agency compiling such general intelligence. Of course, it is not a violation of the law to be a member of the Communist Party and we have had no specific authority to make such general investigations."

The President said, "It seems to me there must be some way this could be done, Edgar. Have you any suggestions?"

"Yes, there is a way," Hoover said. "In the Appropriation Act[1] under which we operate, the FBI has authority to undertake an investigation for the Department of State when requested to do so by the Secretary of State. We could make the investigation should the Secretary request it of the Attorney General."

Roosevelt frowned. He said it seemed rather odd to him that the President couldn't make such a request himself. He added that he hesitated to have any formal request made by the State Department because of the likelihood of a leak. As far as the authority was concerned, Roosevelt said he would put a hand-written memorandum in his safe stating that the President had instructed Secretary of State Cordell Hull to make a request of the FBI for information on subversive activities.

"I want you to come back tomorrow and talk this over with Cordell and me," Roosevelt said.

Hoover returned to the White House at 1:45 P.M. the next day. He was chatting with the President when Secretary Hull entered the office. Roosevelt stated his concern over the lack of information he had on Communist and Fascist activities and his belief that the FBI should undertake a quiet investigation.

"Edgar says he can do this," the President said, "but the request must come from you to make it legal."

The tall, distinguished Secretary of State from the hills of Tennessee turned to Hoover and said: "Go ahead and investigate the———!" The President threw back his head and laughed.

Roosevelt discussed at length the international character of communism and fascism. He said that he didn't like the reports that Constantine Oumansky (counselor for the Soviet Embassy) had been running around the country, spending very little time in Washington.

Roosevelt said he thought the State Department had a right and a duty to know what was going on in such cases.

"Do you want the request in writing?" Hull asked.

Roosevelt shook his head. He said he wanted the matter to be handled confidentially and it would be sufficient if the three of them were aware of the request. He thought the FBI should coordinate this intelligence investigation with the War Department's Military Intelligence Division, the Office of Naval Intelligence and the State Department. He requested that Hoover give Attorney General Homer Cummings a report on the meetings when Cummings returned to Washington from a trip, since Cummings' approval was also necessary.

One week later, on September 1, Hoover and Secretary Hull met with the President again. The final agreement was reached, and the arrangement was made for coordinating the collection of information. The investigation was to be for intelligence purposes only, and not the type of investigation required in collecting evidence to be presented to a court.[2]

With this understanding, Hoover sent letters marked "Personal and Confidential" to his special agents in charge on September 5, saying:

> The Bureau desires to obtain from all possible sources information concerning subversive activities being conducted in the United States by Communists, Fascists and representatives or advocates of other organizations or groups advocating the overthrow or replacement of the Government of the United States by illegal methods. No investigation should be initiated into cases of this kind in the absence of specific authorization from the Bureau. . . .

Hoover gave Attorney General Cummings a report on the confidential White House conferences when Cummings returned to his office on September 10. "Go ahead with the investigation by all means," Cummings said. "I hope you already have made the necessary preliminary moves."

"Yes, sir," Hoover said. "I have sent letters to the Special Agents in Charge ordering them to begin the quiet inquiry, subject, of course, to your approval."

"That's good," the Attorney General replied. "I would like you to keep me advised in this matter."

Returning to his office, Hoover dictated a "Strictly Confidential" memorandum for his staff, saying:

> In talking with the Attorney General today concerning the radical situation,* I informed him of the conference which I had with the President

* Author's note: In reading hundreds of documents, it has become clear to me that when Hoover or the FBI used the word "radical" through the

on September 1, 1936, at which time the Secretary of State was present, and at which time the Secretary of State, at the President's suggestion, requested of me, the representative of the Department of Justice, to have investigation made of the subversive activities in this country, including communism and fascism. I transmitted this request to the Attorney General, and the Attorney General verbally directed me to proceed with this investigation and to coordinate, as the President suggested, information upon these matters in the possession of the Military Intelligence Division, the Naval Intelligence Division, and the State Department. This, therefore, is the authority upon which to proceed in the conduct of this investigation, which should, of course, be handled in a most discreet and confidential manner.

President Roosevelt was not the only one in his official family troubled by Communist activities and the travels of Oumansky. William Bullitt, American Ambassador to France, called on Attorney General Cummings and Hoover on September 14, to discuss information which he had obtained about the Communist situation while in Moscow as United States Ambassador to the Soviet Union. Bullitt talked of the danger of the Communist movement not only throughout the world but particularly in the United States.

Hoover summed up Bullitt's statements in a memorandum dictated immediately after the conference, saying:

He stated he knew at first hand . . . that Stalin, who heads the Russian Government, is also the one who issued orders to the head of the Third Internationale, and so, consequently, he controls the activities of the Third Internationale.

He was particularly concerned over the activities of Oumansky . . . and pointed out that Oumansky is seldom in Washington, but travels over the United States . . .

Mr. Bullitt told me that the Communist leaders in Russia make every effort to put spies in all foreign government agencies, and particularly those agencies which are engaged in or charged with the responsibility of knowing about subversive activities. He made this statement in connection with the possibility of Communists entering the employ of the Federal Bureau of Investigation.[3]

Hoover also said in this memorandum:

I think it is time to take steps to endeavor to ascertain more definitely the activities of Oumansky in view of the fact that Mr. Bullitt tells me he is

---

1920's and 1930's (they no longer use the term), it was intended to refer specifically to the activities of anarchists, IWW's and Communists—and not to those seeking reforms by Constitutional means or to nonconformists. Actually, Hoover himself has been a radical and a nonconformist in altering the old concepts of the law enforcement profession.

the direct contact with this country for organizations and individuals who are engaged in the subversive movement against the Government of the United States.

So the FBI, quietly and without publicly disclosing the source of its authority, began to check on Communist activities and to chart the rise of Fascist movements in the United States. These investigations would later stir up a hornet's nest of criticism to the effect that the FBI was meddling in the political beliefs and opinions of persons merely because they held radical views contrary to those held by Hoover.

More than three years before Roosevelt ordered this intelligence operation, the FBI had at times been called on to look into the activities of a person or a group engaged in pro-Nazi activities. The FBI then did not have the authority or responsibility for such investigations without an official request. An investigation was made, usually at the request of the Department of Justice, a report was submitted, and that ended the matter until another request was made.

A curious chain of events had led to the first of these limited investigations. The German Embassy had received a letter in March, 1933, signed "Daniel Stern," saying that unless President Roosevelt publicly rebuked the Hitler government for its outrages against the Jews, then, "I notify you that I shall go to Germany and assassinate Hitler."

The German Ambassador, F. W. von Prittwitz, wrote Secretary Hull on March 28, saying:

Mr. Secretary of State:
Enclosed herewith I have the honor to transmit a communication received here, wherein the assassination of the Chancellor of the Reich, Mr. Adolf Hitler, is threatened. I would be grateful if an investigation of the matter could be made and the results thereof communicated to me at its conclusion.
Accept, Mr. Secretary of State, the renewed assurance of my most distinguished respect.

Hull sent the Ambassador's letter and the threatening letter to the Department of Justice and the FBI was instructed to investigate.

The German Ambassador probably wished in the weeks to come that he had never written to Secretary Hull, because that letter was a diplomatic fumble. His request opened the way for the FBI to look into the doings of the pro-Nazi organizations in the course of seeking "Daniel Stern," who, incidentally, never was found. In this case the FBI's information was obtained by an oblique approach, but in any event, it proved to be a valuable reference when the Department of Justice requested additional investigations. And Hoover passed the information on to the President.

President Roosevelt became so concerned over the growth of Fascist organizations that, on May 9, 1934, he called a White House conference attended by Attorney General Cummings, Secretary of the Treasury Morgenthau, Secretary of Labor Perkins, Hoover and Secret Service Chief W. H. Moran. The conference agreed that there should be an investigation of these groups and their activities for intelligence purposes.[4]

Hoover immediately sent orders to his special agents to conduct an intensive and confidential investigation of the Nazi movement, with emphasis on anti-American activities having any connection with German Government officials. The FBI had made investigations of individual cases, but this was the first general intelligence investigation made by the government into Fascist activities in this country. This too was a limited investigation, however. It was not until 1936 that the FBI began a continuing but discreet check on subversive activities covering Fascists and Communists alike.

During the late 1920's and early 1930's, pro-Fascist activities had been confined largely to propaganda. But as the situation steadily deteriorated in Europe and Asia, the situation also worsened at home, and the propagandists were joined by espionage agents. From 1933 to 1937 the FBI investigated an average of 35 espionage cases a year. In fiscal 1938, the total jumped to 250.

The first major espionage case in this period involved Guenther Gustave Rumrich, who had deserted from the U. S. Army in 1936 and then entered the German espionage service.

War Department Intelligence officers called the FBI into the Rumrich case when they received a warning from an American military attaché in London that an effort would be made to steal the United States' secret East Coast defense plans. The identity of the foreign agent was unknown to the military and the FBI.

Soon after this warning was received, New York City detectives and State Department special agents arrested a man who had attempted to obtain American passport forms by representing himself as Secretary of State Hull in a telephone call to the New York Passport Bureau. The man was Guenther Gustave Rumrich. He carried in his pocket a penciled note which identified him as the agent who would attempt to steal the coastal defense plans.

Rumrich was turned over to the FBI, and through him special agents unfolded a Nazi plot to obtain information on America's military strength and defense plans, and on the secrets of the new aircraft carrier, the *Enterprise*. Unfortunately, the story of Rumrich's arrest was leaked

by someone to New York newspapers and Rumrich's confederates
scattered. Eighteen persons were indicted, but only four were convicted.[5] The others were listed as fugitives from justice.

The FBI worked with the Office of Naval Intelligence to nail another
spy, John Semer Farnsworth, a graduate of the U. S. Naval Academy
who was dishonorably discharged from the Navy in 1927 and then became a spy in the pay of the Japanese from 1933 through 1936. The
first tip on Farnsworth's activities came from Fulton Lewis, Jr., a news-
man who heard and believed Farnsworth's drunken talk of a spy career.
Rather than expose the case himself as an exclusive story, he took the
facts to the FBI—a practice followed by other reporters over the years
when security was involved. Farnsworth, the FBI learned, received
some $20,000 for giving the Japanese stolen Navy blueprints, code
books, signal books, sketches of ships and Naval maneuvers, and other
information.

Then columnist Heywood Broun caused a flurry in official Washington in March, 1937, when he wrote that the activities of the German-
American Bund had reached a point where "Actual recruiting is going
on, and there is already a considerable body of storm troops here in
America." These Nazi-like storm troops, he wrote, were drilling and
holding rifle practice and "their loyalty is palpably directed toward
Hitler and the homeland."

President Roosevelt saw the Broun column and sent it to Secretary
of War Harry H. Woodring with a note saying, "I think G-2 ought to
make a definite check on this statement . . ." The President's note was
passed on to the Department of Justice with the War Department's
comment that this was a matter for the civil authorities and not for the
military.

The Justice Department approached the problem gingerly, asking the
FBI whether an investigation could be made quietly and without any
publicity, although the Bund's activities by this time were becoming an
open scandal if not a violation of the law. The FBI told Justice officials
it was doubtful that an investigation could be made without a challenge
from some pro-Nazi organization. But the Department finally did
make the decision to go ahead with the inquiry.

Special agents studied the Bund's activities, membership, political
teachings, organization, affiliations and military-like training program.
They then made a lengthy report to the Department of Justice in the
early part of 1938. The Bund had developed out of a National Socialist
association organized in Chicago and known as "Teutonia." Its leader
was Fritz Kuhn, a successor to Walter Kappe, who later was to recruit
and train eight German saboteurs sent to America in World War II.

The Bund investigation came to a dead end. The Department of

Justice apparently decided that while the Bund's general teachings had a tendency to be subversive, they did not violate any law of the United States.

That's where the matter stood until November, 1938, when the House Special Committee on Un-American Activities—then known as the Dies Committee—demanded an investigation by the State Department to determine whether certain organizations—the Communist Party and the Bund, among others—were not actually unregistered agents of foreign governments, operating in violation of federal law.

The Dies Committee kicked up such a fuss that President Roosevelt discussed its demands at a Cabinet meeting on January 4, 1939. Two days later, the President announced at a news conference that an investigation was under way. The New York *Times*' story of the news conference began: "A Department of Justice decision to investigate Dies Committee charges of alleged violations of criminal statutes by Fascist, Communist and other organizations in this country was announced by President Roosevelt today."

But contrary to the President's announcement, and his wishes, the wheels had not even begun to turn when on March 13 Under Secretary of State Sumner Welles wrote Attorney General Frank Murphy and summed up his recollection of the Cabinet discussion back in January. Welles wrote:

> You may remember that . . . the President decided that an investigation of some of the cases of alleged failure to comply with the law should be undertaken immediately and that it might be well to begin by investigating one Fascist organization, one Communist organization, and one organization not avowedly under the influence of any foreign ideology but in fact under that influence as a result of "boring from within." In his press conference on January 6, the President announced that the investigation was under way.

> It was my understanding . . . that your Department planned to send an investigator immediately to examine our files on the organizations mentioned in Mr. Dies' letter and to consult with officers of this Department, in order that a decision might be reached as to which three of those organizations should be investigated in the first instance. Since those conversations we have heard nothing more of the matter.

Welles' letter produced a brief flurry of activity. Representatives from Justice and State talked things over and decided an inquiry should begin with the activities of the German-American Bund, the Communist Party of America and the American League for Peace and Democracy, the latter listed in Dies's letter as a suspect organization.

All this time the FBI was waiting for instructions from the Department of Justice. Available information was furnished to Department officials. Not until June, 1939, however, did instructions arrive—to start investigations concerning the Communist Party and the German-American Bund under the Foreign Agents Registration Act. The Department added that the American League for Peace and Democracy didn't appear to be covered by the Act and no investigation of it should be conducted.

Meanwhile, a fight was being waged over the question of primary jurisdiction in investigations of subversive activities.

Late in 1938, President Roosevelt had approved a $50,000 appropriation for the FBI to conduct espionage investigations (a sum later raised by Congress to $300,000). Hoover regarded this authorization of funds by the President as giving primary responsibility in the civilian field to the FBI. No similar appropriation was earmarked for any other nonmilitary investigative agency. As a result, the FBI and the War Department's Military Intelligence Division worked out a cooperative program, with approval of the Office of Naval Intelligence, to exchange information in subversive investigations. This arrangement was approved in principle by the new Attorney General, Frank Murphy. On February 7, 1939, the Assistant to the Attorney General, Joseph B. Keenan, informed other investigative agencies of the agreement. He asked that they send any information regarding espionage or subversion to the FBI. Hoover advised his special agents that Keenan's letter meant "all complaints relating to espionage, counterespionage, and sabotage cases should be referred to the Bureau, should be considered within the primary jurisdiction of the Bureau, and should, of course, receive preferred and expeditious attention."

Keenan's letter kicked up an immediate storm. The State Department balked, as did other government departments with investigative agencies. Assistant Secretary of State George S. Messersmith called a conference of representatives from the War Department, Navy, Treasury, Post Office Department and the Justice Department—but no one was invited from the FBI. He announced to the meeting that he had been designated by President Roosevelt to coordinate and control investigations of subversion.

The War Department and Navy Intelligence officers stood up for the FBI as the coordinating agency. Hoover waded into the scrap with a memorandum to Attorney General Murphy saying that Messersmith, at a subsequent conference, wanted to divide espionage investigations among the various agencies. Hoover said in part:

> Of course, this suggestion could not be accepted in so far as the Federal Bureau of Investigation is concerned, in view of the fact that . . . I consider centralization of all information in cases of this type in one agency absolutely essential to the proper conducting of proper investigations.

In the end, President Roosevelt gave his support to Hoover. He sent a confidential directive to Cabinet members on June 26, 1939, which said that the investigation of all espionage, counterespionage and sabotage matters was to be controlled and handled only by the FBI and the Intelligence Divisions of the War Department and the Navy. The heads of these three agencies were to constitute an Interdepartmental Intelligence Coordinating Committee. The President declared further that no other government agency should step into this field of responsibility, but that all other agencies should report subversive activities to the nearest office of the FBI.

This confidential directive by the President sorted out the lines of control and continuing responsibility for the first time. The decision came none too quickly, because on August 24, Germany and Russia signed their ten-year nonaggression pact, which freed the Nazis to make war without fear of an attack from the East. On September 1, the German panzer divisions drove into Poland and the Luftwaffe turned Warsaw into a flaming wreckage. France and Great Britain declared war on Germany on September 3.

On September 6, President Roosevelt disclosed publicly that the FBI had been instructed by him "to take charge of investigative work in matters relating to espionage, sabotage, and violations of the neutrality regulations." He also called on all law enforcement officers to give the FBI any information they received concerning subversive activities.

But while lines of responsibility were now established for domestic intelligence work, there were still no clearly defined areas of responsibility for overseas intelligence operations. The pressing need for a decision in this field grew more evident as the months passed. Hoover discussed the problem with the military intelligence chiefs, with President Roosevelt and with Assistant Secretary of State A. A. Berle, Jr., who was the President's closest adviser and confidant on intelligence matters.

Berle took the problem up with the President on June 24, 1940, and suggested that he had the choice of choosing between the FBI, the Army and the Navy.

Berle reported his conversation with the President in a memorandum to Brigadier General Sherman Miles, Army Intelligence; Rear Admiral W. S. Anderson, Director of Naval Intelligence; and Hoover; with a copy to the White House. Berle said in part:

> The President said that he wished that the field should be divided. The FBI should be responsible for foreign intelligence work in the Western Hemisphere, on the request of the State Department. The existing Military Intelligence and Naval Intelligence branches should cover the rest of the world, as and when necessity arises.

It was understood that the proposed additional foreign intelligence work should not supersede any existing work now being done; and that the FBI might be called in by the State Department for special assignments outside the American Hemisphere, under special circumstances. Aside from this, intelligence outside the American Hemisphere is to be left to the officers of the Army & Navy.

Given this division of authority, the three agencies worked out the details of an agreement which, roughly, gave the Navy responsibility for intelligence coverage in the Pacific; gave the Army responsibility for coverage in Europe, Africa and the Canal Zone; and gave the FBI responsibility in the Western Hemisphere, including Mexico, Central America (except Panama), the Caribbean and South America.

Meantime, the FBI was making preparations for a wartime emergency, to be ready just in case. Hoover warned his staff of the mistakes made by the Bureau and the government in World War I in handling the problems that come with war. He recalled the blunders that resulted in a vigilante system being organized for combating subversion; in the lack of preparedness for dealing with spies and saboteurs; in violations of civil rights during the mass "slacker raids" and the roundup of aliens. He ordered studies made with recommendations which would correct the errors of the past as far as possible.

At the request of the Army and Navy, the FBI surveyed more than 2,200 key industrial plants in the United States in addition to Army and Navy arsenals and aircraft factories. Ways and means of tightening security were recommended to the military and to the management of plants. Methods of sabotage were studied and preventive measures outlined. Suggestions were made on fire prevention and tightening of anti-sabotage guards at vital points of production, and for fingerprinting employees as a means of weeding out those with a criminal record from positions of trust.

As silly as it may seem, one plant official said his company had a phrenologist who could tell by the shape of a man's head and his reactions during an interview whether or not he was disloyal, dishonest or unfitted for his job. "That's what the man reported," an agent said, "and so help me they did employ a phrenologist."

Hoover dispatched a team of FBI special agents to England in 1940 to study British civil defense work and the security lessons learned by the British in the Battle of Britain. After this study, the FBI sent special agents throughout the country to instruct local policemen on the problems they might expect in the event of enemy air attacks and how best to deal with them in the light of British experience.

At the request of the State Department, the FBI was also keeping a watch on the activities of German, Italian and Japanese consular officials as well as the officials of the Soviet Union. Little of this work ever came to the public's attention, but Secretary Hull touched on these activities in his memoirs, saying:

> The Federal Bureau of Investigation had communicated to us in May [1941] that they had uncovered espionage activities by Lieutenant Commander Tachibana, a language officer of the Japanese Government, and asked our attitude toward his arrest. We agreed on May 27, and Tachibana was arrested at Los Angeles. Ambassador Nomura besought us on June 14, in the interest of promoting friendly relations between our two Governments, to permit Tachibana to be deported immediately without trial.
>
> I went carefully into this case and decided to grant Nomura's request. . . .

This was but one of a number of cases. Hull consented to the prosecution of several Japanese in Hawaii who had not registered with the State Department as foreign agents, and the FBI also gave the Administration evidence that German and Italian consular offices throughout the country were being used as centers of propaganda and espionage. In June, 1941, the State Department ordered these consular offices closed.

Early in 1940, the FBI stage-managed one of the strangest espionage and counterespionage dramas ever enacted in this country. It began when William Sebold, a naturalized American, returned from a trip to his native Germany and immediately came to the FBI. Sebold disclosed that the Gestapo had threatened injury to his relatives—his grandfather was a Jew—unless he returned to the United States as a German spy. He agreed and they taught him how to use a short-wave radio, supplied him with a secret code and gave him microphotographic instructions to be passed on to other German agents whom he was to contact in the United States.

William Sebold played his role of a German agent well, a role so realistic that the Gestapo and a ring of spies in America were lured into a trap carefully set by the FBI.

First the FBI arranged for Sebold to send a code message to Germany advising the Gestapo that he had arrived safely. Then FBI Laboratory engineers built a short-wave radio station at Centerport, Long Island. It was registered as an approved amateur station just in case any radio "hams" around the country became suspicious. At 7:50 P.M. on May 20, a contact was made with the Gestapo station in Hamburg, Germany. A flow of messages began between the United States and Germany which gradually led the FBI to the largest spy ring to be uncovered before Pearl Harbor.

Each message transmitted from the secret Long Island station, which was manned by FBI agents, contained enough authentic information to be convincing, but none was sent without first being cleared for security with Army and Navy Intelligence officers. The Germans never suspected the hoax.

The FBI had established Sebold in a mid-Manhattan office after all the "props" had been installed. A mirror on the wall reflected the image of anyone looking into the glass—but in the adjoining room this mirror became a window through which agents took movies of everything that went on in Sebold's office. Hidden microphones carried each word spoken to a recording device. On Sebold's desk was a clock (and behind it a wall calendar) which showed the precise time of the day when Sebold had visitors, who always sat in a chair facing the mirror.

Sebold contacted the German agents and gave them the microphotographic instructions brought from Germany. Visitors drifted in and out of Sebold's office to receive instructions and to turn over to Sebold messages to be relayed to Germany. Among the callers was Fritz Duquesne,[6] a long-time adventurer and German espionage agent whose spy career went back to the early 1900's. Duquesne was the ringleader. He and his confederates were particularly interested in sending information to Germany on production of war materials, ship movements to and from England, military aircraft production, the training of American Air Corps personnel and the delivery of aircraft to Britain. The radio station on Long Island sent and received approximately 500 messages.

This game of cat-and-mouse continued until the FBI was certain the entire espionage ring was known. Then special agents closed in. Thirty-three persons were convicted on espionage or related charges, including the suave Duquesne. "It was like shooting fish in a barrel," one agent said.

Early in October, 1940, Hoover went to the office of Robert H. Jackson, who was then Attorney General and later a Supreme Court Justice. They discussed a proposal advanced by President Roosevelt that Hoover take over the direction of all federal investigative and intelligence agencies, coordinating their work from his FBI headquarters or from a separate office.

That evening Jackson was the main speaker at an FBI National Academy banquet at the Mayflower Hotel. In his talk to the law enforcement officers, Jackson said:

> It is something of a gift in men to see beyond today and see what the tomorrows will bring . . . The Director has been able to take a long-term view of some things, and I was impressed by it this afternoon. I laid before him a little matter which would have resulted in his having some additional power—and most men in Washington are supposed to be just

reaching for that—and he said to me, "General, that plan would be very good for today, but over the years it would be a mistake."

Among those in the banquet hall, only Jackson and Hoover knew the position of personal power which Hoover had rejected.

19: *FDR Signals "Thumbs Down"*

IN 1940, President Roosevelt and Attorney General Robert H. Jackson saved the FBI from being destroyed by attacks as savage as any ever seen in the jungle of Washington politics. Had either of these men wavered under the pressures brought to bear, the FBI's reputation and usefulness might well have been damaged beyond repair. But neither wavered.

J. Edgar Hoover once told a visitor: "No one outside the FBI and the Department of Justice ever knew how close they came to wrecking us."

Who were "they"? The records from the archives of the FBI tell the story, a story of plots and intrigues and insinuations which prompted the New York *Times'* Arthur Krock at the time to write that Hoover was one of those who had ". . . gone through the unpleasant experience of being 'smeared,' the word used in Washington to describe an unfriendly publicity campaign. . . .

"For a time," Krock said, "it seemed as if the FBI director's usefulness might be seriously impaired. But . . . important charges against him were quickly disproved, and the lighter insinuations reduced to their proper level. Despite the hopes of some of Mr. Hoover's critics . . . Attorney General Jackson stood firmly behind the chief of the G-Men."

The main attack began after Hoover went before a House subcommittee on appropriations on January 5 to make his annual report on how the FBI was spending its share of the taxpayer's dollar and performing its duties. In discussing President Roosevelt's proclamation of September 6, 1939, announcing the FBI's broadened responsibility for national security, Hoover said:

. . . when this work was assigned to us we organized . . . the General Intelligence Division, which will have supervision of espionage, sabotage, and other subversive activities, and violations of the neutrality regulations . . . We have also initiated special investigations of persons reported upon as being active in any subversive activity or in movements detrimental to the internal security. In that connection, we have a general index, arranged alphabetically and geographically, available at the Bureau, so that in the event of any greater emergency coming to our country we will be able to locate immediately these various persons who may need to be the subject of further investigation. . . .

Hoover's statement was like the steel point of a dentist's probe touching an exposed nerve in a decayed tooth. The reaction was violent. The first attack came from Representative Vito Marcantonio, left-wing Congressman from New York, who told the House that Hoover's security preparations "lay the foundation . . . for a Gestapo system in the United States." And he added:

. . . By this type of testimony . . . two facts become obvious: First, we are preparing a general raid against civil rights, a blackout against the civil liberties of the American people, a system of terror by index cards such as you have in the Gestapo countries of the world; second, we are engendering a war hysteria which is a menace to the peace of the United States.

An informant gave the FBI a report on a February 6 meeting of Communist leaders in Washington where plans were made for a campaign against Hoover and the FBI. This report said:

It was proposed at this meeting that the campaign should have two principal phases, one an attack upon the Bureau as violating civil liberties and secondly a personal attack upon the Director . . . Communist writers were assigned to this second phase of the campaign. It was also planned at the meeting that the services of certain Congressmen would be enlisted in endeavoring to obtain Congressional restrictions upon the Bureau's activities.

The rumor in Washington at this time was that Hoover had lost his strongest supporter when Attorney General Frank Murphy left the Department of Justice to become an Associate Justice on the Supreme Court—and that the new, liberal Attorney General, Jackson, would put the handcuffs on Hoover and the FBI at the first opportunity.

The storm broke against the FBI on February 6. Special agents arrested ten men and a woman in Detroit and a man in Milwaukee who had been indicted on charges of conspiring to recruit volunteers for the Spanish Loyalist Army.[1] All of them were either admitted Communists, members of known Communist-front organizations or openly Communist sympathizers.

The cry arose across the country that these arrests were an example of the FBI's persecution of people who happened to have political views contrary to those of Hoover. FBI agents were accused of third-degree methods, of smashing into homes of frightened people accused only of a technical violation of the law, and of deliberately humiliating them in a display of contempt for Constitutional rights. Hoover was called a greater menace than "a nest of spies." The FBI was described as an OGPU, a Gestapo, a sinister menace to intellectual freedom. There were doubts raised in the minds of honest people who then voiced these doubts without waiting to hear the facts.

The facts were that in 1937, during the Spanish Civil War, the FBI office in Detroit received reports that members of the Young Communist League and others were recruiting volunteers to serve with the Loyalist Army. Reports were also made in January and April of 1938. All of them were sent by the FBI to the Department of Justice's Criminal Division, asking for instructions. When nothing was heard from these requests, Hoover ordered his agents in Detroit to make no further inquiries.

The Department's Criminal Division advised Hoover on September 1 that an investigation into the Detroit recruiting was "highly desirable." A few days earlier Secretary of State Hull had asked the Department of Justice to look into reports that Communists were running a recruiting service in Detroit. The FBI completed the investigation and sent its findings to the Department of Justice on April 22, 1939—shortly after the Criminal Division instructed the FBI to drop the inquiry.

On July 28, the United States Attorney in Detroit received instructions from the office of Attorney General Frank Murphy ordering him to begin prosecution proceedings on the basis of the FBI report in April. Arrangements were made to present the case to a grand jury in September—but then the Detroit U. S. Attorney received new instructions to hold off action for the time being.

The green light for prosecution was turned on again on December 18, when the Department's Criminal Division sent a telegram to the United States Attorney in Detroit saying:

> Reference letter August 26 re Philip Raymond. It is desired that you proceed with prosecution in this case immediately. Keep Department advised. Also advise if you have any other such cases warranting prosecution and if so furnish briefly statement of each. (signed) O. John Rogge

The Department of Justice decision to prosecute was based on affidavits and statements given to the FBI which contained these allegations: A recruiting program in Detroit was directed by Philip Raymond, the Communist Party's candidate for Governor of Michigan in 1937.

Raymond promised a salary of $300 a month to those who volunteered to fight for the Loyalist cause. All expenses would be paid. Those who signed up were sent by Raymond to be examined by three doctors who were cooperating physicians on the staff of the Detroit Health Department. But these examinations weren't free. The doctors' fees were billed to the City of Detroit, not to Raymond. The volunteers who passed the physical tests were given transportation to New York by Raymond, who purchased their bus and railroad tickets from World Tourists, Inc., a travel agency operated by Jacob Golos, a well-known Communist who later headed a Soviet espionage apparatus. In New York, the volunteers reported to a contact who then arranged for passports to be issued under fictitious names or managed to have the men stowed away on ships sailing for France and Spain. Most of the Americans fought in the Abraham Lincoln Brigade in Spain. When they returned home some of them joined the Veterans of the Abraham Lincoln Brigade while their nonveteran sympathizers joined the Friends of the Abraham Lincoln Brigade.

This, in brief, was the evidence which the United States Attorney in Detroit presented to the Federal Grand Jury. The jury returned secret indictments on February 3, 1940. Secret capiases were issued authorizing the arrests and searches of the defendants incident to the arrests.

Hoover and his men were aware that a roundup of even a dozen people connected with Communist activities would bring protests of political persecution raining on the FBI. For this reason, extraordinary precautions were to be taken in making the arrests. In telephone conferences between Hoover and FBI Inspector Myron E. Gurnea and Special Agent in Charge John S. Bugas,[2] it was agreed the arrests would be made simultaneously at 5:00 A.M., an hour when all the defendants would most likely be found at their homes.

The suspects were to be taken to the FBI office in Detroit. A physician was to be present to examine each person as he entered and left the office, thus removing any chance for anyone to claim he had been beaten, mistreated physically or detained while ill. The defendants were to be placed in separate rooms where possible, but with the doors left open, while being fingerprinted, photographed and questioned. Since the Federal Judge would not be available for the arraignment until 3:00 P.M., breakfast and lunch were to be served. If anyone wanted food or drink between those times, the agents were to send out and get it. A matron was to be in charge of the woman defendant. No agent, in making an arrest, was to permit himself to be left alone with a woman. The agents were told to be courteous and to avoid any arguments.

Inspector Gurnea gave this report, in part, of the instructions given to the agents on the evening before the arrests were made:

> They were advised that it is a well-known Communist policy to cause law enforcement officers as much difficulty as possible during an arrest. They were instructed that, no doubt, the persons being arrested would immediately allege that their Constitutional rights were being violated and would challenge the legality of the warrants, and the arrests in general. The Agents were advised that under no circumstances should they mention Communism, or accuse any persons whom they may encounter of being Communists or in any way affiliated with any of the Communist movements. At this point, it was repeated that any material, merely indicating affiliation with the Communist Party, should not be brought to the office but that such seizures should be confined to any evidence indicating an affiliation with the Spanish Republican Army, the Abraham Lincoln Brigade or the Friends of the Abraham Lincoln Brigade.

The after-action reports gave this account of the arrests:

> The arrests were made simultaneously, and, except for arguments over Constitutional rights and the FBI's authority, were made without any difficulty except in two cases . . . A door was forced in . . . the case of the arrest of Harold Hartley. In this instance, the Agents exhibited to Hartley through a window their credentials and the capias calling for his arrest and played a flashlight thereon in order that he could clearly read and understand the same. After this he still refused to allow Agents to enter . . . Agents allowed him five minutes to open the door. They then forced the door open and arrested him. This, of course, was entirely lawful. . . .

> An agent of the Milwaukee Office telephoned to the known address of Dr. X and informed Dr. X personally, "This is the FBI. We have a warrant for your arrest and there are agents at your door. Go to the door and let them in." Dr. X stated, "Arrest, what for?" to which the agent replied, "That will be explained to you later." The arresting agents who were at the residence of Dr. X at exactly 4 A.M. (5 A.M., Detroit time) heard the telephone ring in the residence and thereafter waited until Dr. X had hung up the telephone. They then knocked on the door, stating, "We are agents of the FBI. We have a warrant for your arrest. Open the door." Dr. X refused to open the door, although agents made this request on several occasions. After his continued refusal, arresting agents forced the door open.

All those arrested, except the woman, were handcuffed—a rule followed by the FBI from the day two years earlier when a suspect arrested on a minor charge, and not handcuffed, had jerked free and shot an agent to death. The handcuffs were removed at the FBI office. Most of the defendants refused to answer any questions until they were permitted to see their lawyers after lunch. At their arraignment, they stood mute. They were placed under bond, and then the Court turned them over to four U. S. marshals who handcuffed them to a chain, a practice used in the Detroit court by the marshals whenever a number of defendants were being taken to jail.

Photographers took pictures of the defendants being led to jail, handcuffed to the chain. Then the storm broke. The FBI was accused of using chain-gang methods, humiliating people who were not criminals. The chain-gang picture brought from one newspaper a sharp editorial criticism that the chaining and handcuffing and early morning arrests had created the impression "of a Gestapo that can haul citizens off to prison and court in ignominy, imposing any kind of conditions the captors wish without accountability . . ." The FBI's denial that it was responsible for the chaining was drowned out in the tumult that followed.

The Detroit Chapter of the International Labor Defense—of which the defendant Hartley was chairman—distributed a pamphlet accusing Hoover of establishing a Gestapo and charging the Army, Navy and FBI with "plotting" to overthrow the American democracy by force and violence in making plans for mobilization in event of war. A story appeared in the *Daily Worker* under Hartley's name in which he accused the FBI agents of "harsh treatment." He said that when he mentioned the Bill of Rights, an agent replied: "We only take orders from the FBI Chief here, Mr. Bugas. The Bill of Rights does not mean a thing."

In a more scholarly fashion, the *New Republic* discussed the arrests in an editorial headed "American OGPU." The magazine said:

> In foreign countries people are forced by their governments to submit to their Gestapos. In this country, Hoover has the voluntary support of all who delight in gangster movies and ten-cent detective magazines . . . Attorney General Jackson might well take to heart what was done toward combating wartime hysteria by some of his predecessors, whom he equals in courage and experience. One of the greatest of the Attorney Generals, Harlan Stone, now on the Supreme Court, reduced the Bureau to its normal size, after it had become swollen under William J. Burns, as it is now swollen under J. Edgar Hoover.[3] When Herbert Hoover became President, he created a commission whose greatest achievement was a thorough study of the lawlessness of law enforcement officials.

There was no mention that Stone had appointed J. Edgar Hoover to his post on the recommendation of Herbert Hoover and that both men had remained close friends of the FBI Director.

Before the *New Republic* went to press with its criticism, Jackson reversed the prosecutive action ordered by Murphy. He announced, on February 16, that he had ordered the indictments dismissed in the Spanish recruiting cases. ". . . I can see no good to come from reviv-

ing in America at this late date the animosities of the Spanish conflict
so long as the struggle has ended and some degree of amnesty at least
is being extended in Spain."

But the heaviest blow was to come from the well-known liberal,
Senator George W. Norris of Nebraska, who was disturbed by the editorial in the *New Republic* and by reports which were being carried to
him. Norris wrote Jackson that the Attorney General would know better than he whether "the legitimate rights and liberties of any of our
people have been frustrated and denied," but he made it clear that he
considered the FBI suspect and he suggested that the Detroit arrests be
investigated.

Norris didn't wait for Jackson to reply to his letter. He told the
Senate on February 26 that recruiting Americans for the Loyalist Army
was merely a technical violation of the law and was not a crime of
"malice." He placed the *New Republic* criticism of the FBI in the *Congressional Record* and then added:

> I am not alleging these matters as facts of which I have personal knowl-
> edge, for I have not. I rely . . . particularly upon the editorial in the
> *New Republic* magazine, for which I think we all have the profoundest
> respect, and which ordinarily is not guilty of making any assertions or
> charges without due and proper investigation.

Many FBI critics had been hopeful that Jackson would take their
side against Hoover and the FBI. But Jackson startled them. He stood
by Hoover. One explanation was given in a column by Joseph Alsop
and Robert Kintner, who reported that Jackson had looked into the
FBI's activities and "to his surprise" discovered that the Bureau was
operated along legitimate lines.[4]

Jackson wrote Norris on March 1, saying:

> These warrants [in the Spanish cases] were given to the Bureau for exe-
> cution under circumstances which warranted the impression that their
> service was of the utmost importance and immediacy. Being given a war-
> rant for the arrest of these parties, the obvious duty of the Bureau was
> to effect their arrests promptly, simultaneously, and without escapes. It
> was also their duty to do so without unnecessary force or humiliation
> . . . I have reviewed the facts so far as they are in my possession, and I
> find nothing to justify any charge of misconduct against the Federal
> Bureau of Investigation. . . .

But Norris refused to accept Jackson's assurances. He wrote the Attorney General that he had talked personally with Harold Hartley,
"one of these unfortunate victims," and had received written statements from quite a number of other defendants. On the basis of these
statements, Norris said:

The prisoners were subjected to third-degree methods from the time they were arrested until three o'clock in the afternoon, when they were taken into court, methods which are not only disgraceful and indefensible, but which could have no other object in view except to break down, to intimidate, to frighten them, and to fill their hearts with fear and trepidation. . . .

Norris insisted that Jackson should make a further investigation, and said that when Jackson had reached a conclusion, "I shall have faith and confidence in that conclusion."

Jackson ordered the investigation. Henry Schweinhaut,[5] Chief of the Civil Liberties Unit of the Department of Justice, spent three weeks interviewing the principals, their relatives, FBI agents, photographers, newspapermen and others who had any connection with the case—a total of ninety-eight persons in all. He found that the photographers, reporters, court attendants, the elevator operator and others were in agreement that the FBI had not chained the prisoners. As for third-degree methods, Schweinhaut said, ". . . I am satisfied that . . . the conduct of the Agents is not subject to justifiable criticism."

Jackson sent the Schweinhaut report to Norris with the comment: "I am of course anxious, as you are, that in law enforcement we do no violence to our traditional civil liberties. I am convinced that if those liberties are generally endangered in this country it is not by the FBI."

But while Norris in March had been willing to accept Jackson's conclusion in the case, he had neither faith nor confidence in the Jackson decision in May. He called the Schweinhaut report a "whitewash" and jabbed at Hoover as the "greatest hound for publicity on the American continent today."

Early in March, an FBI informant had reported that the National Committee of the Communist Party had met in New York City and agreed that "the time is ripe" to make the Detroit cases a national issue. A decision was made, the informant said, to "canvass trade unions and all kinds of progressive organizations throughout the country asking them to demand an investigation of the FBI." [6]

These demands came—in a flood of mimeographed resolutions purportedly adopted by labor groups. They said, "There is every evidence to believe that J. Edgar Hoover is preparing for a repetition of the shameful Palmer raids, in which he participated, with the object of attacking and destroying the various unions." They called on the President and the Attorney General to suspend Hoover pending an investigation.

At the same time, a seventy-six page unsigned memorandum was distributed confidentially to certain writers in Washington. It was titled "The Investigative Work of the FBI With Reference to Activities Based Upon Economic or Political Views or Opinions." But the distributors made a mistake. They gave a copy to a nationally known liberal who took one look at it and brought it to the FBI, although at times he had been a critic of the FBI himself.

"In all fairness, I think you should know the source of some of the criticisms," he said. "I want no part of it."

This memorandum was a carefully and skillfully assembled lawyer's brief designed to "prove" that the FBI was a menace to civil liberties, and that Hoover was actually responsible for the scandalous operations of the Bureau in World War I and during the Harding Administration. Hoover was blamed for the "Red Raids" of Attorney General Palmer and depicted as building an organization which defied the Constitution and the Supreme Court. This memorandum was, in fact, a textbook of insinuations of lawless conduct by the FBI under Hoover, although the author, while known to the FBI, never revealed his identity.

Daniel J. Tobin, President of the International Brotherhood of Teamsters, Chauffeurs, Stablemen and Helpers of America, wrote Hoover that he, Tobin, had been invited to a secret meeting of a group which proposed to petition President Roosevelt, Attorney General Jackson and members of Congress for an investigation of the FBI.

Tobin wrote: "I realize, of course, that all men who are in the public service must pay the price of the victories they have achieved by the unjust and adverse criticism which they received, sometimes from men who are honest at heart such as Senator Norris, but more often from men who are feeling the pinch of law enforcement on themselves, either directly or indirectly." He added that he would not associate himself with any such meeting.

The invitation to which Tobin referred was a letter bearing the signature of Professor Franz Boas of Columbia University, Chairman of the American Committee for Democracy and Intellectual Freedom, and an internationally known anthropologist. The letter said in part: "You are undoubtedly aware of the apprehension with which intelligent people throughout the country have realized the dangerous nature and the scope of the FBI's activities as recently exposed by Senator Norris . . ." Professor Boas' name was being used to rally intellectuals against the FBI.

The FBI was hit from another direction after the Department of Justice gave its approval to proposed legislation which would make it possible for the FBI to use in federal courts evidence obtained from wire taps involving cases of subversion and crimes of violence.[7]

As in the Detroit case, these attacks had a curious origin. They stemmed from a complaint of wire tapping in the 1939 election campaign in Rhode Island. The Department of Justice ordered an investigation and the FBI turned up evidence of wire tapping, but the Department declined prosecution.[8] On the basis of the FBI's findings, Senator Theodore F. Green of Rhode Island asked for a Senate inquiry into wire-tapping practices. His request was acted on favorably by the Senate Interstate Commerce Committee, which issued a report roundly condemning all wire tapping. The name of the FBI was not mentioned, but there were whispers advising reporters that the document was pointing a finger at the FBI.

The committee's action was interpreted promptly and widely as an investigation of the FBI. Senator Green protested that his resolution asking for the inquiry was not aimed against Hoover or the FBI. "As a matter of fact," Green said in a statement, "this investigation into wire-tapping practices was partly the result of evidence uncovered by the Federal Bureau of Investigation in my State."

Again Jackson came to the FBI's defense. He said: "In a limited class of cases, such as kidnaping, extortion, and racketeering . . . it is the opinion of the present Attorney General . . . that wire tapping should be authorized under some appropriate safeguard." And he added ". . . The philosophy underlying the foregoing remarks, which were directed to the activities of the underworld, would seem applicable with even greater force to the activities of persons engaged in espionage, sabotage, and other activities interfering with the national defense."

In the uproar over wire tapping, Jackson announced that upon Hoover's recommendation he was ordering wire tapping discontinued by the FBI. He also said that the Department of Justice would handle no prosecutions for any department of the government in which a wire tap had been used. But President Roosevelt had other ideas. He ordered the FBI to resume wire taps in cases approved by the Attorney General.[9]

The central theme running through all the attacks on the FBI was that Hoover had directed the Palmer "Red Raids" in 1919, when civil liberties were abused, and that the FBI was returning to these same practices.[10] Columnist Ralph McGill predicted, "The disgruntled politicians and the Communists joined in opposition [to Hoover and the FBI] will not go very far."

Representative Emanuel Celler of New York was among those to defend Hoover. He told a radio audience that Hoover had no responsibility in the Palmer raids, adding: "At that time Hoover was a Special Assistant Attorney General, and he handled the prosecution of many cases. He had nothing to do with the arrest or so-called persecution of individuals. He simply handled the cases in the courts as they were presented to him." Celler urged support for a bill, which he had introduced with Jackson's approval, to permit not only the interception of telephone messages in certain cases but also their divulgence as evidence in court.

One of those listening to the Celler broadcast was Attorney Morris Katzeff, then living in Boston, who had been one of the lawyers defending those rounded up for deportation in the Palmer Raids. Katzeff wrote Hoover:

> The cases of 1919 immediately came back to my mind and I also recalled that you had nothing to do with the irregularities and harsh treatment of aliens suspected of being Communists; I also recall a hearing before the then Secretary of Labor Mr. Wilson in Washington at which Charles Recht of New York, Mr. Bachrach of Chicago and I were present at which you deplored as sincerely as we did the incident attending the circumstances connected with arrests of aliens in New England, and I recalled how genuinely I was impressed by your sincerity as well as with your thoroughness in presenting your argument, and I felt it my duty as being one of the very few footloose men up to the present moment who could from personal knowledge say a word in defense of a man unjustly accused of wrongdoing.

The attacks on Hoover and the FBI continued throughout 1940. They began to diminish and lose force after an incident which occurred during the dinner given on March 16, 1940, by the White House correspondents, a black-tie affair which annually draws top-ranking government officials, political leaders and business tycoons.

President Roosevelt was the guest of honor at the head table, which was placed on a raised platform to give the hundreds of diners a view of the Chief Executive. Roosevelt spotted Hoover among the guests and called to him. "Edgar," he said, "what are they trying to do to you on the Hill?"

Hoover shook his head and replied, "I don't know, Mr. President."

Roosevelt grinned and turned his thumbs down on the table. "That's for them," he said.

The word soon spread around Washington that Roosevelt had turned thumbs down on the attackers of Hoover and the FBI.

World War II

20: *The FBI Goes to War*

THE Japanese sea raiders slipped out of Hitokappu Bay in the Kurile Islands on November 25, 1941. The destroyers dashed nervously along the flanks of the column, weaving white ribbons of foam around the six aircraft carriers, the two lumbering battleships, the two heavy cruisers and the supply train. All radios were silent as the pack headed eastward toward Hawaii.

The raiders were seven days out of Hitokappu Bay when the message came: "Niita Kayama Nobore!" (Climb Mount Niitaka—Proceed With Attack!) Now the ships were darkened and no light showed at night.

In the radio room of the task force's flag ship, Commander Ono listened intently to the commercial broadcasts from radio stations KGU and KGMB in Honolulu. He listened carefully hour after hour for any hint of alarm or change in the normal routine of the stations' programs. But he heard nothing unusual.

Japanese officers watched their radiomen plot the bearings of the American patrol planes on reconnaissance from the island of Oahu, where an unsuspecting fleet rested at anchor in Pearl Harbor. The bearings were taken from the pilots' radio chatter to each other. And the charts looked good to the Japanese. All the reconnaissance was being made to the southwest.

The raiders slipped unseen to a point two hundred miles north of Oahu in the pre-dawn hours of December 7. And at daybreak the war planes roared from the carriers like great falcons armed to kill.

The torpedo planes and dive bombers hit the fleet at Pearl Harbor first. Then came the horizontal bombers and after them a third wave of dive bombers. From 7:55 A.M. until 9:45—110 minutes—they blasted the fleet and strafed the neat rows of Army, Navy and Marine planes parked on the aprons of airfields.[1]

The bombs were still falling when the Honolulu Special Agent in Charge, Robert L. Shivers,[2] called the FBI Headquarters in Washington with only a brief delay in getting a connection across the 5,000 miles of ocean and land. It was about 2:30 P.M. in Washington.

The telephone girl at Headquarters switched the urgent call to the FBI's private line to New York City, where J. Edgar Hoover had gone for the week end. And then she put in a call to Griffith Stadium, where other top officials of the FBI were watching the Sunday pro football game between the Washington Redskins and Philadelphia Eagles. The information desk in the Communications Center knew the box in which the men were sitting, and a messenger told Assistant to the Director Edward A. Tamm he was wanted on the phone for an urgent message.

Tamm reached the telephone in time to hear Shivers tell Hoover, "The Japanese are bombing Pearl Harbor. There is no doubt about it —those planes are Japanese. It's war. You may be able to hear the explosions yourself. Listen!" Shivers held the telephone to an open window and Hoover and Tamm heard the crash of bombs and the explosions of the warships.

Shivers gave Hoover a quick summary of the reports he had received of the death and disaster. And the FBI Director ordered Shivers and Tamm to put into effect immediately the war plans which had been worked out months before.

Tamm rushed back to the box and whispered to his colleagues, "The Japs are bombing Pearl Harbor! Come on!" In New York City, Hoover was sped to La Guardia Field to catch a plane back to Washington.

Two days earlier, Hoover had instructed his agents to be ready at any time for "the immediate apprehension of Japanese aliens in your district who have been recommended for custodial detention." Now the whole FBI organization was alerted. Each office knew precisely what to do when the order came for the roundup. But Hoover and his men couldn't move on this job until President Roosevelt had issued an emergency proclamation and Attorney General Francis Biddle had signed the necessary directives giving the FBI authority to act. As Hoover was returning to his office from New York City, Attorney General Biddle was being flown to the Capital from Detroit.

Quietly the FBI had been assembling a list of aliens who were anti-American or who were likely to prove most dangerous in time of war. The list included a total of some 770 Japanese. The FBI field offices knew precisely who these people were and where they could be found. And after the alert, the field men waited impatiently for the roundup order.

From San Francisco, Special Agent in Charge N. J. L. Pieper called Louis Nichols, then an Assistant Director, and said, "The boys are getting jumpy. Shouldn't we start moving?"

"Not yet," Nichols said. "We've got to wait for the papers to be signed after the President issues a proclamation. Don't take anybody into custody but go ahead and put those listed under surveillance. Don't let those people get away from you even if you have to sit on their front door step."

Similar queries and similar orders were being handled by other executives.

When President Roosevelt ordered the detention of enemy aliens that Sunday evening and Biddle signed the necessary papers, an urgent message went over the FBI teletype system:

Immediately take into custody all Japanese who have been classified in A, B, and C categories in material previously transmitted to you. Take immediate action and advise Bureau frequently by teletype as to exact identity of persons arrested. Persons taken into custody should be turned over to nearest representative of Immigration and Naturalization Service.
Hoover.

Across the nation and in Hawaii, Alaska and Puerto Rico, FBI agents began the roundup which was to be followed the next day by the arrest of German and Italian enemy aliens. But this time, in sharp contrast to World War I days, the machinery existed for each arrested alien to have a hearing before a civilian board and to be represented by counsel. The FBI agents also had the help of squads of local police who had studied wartime problems in the FBI-conducted schools started in anticipation of the emergency.

The roundup was a remarkable performance in speed and coordination. The careful advance preparations made it possible to take into custody 3,846 enemy aliens in the first seventy-two hours of the war with no violence.[3]

Hoover ordered the FBI on a twenty-four-hour schedule. All annual leaves were canceled. Protective guards were placed at the Japanese Embassy and at Japanese consulates. Air lines were asked not to carry any Japanese passengers until further notice, and also not to accept air express packages from or to any Japanese because of possible sabotage efforts. FBI offices were instructed to alert industries with war contracts to be on guard against espionage or sabotage.

At the request of the State Department, Hoover issued a stop order on all press service and other communications to Japan and occupied territory. Hoover's authority for these stop orders on communications was challenged by the Federal Communications Commission, which told the communications companies to disregard the FBI instructions for the time being. But the companies abided by the stop order.

In the tumultuous first hours of the war, President Roosevelt had given Hoover verbal instructions to take charge of censorship. This was followed by a memorandum to the Secretaries of War, Navy, State and Treasury, the Postmaster General and the Federal Communications Commission which stated: "I am today directing J. Edgar Hoover, Director of the Federal Bureau of Investigation, to take charge of all censorship arrangements pending such further measures as I shall presently take. Franklin D. Roosevelt."

The President turned to Hoover in this case because the FBI had already mapped out a detailed plan, including voluntary censorship by the press and radio, to be handled by an independent agency responsible only to the President. The plan was based on studies made by FBI agents in England. It happened that a complete chart of organization had come from the printers on the Monday before the Pearl Harbor attack. Hoover's idea was that the Director of Censorship should be a civilian appointed by the President, and that the Army, Navy, FBI and other governmental agencies concerned with censorship should have only advisory powers.

On Monday, December 8, Hoover called a conference of representatives from the State, Post Office, Treasury, and War Departments, the Navy, the Federal Communications Commission and the Office of Facts and Figures, and laid his plan before the group. The Treasury representative raised an objection. Secretary of the Treasury Morgenthau, he said, wanted to retain the right "to censor all tangible communications except the mails." The argument for placing this authority with the Treasury was that President Wilson, in World War I, had delegated the power of censorship to his Secretary of the Treasury.

But Hoover objected to this proposal. He suggested that thought should be given ". . . to the problem of obtaining voluntary and cooperative self-censorship by the press and radio . . ." He said that in his opinion no censorship program would succeed without public support—and that this support could best be gained by enlisting the help of the press and radio in an advisory capacity.

Hoover won backing for his position and the group's policy committee approved a recommendation saying:

> The Director of Censorship and the censorship organization should be under no existing governmental agency and should be free from the control of the Military, Naval or any existing civilian establishments inasmuch

as many government departments will be "customers" of the censorship organization, and no customer should control the administration of the organization. Experience in England has proved particularly that it should be free from Military and Naval control.

The conference also approved Hoover's suggestion that the Director of Censorship should be a newspaper executive. It was recommended that "a permanent Director of Censorship be promptly designated and that he be a civilian, preferably, with newspaper experience and very definitely with executive capacity." This description was tailored to fit Byron Price, Executive News Editor of the Associated Press, and President Roosevelt named Price to take over the job on December 16.

Byron Price set up his censorship organization on the broad base of voluntary cooperation. It was an organization which could be (and was) dismantled immediately after the emergency had ended.[4]

The grave security responsibilities placed on the FBI in war forced Hoover to relax temporarily the rule that new agents had to have a law degree or be accountants. The Bureau had 2,602 agents when the United States went to war, with a total personnel of 7,420. Hoover immediately sent out orders to the field offices to begin interviewing graduates of the FBI National Academy who could meet all qualifications except legal training. The FBI had to be built up to handle the tremendous volume of work, and its agent force was increased to 5,072.[5] The total personnel increased to 13,317 on the active rolls two years after the outbreak of war.

Scores of agents were needed merely to run down the torrent of rumors of espionage and sabotage. The rumors went like this: huge arrows had been cut in the cane fields in Hawaii by Japanese field workers, arrows pointing to military targets; Japanese fishing boats in Hawaii were furnishing food and fuel to enemy submarines; a Japanese fifth column was waiting on the West Coast to rise and give help to an invading army; Japanese-Americans were going to poison the water reservoirs on the West Coast; and Japanese truck gardeners were loading their produce with arsenic.

The FBI, military intelligence officers and local law enforcement officers tracked down the rumors and found them false. There was no enemy sabotage after the Pearl Harbor attack—those who might have been saboteurs were rounded up too swiftly. But each report had to be checked.

It was in this early war excitement that an anonymous memorandum appeared in Washington bearing the title "Is the FBI Asleep at the Switch?" It bore a striking likeness in appearance and content to an anonymous fifty-six-page memorandum which had been handed to a few newsmen in the spring of 1941, "Shall America Have a Permanent,

Large Scale Spy System?" The new memorandum was an effort, by innuendo, to blame the FBI for the lack of preparedness at Pearl Harbor.

"The failure of the armed forces to be on the alert at Pearl Harbor was a failure of Sunday morning, December 7, 1941," the memorandum said. "The failure of our counterespionage forces to be on the alert was a 26-months failure . . . The full facts will not be known, however, unless the President's board looks into the adequacy of the FBI, the agency directed by the President and supposed by the public and Congress, to deal with the fifth column in our territory." [6]

The truth was that in 1940 Hoover had refused to accept primary responsibility for the investigation of espionage, sabotage and subversive activities in Hawaii because the FBI office in Honolulu was not equipped with the man power or experience required for the job at that time. In a conference with Admiral Walter Anderson, Director of the Office of Naval Intelligence, and Brigadier General Sherman Miles, Assistant Chief of Staff of the Army's Intelligence Division, Hoover had recommended a joint responsibility in which the Navy would continue its work until the FBI was able to take over, and his recommendation was approved. At that time the FBI had only nine special agents and five stenographers in the Honolulu office, while the Navy had an intelligence staff of more than a hundred interpreters, translators and officers. Obviously, it would have been folly for the FBI to have assumed the primary burden.

In December of 1940, Hoover wrote to Special Agent Shivers: ". . . the Bureau does not consider it advisable or desirable at this particular time for your office to assume the responsibility for the supervision of all Japanese espionage investigations in the Territory of Hawaii." The FBI Director stressed the point a few months later in another letter to Shivers, saying: "The Bureau is not yet prepared to handle the investigation of Japanese activity exclusively on the mainland, and consequently the Bureau cannot authorize the assumption by your office of exclusive jurisdiction in matters relating to Japanese activities in the Hawaiian Islands."

The problem of jurisdiction was reviewed in early 1941 by the Army, Navy and FBI and a recommendation made ". . . that the present program of the joint operation in the coverage of Japanese espionage be continued and that the Federal Bureau of Investigation continue to extend its operations in this field." This was the agreement in effect on December 7.

But while these agencies were reaching their working agreement, a backstage struggle was going on between the FBI and the Federal Communications Commission (FCC) over the FBI's right to make security checks on coded messages being sent to Tokyo, Berlin, Rome, Moscow and other world capitals. It had begun in September, 1939, when Hoover suggested to FCC Chairman James Lawrence Fly the need of an arrangement whereby the FBI could check on these communications, inasmuch as the President had given the FBI responsibility for coordinating the security effort.

At the heart of the controversy was the FCC's stand that wire tapping or interception of messages, even in the name of national security, was illegal, an interpretation of the law not shared by the Department of Justice, which held that authorized wire taps and intercepts were entirely legal as long as the information obtained was not divulged to unauthorized persons.[7]

When the FBI and FCC had not come to agreement in mid-1941, Hoover appealed to Attorney General Robert Jackson. He asked that a proclamation be drafted for President Roosevelt's approval which would give the FBI access to international communications. Hoover had White House assurances that the proclamation would be signed and Department attorneys were working on a final draft giving the FBI this authority, when the Japanese attacked at Pearl Harbor. But then it was no longer needed.

This dispute over security checks on coded messages was only part of the conflict between the FBI and FCC at that time. There was also friction over the FCC's refusal to turn over to the FBI the fingerprint cards of some 200,000 radio operators and communications employees. Chairman Fly said the prints had been taken merely to check the citizenship of the workers and ". . . the turning over of fingerprints in a block to your Bureau might be regarded by the persons fingerprinted as a serious breach of faith on the part of the Commission . . ." He argued that to give these prints to the FBI would be similar to turning over private telegraph messages to unauthorized persons—and besides, the workers' union leaders objected to the transfer.

Attorney General Biddle intervened after the war began. He wrote Fly on January 2, 1942:

> . . . The situation has materially changed in recent days. The evidence is strong that messages have been surreptitiously transmitted to our enemies by radio, and that military attacks upon the territory of this country may have been furthered and facilitated thereby . . . Please think this over; I should hate to have something serious happen which might have been so easily avoided.

Fly replied that the Commission agreed that the fingerprints should be checked by the FBI. But he insisted that the cards should not be kept in the FBI's permanent files, as "it would be unfortunate if the employees were subjected to disclosure of past misdemeanors and other crimes which have nothing to do with security matters."

Biddle refused to accept anything less than the permanent filing of the cards with the FBI. He wrote to Fly, saying: ". . . If there is anyone in a position to do real harm in the present state of affairs, certainly the radio operator is included. I conceive it my duty not to overlook any source of information which bears upon our national security, and to do all in my power to obtain it." Biddle also noted that unless the cards were filed permanently with the FBI, a person could be discharged for subversion by one government agency and hired by another with no one the wiser.

Nearly a year after the dispute began, the FBI received the fingerprint cards from the FCC.

Those were days of conflict and pressures, when men's nerves were rubbed raw as they drove themselves to the point of exhaustion. They were days when fear bred hysteria and when hysteria—as it did in World War I—caused men's judgment to falter.

Such was the case in the decision to move some 120,000 Japanese-Americans from their homes and farms on the West Coast to relocation centers. It was a tragic upheaval which Hoover looked upon as a mixture of politics and hysteria and not as an urgent measure of national defense.

The FBI Director first heard of the evacuation proposal when he was called to the office of Secretary of the Treasury Morgenthau on the evening of December 10 for a talk with the Secretary and two other Treasury officials. A memorandum of the meeting written by Hoover to Attorney General Biddle tells the basic story:

. . . The Secretary stated that he had been in communication with his representatives in San Francisco and as a result had ascertained that the task which they were carrying on [freezing Japanese assets and businesses] was an enormous one and that he believed more drastic measures should be taken in order to adequately cover and complete it. The Secretary then put in a call to Mr. X, one of his representatives in San Francisco, and this conversation was heard by all in the Secretary's office . . . It was the opinion of Mr. X that there should be a round-up of the Japanese in San Francisco, Los Angeles and in the bay cities of San Francisco, as well as in certain sections of the San Joaquin Valley . . . The Secretary inquired of me as to whether this could be done . . .

I suggested to Secretary Morgenthau that he call you by phone. I told the Secretary that I felt that you would be reluctant to approve any such program unless there were sufficient facts upon which to justify the cases of the persons arrested, as I believed you would be opposed to any "drag-net" or "round-up" procedure. I pointed out to the Secretary that in the arrests which had already been made of the Japanese, German, and Italian alien enemies, factual cases had had to be prepared on each one of them prior to their arrests and that these had to be approved by the Attorney General, and that of course citizens of the United States were not being included in any arrests as the authority to make arrests was limited to alien enemies and unless there were specific actions upon which criminal complaints could be filed, you had not approved the arresting of any citizens of the United States.

The Secretary then called you . . . and you were in accord that the matter should be further considered and that certainly no action should be taken last night of the character recommended by the Treasury Agents in San Francisco . . .

But the snowball had started. With the hysteria there were the cold calculations of men who wanted the Japanese moved for economic reasons and because of racial prejudices. The decisions for the movement were made in the upper reaches of the Administration. And so it was that tens of thousands of loyal Japanese-American citizens made the sad journey from their homes after a directive was issued giving the Army authority for the roundup.

Hoover put his finger on the real reason for the evacuation when he told Biddle in a memorandum:

The necessity for mass evacuation is based primarily upon public and political pressure rather than on factual data. Public hysteria and, in some instances, the comments of the press, and radio announcers, have resulted in a tremendous amount of pressure being brought to bear on Governor Olson and Earl Warren, Attorney General of the State, and on the military authorities. It is interesting to observe that little mention has been made of the mass evacuation of enemy aliens.

This was a case in which the FBI, after many months of investigation, had tagged and arrested 733 Japanese aliens in all parts of the nation by 6:30 A.M., on December 8. Those were the Japanese considered by the FBI to be dangerous to the nation's security. The evacuation swept up some 120,000 people of Japanese ancestry—the great majority of them citizens—on the West Coast alone.

In this hysteria, Hoover turned aside a flood of offers from citizens' and civilian groups across the country who wanted to resurrect the old American Protective League of World War I. The FBI Director saw no place for vigilantism in World War II.

21: *Espionage, Limited*

EVEN as the oily black clouds of destruction mushroomed above the shattered fleet at Pearl Harbor, a thin spire of gray smoke was rising from the yard of the Japanese Consulate in Honolulu. This smoke came from a small fire tended by Consul General Nagao Kita and his Vice Consul, Atojiro Okuda. They were burning the Consulate's secret code books and the messages which had passed between Kita and Foreign Minister Togo in those last days before treachery reached its flaming climax.

Nagao Kita. It's a name to remember in the espionage of World War II. If any man can be named as the most effective enemy agent in the Pearl Harbor attack, it was Kita. Behind the curtain of diplomatic immunity he supplied Tokyo with a running account of last-minute ship movements in and out of Pearl Harbor. And now that the blow was struck, he was trying to destroy the evidence.

But paper in bulk burns slowly. While the flames at the Consulate were being fed by Kita and Okuda, Special Agent in Charge Shivers asked the Honolulu Police Department to place a guard at the Consulate. The guard saw the papers being burned. He rushed in and grabbed a code book and a bundle of messages from the protesting Japanese. The papers were turned over to Shivers, who gave them to the Navy to decode, along with Consulate messages obtained from the commercial communications companies—messages which had been denied to the FBI until the Japanese struck.[1]

When Shivers saw the uncoded messages, he exclaimed to another agent, "My God, if we'd had these earlier! Look at this!" And he handed the messages to the agent:

#0245 (1) "PA" 3 December, 1941
FROM: KITA
TO: FOREIGN MINISTER, TOKYO
(Secret Military message No.) (By Chief of Consulate's Code).
To: Chief of Third Section, Naval General Staff
From: FUJII

Re signals I wish to simplify communications as follows:

1. *Code* (following 3 section 8 line table)
    1. Battle force, including scouting force, are about to put to sea—
    2. Several aircraft carriers plan to put to sea.
    3. All battle force has sailed 1st-3rd dates inc.
    4. Several aircraft carriers have sailed (1st to 3rd)
    5. All aircraft carriers have sailed (1st to 3rd)
    6. All battle force have sailed, 4th-6th dates inc.

7. Several aircraft carriers have sailed (4th to 6th)
8. All aircraft carriers have sailed (4th to 6th)

2. *Signal*

Light in Lanikai beach house at night—

One light from 8 P.M. to 9 P.M. indicates "1". From 9 P.M. to 10 P.M. indicates "2". The below signals until midnight, in order to indicate 3 and 4. Two lights, according to the time, indicates 5, 6, 7, 8. When not in accordance with (lights) above 1 full automobile headlight and one half light indicates 1, 2, 3, 4. Two full lights indicate 5, 6, 7, 8.

2. On the Lanikai coast during daytime from 8 A.M. until noon every hour 1 piece linen cloth (sheet) indicates 1, 2, 3, 4. Two pieces linen cloth indicate 5, 6, 7, 8.

3. In Lanikai bay during daytime in front of harbor (offing) a star boat with one star on sail indicates 1, 2, 3, 4; a star and "III" indicates 5, 6, 7, 8.

4. Light in dormer window of Kalama house from 7 P.M. to 1 A.M. every hour indicates 3, 4, 5, 6, 7, 8. . . .

FROM: FOREIGN MINISTER   December 3, 1941
TO: KITA, CONSUL, HONOLULU
STRICTLY SECRET

WOULD LIKE YOU TO HOLD ON YOUR LIST OF CODE WORDS (ALSO THOSE USED IN CONNECTION WITH RADIO BROADCAST) RIGHT UP UNTIL THE LAST MINUTE. WHEN THE BREAK COMES BURN IMMEDIATELY AND WIRE US TO THAT EFFECT.

TOGO

FROM: KITA   December 5, 1941
TO: FOREIGN MINISTER, TOKYO

1. The three battleships mentioned in your X239 of Friday morning, the 5th entered port. They expect to depart port on the 8th.
2. On the same day the LEXINGTON and 5 heavy cruisers departed.
3. The following warships were anchored on the afternoon of the 5th:

        8 Battleships
        3 Light cruisers
        16 Destroyers

Coming in were 4 cruisers of the Honolulu type and 2 destroyers.

KITA

FROM: TOGO, FOREIGN MINISTER   December 6, 1941
TO: CONSUL, HONOLULU

PLEASE INFORM US IMMEDIATELY OF ANY RUMORS OF THE MOVEMENTS OF WARSHIPS AFTER THE 4TH.

TOGO

Here was evidence of espionage. The message sent by Kita to Tokyo on December 3 proved that Kita had arranged for someone to signal Japanese submarines and give them information on the American fleet. And the finger of suspicion pointed to Bernard Julius Otto Kuehn as Kita's confederate because Kuehn had a house at Lanikai, a house at Kalama with a dormer window and a boat with a star on the sail.

Otto Kuehn, a German national, had first come to the FBI's attention in 1939 because of persistent rumors that he had an abnormally large income for a man with no profession or known business connection. Such talk gets around in a community the size of Honolulu. And it was no secret to the FBI that Kuehn had deposited more than $70,000 in a Honolulu bank from 1936 to 1939. He had once been a member of the Nazi Party.

Kuehn explained to friends that his income came from family inheritances, but in tracing the money the FBI began to suspect it had come to Kuehn from Japanese sources in Berlin. These suspicions increased when the Army advised the FBI that the Japanese Consul General was known to have asked his Foreign Office for an opinion on the reliability of a couple in Hawaii named "Friedell."

The FBI could find no one named "Friedell." But agents noted that Mrs. Kuehn's first name was Friedel, spelled with one "l." This similarity in names seemed more than coincidence in view of the fact that the Army's tip came a short time after Mrs. Kuehn's return from a trip to Tokyo.

Still, there was no tangible evidence of espionage by Kuehn until the Consulate messages had been translated. Then Kuehn confessed. He admitted he was the source of the code for signaling to the submarines, but he claimed it was never used so far as he knew.

Kuehn told agents:

> . . . It was also arranged [with Kita] that this same set of signals could be given by short wave radio and arrangements were made that if the Consulate desired to contact me they could do so by sending me a postcard signed "Jimmie," to my Box No. 1476 at Honolulu . . . On the same occasion that I transmitted this simplified system of signalling I had also advised the Consulate that there were seven battleships, six cruisers, two aircraft carriers, forty destroyers, and twenty-seven submarines, or some similar figure, in Hawaiian waters . . .[2]

Kuehn also told of receiving some $30,000 in 1940–1941 from sources in Tokyo, money which he claimed represented transfers from property income in Germany. He said the last $14,000 payment was handed to him by a strange Japanese, and that his wife hid all the money.

"I don't know where she has it hidden," Kuehn said. But there was testimony indicating that the stranger who gave Kuehn the $14,000 was Vice Consul Okuda's associate, Consulate Secretary Tadasi Morimura.

A military commission operating under martial law listened to Kuehn's story and then sentenced him to be shot to death "by musketry." However, the sentence was later commuted by the military governor to fifty years at hard labor.[3]

Kuehn was one of ninety-one persons convicted of spying against the United States from 1938 to 1945. And the shame of it was that sixty-four of them were American citizens betraying their own country. The greater number worked for the Hitler government because of loyalty to Germany. A few others were mere adventurers. A few were recruited by threats of death or injury to loved ones held by the Nazis. A few became enemy agents because they saw a way to make easy money.

The Nazis tried desperately to establish an espionage and sabotage apparatus in the United States to equal the spy ring organized by von Bernstorff, von Papen and Boy-Ed before World War I. But this time the FBI was alert to the threat. Even before the war began the FBI had assembled through information obtained by its own agents, and with the cooperation of the British and American military intelligence services, a clear picture of Nazi espionage methods.

Most of the Nazi spies trained in the espionage school at Klopstock Pension, Hamburg, entered the United States in 1939 and early 1940, while this country was at peace. Some were ex-army officers. Some were trained in professions such as engineering, medicine, finance, photography and education.

One of the Nazis' most trusted prewar agents was Kurt Frederick Ludwig, whose birthplace was Fremont, Ohio, but who spent most of his life in Germany. Ludwig was a friend of Robert Ley, Hitler's "master of German labor," and he was sent to the United States in 1940 to organize a spy ring.

Ludwig was a man with a hundred aliases. The FBI got on his trail when British censors in Bermuda intercepted a suspicious letter in January, 1941, addressed to a person in Spain. On the back of the letter was found secret writing giving information on supplies being shipped to England, and it was signed "Joe K."

The FBI's problem was to find the mysterious "Joe K" somewhere among the tens of millions of Americans—and the name was the only clue. It appeared hopeless until another letter was intercepted which said that "Phil" had been injured fatally in a traffic accident on March 18 and had died at St. Vincent's Hospital in New York City.

This gave the agents something tangible to pursue. They found that a Julio Lopez Lido had been in a traffic accident on March 18, and witnesses said that a man with Lido had grabbed the injured man's brief case and hurried from the scene. Agents subsequently learned that Lido's true name had been Ulrich von der Osten, and in von der Osten's papers they found a name here, an address there, and a scribbled telephone number which, when put together, unmasked Ludwig as the writer of the "Joe K" letters.

Agents caught Ludwig on the West Coast as he was trying to flee aboard a ship. From Ludwig the trail led to others, one of whom was Paul T. Borchardt, a scholarly ex-officer of the German Army who had taught young Nazi officers the science of geopolitics at the Geographic Military Seminary in Germany before coming to the United States in 1940. Borchardt became the clearinghouse agent for Ludwig, assessing the military, economic and political value of information before it was sent to Germany.[4]

And there was the improbable "doll woman," who wrote such gentle and disarming letters about her dolls. But then one of her letters was returned from Buenos Aires marked "Unknown at This Address." The mailman brought the letter to Mrs. Sara G., of Portland, Oregon, whose name was given on the return address. The letter was dated May 20, 1942. Mrs. G. brought the letter to the FBI.

"I never saw the letter before," Mrs. G. said. "I don't know anyone in Buenos Aires."

The letter looked innocent enough. It said, in part:

I just secured a lovely Siamese Temple Dancer, it had been damaged, that is tore in the middle. But it is now repaired and I like it very much. I could not get a mate for this Siam dancer, so I am redressing just a small plain ordinary doll into a second Siam doll . . .

And then other doll letters were intercepted by censors, apparently written by the same person. In the FBI Laboratory, cryptographers studied the "doll" letters and finally concluded that "Siamese Temple Dancer" meant "aircraft carrier warship" and "doll" meant "warship." And then the talk of dolls assumed a sinister meaning:

I just secured information of a fine aircraft carrier warship, it had been damaged, that is torpedoed in the middle. But it is now repaired and I like it very much. They could not get a mate for this so a plain ordinary warship is being converted into a second aircraft carrier . . .

Agents noted that this letter had been written a few days after the aircraft carrier USS *Saratoga* left Puget Sound for San Diego.

But the gentle doll lover made a mistake. In a moment of spite, she used as a return address the name of Mrs. M., a woman with whom she had had a spat. When an FBI agent called on Mrs. M. to check on the letter, she knew nothing about it. Certainly she hadn't written the letter.

"Do you have any idea who might use your name?" the agent asked.

Mrs. M. thought for a moment and then her eyes blazed. "I'll bet it's that Velvalee Dickinson in New York. I bought some dolls from her and because I couldn't pay her right away she's been after me with some nasty letters." The FBI didn't regard a woman's intuition as a reliable tool in espionage, but in this case agents learned the lesson that it never pays to underestimate the power of a woman.

Letters written by Velvalee Dickinson were compared with one of the letters mailed to South America. They were written on the same typewriter.

At first Velvalee Dickinson claimed that the $100 bills she was found to be taking from a safe-deposit box were left to her as part of her husband's estate. Then she changed her story, saying that her late husband had been paid $25,000 by the Japanese Naval Attaché, Ichiro Yokoyama, on November 26, 1941, to furnish information to the Japanese. She insisted she had not supplied information herself, although the FBI's evidence all pointed to Mrs. Dickinson and not her husband.

Mrs. Dickinson was indicted on espionage charges, but the U. S. Attorney handling the case decided to accept her plea of guilty to violating censorship because the evidence was "circumstantial." In passing sentence, Judge Shackelford Miller said:

> It is hard to believe that some people do not realize that our nation is engaged in a life and death struggle . . . [you] were certainly engaged in espionage . . . You were fortunate that the Government did not have you tried on espionage charges. The penalty for such a conviction would have been death or life imprisonment . . .

In uncovering spy activities, the FBI also uncovered espionage tools resembling a magician's props for parlor tricks. One enemy agent was caught with a box of ordinary-looking safety matches. Most of the matches were just that, but four of them turned out to be tiny pencils which wrote invisibly. Messages were sealed into fountain pens whose barrels had to be broken to extract the note. Codes were concealed in books and magazines by minute pin pricks through certain letters.

But one of the FBI's most exciting achievements was in uncovering the Nazi secret of the "micro-dots," perhaps the cleverest espionage weapon of World War II.

Early in 1940 the FBI received a tip from a double agent that the Germans were developing a new method for slipping information from

Allied countries. He told a story of attending the espionage school at Klopstock Pension and of hearing Dr. Hugo Sebold, the school's director, say in a final lecture:

> The greatest problem of der Führer's agents in North and South America is keeping in touch with us . . . but before long we shall be communicating back and forth throughout the world with impunity . . .

The double agent said the method had something to do with a new photographic process in which full-page messages would be transmitted on dots no bigger than the head of a pin. In fact he had been shown one under a microscope and told to watch for these dots in the messages he would receive. But he could give no further information.

Then a young Balkan arrived in New York City from South America. He checked into his hotel and didn't appear surprised when he found two FBI agents waiting for him in his room. There was no reason for surprise, because, even though recruited by the Germans as an espionage agent, it can now be revealed that he was working for the FBI.

"Did you bring them?" an agent asked.

The young man pulled from his pocket four blank telegraph messages. The papers were sent to the FBI Laboratory in Washington and under a fluorescent lamp a Laboratory technician saw tiny black dots embedded in the paper. He pried one of them loose; it was a dot no bigger than the period at the end of this sentence.

Under a microscope that enlarged the tiny object two hundred times, the technician saw a full-page message reproduced. He pried other "periods" loose from the papers and found all of them were messages reduced to midget size.[5]

This was the secret of the "dots," a triumph in photography.

Discovery of the micro-dot secret opened a door through which the FBI got onto the trail of espionage agents and their confederates, a trail that led through the United States and South America, and helped the FBI break up a German espionage ring in Mexico in cooperation with the Mexican Government.

One of the most successful double agents developed by the FBI had the code name of ND98. He was operating an import-export business in Germany when he was recruited for espionage by the Nazis. Like the others, he was schooled in secret writing, telegraphy and codes, and given instructions reproduced on the easily hidden microphotographs.

One day in 1941, ND98 was summoned to the Abwehr [6] office in Hamburg. A Nazi official told him:

> You will go to Uruguay and set up a radio transmitter. Here are the names of three persons who will send you information from America

concerning war production and military installations. Contact us when you have the radio ready. Here are your papers and instructions.

ND98 had a pleasant voyage to Montevideo. But once he was certain that he wasn't being watched, he met a U. S. State Department official. ND98 was willing to sell his services. Was the United States interested?

A few days later ND98 advised his Nazi espionage bosses:

Impossible to establish radio station and obtain information desired. Am going to United States where I will be able to operate more freely. Will contact you.

And then he proceeded to New York City, where he was taken in tow by the FBI.

Under FBI guidance, ND98 made the radio contact with Germany on February 20, 1942, from a secluded Long Island radio station similar to the one the FBI had set up for double-agent William Sebold twenty-one months earlier. The Nazis asked for information as quickly as possible on aircraft, ship and arms production and troop and cargo movements, and for any reports on new weapons.[7]

After a decent interval, the radio on Long Island sent a signal across the Atlantic. It was acknowledged by the German station at Hamburg. And ND98 began feeding information to Germany—information carefully prepared by the FBI and screened for security or furnished by the Joint Security Control operated under the direction of the Joint Chiefs of Staff.

The operation worked so smoothly that the FBI decided to put out a tentative feeler designed to trap other German spies. ND98 sent a message: "Urgently need help. Can you have reliable agents report to me?"

The feeler didn't succeed. The station in Hamburg radioed back: "You and your work too valuable to have you identified with anyone else."

But in August of 1943, the Hamburg station was grumbling that while ND98's information was good, it was certainly expensive. By this time the Nazis had paid him approximately $34,000, which was turned over to the Alien Property Custodian.[8]

ND98 replied: "Sorry you regard information as too expensive. If not satisfactory, will be glad to withdraw as strain and danger are great." The Abwehr hurriedly assured ND98 that not only was his work satisfactory but he would receive another $20,000 in due time.

ND98 acknowledged receipt of the promised bonus with a message in November broadly hinting that the United States planned a large-scale attack against the Northern Kurile Islands, a message which the

Joint Chiefs of Staff advised the FBI was dangerously close to the truth. The attack on the Kuriles, however, was to be merely a feint while the main American force hit the Marshall Islands. Just as expected, the Germans relayed the message to Japan. The Joint Chiefs later advised the FBI that there was reason to believe the information sent through ND98 had contributed to the successful attack on the Marshalls in February, 1944.

Among the final hoaxes played on the Nazis were a series of messages sent just before the Allied invasion of Normandy on June 6, 1944. The Germans were told that invasion plans had been delayed by a breakdown in the production of invasion boats and that troops had sailed from New York for the Mediterranean.

Five days before the Normandy invasion, ND98 radioed Hamburg:

Nevi reports that express liners Ile de France and New Amsterdam will leave New York.

Harbor for undisclosed Mediterranean destination within next few days. Appearing of highest importance possibly indicating some plan change. It appears that a force.

Consisting of a number of infantry and armored divisions originally scheduled for United Kingdom are being.

Diverted for a special operation. Will make every effort to ascertain further details.

At least ND98 added to the confusion of reports fed to the Germans on the Allied invasion plans. And for his war effort, Double Agent ND98 received $32,000 in salary, bonuses and expenses. The $55,000 supplied by the Germans was more than enough to cover the cost of the entire operation.[9]

The success of the Long Island radio operation is reflected in the log of radio messages sent from the Long Island station, which shows that the Germans doggedly maintained contact with ND98 up to the time the British captured Hamburg on May 2, 1945.[10]

22: *Why the Saboteurs Failed*

HITLER boasted in 1940 that his armies and air force were invincible. But even at the peak of the Nazi power in Europe, the German High Command was secretly worried. Air Marshal Hermann Goering and S. S. Chief Heinrich Himmler, among others, were complaining bitterly about the failure of the Abwehr to establish reliable agents in the United States.

The Abwehr chiefs were in an embarrassing position. Their espionage agents were being trapped singly and in groups by American counterespionage. Something had to be done to replace these agents, and also to cripple the American industrial giant by sabotage before it became too great a threat. All that the Fuehrer needed was time to consolidate his gains in Europe—and then it would be too late for the United States to intervene. So the Nazis reasoned.

The Abwehr decided on a bold gamble: agents who had once lived in America would be chosen, men who knew the country and its customs well. Some would be trained in espionage and others in sabotage. Then they would be slipped into the United States by submarines with enough money and sabotage supplies to last them for two years.

The plan was laid before Admiral Doenitz. He finally agreed to cooperate, with the understanding that only the best agents would be carried by the U-boats and that the agents would supply information of value to the German Navy, particularly to his U-boat commanders.[1]

The Abwehr agreed to Doenitz's conditions. The task of recruiting two of the sabotage teams was given to pudgy, bull-necked Lieutenant Walter Kappe, the same Walter Kappe who had come to the FBI's attention in the early 1930's when he was helping to promote the "Teutonia" association in Chicago and later the German-American Bund. Kappe had returned to Germany from the United States in 1937. At the outbreak of war, he had joined the German intelligence service, specializing in American affairs.

Kappe picked eight men from a group of prospects who had been thoroughly investigated and approved by the Abwehr. The oldest of the eight was George Dasch, thirty-nine, who worked in the German Foreign Office as a radio monitor. Dasch could have become an American citizen in September, 1939, by taking the last step in obtaining citizenship, the oath of allegiance to his adopted country. But he had returned to Germany before he was notified to appear in Federal Court in New York City for the oath-taking ceremony. The German Government had financed his return.

Dasch and his seven companions-to-be, who also knew America

well, entered the Nazi sabotage school at Quentz Lake, near Berlin, in April, 1942. They were taught in theory and in practice how to use explosives, incendiaries, detonators and timing devices. They were taught how to wreck an industrial machine or an engine with abrasive material, and how to place an explosive charge to get the maximum damage to a bridge or a plant. Each man memorized the location of the targets, most of them aluminum plants, Ohio River locks and railroads. They rehearsed phony life stories as an actor learns his lines for a play. And these life stories were documented with false birth certificates, draft deferment cards, Social Security cards, and automobile drivers' licenses.

At last the men were ready. Lieutenant Kappe took his pupils from Quentz Lake to the submarine base at Lorient, France, where the final preparations were made. Dasch was the leader of team Number 1, which included Ernest Burger, thirty-five; Heinrich Heinck, thirty-four; and Richard Quirin, thirty-four. Team Number 2 was under the command of thirty-two-year-old Edward Kerling. His companions were Herman Neubauer, thirty-two; Werner Thiel, thirty-five; and twenty-two-year-old Herbert Haupt.

Kappe gave each team leader $50,000 to be used as a general fund, plus another $20,000 each to be divided equally among the men as needed. In addition, there was a money belt for each containing $4,000 and a wallet stuffed with $400 in small bills. In all, the saboteurs carried a small fortune of $175,200, most of it in fifty-dollar bills.

Kerling and his men boarded a submarine, and on the night of May 26 the raider slipped out to sea. Two nights later, U-boat Number 202, the *Innsbruck,* left the submarine base carrying Dasch and his team. Each group carried four waterproofed boxes containing high explosives, TNT molded to look like pieces of coal, fuses, detonators, primers and an assortment of mechanical and chemical timing devices.

After reaching the United States, the men were to split up in pairs. The Dasch team's primary sabotage targets were the Aluminum Company of America plant in Alcoa, Tennessee; an aluminum plant at East St. Louis, Illinois; the Cryolite plant at Philadelphia; and the locks on the Ohio River from Pittsburgh to Louisville, Kentucky. Kerling and his men were to concentrate on railroad sabotage. They were to place explosives in the Pennsylvania Railroad station at Newark. N. J.; attempt to blow up a section of the Hell Gate railroad bridge across the East River in New York City; and disrupt facilities of the Chesapeake and Ohio Railroad. They were not to make any effort to conceal the fact that their destruction was the work of saboteurs. Part of their job was to create fear and confusion while slowing up rail shipments and production in the light-metals industry in particular.

Sixteen days and sixteen nights after leaving Lorient, the *Innsbruck* surfaced off the beach near the town of Amagansett, Long Island. The U-boat moved slowly through a heavy fog to a point about 440 yards offshore, and then the motors were stilled. It was almost midnight on Friday, June 12, when seamen scrambled on deck and inflated a rubber boat. The four saboteurs, dressed in German Marine fatigue uniforms and unarmed, climbed into the boat. Two seamen manned the oars and the boat rode through the surf; the Germans scrambled onto the beach. In the confusion the seamen dropped their oars and the boat was swamped, but the equipment was hauled to safety. The seamen struggled frantically to haul the boat onto the beach and empty it of water while the saboteurs quickly changed to civilian clothes.

At about the same time the saboteurs were landing, twenty-one-year-old Seaman 2/c John Cullen was leaving the Amagansett Coast Guard station to make the midnight beach patrol. He was alone and unarmed and the fog swirled around him on the lonely stretch of sand. The beam from his flashlight was a white cone stretching into gray nothingness. He could see only a few yards in any direction.

Dasch saw the light approaching. He was horrified. The man must not see the uniformed submariners at the water's edge. Dasch hurried forward to intercept Cullen and recognized the Coast Guard uniform.

"What's going on here?" demanded Cullen. "Who are you?" He saw that two men were struggling with an object in the water.

Dasch said casually, "There's nothing wrong. We're fishermen. Our boat ran aground and we're going to wait here until daylight." He explained that he and his friends had left East Hampton intending to go to Montauk Point when they became lost in the fog.

Cullen exclaimed, "What do you mean East Hampton and Montauk Point? Do you know where you are?"

"I thought you should know," Dasch said. "Where is your station?"

"It's right up there. My station is Amagansett."

Dasch, who knew Long Island well, realized that the skipper of the *Innsbruck* had crossed more than three thousand miles of the Atlantic and missed his target of East Hampton by only three miles. But that three-mile error was endangering the entire expedition. For a moment Dasch considered the idea of luring Cullen to the rubber boat and then shanghaiing him aboard the submarine. He decided to try bribery instead.

Cullen said, "It will be four hours until sunup. You had better come with me to the station."

Dasch nodded and walked up the beach with Cullen but then he stopped. "Wait a minute," he said. "I'm not going with you."

"You'll have to go," the youth retorted.

"Now, listen," Dasch growled. "How old are you? Do you have a father and mother? I don't want to kill you. You don't know what this is all about. Why don't you forget it? Here is some money. Go out and have yourself a good time."

"I don't want the money," Cullen said. But then from out of the fog a man ran up to Dasch and said something in German. Dasch clapped his hand over the man's mouth and snapped, "Shut up!"

Cullen was thoroughly alarmed now. He didn't know how many men were out there in the fog or what they might do to him. He had no way to defend himself from a gang attack.

Dasch grabbed Cullen by the arm and said, "Come over here!" He shoved a wad of bills into the Coast Guardsman's hand and stared at him. "Look in my eyes! Look in my eyes! Would you know me if you ever saw me again?"

"No," Cullen said. "I have never seen you before."

"You might see me in East Hampton."

Cullen began backing away. "I never saw you," he said. Once out of sight of Dasch, Cullen turned and ran for his station to sound the alarm.[2]

Dasch returned to his companions. "It's all right," he said. "I fixed everything."

Quickly the four saboteurs buried the clothing and boxes of equipment in the sand dunes, taking a bearing on a crude cross—a slab of wood nailed to a post sticking from the sand. Then they walked across the dunes to a macadam road. Hiding in the dunes whenever a car passed, they waited for daybreak.

Back at the Coast Guard station, Cullen aroused four of his mates and told them what had happened. He showed them the money— $260. The five men armed themselves and went back to the beach but they found nothing. The only sound came from engines throbbing out on the fog-shrouded water.

"Three of us laid around on the top of the beach where I had seen him [Dasch]," Cullen said later. "We stayed there for a while and then we heard these motors out on the water, but we couldn't see anything. We thought they were coming back . . . The motors cut off and we did not hear them . . ."

The motors they heard were those of the *Innsbruck,* which was stuck on a sand bar. The U-boat floated free with the tide.

At daybreak, Coast Guardsmen from the Amagansett station again returned to the beach. They found footprints and followed them into the dunes, where they found the buried cache of equipment and the German uniforms. The saboteurs had been too excited to smooth the sand and cover their tracks. A truck was called and the boxes were taken to the station for closer examination.

While the Coast Guardsmen were discovering the buried boxes, Dasch and his companions were walking across the fields to the tracks of the Long Island Railroad. They followed the tracks to the Amagansett station but it was locked. The four men sat on the platform waiting. It was 5:30 A.M.

Finally the ticket agent opened the station and Dasch bought four tickets.

"You're out early this morning," the ticket agent said genially.

"Yes," Dasch said, "We've been fishing."

The saboteurs boarded the 6:57.

In the city, Dasch and Burger registered at the Governor Clinton Hotel. Heinck and Quirin checked into the Hotel Martinique under the names "Henry Kayner" and "Richard Quintas."

Warning that enemy agents had landed on Long Island reached the FBI shortly before noon, almost twelve hours after the landing. The warning came when Assistant Special Agent in Charge T. J. Donegan of the New York FBI office received a telephone call asking him to come to the office of Coast Guard Captain J. S. Bayliss. There he learned what had happened on the beach and he saw the cases of sabotage equipment. Coast Guard and Naval officers at the meeting agreed the FBI should take over the responsibility of running down the spies. Director Hoover ordered the FBI into action.

Hoover had a vivid memory of the terrible Black Tom explosion in World War I, the bomb explosions, and the fires that wiped out chemical and powder plants. He was fearful these things might happen again with enemy agents at large.

The day after their landing, Dasch and Burger sat in Dasch's hotel room and talked. The blood-pounding excitement was gone now. In their hearts they knew they were hunted men. They were well aware that death was the usual penalty for wartime espionage and sabotage, and their courage was oozing away.

Dasch told Burger, "I'm going to notify the FBI. I'm going to Washington and tell them everything." Burger nodded. He had had enough.

On Sunday evening, an agent in the New York FBI office received a mysterious telephone call.

"I am Franz Daniel Pastorious," a man said. "I want you to know that I shall get in touch with your Washington office next Thursday or Friday. I have some important information."

"What is your information?" the agent asked. The only reply was a click, and the line went dead. The agent shrugged. Another screwball call. But he made the usual memorandum for the record.

It was 10 A.M. on Friday, June 19, when the man who called himself Pastorious rang the FBI Headquarters and asked to speak to Hoover.

"I'm the man who called your New York office last Sunday," the caller said. "My real name is George John Dasch. I have just arrived from Germany with some important information. I am in room 351 at the Mayflower Hotel."

Within a matter of minutes, two FBI agents were at the hotel. They brought Dasch to Headquarters, where he poured out the story of the sabotage school, Kappe, the voyage by submarine, the landing, the meeting with Cullen and, finally, the decision with Burger to quit the game. He told them of Edward Kerling and his team, who, he supposed, were loose somewhere in the United States. He gave the agents a handkerchief on which had been written, in secret ink, the names of persons he was told to contact in the United States.

Where had he been since making the call to the FBI in New York? He had been shopping and playing pinochle with old friends.

Kerling had better luck in landing than Dasch. His team landed undetected just before dawn on June 17 at Ponte Vedra Beach about twenty-five miles south of Jacksonville, Fla. They buried their boxes of equipment near the beach and then, about noon, caught a bus into Jacksonville, where they spent the night in hotels. Kerling and Thiel went to New York by way of Cincinnati, Haupt and Neubauer to Chicago, traveling by train.

From the records of previous investigations [3] made of persons who had returned to Germany before the war, FBI agents located relatives and friends of the saboteurs and kept them under surveillance. Burger was followed in New York City and, not realizing he was being trailed, led agents to Heinck and Quirin. Kerling and Thiel were caught in New York City when Kerling contacted a man whose name was listed on Dasch's handkerchief. Neubauer was found in Chicago registered at a hotel under the alias H. Nicholas, a name supplied by Dasch.

As the net closed, young Haupt made a bold effort to throw agents off his trail. One day he walked into the Chicago FBI office and asked to see the Agent in Charge. Even at that time he was being shadowed.

"I understand the FBI has been inquiring about my selective-service status," Haupt said. "There has been a misunderstanding. I went to Mexico to avoid being forced into marriage and that caused trouble with my draft board. But I've got it all straightened out now and I'd like permission to go to work."

"We're no longer interested in your case," the agent told Haupt. "Since you've got things straight, you're free to do whatever you wish as far as we're concerned."

But when Haupt walked from the office he was followed. Before arresting him the FBI wanted to know whether or not he had enlisted any helpers or had made any contacts with other enemy agents.

Fourteen days after the first saboteurs had landed on Long Island, all eight of them were in the custody of the FBI. The Nazis' grandiose scheme of sabotage had failed. In two weeks on American soil, the men had managed to spend only $611.38 of the $175,200 treasury.

Immediately after hearing of the landing of the saboteurs, Hoover informed the White House and the Attorney General. FDR told Hoover that when the saboteurs were caught, the news should be made public as quickly as possible in order to discourage any further landings.

Hoover's announcement of the capture of the eight saboteurs was a jolt to Nazi sabotage hopes. Admiral Doenitz was so enraged that his submarines had been risked in such an abortive venture [4] that for months he refused to listen to any more Abwehr plans that called for U-boat transportation.[5]

But Doenitz did give in to the entreaties of the political intelligence section of the Abwehr late in 1944. This time one of his U-boats carried espionage agents Erich Gimpel, a radio expert, and William Curtis Colepaugh, a renegade American who had found the Nazi ideologies to his liking. Both men had been given espionage training. Between them they carried $60,000 in American money.

Gimpel and Colepaugh were landed at Crab Tree Point, Maine, about 11:00 P.M. on November 29, during a snowstorm. Curiously, neither man had remembered to bring an overcoat or a hat. They bent their heads to the wind and walked inland until they came to Highway 1. They flagged an automobile, which happened to be a taxi, and the driver agreed to drive them the thirty-five miles into Bangor, Maine. Early the next morning Gimpel and Colepaugh were en route to New York City.

The FBI got on the trail of Gimpel and Colepaugh because several people, including an eighteen-year-old son of a deputy sheriff, thought it was strange that two men without hats or overcoats should be walking from the beach in a snowstorm. Their suspicions were reported to the FBI.

The incident might have had no significance except that Boston FBI agents knew that a British freighter, the *Cornwallis,* had been torpedoed and sunk on December 3 off the Maine coast near Bar Harbor. They reasoned that a submarine operating in that area could easily have dropped spies on the beach; and the suspicions of the young man set them to searching for the two strangers.

But Colepaugh, like Dasch and Burger, tossed in the towel in the first round. He slipped away from Gimpel and went to the home of a friend in Richmond Hill, New York. He confessed that he was a spy and the friend called the FBI on December 26.

Colepaugh was talkative. He told agents he had ditched Gimpel in the city and didn't know where he could be found. But he recalled that Gimpel had a habit of buying Peruvian newspapers at a subway newsstand at Times Square. Colepaugh remembered also that Gimpel had a peculiar habit of tucking dollar bills in the breast pocket of his suit coat. Gimpel, he said, was using the name "Edward Green" as an alias.

FBI offices across the nation were given Gimpel's description when it was found that he had left the apartment where he and Colepaugh had lived. Agents began checking hotels. They checked with ticket agents, airlines, general delivery windows at post offices, and at newsstands handling South American papers. An "Edward Green" was registered at a New York hotel, but the man didn't use the room and after two days the hotel gave it to another guest.

The search ended at the Times Square newsstand. Four days after Colepaugh's confession, two agents saw a man approach the newsstand which had been under twenty-four-hour surveillance. He fitted the description given by Colepaugh. The man selected a magazine and then reached into the breast pocket of his suit and pulled out a bill. The agents nodded to each other.

Gimpel tried to bully his way out of the arrest. But it was no use. The agents found $10,000 in cash in his pockets and ninety-nine small diamonds wrapped in tissue paper. Another $44,000 was found in his hotel room. Gimpel confessed.[6]

Throughout the war years the FBI investigated 19,649 cases in which sabotage was suspected, but there was not a single case of enemy-directed sabotage to be found. The enemy was never able to establish an apparatus for espionage and sabotage such as the Germans had in World War I. The suspected sabotage cases were, for the most part, industrial accidents caused by fatigue, carelessness, spite, a momentary burst of anger or horseplay among workers. But each accident affecting the war effort, and reported to the FBI, had to be investigated.

There was the case in which a trainload of soldiers was derailed. The investigation disclosed it was done by three small boys "just for the fun of it." A Kalamazoo worker loosened the cutting tool of his machine to spite a night-shift worker who had left the machine in poor working condition for him. An amorous nineteen-year-old bashed an electric steel furnace with a sledge hammer until the brick lining collapsed and the furnace was ruined—because he wanted to get off early to meet his girl friend. An explosion wrecked a hoist at a mine in Kentucky—the work of a former employee who wanted to get revenge on the mine superintendent. An Arkansas box plant was destroyed by a worker who had been fired. A twenty-one-year-old Naval inspector at an aircraft factory was found responsible for 150 acts of sabotage to aircraft; he didn't like plant inspectors and enjoyed causing them trouble.

Hoover urged the Department of Justice to take action under the federal sabotage laws against those who deliberately slowed down war production, regardless of whether union or nonunion workers were involved. He argued also that acts of carelessness and personal spite, when they damaged war production, had the effect of deliberate sabotage. There was the case, cited by Hoover, in which a worker in a sudden fit of temper plunged a spike into an airplane fuel tank, an act which might have cost the lives of a bomber crew had the damage not been discovered. Hoover felt a stern policy would discourage horseplay and carelessness. But the Department took the position that a get-tough policy toward workers in war industries would do more harm than good.

Even before the United States entered the war, the FBI had, at the request of the Army and Navy, developed a system of cooperation with workmen in defense plants as a check against sabotage and slowdowns in plants with government war contracts. In World War I the Navy had initiated a plant protection program as a means of reducing the fires, explosions, accidents and labor frictions which affected war production, and the Navy plan had been adopted by the Army and the U. S. Shipping Board's Emergency Fleet Corporation. In 1931, the military agreed that in another emergency this work should be handled by the FBI.

It was through these specially designated workmen who furnished information to the FBI that it was possible to determine in hundreds of cases that accidents—not enemy sabotage—were responsible for damaged material, machinery and plant equipment. The informants were volunteers.

In this program Attorney General Robert H. Jackson authorized the FBI to recommend to plant managers on the Army and Navy production priority lists that their employees be fingerprinted. And Jackson also authorized the Bureau to give the Armed Services copies of reports on any workers in defense plants found to have a criminal record. It was through this antisabotage machinery that the FBI learned early in the war of the extent of Communist infiltration of some labor unions and was forewarned of the scope of the Communist Party's activities.

The plant informant program was roundly attacked in some quarters as a spy system directed against labor. The FBI's instructions to informants were: "The FBI is not interested in matters involving the relationship between employers and employees as such or regular labor activities, but only in matters affecting the national defense." But denials would not still the accusations.

The untold story back of the FBI's antisabotage and antiespionage precautions was that Hoover had two primary motives in initiating them: first, there must not be any enemy espionage and sabotage such as there had been in World War I; and second, there must not be permitted to develop any vigilante system of wartime law enforcement. The records of the FBI reveal Hoover's motives to be that simple.

After the Pearl Harbor attack, the FBI was flooded with offers from citizens who wanted to help in the war effort. In Hollywood, movie magnate Cecil B. DeMille offered to organize, head and finance an "FBI unit" throughout the picture industry. The proposal was relayed to Hoover by James Roosevelt, the President's son.

"I appreciate deeply the very generous and patriotic offer made by DeMille," Hoover informed his Special Agent in Charge at Los Angeles, "but at the present time it does not seem necessary for us to avail ourselves of it as we have the situation well in hand . . . I do not think the present situation warrants the establishment of any so-called auxiliary of the FBI. . . ."

Hoover knew that proper law enforcement and protection against subversion depended on information, not vigilantes. He knew the FBI had to have reliable sources of information to build up a sound security system. He was reasonably sure, also, that if professional law enforcement officers failed to do the job properly, then amateurs would take over. No matter how patriotic and well meaning they might be, they were not equipped by training or experience for the job.

During the summer of 1940, the American Legion considered a plan under which 11,000 Legion posts would organize their own investigative agency to help combat subversion. In brief, each post would name two or more members who would be given special badges, a manual of instructions and credentials of identification. This force would investigate subversive activities and report to local law enforcement agencies.

American Legion leaders laid their plan before Attorney General Jackson but Jackson took the position that patriotic groups and individuals shouldn't engage in investigative activities, which was a job for professionals. He suggested that any information having to do with subversion be turned over to the FBI.

Some Legionnaires felt they were being shut out of the national defense effort and began actively campaigning within the organization for an investigative corps. It was at this point that Hoover laid before American Legion officers a counter-plan to enlist the help of the Le-

gionnaires but at the same time avoid the growth of a vigilante movement. The FBI plan suggested a liaison arrangement between Post
Commanders and Special Agents in Charge of field divisions for discussions of national defense problems. Whenever a Legionnaire was in a
position to furnish confidential information about a particular problem, he would be designated to make reports to the FBI; but any investigation would be made by the FBI, not the Legionnaire.

The proposal was accepted by the American Legion at its conference in Indianapolis in November, 1940, and this acceptance laid the
basis for the wartime cooperation between the FBI and the Legion.
The Legion's cooperation was typical of the aid given the FBI by many
civic, fraternal and professional groups.

The security program also included local law enforcement officers,
who were drawn together for courses of instruction on such problems
as convoy traffic, protection of public utilities, civil defense organization and the investigation of espionage, sabotage and subversion. The
lessons taught were based largely on the British wartime experiences.
These schools were attended by 73,164 law enforcement officers from
1940 to 1942.

From this security network the FBI received information not only
from the military intelligence services, but also from workers in industry, the Legion, police officers and others who were mobilized for
the war effort. Against this alignment, saboteurs made little headway.

Those were tense and exciting years in which odd stories unfolded.
But there was no greater oddity than the FBI's brief adventure into
the realm of helping the Navy "kill" an enemy submarine.

Two weeks after the Pearl Harbor attack, operators at the Radio
Corporation of America, Communications (RCAC), radio station at
Point Reyes, some forty-five miles northwest of San Francisco, heard
two strange radio stations exchanging messages. Checking with directional antenna, they figured that the strong station was probably a land
station in Japan and the weaker station a submarine not far off the
California coast.

They told their story to an FBI agent. "When you're not busy," the
agent said, "how about monitoring that wave length? If you hear anything, give us a call." The operators agreed.

Five days later, shortly before noon on December 26, one of the
RCAC operators called the San Francisco FBI office.

"That station is sending again," he said. "Sounds like a mobile
marine unit at 6908 kilocycles and it could be close."

The FBI agents quickly called the FCC monitoring station at Portland, Oregon, the radio room of the Pan American Airways System at
Treasure Island in San Francisco Bay, and the FCC monitoring station

at Santa Ana, near Los Angeles. These stations were asked to tune in and take a directional reading on the strange station. The telephone lines were held open.

The bearings taken by the FCC stations were given to the Pan American radio room. In less than five minutes, the operator called and said: "According to my charting, that offshore station is sending from 40 degrees 1 minute north latitude and 124 degrees 6 minutes west longitude. That's about eight miles off the coast of California at Point Mendocine—about 200 miles northwest of here." The position of the suspect station was telephoned to the Pacific Naval Coastal Frontier office, which relayed the information to a PBY patrol bomber. Ten minutes later the Navy called to report receipt of a message from the plane: "Attacking enemy submarine Opal 18."

The submarine spotted the PBY and crash dived. The plane dropped one bomb behind the submarine and then placed another in its forward track. In less than two minutes, Army bombers arrived and depth charges were dropped. An oil slick spread over the water. The Navy bomber crew reported their belief that the first bomb had exploded close enough to open the submarine's plates, and that the craft had been destroyed.

Maybe. Maybe not. But FBI men like to think they helped get one enemy submarine.

23 : *The Perilous Fight South of the Border*

You are a better judge than I as to whether the time has come to tell the story of the western hemisphere operation. Told or not, it is the story of a great piece of work. I do not think a similar operation has ever been carried on; and I can personally attest to the brilliance of its results.

> (*From a 1946 letter written by former Assistant Secretary of State Adolf A. Berle, Jr., to FBI Director J. Edgar Hoover.*)

For more than sixteen years the FBI has remained silent about its amazing operation in which special agents often risked their lives [1] in helping smash the Nazis' World War II spy networks in Central and South America.

The story began in 1940, when President Roosevelt and others in his Administration realized with grave concern, from evidence obtained in spy cases, that Axis agents had established a string of espionage bases from Mexico City southward to the Strait of Magellan.

Actually, South America had become a staging ground for Nazi spies being slipped into the United States. Information on American defense and industrial efforts was being funneled through South America to Germany. Clandestine radio stations beamed on Hamburg, Cologne and Brussels were pumping military, political and economic reports to the Nazis' spy headquarters. And some Germans had turned from daydreams of *"lebensraum"* to the practical planning of ways and means to conquer South America for Hitler.

Long before Hitler's star had begun to rise, Germans had migrated to South America and settled in the growing countries in colonies which, for the most part, clung to German customs, language and culture. In the late 1930's, an estimated 360,000 German nationals and native-born descendants lived in Brazil, 194,000 in Argentina and 129,000 in Chile. The concentrations were mostly in areas like the state of Santa Catarina in Southern Brazil, the Misiones District of Northern Argentina and the Valdivia region of South Central Chile.

The Nazi movement took hold in these areas. Germans wore the uniforms of storm troopers and carried the Nazi flag on ceremonial occasions. There were German youth movements, a German labor front, a German Workers' Party, and a German war veterans' organization.

As early as 1911, Richard Tannenberg, in his book *Greater Germany: Work of the Twentieth Century,* advanced the theory that much of Brazil and Argentina, and all of Uruguay, Paraguay and eastern Bolivia one day would be a German-controlled colony in the New World. And then a former German soldier and one of the leading Nazis in South America, Arnold Fuhrmann, drew up a plan for the Nazi conquest of Uruguay by troops recruited in Uruguay and Argentina.[2]

The FBI, through its own counterespionage and from reports by other intelligence agencies and the British, realized that the best way to control Nazi espionage in the United States was to wipe out the spy nests in Latin America. But this could be done only through cooperation with and by the Central and South American governments. It would be an operation calling for skill and diplomacy, because it would have to achieve results without embarrassing either the United States or any of our southern neighbors.

FBI Director Hoover discussed the problem early in May with Assistant Secretary of State Adolf A. Berle, Jr., and again in early June with Berle, General Sherman Miles, Assistant Chief of Staff of Army G-2, and Admiral Walter S. Anderson, Director of Naval Intelligence. Out of these meetings came a proposal for the organization of a Special Intelligence Service (SIS) to operate in the foreign field. Berle agreed to lay the plan before the State Department and the President, to get their approval.

It was agreed that the Special Intelligence Service would act as a service agency, furnishing the State Department, the military, the FBI and other governmental agencies with information having to do with financial, economic, political and subversive activities detrimental to the security of the United States. Army and Navy intelligence would continue coverage in their own specialized fields.

When Berle called on the President for a decision on areas of responsibility in foreign intelligence, Roosevelt decided that Hoover and his men would be responsible for nonmilitary intelligence coverage in the Western Hemisphere. On June 24, he issued a directive setting forth the lines of responsibility, and in less than thirty days the FBI had organized an SIS operation and agents were soon drifting south. Most of them were men who had developed special skills in undercover work, and they went south secretly as undercover agents. Later others were openly attached to embassies or were stationed at strategic points as liaison officers with the national and local police forces, with approval of the governments involved.[3]

One undercover agent went to South America as a soap salesman for an American concern whose officials never suspected his role with the FBI. He sold so much soap within a few months that the company had to expand its import and distribution operations and then settle a dispute over the franchise. A local businessman who had been with a firm which had given up the franchise was howling to get it back. Meantime the demon soap salesman had made valuable contacts in business and government circles.

One young man opened a stockbrokerage business, bought a membership in the stock exchange and sent out a stock-market report that drew favorable attention in Argentine business circles. He had wire communications with New York and soon his margin accounts for customers dealing with the New York Stock Exchange were well above $600,000. He turned a neat profit, but his reports to the FBI were even more informative than the reports to his stock customers.

In another Argentine city, a boyish-looking American arrived to work as a reporter. He joined local clubs and soon he was sending articles to the United States and receiving favorable comment from publications interested in Latin American affairs. This particular young reporter was an FBI agent whom we shall call George Stevens. One of his favorite hangouts was a small hotel operated by a man whose parents still lived in a country overrun by the Nazis, but who refused to be blackmailed into becoming a spy.

The innkeeper was the leader of an organization whose members were scattered throughout the city in businesses of their own and in every important utility, private business and government agency in town. Somehow the innkeeper seemed to absorb all the talk that passed across his tables in the course of a day. Stevens decided to try to enlist his help. He went to the inn.

Over a cup of coffee, Stevens said, "I would like to do a series of stories on the national groups in the city. I'd like your help in gathering the information." He watched closely to see what the man's reaction would be.

The man looked at the young American for a full minute. Then he said quietly, "If I give you this information, will it reach the right people?"

Stevens nodded. "Yes. And I promise you'll never be embarrassed." There was no other agreement or explanation. None was needed. They understood each other.

"I never knew anyone like this man," Stevens recalled later. "His people trusted him so completely that if he had told them to jump off a cliff, they would have done it.

"At least once a week the police would follow me. But I always knew in advance when I was to be followed—and that was always the day I worked hard at being a reporter. That was always the day, too, when I would call on the chief of detectives, telling him I just happened to be passing by and would he have a cup of coffee with me. It must have driven the guy nuts—and the detectives who were trailing me, too. They never knew I was being tipped by the innkeeper, who had a well-placed friend at the police station.

"One day our people got word to me that two Germans suspected of espionage had driven by automobile into a neighboring country. I was supposed to find out who they were, where they had gone, whom they had seen, and if they were coming back. That's a pretty tough assignment when you don't even know the names of the men.

"Well, I went to my friend. He said to come back in a few days. I went back. He said come back later. I went back later. He shook his head. I said, 'This time I asked too much, didn't I?' He said, 'Come back tomorrow.' I figured he was stalling.

"When I returned, he gave me a typewritten report identifying the Germans. He had the license number of their car and the serial number of the engine. He knew where they had gone and he even had the

gist of their conversation as they drove as well as the fact they were
to meet later in Argentina. And instead of two Germans there had
been three Germans. It was one of the most detailed reports I ever
saw and it helped uncover an espionage ring.

" 'Would you mind telling me how you got it?' I asked him.

"He smiled and said: 'The man who drove their car was one of my
men. When those people ask for a car in this city, the driver always is
my man.' "

Stevens recalled that once he almost wrecked his relationship with
the innkeeper. "He did so much for us I offered to pay for the information. I thought he was going to throw me out of his place. But he
cooled off and said: 'What I do for you, I do from my heart—not
for money.' I finally got out of an awkward situation by saying I
didn't mean he should take money personally but that I felt he should
allow me to help pay the expense of gathering information for us. He
was a good friend and a good ally."

Most of the Central and South American governments willingly
helped in the counterespionage program, but there were places, such
as Argentina, where hostile police and government officials made the
work difficult and dangerous. There agents frequently found themselves shadowed and informants caught by the police told of inquisi-
tions with the *picana electrica,* the electric spur, which caused an agony
of pain when inserted into a sensitive part of the body.

Until Argentina severed relations with the Axis in 1944, the SIS
kept a battered old motor launch hidden on the Rio de la Plata in
Buenos Aires harbor. Frequently at night an undercover agent or an
informant sought by the police would slip through the shadows along
the water front. There would be a whispered conversation with the
boat's native skipper. And soon "Crandall's Navy," as FBI agents had
dubbed the boat in honor of the agent who conceived the escape idea,
would slide out of hiding and, dodging the harbor patrol, carry the
hunted man and his information upstream toward the Parana and then
to the safety of Montevideo, Uruguay.

SIS agents penetrated the "Green Hell" of the Choco jungle in Colombia trailing platinum smugglers. They tramped the rugged coasts
looking for submarine hiding places. They traveled by canoe on the
headwaters of the Amazon, where the tributaries are infested with pira-
nhas, the vicious little man-eating fish. They helped track down the loca-
tions of hidden radios and, working with the State Department, Army
and Naval intelligence, the British and local police, pieced together
the astonishing story of one of the Germans' greatest spy networks.

Out of the mass of information came a clear picture. The Nazis'
intelligence apparatus in the Western Hemisphere was centered pri-

marily in Brazil, Argentina, Chile and Mexico, although it extended into every Central and South American country. Mexico's chief importance was in the country's proximity to the United States.

This was the situation which confronted the United States as the war clouds gathered. The United States' own "soft underbelly" was exposed in a time of crisis unless the Americas stood together.

Brazil severed diplomatic relations with the Axis in early 1942. That was the signal for SIS agents to join forces with the Brazilian authorities in their cleanup of Nazi spy rings which operated six clandestine radio stations in Brazil alone. Messages between these stations and German stations in Europe had been intercepted for months by FCC and FBI monitoring stations. The messages had been decoded and analyzed for the benefit of SIS agents in Brazil and the information had been given to the State Department. Most of the Axis agents and their cover names were known to the Americans. But when Brazil broke with the Axis, the police and SIS agents had not yet identified the mystery man who directed a spy ring which operated around a clandestine radio station known by its call letters, CIT.

The mystery man was Josef Jacob Johannes Starziczny, engineer and scientist. The Nazis recruited Starziczny to espionage in 1940 and trained him in secret writing, codes and radio telegraphy. The original plan was to drop him by parachute into England, but Starziczny's courage failed him and he was sent to Brazil instead, under the name Niels Christian Christensen.

This little man who peered owlishly through thick glasses arrived in Rio de Janeiro on April 6, 1941, aboard the SS *Hermes*. He smuggled ashore a black leather bag containing a radio transmitter, four code books and microphotographic instructions. He also carried a letter of introduction to Otto Uebele, the German consul in Santos and manager of Theodor Wille and Company. The letter ordered Uebele to advance Christensen $5,000 and to help him in his mission. A month later a secret radio station using the call letters CIT went on the air with messages to Germany. Starziczny was in operation.

Some people are string savers. Starziczny, alias Christensen, was a man who squirreled away every paper and document he received. Despite orders to destroy messages and letters in his espionage work, the neat and orderly little man filed them away in neat and orderly fashion.

This weakness for saving papers was a time bomb for German espionage in Brazil. And Starziczny lit the fuse when he went to Santos, Brazil, to install a transmitter and found he needed a wave meter. He went to a small radio shop to make the purchase in December, 1941.

"I don't have one in stock," the shopkeeper said, "but if you will leave your name and address, I shall forward it to you."

Starziczny wrote on a piece of paper, "O. Mendes, Hotel Santos, Santos."

The shopkeeper was suspicious of Mr. Mendes. Brazilian authorities had warned dealers to be cautious in selling radio parts and accessories to strangers. The shopkeeper called in the police and gave them the name and address.

There was no "O. Mendes" registered at the Hotel Santos, of course. But in mid-February, 1942, the shopkeeper received a call from a Santos firm asking about the wave meter ordered by Mendes. This same firm, the shopkeeper recalled, had made an earlier purchase of a transmitter and a wave meter and these facts were passed on to the SIS.

Police, working closely with the SIS and the State Department, traced these purchases from collaborator to collaborator until the description of "O. Mendes" began to merge with that of Niels Christian Christensen, the "Danish" engineer in Rio de Janeiro. Christensen was arrested and it was found that his true identity was Starziczny.

Starziczny's home and his safe-deposit box at the bank were a treasure house of espionage information. He had kept messages, codes, secret instructions—and the names of other agents. An unregistered radio transmitter was found hidden in a trunk.

Starziczny's arrest was a blow to the Nazis. But the most shattering blow came with exposure of the operations of a spy ring centered around the radio station CEL.

The chief of the CEL ring was handsome and urbane Albrecht Gustav Engels, who worked closely with the German Embassy through Hermann Bohny, the German Naval Attaché stationed in Rio de Janeiro.

Engels was ranking executive and director of an electric light and power company, and a man with many important connections throughout South America. He was a loyal German and he was disturbed, perhaps even alarmed, when Erich Leonhardt Immer returned from Germany in 1940 and informed him that he, Immer, was to direct an espionage operation in Brazil. Engels was shocked that his government should trust such an important mission to a nobody, a man he regarded as having the caliber of a "third-class clerk," even though he was an engineer by profession.

Engels' judgment of Immer was harsh; but in looking down his Prussian nose, Engels had seen Immer for what he was—an inept and not overintelligent fellow who was undertaking an assignment which should have been entrusted only to his intellectual betters.

Immer made his first mistake soon after he began enlisting his agents. He gave a micro-dot to one of his agents, and the agent took it to a German optician to have it read under his microscope. The optician was so startled by this stupid bit of work that he notified the German Embassy of the incident. Bohny was furious that Immer should have chosen an agent with such total lack of discretion and risked exposure of the entire espionage effort.

Soon after the micro-dot incident, Immer received a message which ordered him to return to Germany immediately. He hurried back, doubtless expecting important conferences and new instructions. One can only guess at what happened when he checked into the Abwehr headquarters in Berlin and was ushered into the office of his superior. The little scene probably went something like this:

Immer's superior looks at the visitor in astonishment. "What are you doing here? Why aren't you in Rio de Janeiro?"

"Because, sir, you ordered me to return."

"Don't be ridiculous. I didn't order your return."

Immer, now thoroughly confused and frightened, pulls a message from his pocket.

"But here is your message!"

His superior looks at the message. "You fool! I didn't send any such orders!" He throws the paper back to Immer, who looks at it stupidly. The Abwehr chief shouts: "Get out!" And Immer, dazed, stumbles out. . . . Later he wrote bitterly to a friend that he had been tricked by Engels and Bohny.

The Engels-Bohny combination was a potent one. They kept Germany advised on shipping, economic and political affairs in the Americas, and the construction of the giant international airport at Natal, Brazil, through which American bombers and aircraft were to be shuttled en route to the Middle East.

Messages such as these were received and sent:

From: ALD   10/7/41
To: CEL

PROCURING OF THE FOLLOWING UNITED STATES JOURNALS IS OF THE GREATEST INTEREST: ARMY NAVY JOURNAL, MARINE ENGINEERING AND SHIPPING REVIEW, PACIFIC MARINE REVIEW, MARINE NEWS, ARMY NAVY REGISTER. HEREIN THERE ARE DISCUSSIONS ABOUT SHIP CONSTRUCTION AND REPAIR NEWS OF ESPECIAL VALUE. 63. STEIN.

From: CEL   9/29/41
To: ALD

ESKADELEGATE [4] WITH CARGO OF ORE LEFT ON NOVEMBER 28 AT 15 O'CLOCK BRAZIL TIME DECLARED FOR ENGLAND. TURNED ON THE HIGH SEAS ON THE COURSE FOR SOUTH AFRICA. PROFILE CHANGED BY ONLY ONE MAST. ALFREDO.

From: CEL   11/11–12/41
To: ALD

AUXILIARY SHIP BALTAVIA ARRIVED 11/8 DOCKED 11/10 WITH SLIGHT
DAMAGE TO THE MACHINERY. . . . LEFT FOR RIO GRANDE. HUMBERTO.

From: CEL   12/3/41
To: ALD

REPORTS ANNOUNCEMENTS OF FLIGHTS [FROM] NATAL [TO] AFRICA.
MACHINES ARE BOEING B 17 OR CONSOLIDATED B 24. OF THESE TYPES
FIVE WERE FLOWN OVER FROM NOVEMBER 16 TO NOVEMBER 26.
DIVERGENCIES ARE TO BE EXPLAINED BY THE LACK OF KNOWLEDGE OF
THESE TYPES BY THE OBSERVERS. WE ARE CURRENTLY ENGAGED IN RE-
MOVING THE DISADVANTAGEOUS CONDITION. ALFRE[DO].

From: CEL   February 18, 1942
To: ALD

SERVICE INTERRUPTED AND MOVED, SINCE DISCOVERED BY AMERICANS.
SECOND STATION IN CONSTRUCTION. ONE TRANSMITTER IN RESERVE.
FURTHER 2 STATIONS SOON READY FOR SERVICE. SALOMON ARRESTED,
WERE ABLE TO GET OUT HIS TRANSMITTER. TRANSMITTER FREDERICO
TOO VOLUMINOUS.

But in March, 1942—slightly more than a month after Brazil severed
relations with the Axis—Brazilian police armed with SIS information
began the roundup of the Nazi espionage agents and their helpers. Six
espionage radio rings were broken up and eighty-six agents convicted
in Brazilian courts.[5]

The arrests smashed the Brazilian spy net, but then the Nazis' field
headquarters for espionage simply shifted to Argentina and Chile. And
SIS agents concentrated on uncovering their operations in these countries. The task was a difficult and sensitive one, largely because the SIS
men could not make arrests or interfere in any way with the Axis
agents' operations. All they could do in some cases was collect the information and pass it on to the American Ambassadors, who then laid
the facts before the governments concerned.

So far as security measures were concerned, most Central and South
American countries at the start of World War II were as unprepared
as the United States had been at the outbreak of World War I; and for
that reason most of them welcomed the American offer of FBI help in
training police and organizing antiespionage and antisabotage defenses.[6]

The SIS prepared security recommendations for one good neighbor
and finally an agent laid the plan before the country's president, who
looked it over carefully. The agent explained the procedures used in
the United States to control enemy aliens and tighten security.

Finally the president exclaimed, "It would be easy to put into effect such a program in the United States. Mr. Roosevelt would merely press a button, an aide would rush to his desk, the President would tell him what was wanted and it would be done. But here, I press a button and what happens? Nothing! The buzzer won't even work."

Nevertheless, the SIS helped to get buzzers to working in a good many places despite minor misunderstandings. One case of misunderstanding involved an SIS agent whose name and face and family were as Irish as the shamrock. His name was Kelly.

When Kelly got to the border of one Latin country, he gave the immigration officer his name, occupation and life history. The immigration officer didn't ask Kelly his religion. He merely wrote down "Protestant." To him, all North Americans were Protestants. Kelly protested. The border official questioned Kelly's knowledge of Church rituals, and Kelly—whose uncle was a Monseigneur—gave him the works. The official listened gravely and then wrote after the word "Protestant"— "Claims to be a Catholic."

Because of the importance of their work, FBI agents were exempt from military duty even though many of them asked to be permitted to go into uniform. And being without a uniform at times was an embarrassment when some drunk or loud-mouthed patriot drew attention to their civilian clothes.

In one case, an SIS agent working in Mexico went to a mountain resort on an espionage investigation. An American with a brassy voice tuned to hundred-proof volume demanded repeatedly to know why he wasn't in uniform. Finally the agent drew the drunk to one side and whispered, "Confidentially, I'm wanted for murder. I killed a man in the States. He was asking too many questions." There were no more questions.

The SIS worked closely with British Intelligence. The cooperation was particularly effective in keeping a check on the Nazis' courier system. These couriers traveled by Spanish ships, carrying espionage information and contraband such as platinum. The British often tipped the SIS to the arrival of couriers from Spain—and then the SIS tipped the British when couriers left. Many of them were arrested by the British when their ships stopped at Trinidad.

The SIS succeeded in planting double agents in the courier system, agents who made it possible for the SIS men to photograph more than 500 pages of coded messages, and check some 4,000 photographic negatives containing economic and political information. Often the original messages were taken from the double agents, who then delivered substitute messages.

On one occasion a Nazi courier prepared to board a ship bound for Spain with 750 grams of insulin concealed in his luggage. He is probably wondering to this day how it happened that en route to Germany the insulin was transformed into talcum powder.

The SIS operation was remarkably smooth. But at the start of World War II friction developed between the FBI and the Office of Strategic Services. This development threatened to eliminate the SIS from the intelligence field at a time when its agents were closing in on the South American spy rings.

When the dispute was carried to President Roosevelt, he directed that the FBI continue to have sole responsibility for the civilian intelligence operation in the Western Hemisphere, with the Army and Navy working in the military field.

24: *Outsmarting the Enemy*

EARLY in 1944, FBI Director J. Edgar Hoover received a disturbing report from South America warning that his top SIS undercover agents in Argentina were in grave danger of arrest and torture by the political police of President Pedro Ramirez, whose government, if not pro-Nazi, was enthusiastically anti-United States. Five SIS informants were being held secretly by Argentine police and there was a possibility that they might disclose the identities of SIS agents.

Relations between the United States and Argentina had deteriorated to the point where a diplomatic rupture seemed likely. Argentina refused to make common cause with sister states whose sympathies were with the Allies, and the State Department had alerted the FBI to be prepared for a break with Argentina at any time.

It was vitally important to keep undercover agents in Argentina because the country had become the hub of Nazi espionage operations. To leave Argentina uncovered would create a serious gap in the United States intelligence system covering the Western Hemisphere.

The report sent to Hoover by one of his FBI inspectors said in part:

I am . . . concerned with the tremendous danger of one of our agents being picked up in Argentina, tortured into a full confession (which I think the present Argentine regime would most gleefully and effectively use as a *cause célèbre*) with consequent publicity throughout the entire world. The repercussions of such an incident might well be terrific insofar as Latin American relations are concerned. It would add tremendous prestige and strength to Argentina's present position and would place the Bureau in a very unfortunate position of the traditional "goat," always the fate of him who gets caught and is thereby subjected to ridicule and criticism. I do not think we can ignore overwhelming evidence which we have to the effect that the German agents are working hand-in-hand with the present Argentine regime and would undoubtedly be most happy to very effectively embarrass the American Government by such means . . . Should there be a break in diplomatic relations, I expect that virtually all Americans in Argentina without diplomatic protection will come in for some very rough handling . . .

The agents themselves were willing to accept the dangers. But Hoover, as a combat commander often had to do, was forced to weigh the potential gain against the possible losses. Hoover made his decision. The five agents who were in immediate danger were ordered to other assignments. From Buenos Aires came a coded message saying:

REFERENCE YOUR RADIOGRAM 772. ALL NECESSARY PREPARATIONS NOW UNDER WAY FOR EARLY DEPARTURE OF 241, 243, 582, 361, and 363 TO MONTEVIDEO . . .

One by one, the SIS agents slipped out of Buenos Aires by the underground which they had arranged for just such emergencies. "Crandall's Navy" shuttled them across the Rio de la Plata to friendly Uruguay. And this ended, for these five, at least, an exciting chapter in counterespionage against the Nazis in Argentina. But their places were taken by others, and the dangerous game went on.

The game went on endlessly. Sometimes it was a bloodless economic war. Those who cooperated with the enemy had to be hurt—to make them stop hurting us. Business firms and individuals who ranged themselves on the side of the Axis were likely to face economic starvation. This starvation was achieved by the use of the U. S. Government's dreaded "black list," which had the official and harmless-sounding title of "The Proclaimed List of Certain Blocked Nationals." The British had a similar list, and so did the French until the fall of France.

Any person or firm whose name appeared on the United States black list as a collaborator with the Axis found the list anything but harmless. It meant that the U. S. Government wouldn't do business with them, or if possible, permit anyone else to do business with them. The black list was a powerful economic weapon in the hands of the Allies in discouraging individuals and firms from becoming chummy with enemy representatives.

Efforts were made by some businesses to dodge the embargo. In one case a Venezuelan company controlled by the German I. G. Far-benindustrie was badly in need of pharmaceutical products. Without them, the company's competitor would inevitably begin to take over the market. So the firm arranged to have more than $23,000 worth of supplies shipped from Argentina to a phony consignee in Venezuela.

The SIS agent in Caracas informed the American Embassy, which notified the Venezuelan police. When the cargo arrived aboard the SS *Rio Grande,* the police denied permission for it to be unloaded. The ship sailed on to San Juan, Puerto Rico. There the cargo was seized by U. S. Customs officials on orders from the Alien Property Custodian.

As the espionage fight shifted from Brazil to Chile in the spring of 1942, SIS gathered evidence against a radio spy ring known by the call letters PYL, a ring which started operations under the direction of General Friedrich Wolf, the German Military Attaché in Chile. When Wolf was transferred from Chile to Argentina, he was succeeded by Major Ludwig Von Bohlen, a veteran of World War I. Von Bohlen had been born in Chile and had once served as secretary to a high government official, a position that gave him many important connec-tions even before the Nazis recruited him for espionage.

Station PYL began its operations early in 1941, acting largely as a clearinghouse and relay point for information gathered by the German agents along the Pacific Coast from Chile to Mexico. The PYL transmitter was hidden in a small building on a farm outside Quilpue, near Valparaiso, and it operated for months without serious interrup-tion. But the SIS had been watching the PYL operation.

After the breakup of the Brazilian rings, the SIS collected a formi-dable display of evidence against the PYL group. This evidence was turned over to the State Department, which notified the Chilean Mini-ster of Foreign Affairs of what was going on. Station PYL went silent. But Chile did nothing against the ring until the State Department obliquely protested against the lenient attitude toward Axis agents.

Acting Secretary of State Sumner Welles said in a speech on Octo-ber 8, 1942:

> . . . I cannot believe that these two Republics [Argentina and Chile] will continue long to permit their brothers and neighbors of the Americas, engaged as they are in a life and death struggle to preserve the liberties and the integrity of the New World, to be stabbed in the back by Axis emissaries operating in the territory . . .

Welles' speech nudged the Chilean Government into action, but by this time most of the PYL ring had fled into Argentina.

Chile severed relations with the Axis in January, 1943, largely as a result of the angry outcry raised by the publicity given the exposé of the PYL espionage group. But in April the FBI and FCC monitoring stations picked up messages from another secret station somewhere in Santiago, Chile, a station with the call letters PQZ.

And so the search began again. This time the SIS encountered one of the best-organized espionage rings in all of South America. The ring had agents not only in Chile but also in Peru, Bolivia and Brazil. It had been organized by Von Bohlen, who remained in Chile until September of 1943, even though diplomatic relations had been broken in January.

When Von Bohlen left for Germany, he turned over the operation and some $200,000 to Bernardo Timmerman, one of his chief lieutenants.

Bit by bit, the operations of the PQZ ring were exposed. An intercepted letter from one spy led to the location of another spy. Information picked up by a State Department official, added to the information obtained by the SIS, filled in gaps of the investigations by Chilean police. And the trail finally led to Timmerman in February, 1944. The PQZ ring was broken.

Curiously, Major Von Bohlen was another German espionage agent who couldn't resist leaving evidence on paper, even while criticizing others for such carelessness. After the breakup of the PYL group, he carefully studied the weaknesses of the ring and wrote a paper entitled "Experiences Gained From The Valparaiso Process." He wrote:

1. The cardinal mistake was the insufficiency of the original key and the transmission of the second key together with the first. If the communication identification word had not been deciphered, the code would not have been broken.

2. Although after the receipt of the memorandum, weeks even months were available in which to hide all clues, the proper steps were not taken notwithstanding strict orders in this regard. For example, parts were found in Quilpue and stenographic notes were discovered in a trunk belonging to Sz. . . . In this connection Bl. disappointed us in his lack of self-discipline and Sz. through his stenographic diary, the keeping of which was unnecessary. Sz. had also sent papers to another place for safekeeping, which we were able to obtain possession of in time. His stenographic notes were not only damaging to the case but he thereby involved some of his co-workers and in the end his former fiancée and another lady were also connected with the affair . . .

The papers left behind by Von Bohlen were extremely valuable in locating other Nazi spies.

The danger of enemy radio stations to the Allied cause was never better illustrated than in the case of the great liner, the *Queen Mary,* which became a troop transport and a prize to be hunted by the U-boats.

The big ship arrived in Rio de Janeiro on March 6, 1942, en route overseas with 10,000 troops aboard. And on the same day an FBI radio monitoring station intercepted a message from the Nazis' station CIT which said: "Queen Mary arrived here today at 10:00 . . . she must [go] to the cellar."

Two days later at 10:52 P.M., GMT, station CEL informed station ALD in Hamburg: "Queen Mary sailed on March 8, 18 o'clock local time."

And the next day CIT's operator pounded out a message saying: "With Queen Mary falls Churchill . . . Good luck."

And so the sea raiders were alerted that the *Queen Mary* was loose in the Atlantic with a cargo whose loss would be a staggering blow to the Allies. And she was traveling without a convoy.

The intercepted messages were turned over to the State Department, the Office of Naval Intelligence and Army Intelligence by the FBI. And then Brazilian police on March 10 arrested Josef Jacob Johannes Starziczny—the same Starziczny who squirreled away his spy documents—and found a copy of the message sent by station CIT reporting the *Queen Mary*'s movements. The American Embassy reported the message to the British Embassy in Rio de Janeiro.

On March 15, the official Italian news agency Stefani broadcast a report which said:

> In Argentine maritime circles it is affirmed that the British trans-Atlantic [liner] *Queen Mary,* which left Rio de Janeiro a few days ago with 10,000 North American soldiers aboard headed for an unknown destination, was torpedoed. The ship was damaged heavily and tried to reach the British base at Falkland Islands.

But the *Queen Mary* had dodged the U-boats, saved by the prompt warning which resulted from the intercepted messages.

At the peak of the SIS operation, the organization had a total of 360 agents. Nine of the ten republics of South America had asked that agents be assigned to act as technical advisers on police matters and counterespionage. They made antisabotage surveys of more than 150 industrial plants, utilities and other centers regarded as highly important to the Allied war effort; and they recommended measures for tighter security.

But in all the SIS activity, there was none which produced better results, perhaps, than the battle of wits with the smugglers of platinum, a metal which is an essential material for equipping and maintaining a a war machine.[1]

Only five nations in the world produce platinum in quantity—
Colombia, Canada, Russia, the United States and the Union of South
Africa. The German war machine needed platinum badly, and the
Nazis reached out to Colombia to get it because Colombia was
the only one of the platinum-producing countries not at war with
the Reich in 1942.

About 22,850 troy ounces of Colombia's annual platinum production
came from the big dredges of the Choco Pacifico Company and another 12,150 ounces came from some 30,000 natives who panned it
from streams much like the Klondike miners panned their gold.

From 1936 until 1941, a German named Theodore C. Barth had
just about cornered the "native" platinum production in Colombia by
the simple expedient of paying from 20 to 30 percent above the official
market price. But Barth's monopoly collapsed when German funds
were frozen in the United States in June of 1941. And the smugglers
moved in.

The price of platinum jumped to $2,338.10 a pound in the black
market in August, 1942—almost four times the official price. A four-
and-a-half-inch cube of placer platinum weighing sixty-six pounds
was worth $154,314.60.

The United States, by agreement with the Colombian Government,
was supposed to receive all the country's platinum whether it came
from the Choco Pacifico Company or from the natives. There was no
difficulty about the company's production because it automatically went
to the government's collection agency, but controlling the "native"
production was the key to blocking the flow of platinum to the Germans. And the natives in the back country were usually willing to sell
to the highest bidder. The Colombian Government issued decrees and
threatened severe punishment for those who failed to turn in their
platinum to the government, but there was no effective machinery for
enforcement and the smugglers knew it. And so the SIS moved in.

The trails in smuggling cases reached from the wild green jungles of
Colombia to the luxurious home of a smuggler living near the smooth
greens of California's Monterey Peninsula Country Club.

One day in March, 1943, the FBI radio operator in Quito, Ecuador,
tapped out a long message to FBI Headquarters in Washington referring
to "possible platinum smuggling" by a man named Harold Ebury, said
to be a British citizen, and by an Austrian who was not as discreet as
he thought when he began asking about the chances of buying black-
market platinum. SIS agents in Quito had learned that the Austrian was
an associate of Ebury, who had often been in Ecuador claiming to be
dealing in *trigo* (wheat).

Upon receipt of this message the FBI searched its files. They found a report written on Ebury after he arrived in Seattle from the Orient carrying a considerable amount of Japanese currency which he had sent to Argentina prior to the war. Ebury had claimed to be an international banker, but the British had advised the FBI that Ebury was a suspected smuggler.

SIS agents in Quito were ordered to give the Ebury case "preferred attention." They dug into the doings of the mysterious Mr. Ebury and his South American associates, to find that the ring was organized to smuggle platinum from Colombia by way of Ecuador to Argentina. The end of the line, so far as the agents could learn at the time, was a tailor's shop on Florin Street in Buenos Aires. They learned that the shop's owner had received a cablegram from Ebury saying that he would arrive soon by way of Quito.

As lead after lead was developed, it became clear that Ebury, living in California, was directing smuggling operations in South America. Agents trailed one smuggler from Ecuador to Argentina by way of Bolivia to learn the smugglers' routes. He was permitted to sell the metal and it was traced to a refining firm with a German name.

The FBI closed in on Ebury on July 17, 1943. Agents found him at his Monterey Peninsula home. He ushered them into his living room and, quite coolly, talked of his world travels and his plans to go to Ecuador to establish an import-export business. The agents pressed Ebury for more details of his business activities and it became obvious to Ebury that these men knew more than he had realized.

Finally he smiled, leaned back in his chair, and said, "Yes, gentlemen, I smuggled platinum to Buenos Aires twice. I'll tell you everything. Where do you want me to begin?"

Ebury reckoned that during his career he had handled perhaps a half-ton of platinum. He admitted that when he used the word "cloth" in his correspondence he was referring to platinum, and that the figure $1,300 meant 1,300 grams of platinum. But he denied that any of the platinum, to his knowledge, was destined for the Axis. He admitted in court that he had smuggled platinum from Ecuador to Argentina, but his action involved no crime committed in the United States. He pleaded guilty, however, to censorship violations by the use of codes in his letters, and was sentenced to serve eighteen months in prison.

But while SIS agents were marking the Ebury case closed, they were opening nineteen new smuggling cases as a result of leads turned up in that one investigation. The Ebury disclosures threw fear into the smugglers for a time, but then the rings began operating again, and in 1944, Director Hoover ordered four more SIS agents into Colombia to aid in breaking up the traffic. Arrangements were made for the agents to have a conference with President Alfonso Lopez of Colombia, and they laid before him a suggested decree. As one of the agents put it, "We made it tough. We figured if we got fifty percent of what we asked, we'd be lucky. But after he read our proposal, he put a heading on it, signed it, and that was his decree."

The agents divided the country into four operational areas and then went to work. Agent George Stevens' area was the wild jungle country at the foot of the Andes mountains.

"I flew in with the pilot of an old Ford Tri-Motor plane," Stevens recalled. "There was no compass or radio. The plane was equipped with pontoons and the pilot skidded it over the water and the mud flats to land. I asked him, 'How will you find your way back to Barranquilla without a compass or radio?' He grinned and said, 'I'll just follow the river to the coast and then turn right. Can't miss it.' I said, 'What if a storm comes up?' He said, 'Oh, I just set down on the river, tie up, and fish.'

"They finally got him a brand-new plane and it was a beauty. But he cracked it up. Last report I had of him he was back flying the old Ford Tri-Motor. Still is, for all I know.

"It didn't take long to discover the smugglers had a system of sending a man around to the natives to collect the platinum panned by each of them. Then he would take it over the mountains to Ecuador and it would go out that way. I developed sources of information among the natives while my partners were working other areas."

Stevens learned that one group of smugglers was using a Spaniard, a truck driver, as a courier. He sent word to the Spaniard that he wanted to see him.

"When the man came in, I laid it on the table," Stevens said. "I told him the new government decree called for imprisonment or deportation of any alien found smuggling platinum. He was an alien and there was a good chance that he not only would be deported—but he would lose his home and his truck and everything else he owned.

"I told him, 'You can take your choice—you play on our team or else.' He worked with us and continued his work as a courier. Through him we prevented another ring from going into high gear."

In tracing the platinum from its source to the ultimate user, SIS agents from 1942 to July 1, 1944, were able to account for all but 2,507 troy ounces of the metal and presumably that amount could have reached Germany. But the German war machine in that same period needed 137,500 troy ounces of platinum according to official estimates. The barriers set up by the Colombian Government based upon information furnished by the SIS limited the Nazis to less than 2 percent of their platinum needs.

The battle against the smugglers and enemy espionage was going full blast in early 1944, when FBI Director Hoover received confidential reports from the Pentagon and the State Department which alarmed him. The reports came from sources too reliable to be doubted and both had the same documented story: arrangements were being made for the Communists' secret police, the NKVD, to set up an office in Washington.

Without prior clearance from the White House, Secretary of State Hull or the Joint Chiefs of Staff, the Office of Strategic Services had agreed with Russia's Commissar of Foreign Affairs Molotov for an exchange of missions which would permit OSS men to go to Moscow and NKVD men to come to Washington.

Presumably, each agency would act only in a liaison capacity in the interchange of intelligence. But Hoover knew that each country which had tried such cooperation with the Russians had found itself in trouble trying to curb the NKVD's efforts at espionage.

Hoover sent a special messenger to the White House with the following confidential letter dated February 10, 1944, to Harry L. Hopkins, the President's close friend and aide:

Dear Harry:

I have just learned from a confidential but reliable source that a liaison arrangement has been perfected between the Office of Strategic Services and the Soviet Secret Police (NKVD) whereby officers will be exchanged between these services. The Office of Strategic Services is going to assign men to Moscow and in turn the NKVD will set up an office in Washington, D. C. This agreement, I am advised . . . has gone so far that War Department officials now feel they cannot change the program.

I wanted to bring this situation to your attention at once because I think it is a highly dangerous and most undesirable procedure to establish in the United States a unit of the Russian Secret Service which has admittedly for its purpose the penetration into the official secrets of various government agencies. The history of the NKVD in Great Britain showed clearly that the fundamental purpose of its operations there was to surreptitiously obtain the official secrets of the British Government. I am informed that various other countries where the NKVD has operated have had a similar experience with it.

I feel that it will be highly dangerous to our governmental operations to have an agency such as the NKVD officially authorized to operate in the United States where quite obviously it will be able to function without any appropriate restraint upon its activities. In view of the potential danger in this situation I wanted to bring it to your attention and I will advise you of any further information which I receive about the matter.

Sincerely,
J. Edgar Hoover

Hoover sent a memorandum to Attorney General Biddle advising him of this development. He passed on to Biddle the same warning he had given Hopkins, adding:

As a matter of fact, secret agents of this agency in the United States operating surreptitiously have been engaged in attempting to obtain highly confidential information concerning War Department secrets. I think that the establishment of a recognized unit of the NKVD in the United States will be a serious threat to the internal security of the country . . .

The "War Department secrets" to which Hoover referred were the secrets of the atomic bomb, which were being guarded by the Army's Manhattan Engineer District.

The exchange of intelligence missions was blocked by the White House and quietly forgotten by everyone concerned.

As the war neared an end, the problem of postwar intelligence began to loom large. There was general agreement that the system which had mushroomed under the pressures of war should be overhauled. The question was what form the system would take and where the responsibility for the field operations should rest.

It was at this point—in April of 1945—that the Budget Bureau Director, Harold D. Smith, advised the new President, Harry S. Truman, that the Budget Bureau was staffed with experts on intelligence.

As Truman recalled in his memoirs:

. . . I was now told that the Budget Bureau itself had some experienced and competent people who had become specialists in the problems of intelligence organization . . . Smith suggested, and I agreed, that studies should be undertaken at once by his specially trained experts in this field . . .

At this time, the Joint Chiefs of Staff, the OSS and the FBI were also making their own studies. And it soon became apparent that there was a wide spread of opinion as to how the nation's intelligence organization should operate.

The Budget Bureau's plan was to make the Department of State the "locus of coordination" in espionage and counterespionage work, with security operations distributed among the Army, Navy, FBI, State Department, Securities and Exchange Commission, Alien Property Custodian, Foreign Funds Control and—in loyalty-type investigations—the Civil Service Commission, Coast Guard, Provost Marshal General, Treasury Department and others. Just about every Tom, Dick and Harry in government would have a hand in it.

The OSS and the Joint Chiefs of Staff favored plans calling for a new executive agency headed by a director with power to set up a world-wide organization, to draft specialists from other intelligence agencies, and to inspect the organization and operation of any other investigative agency. The FBI plan was simply to expand the wartime Western Hemisphere intelligence system to a world-wide basis. This meant that the Army and Navy would continue to handle matters of importance to the military while the FBI would operate in the civilian field. The operations would be coordinated and evaluated by a committee composed of representatives from the Army, Navy, FBI and the State Department.

It was in this climate of disagreement in January, 1946, that President Truman directed the formation of a National Intelligence Authority.[2] At the working level was a Central Intelligence Group (CIG) to plan, develop and coordinate the United States' overseas intelligence operations. The President named Admiral Sidney W. Souers the first Director of Central Intelligence.

The Truman directive left an area of doubt as to whether the new agency would enter active intelligence operations itself, or whether it would act solely as a coordinating and evaluating agency and leave the field operations to existing intelligence agencies. But Hoover had no doubt on one score: an effort was under way to remove the FBI from the field of foreign intelligence.

Souers operated the Central Intelligence Group as a coordinating and evaluating agency, but when he was succeeded by General Hoyt Vandenberg in June, 1946, the new director quickly moved to establish a world-wide operation of his own. A directive was drawn by the National Intelligence Authority giving Vandenberg authority to take over basic intelligence research and analysis and to conduct all foreign espionage and counterespionage.

Word that the FBI was being withdrawn from foreign intelligence brought a deluge of letters from the heads of foreign missions in South America protesting withdrawal of the FBI. Many of them said the breakup of SIS was foolhardy since it had become so well established. One State Department official summed up the general attitude in a memorandum to his superiors which said: "In my experience no coordination has been achieved in the intelligence field to compare with that of the FBI and the Department of State in the field of Latin American intelligence. . . ."

But the decision to disband the SIS operation had been made in the top echelons of government. The FBI had no choice but to accept it. And so ended the story of the FBI's Special Intelligence Service.[3]

25 : *The Princess Was No Pauper*

NO STORY of international intrigue in fact or fiction would be complete without the clever, scheming female who moves through glittering drawing rooms and chancelleries as a courier and adviser to men spinning plots for power and conquest.

And so we can hardly overlook titian-haired Steffi Richter, better known as Her Serene Highness Princess Stefanie Hohenlohe-Waldenburg Schillingsfurst. The Princess was a handmaiden of the appeasers in events leading to the betrayal of Czechoslovakia at Munich. Then in 1940 she arranged a meeting in San Francisco between a mysterious British visitor and Hitler's most trusted agent, Captain Fritz Wiedemann, where plans were discussed for setting up a monarchy in Germany. The Englishman felt that both the English and German peoples would be surprised if they knew how easily a satisfactory peace could be arranged between the right people.

But we get ahead of our story. . . .

Steffi Richter, a commoner, captured the fancy of a Hungarian Prince. As the seventeen-year-old daughter of a Viennese lawyer curtsied to herself in the privacy of her room and addressed herself as "your Serene Highness," she knew that the dreams she saw in the mirror would come true. The man in her dream was Prince Friedrich François Augustin Marie Hohenlohe-Waldenburg, an officer in the Austrian Army. Steffi and her Prince were married in London in 1914, and they were divorced six years later. Steffi said there was another woman. The Prince didn't say. But Steffi retained her royal title and soon became a familiar figure flitting through the capitals of Europe. London became her base of operations and she ran with the Cliveden set, which was willing to play footsie with the Nazis. She was a favorite with Adolf Hitler—and an intimate friend of the Fuehrer's personal Adjutant, Captain Wiedemann, who had been Corporal Hitler's commanding officer in World War I.

A good many people must have wondered where the Princess got the money to entertain so lavishly and to travel so extensively. At least part of the mystery became clear in 1939, when Stefanie filed suit in London against Lord Rothermere, a wealthy English publisher. She claimed he had reneged on a contract to pay her $20,000 a year for life if she would act as his personal "ambassadress" to Hitler and other government heads in Europe. Stefanie later claimed that she inspired Rothermere to seek the restoration of the monarchy in Hungary—but that she simply would have nothing to do with Rothermere's ambition to place a relative on the Hungarian throne.

Lord Rothermere admitted that from 1932 until January, 1938, he had paid Stefanie not $20,000 a year but a total of some $250,000, not including expensive gifts which she had purchased and had billed to him. His attorney argued that the agreement was a social arrangement, not a legal contract, and he hinted broadly that the lady was "flirting with blackmail" in pressing her claim.

Mr. Justice Tucker listened to all the arguments and ruled that there was no evidence to prove Rothermere had made a lifetime contract with the Princess.

Introduced in evidence was a particularly interesting letter written by Captain Wiedemann to Lord Rothermere expressing Hitler's appreciation of the Princess' acts in introducing Lord Rothermere to him. Wiedemann further reported that "it was her groundwork which made the Munich agreement possible."

The Princess' account of events preceding the Munich agreement was related in part by Her Serene Highness to FBI agents. Her story was this:

> She was summoned by Field Marshal Hermann Goering to his medieval castle Karin Hall in June, 1938. Goering and the Princess "discussed a meeting between a representative of Germany and Lord Halifax in the interest of preserving peace . . . Such a meeting would necessarily have to be arranged without the knowledge of Herr Von Ribbentrop, the foreign minister." The two discussed various Nazis to make the contact. They agreed that Captain Wiedemann was just the man for so delicate a mission. Goering, according to the Princess, had conceived the idea that he could bring about a better understanding between Germany and England and thus avert war in spite of Von Ribbentrop.

The Princess then persuaded Wiedemann to obtain Hitler's consent to permit him to go to London to see Lord Halifax to pave the way for the Goering visit.

Once plans were made in Germany, the Princess hurried to London. She encountered no difficulty in arranging a conference with Lord Halifax, "who was most agreeable to having an unofficial conference with Wiedemann in London with a view to preserving peace and furthering understanding between Hitler and England."

Wiedemann, with the full approval of Hitler, arrived in London to discuss the issues between the two countries. As the Princess later recounted, "Although I was not present during this conference between Halifax and Wiedemann, I understood that the conference was most successful." But the Goering visit never materialized because news of the Wiedemann visit leaked out and Von Ribbentrop intervened. The conference between the leaders of Germany and England later occurred at Munich.

Stefanie vigorously denied reports, however, that she had a connection with the meeting between Lord Runciman and the Czech Nazi, Konrad Henlein, where German claims to the Sudetenland of Czechoslovakia were given sympathetic consideration. And during the Munich crisis she was at her part-time home, Schloss Leopoldskron, just across the valley from Berchtesgaden, entertaining lavishly. At night, she could see the lights of Hitler's mountain retreat winking in the distance.

The Princess later claimed she had never met Hitler before her employment by Rothermere and that her first meeting with Hitler was at Rothermere's request and in his service. When she broke with Lord Rothermere she related how his admiration for Hitler grew and how "he stood in the front rank of England's appeasers and praised Hitler after Munich."

Stefanie explained her role as that of "a glorified messenger," although Hitler presented her with a golden Swastika, the Order of the German Red Cross, a personally autographed photograph inscribed "In memory of a visit to Berchtesgaden," and once wrote her to say:

> . . . I have been informed how sincerely and warm-heartedly you also championed New Germany in the past year and her necessity for living. I know very well that many embarrassments resulted from this. Therefore I should like to express to you, highly esteemed Princess, my sincere thanks for the great understanding you always have shown for our people generally and for my work especially . . .

After the infamous Munich appeasement, the FBI was particularly interested to learn that Hitler was sending Captain Wiedemann to the United States to be his consul general in San Francisco. It seemed odd that Hitler's most trusted aide should be appointed to such a modest post after his brilliant achievements in pre-Munich diplomacy. Wiedemann arrived from Germany aboard the Hamburg-American liner SS *Hamburg* on March 4, 1939, and told reporters: "My only intention and wish is to act as an intermediary in creating good will between our two countries . . ."

Wiedemann's arrival coincided with Germany's final preparations for the plunge into war. And then the FBI was informed that the Captain's mission was not as innocent as he made it appear. A warning was relayed from Brussels by way of the State Department which quoted two of Hitler's close associates as saying that Wiedemann's mission was to organize pro-German and anti-Jewish propaganda in the United States, encourage fascism in Mexico, and convert the San Francisco Consulate into a headquarters for German-Japanese espionage.

Another disturbing report, too, was that Wiedemann would be joined by the Princess Stefanie—which would bring together once again the team which had worked so smoothly in arranging the Munich preliminaries.

The Princess arrived in New York in December, soon after losing her suit against Lord Rothermere. She laughed off a reporter's questions about her past political activities. "I have as much to do with politics as a rope dancer," she said. "I don't even read half the news in the daily papers." It seemed the Princess was interested solely in writing her memoirs and finding "peace and quiet." Nothing more.

Despite these disarming statements, the FBI kept a close watch on Wiedemann and the Princess from the time both of them set foot on American soil. And it was no surprise to agents when Stefanie arrived in Fresno, California, where she met Captain Wiedemann at a restaurant on May 29. The two of them drove to Sequoia National Park and the next day they arrived in Hillsborough, a San Francisco suburb, where the Princess became the house guest of Captain and Mrs. Wiedemann. The FBI was able to develop sources of information which gave a virtual running account of their activities from day to day.

The Department of Justice had received a warning of the danger that Wiedemann might be another Count von Papen in case of a war between Germany and the United States. It was recalled that von Papen had been one of Germany's most effective espionage agents in World War I.

But then the FBI began receiving reports that Wiedemann was trying to get in touch with someone from British Intelligence. A British diplomat contacted Wiedemann informally and found that the Captain was losing faith in his one-time corporal. Hitler was beginning to ignore the advice of his generals, and to an old soldier like Wiedemann, the generals were more reliable than intuition. Wiedemann wanted to know how harshly England would deal with Germany if the war should end. Obviously he feared Hitler's defeat and hoped to save Germany from harsh peace terms.

Wiedemann's peace feelers brought action. On November 26, 1940, a titled Englishman checked into Room 1026 at the Mark Hopkins Hotel in San Francisco. He was a well-known international banker, and the FBI knew that he had contacts with the British Intelligence in the United States. The first visitor to Room 1026 was Her Serene Highness, Princess Stefanie, acting very unlike a politically naïve rope dancer.

The Englishman—whom we'll call Sir John—and the Princess talked for two hours and forty-five minutes that afternoon, and then met again after dinner. They were joined the next evening by Captain Wiedemann.

Later, confidential informants were able to give the FBI a full account of these talks, the substance of them being as follows:

> Sir John told the Princess he represented a group of Englishmen who believed satisfactory peace terms could be arranged between Britain and Germany before the United States was drawn into the war. They discussed the possibility of the Princess' going to Berlin to place a peace proposal before Hitler and Foreign Minister Joachim Von Ribbentrop.

> The Princess was confident that she could make Hitler realize he was butting against a stone wall and that at the opportune time he should align himself with England to achieve lasting peace. Sir John said he would recommend to Number 10 Downing Street that Stefanie's visit to Berlin be given unofficial approval by the British Government.

> When Wiedemann entered the conversations, the idea of dealing with Hitler was pushed into the background and the trio discussed the possibility of reestablishing the German monarchy with the support of the German Army. There was agreement that Hitler couldn't be trusted and that any lasting peace would have to be made with a stable group which could be relied upon to keep its promises.

> Stefanie suggested a point-blank alliance between Hitler and England, and wondered why England couldn't make such an agreement and then "fool" Hitler. But Stefanie's idea of a double-cross was rejected by the two men, who thought the best thing would be to enlist the Army's help, overthrow Hitler, and then put a king back on the German throne—perhaps Crown Prince Wilhelm Hohenzollern, whom the Princess called "Little Willy." Sir John thought the German-British accord would be easier to achieve with France out of the way—although the agreement would recognize the need for reestablishing France and Poland.

The English visitor left the hotel shortly after noon, November 28, and caught a plane to Washington, where he hurried to the British Embassy.[1]

Three weeks after the San Francisco meeting, Stefanie found herself in trouble with the United States Government. Her request for permission to remain in the country was rejected. The Princess fought deportation with tears, entreaties, a collapse from an overdose of sedatives, and lawyers. One of her attorneys said forty-two countries had been asked to give her a visa and forty-two countries had said no.

Major Lemuel B. Schofield, head of the U. S. Immigration and Naturalization Service, was, as one of his officials said, "tough as hell" about the Hohenlohe case and thought the Princess should be held without bail. Immigration officers took her into custody on March 8, 1941, but when she became hysterical they took her to a hospital room at the Immigration headquarters in San Francisco.

Major Schofield came to San Francisco to interview the Princess himself. He talked with her at length. And there it was that the Major's sternness was dissolved by the royal tears and Stefanie's story that she was merely the victim of a lying press.[2] The Princess was released by Immigration officers and Major Schofield announced that she had given the government some "interesting information" and had promised to cooperate in the future. The Princess' trying ordeal appeared to be over.

The Princess was visiting in Philadelphia under the name "Mary Reihert" when she was arrested by FBI agents the day after the Pearl Harbor attack. She was held by the Immigration and Naturalization Service at Gloucester City, New Jersey, as an enemy alien. Then reports reached President Roosevelt that the Princess was receiving special treatment. He sent a memorandum to the Attorney General which closed with, "Honestly, this is getting to be the kind of scandal that calls for very drastic and immediate action."

The Attorney General ordered Stefanie interned on February 13, 1942, and later she was sent to an internment camp at Seagoville, Texas.

Despite the kindness and thoughtfulness shown to Her Serene Highness while she was in internment, she became fretful. Seagoville was no gilded cage for a princess. She exploded to an FBI agent: "I'm sick and tired of this whole thing. I want an interview with your Mr. Hoover or someone close to him." It seemed she had a lot of information about Lord Rothermere, Fritz Wiedemann and other patrons which she wanted to confide to the FBI. She talked to an agent for five days but she didn't see Hoover.

Princess Stefanie was paroled from Seagoville soon after the war in Europe ended, and within a comparatively short time she was entertaining and being entertained in New York and Philadelphia social circles. The annoying interlude known as World War II was over and the Princess had adjusted nicely.

The FBI's investigations in the Hohenlohe episode, in which President Roosevelt maintained a keen interest, ranged over a period of more than four years. Like the case of the Nazi saboteurs, they became a part of the fabric of the Bureau's wartime story.

26: *A Contrast in Wars*

THE FBI's handling of law enforcement and security problems in World War II was in startling contrast to the blundering in World War I. Something tremendously important had happened to the FBI itself between the wars. And yet this change went almost unnoticed in the excitement of the conflict.

There were no cries in the second war protesting mass raids in violation of civil rights. There were no vigilantes taking over the duties of law enforcement officers in hunting spies, saboteurs and draft dodgers. There were no armed rebellions against military service and no mass evasion of military duty such as there had been in the first great war.

Perhaps the sharpest contrast between the two wars was in the FBI's enforcement of the Selective Training and Service Act. At the end of the first conflict, about 295,000 men were still classified on Selective Service rolls as draft dodgers. But there were only 8,836 draft evaders still at large at the end of the second war. The plans made by Hoover and his men for cooperation with local law enforcement agencies and the American Legion brought results while avoiding the old mistakes of 1917–1918.

The FBI policy in enforcing the draft was to get men in uniform, and not into jails. Prosecution of delinquents was reserved for cases in which there was evidence of willful evasion of duty.[1]

Such raids as the big "slacker raids" of 1918, which rounded up some 50,000 men in New York City alone, were banned by Hoover in World War II. The biggest roundup was made in 1943, when the FBI and local police arrested 779 men in thirty-nine cities—and then only after each case had been carefully investigated. The greatest number of arrests in this roundup was made in New York City, where 161 were seized. These arrests caused hardly a ripple.

In most cases, draft evasions were the result of ignorance or carelessness and not deliberate efforts to escape military service. A New York editor didn't know he had to carry his registration card until he was arrested for not having it. A Denver mother burned her son's registration card with the trash. A Cleveland housewife tossed out her husband's draft questionnaire and he forgot all about it until an FBI agent knocked on his door. There were thousands of such cases.[2]

But in addition to the careless and the ignorant there were other thousands who tried desperately—and usually without success—to escape war duty by self-mutilation, feigned illness, flight to Mexico, adopting aliases and scores of other evasions. In Arkansas, a farm family fought off "the law" with a double-bladed ax, a coal shovel, an iron poker, chunks of stove wood and anything else that could be thrown or swung to protect a draft-age youth. The law finally won.

The problem of dealing with conscientious objectors was studied carefully in a Department of Justice conference in 1940, and it was agreed that the FBI should handle the investigations of these cases to determine "the character and good faith of the objections of the person concerned." The time required for these investigations alone was tremendous, but time and effort were the only way to sift the sincere objectors from the frauds. The conscientious objectors were known in World War I as "conchies" and the nickname was a word of contempt implying cowardice. But the majority of those claiming conscientious objections to combat duty in World War II accepted noncombatant service in the medical corps or offered themselves as human "guinea pigs" in medical experiments. The FBI's approach to this problem helped establish a better understanding of the sincere objector while closing the door against frauds.

The result of all this was that although the FBI had been under heavy fire in 1918 for its handling of the draft-evasion problem, the opposite was true twenty-five years later. In 1943 the American Civil Liberties Union issued a pamphlet which said in part:

> The striking contrast between the state of civil liberty in the first eighteen months of World War II and in World War I offers strong evidence to support the thesis that our democracy can fight even the greatest of wars and still maintain the essentials of liberty.

While men were fighting and dying for the essentials of liberty, there were vermin to be found. Among them were Amerigo Antonelli and his henchmen, who deliberately made defective grenades to squeeze another dollar of profit from war contracts. When some GI died because of a defective grenade—perhaps it was an Antonelli-made grenade.

Antonelli was president of the Antonelli Fireworks Company at Spencerport, New York. In the five years before World War II, his reported income averaged about $2,000 a year. He was given government contracts to manufacture grenades and incendiary bombs, and the Antonelli salary jumped to $26,000 a year plus profits.

The military inspectors had trouble with Antonelli and his foremen from the start. Rejected grenades and bombs were supposed to be tossed into boxes where they could not become mixed with the good ones. But those rejects kept coming back down the assembly line again and again or turning up in the boxes of approved grenades and bombs.

At last the FBI was called into the case.[3] Agents put together a damning story as employee after employee swore he had orders to put only three charges of powder into grenades which were supposed to have four charges—and only two charges of thermite in bombs supposed to carry three charges. One girl said she was told, "The hell with what the bombs are like, get out more bombs." Similar stories were given to agents by others, who also told of spilled powder being swept up from the floor and then poured into the grenades, dirt and all.[4]

No better than Antonelli were those Collyer Insulated Wire Company officials of Rhode Island who were responsible for working out a scheme to palm off defective electrical wire on the government, wire which would be used aboard ships and by the Army Signal Corps.

Special agents of the FBI became suspicious during the course of an investigation at the Collyer plant when they noticed signs that switches had been removed and the wiring changed on panels on which voltmeters were installed. There were signs, too, that switches had been removed from an electrical circuit on which galvanometers—the instruments used in testing the wire and cable—were operated.

The agents found the reason for these changes—a hurried effort to hide fraud. Some company officials and employees had been very cleverly using electrical sleight-of-hand to fool the inspectors. By changing the wiring and using an extra switch, the culprits could send 500 volts through a cable and make the voltmeter read 2,000 volts. The inspector would approve the cable as being capable of withstanding a 2,000-volt charge. And in testing the leakage of electricity through the insulation, similar sleight-of-hand was used to alter the galvanometer readings.

Agents found that the company representatives were testing the same sample of good wire more than once as a way to get tags of approval on defective reels of wire. The bad reels of wire would be kept from sight and later the "approved" tags would be switched to the wire which couldn't pass examination. One shipment of Collyer wire was traced to the U. S. Marine Corps supply depot at Barstow, California. An FBI Laboratory expert flew to Barstow and made tests of 400 reels of wire. He found that 127 of the 400 reels failed the voltage test and 204 failed the insulation-resistance test.

If a company commander on a battlefront suddenly lost contact with his battalion because his telephone line failed—or a fire started aboard a ship at sea from defective wiring—perhaps it might have been the wire made by the Collyer Insulated Wire Company.[5]

Along with such frauds as these and the multitude of other problems [6] brought by the war, the FBI had the continuing worry that escaped prisoners of war might be recruited to espionage or sabotage. The United States had been in the conflict less than a year when Assistant Secretary of War John J. McCloy wrote:

> The War Department has arranged with the Department of Justice that the Federal Bureau of Investigation shall assume responsibility for coordinating the search for escaped internees and prisoners of war. . . .

This arrangement was made at Hoover's suggestion.

Over a period of months, the FBI Director pressed for tighter security over the prisoner-of-war centers policed by the Army. Usually the escaped prisoners were caught within twenty-four hours by local police, the Army or the FBI.

The fact that Nazi sympathizers were willing to give shelter to escaped prisoners of war was disclosed early in 1942 when Lieutenant Hans Peter Krug, a young German bomber pilot, escaped from a Canadian prisoner-of-war camp and slipped into the United States.

Krug's prison pals helped him by fashioning a figure from straw and newspapers. They carried this dummy into the line-up of prisoners. Crude as it was, it covered Krug's absence long enough for him to escape. He made his way to Windsor, Ontario, and rowed across the Detroit River in a stolen boat to Belle Isle in Detroit.

Krug carried with him a slip of paper bearing the name of Margareta Johanna Bertelmann and a street address. The slip of paper had been found by a German prisoner at the camp, concealed in a pair of woolen socks sent in a gift package.

Krug made his way to the Bertelmann home. He knocked and when Mrs. Bertelmann came to the door he asked for a drink of water. Once inside, Krug identified himself. He produced the silver epaulets he had cut from his Nazi uniform.

"These will identify me as an officer of the German Luftwaffe," he told her. And Mrs. Bertelmann accepted the identification.

After giving him breakfast, Mrs. Bertelmann told Krug she knew the man who could help him in his escape. The man was Max Stephan, a naturalized American, who operated a restaurant in Detroit. Before the war, the restaurant had been a meeting place for members of the German-American Bund. Stephan took Krug under his wing, bought him a bus ticket to Chicago, gave him money and shelter, and then advised him how he should act to avoid suspicion. Stephan helped the escaped German on his way, and Krug proceeded by stages toward the Mexican border. He hoped to slip into Mexico and then return to Germany.

But when he registered in a small hotel in San Antonio as "Jean Ette," the hotel clerk recognized him from a picture he had seen on an FBI wanted notice. Two special agents and two San Antonio policemen arrested Krug.

The arrest of Krug led also to the arrest of Max Stephan, who was charged with treason. Stephan was convicted—the first man to be convicted by the federal government under the Treason Statute since 1794, when the leader of the Pennsylvania "Whiskey Rebellion" was found guilty of trying to nullify a law imposing a tax on whiskey. Stephan was sentenced to death, but President Roosevelt commuted the sentence to life imprisonment.

As the number of prisoners of war in the United States climbed to 175,000 and then to more than 400,000, Hoover became increasingly concerned about the dangers of sabotage and espionage by escaped prisoners. At one time the prisoners were escaping at the rate of seventy-five a month.

Hoover's notes to the Attorney General and the White House urging tighter security around the prison camps became more insistent. But his alarm was not shared in other quarters until word was sent by American officials in London to Harry Hopkins at the White House late in December, 1944, warning that the President's life might be in danger.

The British Secret Service had received reliable information indicating that the Germans would probably drop parachutists behind the Allied battle lines and in London and Paris during the Christmas holidays. General Eisenhower had been reported marked for assassination. The London report further indicated that an attempt might even be made to assassinate President Roosevelt while prisoners of war created confusion with a mass escape from the American prison camps.

Hopkins told the FBI he had given this information to General George C. Marshall, Admiral Ernest J. King and to Mike Riley, then chief of the White House Secret Service detail.

The alert from overseas brought a tighter security.[7]

The great war came to an end and nations weary of the struggle began laying down their arms and breaking up their armies—except in Russia. The United States' armies were demobilized, the vast air fleets were junked and the warships "mothballed." Peace—it was wonderful.

But there was no peace for the FBI.

War's Aftermath

27: *Postwar Crime*

THE insistent ringing of the doorbell brought Sister Morand hurrying to the door of the French Institute of Notre Dame de Scion, an exclusive school for small children in Kansas City, Missouri. It was about 10:55 A.M., September 28, 1953.

Sister Morand opened the door and saw that the visitor was a plump, middle-aged woman, obviously in a state of emotional upset. The woman apologized for her nervousness and hurriedly explained that she was the aunt of little Bobby Greenlease, Jr., one of the students.

A terrible thing had happened, she said. Bobby's mother had suffered a heart attack and had been taken to St. Mary's Hospital where she was calling for her son. The boy had to be taken to his mother at once.

Sister Morand murmured her sympathies and invited the woman to wait in the chapel while she went upstairs after Bobby. She told the boy an aunt had called for him, but said nothing to him about the heart attack.

When Bobby came downstairs he gave no sign that the woman who came from the chapel was a stranger to him. The visitor told Sister Morand she had prayed for Mrs. Greenlease's recovery and added, "I'm not a Catholic and I don't know whether God heard my prayers."

She put an arm around Bobby's shoulders and was holding him by the hand as they walked from the school and entered a waiting cab. The driver let them out at the Katz Parking lot at 40th and Main Street in downtown Kansas City. Quickly the woman led the six-year-old to a Plymouth station wagon in which a ruddy-faced man with a dim scar on his forehead was waiting. The station wagon swung from the parking lot but it didn't head toward St. Mary's Hospital.

At about this time a Sister was calling from the Institute to ask about Mrs. Greenlease's condition. She was stunned to learn that Mrs. Greenlease was at home and well, and that Mrs. Greenlease knew nothing of a strange woman who had taken her son from the school. Mrs. Greenlease called her husband, a wealthy automobile dealer, and he rushed home. He notified the Kansas City police, who in turn reported the kidnaping to the FBI.

During these frantic calls, the station wagon drove in a southerly direction out of Kansas City onto Highway 169. The man at the wheel was thirty-four-year-old Carl Austin Hall, the ne'er-do-well son of a respected lawyer. The woman was Bonnie Brown Heady, his forty-one-year-old paramour. Hall had squandered his parents' estate and then served sixteen months of a five-year sentence for first-degree robbery of taxicab drivers in Kansas City. He had been paroled from the Missouri State Prison on April 24, 1953.

He had met Bonnie Heady soon after he got out of prison and had gone to live with her at her home in St. Joseph, Missouri. Each of them drank about a fifth of whiskey a day and between their drunken stupors they planned the kidnaping of the Greenlease boy.

Now the kidnaping had been done, they carried out the remainder of their plan.

The station wagon swung off the main highway onto a side road. After driving about two miles, the car turned into a remote lane and halted. Bonnie Heady got out and walked into the field and Carl Hall turned to the boy beside him. His fingers gripped the youngster's neck and he tried to strangle the life out of him. But the fighting, squirming boy fought savagely for breath. Then Hall reached in his pocket.

He told FBI agents later, "I had the gun in my coat pocket. I pulled it out and I shot once trying to hit him in the heart. I don't know whether I hit him or not for he was still alive . . . I shot him through the head on the second shot.

"I took him out of the car, laid him on the ground and put him in a plastic bag. I remember a lot of blood there. This farm where the killing occurred is about two miles south and two miles west of the state line and in the state of Kansas."

Bonnie Heady came back to the station wagon. She helped Hall lift the body into the back seat. Then they drove to her home in St. Joseph and parked the car in the garage.

The grave had already been dug beside the house. They dumped the body into the trench and Hall poured a sack of quicklime over it. They covered the body with earth. Next day Bonnie Heady and Carl

Hall bought chrysanthemums and planted them in the freshly turned loam beside the house.

The first extortion letter these two sent to the Greenleases said:

Your boy been kidnapped get $600,000 in $20's—$10's—Fed. Res. notes from all twelve districts we realize it takes few days to get that amount. Boy will be in good hands—when you have money ready put ad in K. C. Star. M—will meet you in Chicago next Sunday—Signed Mr. G.

Do not call police or try to use chemicals on bills or take numbers. Do not try to use any radio to catch us or boy dies. If you try to trap us your wife your other child and yourself will be killed you will be watched all of the time. You will be told later how to contact us with money. When you get this note let us know by driving up and down main St. between 39 & 29 for 20 minutes with white rag on car aeriel.

If do exactly as we say an try no tricks, your boy will be back safe withen 24 hrs—afer we check money

Deliver money in army duefel bag. Be ready to deliver at once on contact.—

M

$400,000 in 20's
$200,000 in 10's

The FBI was in close touch with the Greenlease family and with the Kansas City police, but nothing was done to hinder the Greenleases' contacting the kidnapers, since this was the family's wish.

Then began one of the most cruel and sadistic chains of letters and messages ever transmitted in American criminal history—all holding out the promise of the boy's safe return if the money were delivered.

There were telephone calls from the mysterious "M," and further letters in which instructions were given for delivery of the money. But in each case something always went wrong.

On one call, "M" talked to friends of the Greenleases until Mrs. Greenlease demanded to talk to him. The conversation has been reconstructed like this:

Mrs. G. "M, this is Mrs. Greenlease."

Voice. "Speaking."

Mrs. G. "We have the money but we must know our boy is alive and well. Can you give me that? Can you give me anything that will make me know that?"

Voice. ". . . A reasonable request, but to be frank with you, the boy has been just about to drive us crazy. We couldn't risk taking him to a phone."

Mrs. G. "Well, I can imagine that. Would you do this? Would you ask him two questions? Give me the answer of two questions?"

Voice. "Speaking."

Mrs. G. ". . . if I had the answer to these two questions, I would know my boy is alive."

Voice. "All right."

Mrs. G. "Ask him what is the name of our driver in Europe this summer."

Voice. "All right."

Mrs. G. "And the second question, what did you build with your monkey blocks in your playroom the last night you were home . . . If I can get those answers from you, I'll know you have him and he is alive, which is the thing you know that I want."

Voice. "We have the boy. He is alive. Believe me. He's been driving us nuts."

Mrs. G. "Well, I can imagine that. He's such an active youngster."

Voice. "He's been driving us nuts."

Mrs. G. "Could you get those answers?"

Voice. "All right."

Notes from Hall to the Greenlease go-betweens were left under rocks marked with crayons. Letters were left taped to the under side of mail boxes. One note would give directions as to the location of another note, and so on until those trying to follow the instructions became confused. Telephone instructions were confused, too. Once the $600,000 in ransom money—weighing eighty-five pounds—was left beside a country lane and Hall failed to find it. The duffel bag was retrieved by the friends of the Greenleases, who then had to go through the agony of waiting for another message.

The fourteenth telephone call was received from "M" at the Greenlease home at 8:28 P.M., on October 4, 1953. The call was taken by Robert Ledterman, a close friend of the Greenleases. And this call went something like this:

Ledterman. "Greenlease residence. Ledterman speaking."

Voice. "How are you?"

Ledterman. "Fine. How are you tonight?"

Voice. "A little late."

Ledterman. "You said eight o'clock. Are we all set?"

Voice. "We're all set. We have a perfect plan. It couldn't be any . . ."

Ledterman. "How's that now? Give me that again."

Voice. "There could not be any mistake. This is a perfect plan. It will have to be a little later. I am sorry, too, but we want to make sure there's no mix-up this time."

Ledterman. "Yes. Let's get things over—say, by the way, M, did the boy answer any of those questions?"

Voice. "No . . . I couldn't . . . we didn't get anything from him."

Ledterman. "Couldn't get anything from him?"

Voice. "He wouldn't talk . . . I'll tell you this much. You will get him in Pittsburg, Kansas."

Ledterman. "You're not bunking me in that, are you?"

Voice. "That's the gospel truth . . ."

It was about midnight when Ledterman and Norbert S. O'Neill, another friend of the Greenleases, dropped the duffel bag of money at a bridge near the junction of Highways 40 and 10E near Kansas City.

Soon after they returned from their mission, the Greenlease telephone rang again. "M" reported he had picked up the money but hadn't had time to count it. Ledterman assured him it was all there as promised.

Voice. "Well, I am sure of that. You can tell his mother that she will see him as we promised within twenty-four hours . . . We will certainly be very glad to send him back."

The cruel hoax was played by Carl Hall and Bonnie Heady to the very end.

Once they had the money, they went on a drinking spree in St. Louis. Hall bought two metal suitcases and transferred the ransom money from the duffel bag which he dropped in an ash pit in south St. Louis (where it was later found by FBI agents).

The day after the payoff, Hall took Bonnie to an apartment on Arsenal Street in St. Louis. But as soon as Bonnie fell into a drunken sleep, he slipped out with the money, leaving only $2,000 of it in her purse.

Hall and Heady had less than two days of freedom after picking up the ransom money. Hall became too friendly with a taxi driver, who tipped St. Louis police that he could give them "something hot." Police arrested Hall and Heady on the evening of October 6, 1953.

But of the $600,000 paid to the kidnapers, only $295,140 was recovered by the FBI.

Hall finally gave police and FBI agents a full confession. Agents found the boy's body in the shallow grave and it was identified by the family dentist. Bloodstains were found on the basement floor and steps of Bonnie Heady's home and also on a nylon blouse and a fiber rug. They found thirty-eight-caliber shell casings which the FBI Laboratory established had been fired from the thirty-eight-caliber snub-nose Smith & Wesson revolver found on Hall at the time of his arrest. A lead bullet was recovered from the floor mat of the station wagon owned by Bonnie Heady and the Laboratory reported that it had been fired from Hall's revolver.

As for Bonnie Heady, she admitted to agents and police that she had assisted Hall in preparing the ransom notes and that she had taken Bobby Greenlease from the school. But she tried to place all the blame of the killing on Hall.

Carl Hall and his paramour pleaded guilty in the Federal Court at Kansas City to a charge of kidnaping for ransom. A jury then heard the evidence and on November 19, 1953, the jury recommended death.

Judge Albert L. Reeves said: "I think the verdict fits the evidence. It is the most cold-blooded, brutal murder I have ever tried."

The killers of little Bobby Greenlease were executed together in Missouri's lethal gas chamber at the Jefferson City State Penitentiary on December 18, 1953. Hall was pronounced dead at 12:12 A.M. and Bonnie Heady died twenty seconds later.

The ransom money was paid in 40,000 bills wrapped into forty bundles. But in the late summer of 1956 the FBI had not been able to find $301,960 of the money, which disappeared at some point between the time of the payoff and the time the two metal suitcases were brought into the Eleventh Precinct Station in St. Louis after Hall's arrest. The search for the money still goes on.

This shocking kidnap-murder case is merely an example of the post-war crime problem which confronted the FBI and local law enforcement officers in the wake of World War II.

Hoover had foreseen the crime wave which would include such crimes as the Greenlease kidnaping and the Denver plane crash murders. One barometer was the rising rate of wartime juvenile delinquency.

Hoover said in 1944:

It is well to analyze the conditions that breed crime today, in order that we may prevent it tomorrow. One of the primary causes of the alarming increase in crime among our young people, for example, has been the disintegration of the home as a guiding influence. The tremendous number of parents who have entered the armed services and war industries no longer can exercise sufficient control over their sons and daughters. The mushrooming of industrial cities, where facilities for recreation and wholesome living are inadequate, deprives thousands of children of the benefits of a normal way of life.

The migration of workers from small towns and farms to cities and defense centers often brought a moral letdown. The parents' authority over their children was relaxed. Families were crowded into slum-like areas where many boys and girls had little chance for a normal life. Girls became "khaki-wacky" and teen-agers began looking for excitement without a steady hand to guide them. The problem wasn't confined to those living on the wrong side of the tracks.[1] It was found in the better neighborhoods, too, among well-to-do families in which parents and children drifted apart and suddenly found they didn't understand each other.

Much of the crime increase could be accounted for by the increase in the nation's population. But that wasn't the whole answer by any means, because the percentage increase in crime in the postwar years was greater than the percentage increase in population. From 1945 to 1955, population increased 24.3 percent while crime increased 44.5 percent.

A few statistics tell a part of the story. The major crimes committed in 355 cities in the prewar years 1937–1939 averaged 630,257 each year. These were crimes of murder, manslaughter, rape, robbery, aggravated assault, burglary, larceny and automobile theft. In these same cities, the major crimes in the postwar years 1946–1955 averaged almost 800,000 each year, or an increase of 26.8 percent over the prewar years. Across the nation, major crimes climbed above the 2,000,-000 mark for the first time in 1952. Three years later the major crime rate was over the 2,200,000 level and property loss in burglaries, robberies, auto thefts and other larcenies was close to $400,000,000. In 1955, a serious crime was committed on an average of every 13.9 seconds in the day.

The most shameful part of the postwar crime record was the number of teen-age children involved in major law violations. Out of 1,861,764 persons arrested in 1,477 cities in 1955 for major crimes, it was found that one out of every ten was under eighteen years of age. Boys and girls under eighteen were involved in 42.3 percent of the arrests made for major crimes; and almost half of these were under fifteen. The reports showed that 62.2 percent of those arrested in 1955 for automobile thefts and 52.7 percent of those arrested for burglary had not reached their eighteenth birthday.

The bare statistics standing by themselves gave the frightening impression that young people had no moral restraints and were running wild. Such an impression was false, of course, but the situation was disgraceful and there was confusion across the land. Almost every state had its own definition of a juvenile delinquent and its own legal rules for handling youthful law violators.

The FBI's early interest in the youth problem was rooted primarily in the fact that until juvenile delinquency was controlled there was little likelihood that the adult crime problem could be solved. The records showed that the juvenile delinquent too frequently became the adult criminal.

As early as 1946, Hoover considered the problem so pressing that he directed the organization of an FBI Juvenile Delinquency Instructors School in which special agents were assigned to a broad research project, supplemented by lectures from well-known authorities in the field of juvenile delinquency. The agents equipped themselves to lecture to local police groups on the latest developments in handling juveniles, the psychological problems involved in juvenile delinquency, how to organize boys' clubs, what other agencies were doing in this field and related subjects. Many of the agents had already gained practical experience in dealing with young people in boys' clubs, the Boy Scouts and church work. Some of them had experience as parole and probation officers before joining the FBI.

The information gathered in these studies is being made available through FBI training schools to police departments to help them in developing their own programs to combat juvenile delinquency.

But in their work, Hoover and his men are aware that the basic solution rests with the mothers and fathers themselves and not with any law enforcement agency. In an article for the *Syracuse Law Review* Hoover expressed the parent problem in this way:

> Criminal behavior is learned behavior. The child and the adolescent are impressionable, and their active minds develop codes of morality no higher than those to which they are exposed. The environment which the adult community provides its growing children is the most important factor underlying the behavior patterns cultivated by the normal child.

Along with the increase in juvenile delinquency, there was a steady increase in bank robberies. Old-time gangs like the Dillingers, Karpises, "Baby Face" Nelsons, and "Pretty Boy" Floyds of the gangster era no longer roamed the country. But the professional bank robbers still operated, and they had been joined by a growing number of amateurs even more vicious and dangerous than the professionals because they were less predictable in handling weapons.

In a few cases, such as the Brink's robbery, the planning was professional and each move was carefully mapped out in advance in the meticulous manner of "Eddie" Bentz, who operated in the early 1930's. Bentz was one of the first to use getaway charts and to study a bank and its employees' habits thoroughly before making a move.

"I always study the financial reports of a bank," Eddie once said. "How can you know what you are doing unless you know how much in bonds and cash are kept at hand?"

If nothing else, Eddie was thorough. He spent days and sometimes weeks in "casing" a bank, charting employees' movements and diagraming the escape routes. He read the law enforcement journals to keep abreast of the latest developments.

"I sometimes change my brand of cigarettes, too," Eddie told a friend, "because the G-Men pay attention to such details."

The postwar bank-robbery problem found the amateurs—and not the Bentzes—in the majority. In some respects this made the FBI's work harder, because the amateur often had no past crime record and identification was more difficult. But the amateur left more clues and made more mistakes—like the robber who got excited and ran through the wrong door into a barred room rather than a back alley.

The FBI found that greed for easy money wasn't confined to any age bracket. Bank robbers, the records show, came in all ages from teen-agers to grandpas. And even some families tried it. In Wisconsin, a mother, her twenty-four-year-old son, fourteen-year-old daughter, and two others outside the family planned a robbery and carried it off, escaping with $11,533.93. The daughter, who carried a gun in the robbery, afterward returned to her grade school with a note for the teacher, signed by her mother: "Please excuse Marguerite, she was sick with a cold." The brother was quite proud of his young sister. "I don't know what she would have done if somebody had started shooting," he said after the gang's arrest, "but I think she would have done all right."

The FBI found, too, that some bank robbers shuddered when they saw that a bank had hired women or elderly men as tellers. "They're so unpredictable," one bank robber, Clyde Milton Johnson, told agents after his arrest. "You take a dame or an old man and you never know what they're going to do. I almost backed out of one job when I saw the bank had two women tellers.

"I'll tell you what I mean. I went into a savings and loan company office and pointed my gun at this old man sitting there in his cage. You know what he did? He just sat there.

"I shoved the gun right under his nose and said, 'I mean business!'

"He said: 'I don't have anything to do with the money,' and he pointed to the guy in the next cage.

"Well, I figured the old guy would stay put, so I put my gun on the other guy. Then this old man got up and started toward the door. I yelled: 'Where the hell do you think you're going?'

"He looked over his shoulder and said, 'I'm going for a policeman,' and he kept going."

Johnson shook his head. "What are you going to do with people like that?"

Johnson's complaint was underscored in another case in which a bank robber exhibited a pistol to a woman teller and pushed a note through the window which read: "Fill this bag with money or die."

The woman read the note and exclaimed: "Why pick on me?" Then she calmly squatted down behind the protection of her counter. The baffled robber fled, no doubt disgusted with the unpredictable reactions of the female of the species.

But the amusing incidents could never obscure the trail of death and terror left behind by the bank robbers, who remained a postwar problem of considerable magnitude when the total robberies and attempted robberies were added up.

In the excitement that goes with a bank robbery, identification of the bandit becomes difficult at times and the FBI has learned that the most "positive" identifications can't always be accepted without checks and double checks. This lesson was driven home when L. H. was arrested in Connecticut by State Police as a parole violator. Questioning developed him as a suspect in a $25,900 bank robbery and he was identified by six witnesses as the bandit. The witnesses repeated their positive identifications to FBI agents. L. H. was convicted by a federal jury on May 20, 1953, although he maintained that he was innocent and that at the time of the robbery he had been at home with his wife.

Ten months later a man in Indiana confessed to the Connecticut robbery and cleared L. H., who was turned over to state authorities on an armed-robbery charge, but the state witnesses refused to identify him and he later received $4,000 for the erroneous bank robbery conviction.

Another persistent crime problem for the FBI was the tremendous number of automobiles stolen and then transported in interstate commerce. From 1935 through 1955 it is estimated that more than 4,000,-000 automobiles were stolen in the United States. In 1955 alone, there were 227,150 automobile thefts.

Back in 1919, Representative Newton of Missouri had been shocked to learn that in the previous year 29,399 automobiles had been stolen in twenty-one cities and 5,541 of the cars—worth more than $5,000,-000—had never been recovered. Newton told his colleagues: "There is no class of criminals enjoying more lucrative gain as a reward for their industry than the automobile thieves of the country," and he demanded that Congress act to curb the thieves by making it a federal offense to transport a stolen automobile across a state line. Some lawmakers professed to see in this proposed legislation a threat to states' rights, but the need for federal jurisdiction was so evident that Congress passed the National Motor Vehicle Theft Act (Dyer Act) in that year. Even in those early days of the automobile, the theft problem was too great for local authorities, whose jurisdiction ended as soon as the chase for a stolen car reached a state line.

The Dyer Act was to prove a greater weapon against criminals than

Congress anticipated. When Dillinger and the other gangsters went on their rampage in the early 1930's, it was often the theft of a car which put the G-Men on their trail. Once they crossed a state boundary with a stolen automobile, the FBI had legal authority to go after them— and did.

Most car thefts such as those in which youngsters steal a car for a joy-ride, have been local police problems. The FBI has concentrated largely on tracking down those who have stolen cars for use in crimes, and also professional automobile rings who make stolen cars a lucrative criminal business.

In making tens of thousands of investigations, the FBI has on a few occasions arrested the wrong person. Sometimes an agent has made inadequate investigation or a set of circumstances has been such that for a time Justice stumbled and her scales were off balance.

In one case, a Chevrolet automobile stolen in Fort Worth, Texas, was located in a garage in Cantillo, Texas. The agent's first checks indicated that R. A. was possibly the man they were after. The garage operator was shown photographs of five men and he picked out R. A. as the man he believed had left the car in his garage. He added that he wouldn't make a positive statement of identification until he saw R. A. in person. However, the circumstances were such that the U. S. Attorney in Texas agreed there was sufficient cause to have a warrant issued for R. A.'s arrest. After process was obtained, the FBI office at El Paso asked agents in Montana to locate and arrest R. A.

R. A. was arrested in Montana, at 10:00 P.M., May 17, 1956. There was no doubt about R. A. being the same person whose arrest had been asked by the El Paso office, because his physical description and past criminal record fit El Paso's specifications.

But R. A. insisted he was working in Montana on the day the Chevrolet had been stolen, and in checking his story, agents found that it was true. He had been working in Bozeman on that day, and could not possibly have been guilty of the theft.

In less than twenty-four hours from the time of his arrest, R. A. was released from jail. Headquarters in Washington gave the agents responsible for the mistake a dressing down for not taking greater care in their investigations before making an arrest.

But while the FBI's assault against postwar criminals was perhaps one of the most spectacular parts of the Bureau's work, the G-Men were by no means entirely absorbed with crime.[2] They were responsible also for fact-finding in an astonishingly broad range of civil litigation. A book could be written about this field of FBI activity alone, in which special agents produced evidence to save the government more than

$601,975,128 from 1945 to 1955 by exposing false claims and fraud against the government, auditing renegotiated contracts, proving ability to pay fines, and establishing the nonliability of the federal government in personal-injury and property-damage claims.

Many of these investigations were intricate exercises in accounting and finance. Others fell into the pattern of careful observation and documentation of evidence to refute false claims. Such was the case of a veteran, a farmer, who claimed that his war-risk insurance was payable inasmuch as he had become permanently and totally disabled.

A special agent drove into the country and spent several hours observing the farmer.

The farmer was plowing with a team of mules, keeping his plow in a deep, straight furrow. After plowing quite a while, he picked up heavy sacks of fertilizer and carried them across the field. He was spreading the fertilizer when something frightened the team of mules. They broke away, dragging the plow behind them. The farmer took out after the mules, ran them down after a hundred-yard sprint, and brought them back. Then he went on with the plowing.

The agent's photographic record of this busy day on the farm was a convincing argument against the veteran. The claim was not allowed.

Through the postwar years—just as in the prewar years—every case among the thousands handled by the FBI was scanned by the Bureau's critics for some evidence that civil rights were being ignored or violated. Never, perhaps, had the actions of an investigative agency been under so critical a microscope over so long a period of time—and with so little satisfaction to the critics.

28: *To Secure These Rights*

ALMOST everyone in Newton, Georgia, was asleep when Sheriff M. Claud Screws's automobile rolled into the courthouse square and stopped. Three men stepped from the car and were joined by another. The men were the sheriff, a policeman, a deputy sheriff and a thirty-year-old Negro prisoner named Robert Hall, who had been arrested on a warrant charging the theft of an automobile tire.

Hall was handcuffed, but suddenly—according to the evidence—the three officers began to beat their prisoner. They slugged him with their fists and there was the thump of a two-pound iron blackjack crunching into Hall's skull. The prisoner fell but still the three men beat and kicked him for at least fifteen minutes, perhaps thirty. Later they claimed the prisoner had used insulting language and appeared to have reached for a pistol. That was the defense they gave.

At last they stopped hitting the man. They dragged him, feet first, across the courthouse yard to the jail. They heaved the victim into a cell.

An eyewitness said:

He was bloody and full of dirt and he was unconscious but crawling around on his all fours. The back of his head was beaten to a pulp and he was in a pool of blood. His head was swollen so that his eyes were closed . . . There was a hole in his left temple. There was a gash about an inch and one-half in the top right side of his head . . .

An ambulance from Albany was called to the jail. The ambulance attendant took one look at the prisoner and asked, "Was he in a wreck?"

"Yeah," somebody said. "Yeah. He was in a wreck."

Robert Hall died a few minutes after the ambulance arrived at the hospital.

The brutal treatment of Hall was as revolting to the great majority of Southerners as it was to those in the North, the East and the West who respect the Constitutional guarantees of rights which include a trial by jury rather than a trial by ordeal.

But in their savagery did the three officers deny their victim his civil rights in violation of a federal law—or was this episode merely a case of police brutality, punishable by the state and not by the federal government?

At the request of the Department of Justice, the FBI investigated the death to determine whether or not the officers had violated a federal law which forbade anyone "acting under the color of law" to willfully deprive another of the rights, privileges or immunities guaranteed by the Constitution or the laws of the United States.[1]

A federal grand jury thought Hall had been denied his Constitutional rights and an indictment was brought against Sheriff Screws and his two companions. A federal petit jury heard the evidence and convicted the trio. The conviction was upheld by the Circuit Court of Appeals.

The United States Supreme Court called the case "a shocking and revolting episode in law enforcement," but it also—by a five-to-four decision—ordered a new trial for the defendants. The majority ruled that the trial judge should have instructed the jury to convict only if the officers had beaten Hall with the specific intent and purpose of denying their prisoner a Constitutional right.[2]

The defendants were acquitted in their second trial when the government was unable to prove that they had "willfully" denied Hall his civil rights.

The Screws case and others prompted FBI Director Hoover to warn:

We can have the Constitution, the best laws in the land, and the most honest reviews by the courts—but unless the law enforcement profession is steeped in the democratic tradition, maintains the highest in ethics, and makes its work a career of honor, civil liberties will continually—and without end—be violated.

In addition to being an example of cruel and inhuman treatment, the Screws case underlined one of the most misunderstood facets of law enforcement—the FBI's responsibilities and limitations in the field of civil rights.

The Constitutional Amendments known as the Bill of Rights provide for freedom of religion, speech, press, assembly and petition; freedom to keep and bear arms, from enforced quartering of troops, from unlawful search and seizure; freedom from being a witness against oneself; freedom from excessive bail or fines; from being deprived of due process; from cruel and unusual punishment; and the right to a speedy and public trial by jury. These are primarily guarantees against oppression of individuals by the federal government. The relationships between private persons are matters which are largely reserved to the states.

An example of the line drawn between federal and state jurisdiction in civil rights cases was the attempt by Congress in 1871 to abolish lynchings and mob actions by means of a law making it a federal crime for two or more persons to conspire to deny others the due process of law. The Act was aimed primarily against the Ku Klux Klan.

However, the United States Supreme Court held that the criminal conspiracy section of the Act was void. The court ruled [3] that while the Fourteenth Amendment prohibited a state from abridging the rights of a citizen, the Amendment did not cover the acts of private individuals. Thus a mob might lynch a victim in violation of every concept of decency and fair play, but this action did not necessarily mean that the mob had violated a federal law. And unless a federal law were violated, then the FBI had no jurisdiction.

The two basic civil rights statutes which more or less form the framework of the FBI's responsibilities in this field are found in Sections 241 and 242 of Title 18, United States Code. Section 241 deals for the most part with involuntary servitude, peonage and voting rights. Section 242 applies largely to the actions of law enforcement officers who, "under color of law," willfully deny a person the rights guaranteed by law and the Constitution.

There has been no area more sensitive for the FBI than that of civil rights, where investigations touch jealously guarded states' rights and where the passions of men are easily aroused. Some groups have accused the FBI of meddling in the states' affairs, while others have denounced the Bureau for not plunging deeper into this field and being more aggressive.[4]

Hoover told a House Appropriations Subcommittee early in 1956:

> In civil rights cases the Bureau is in a situation that if it obtains facts which result in prosecution it is unpopular and if it doesn't obtain facts, it is unpopular. Our sole purpose is to do our job objectively.

The Attorney General has established the procedures followed by the FBI in civil rights cases:

1. A preliminary investigation is made whenever a complaint is received alleging a violation of federal civil rights statutes.

2. The results of the inquiry are given to the Criminal Division of the Department of Justice for study.

3. If the Criminal Division decides that the case is not a violation of federal law or that federal action is not warranted, the FBI takes no further action.

4. If the Criminal Division decides there has been a violation, a full investigation is made and all evidence is gathered for use in prosecution.

5. In no case does the FBI recommend what action the Department should take.

Heavy pressure was put on the federal government in 1955 to have the FBI investigate the murder of Emmett Louis Till, a fourteen-year-old Negro youth from Chicago who was slain in Mississippi after he allegedly made indecent remarks to a white woman, Mrs. Roy Bryant, at a country store. Seven days after the incident at the store, Till's body was found floating in the Tallahatchie River. He had been shot through the head. A cotton gin fan had been tied about his neck and his body dumped into the river. Witnesses said Mrs. Bryant's husband and his half brother, J. W. Milam, had seized young Till in the home of his uncle and taken him away with them into the night. The two were indicted for murder, but a jury acquitted them.

The death of young Till was a brutal, savage and shameful murder beyond a reasonable doubt. But the Justice Department's Criminal Division decided that the FBI should not enter the case inasmuch as the available preliminary facts revealed no indication of a violation of federal civil rights statutes.

The reasoning behind this decision was that while murder no doubt had been done, the federal government had no authority to investigate and prosecute murder unless a federal law had been violated. Unless and until Congress passed a law covering such cases, federal intervention would be an invasion of the states' rights.

The clamor for federal intervention in civil rights cases such as the Till case was like an echo from the early 1930's, when the cry rang out for a federalized police force to stamp out gangsterism. But the real answer to the problem is stronger local law enforcement backed by intelligent public opinion.

One of the greatest barriers encountered by the FBI in civil rights violations has been local prejudice. Juries have refused to convict even when defendants confessed. Witnesses' lips have been sealed by fear or by sympathy for the accused. Authorities have refused to cooperate. And public opinion has been apathetic toward seeing justice done.

One of the most shocking cases of a jury's refusal to convict occurred in 1947 in South Carolina, after a cab driver was fatally stabbed near the town of Liberty. A Negro suspect named Willie Earle was arrested and taken to the Pickens County jail for questioning. He protested his innocence.

The word spread that Earle was being held for the crime. Angry cab drivers in Greenville, South Carolina, began to discuss the death of a brother driver. Soon the crowd had become a mob armed with shotguns and knives and the mob was racing for the Pickens County jail. They pushed their way into the jailer's living quarters at the jail and forced him to unlock Earle's cell.

Willie Earle was dragged from his cell and pushed into an automobile. Near the Saluda Dam the caravan halted and the prisoner "confessed" to the crime. Then he was taken to a point on Bramlett Road in Greenville County and pulled from the car. The mob beat Willie Earle and stabbed him with knives. One man broke the butt of a shotgun over his head. Knives carved chunks of flesh from his body and finally shotgun blasts snuffed out the last small flame of life. Then the self-appointed executioners went home.

The Justice Department authorized the FBI to conduct a full investigation of the lynching because Earle had been in custody of an officer and there was the possibility that his civil rights had been denied "under color of law" by the jailer's willingly giving help to the mob or being derelict in his duty. The FBI's investigation exonerated the jailer.

The FBI joined forces with local law enforcement officers in the investigation and twenty-eight persons were identified as having been in the mob. They were arrested on state warrants charging them with murder—and twenty-six of the defendants confessed to taking part in the lynching. South Carolinians generally were outraged. Governor J. Strom Thurmond named a special prosecutor to see that justice was done. The defense offered no testimony. But the jury found all twenty-eight defendants "not guilty," despite the confessions.

Whenever a police officer or an official of a state institution is accused of a possible civil rights violation, the FBI investigates if the Criminal Division of the Department so instructs. The investigation goes forward regardless of whether the state authorities have taken action or failed to take action in the case, although as a matter of policy the Department of Justice invariably stands aside if the state indicates it desires to take action.

Civil rights enforcement has led the FBI into sharp conflict at times, not only with police officers with whom the FBI has worked for years, but also with the governors of states.

In one widely publicized dispute, the FBI—at the Department's request—made a preliminary inquiry in 1952 into an alleged civil rights violation at the Gainesville, Texas, State School for Girls. An FBI agent called on the school superintendent, who cooperated in helping round up the facts. As it turned out, a girl inmate had rebelled against the school's discipline and had been kept in confinement, but the FBI found no basis for the charge of a civil rights violation. The FBI report supported the state's own findings.

A year later Governor Allan Shivers cited the Gainesville investigation as an example of FBI "snooping" into cases already investigated by state authorities, and charged the FBI with failure to consult the proper state officials before making the inquiries.[5]

Hoover denied that his agents had failed to notify the proper authorities in advance of the inquiry, and he wrote Shivers:

> . . . We of the FBI certainly have no apologies to make to anyone for doing our duty in carrying out the instructions of the Attorney General in enforcing the law of the land. Should the day ever come when the Director of the Federal Bureau of Investigation has the discretion of choosing those laws which his service will enforce, then indeed we will have a Gestapo, and I can assure you I would have no part of it.

The Shivers incident came after Governor John S. Fine of Pennsylvania and Governor John S. Battle of Virginia, speaking in Seattle before the annual Governors' Conference, criticized the FBI for an invasion of the police powers of their states. Both were referring to FBI investigations of alleged brutal treatment of inmates in their state institutions.

Fine argued in this manner:

It should be noted that this interference by the executive branch of the Federal Government is closely paralleled by the interference of the judicial branch through the writ of habeas corpus. Conceivably, we could now have a situation where a prisoner complained that he is being deprived of his constitutional rights and have the FBI gather the evidence for him that would lead to his release by writ of habeas corpus.

The question, therefore, is whether the Federal Government should continue to treat the States as quasi-criminals upon the complaint of those persons whom the state has found to be unfit for society or those the state has confined to help them and to protect the rest of its citizens.

Hoover replied to this attack by declaring that the governors were criticizing the FBI for enforcing an Act of Congress and carrying out instructions given by the Department of Justice.

He added:

. . . it would appear that if the Governors are opposed to this law, their recourse would be to go to Congress and seek the repeal of the law rather than level their attacks upon the FBI . . .

The American Civil Liberties Union came to the FBI's defense with a letter to Fine which said in part:

. . . We are at a loss to understand why the FBI, which, over-all, has made an excellent record of enforcing these constitutional rights, should be the subject of such an attack—especially as your speech indicated no criticism of the FBI's investigative procedures, but emphasized opposition to its coming on to the scene at all . . . Certainly the federal government has the power to protect its citizens from deprivation of their rights and when such occasions arise, it is its duty to act.

Enforcement of the civil rights statutes created a difficult situation for the FBI in 1953, when the New York City Police Commissioner at that time, George P. Monaghan, refused to permit agents to question members of his force who had been accused of brutal treatment of prisoners in violation of their rights. Monaghan's position was that FBI investigations were having a bad effect on the morale of the New York City police—and besides, the case in which the FBI was interested had already been investigated by his own Department, the officers cleared, and a report sent to the U. S. Attorney for the Southern District of New York.

It developed that Monaghan had reached an agreement with the United States Attorney and the Department of Justice's Criminal Division whereby the Justice Department would refer civil rights complaints to the New York Police Department. The Police Department would make its own investigation, and a report would be forwarded to the Justice Department through the United States Attorney. In case the

Justice Department wasn't satisfied with the results of the inquiry, it could then take whatever steps were deemed necessary. The arrangement had been made without any notice to the FBI.

Hoover protested to the Attorney General, James McGranery, that this agreement in effect gave the New York City police special exemption in civil rights investigations. He argued that the New York City police should not be on a different basis from the police in other parts of the country. McGranery ordered the agreement revoked, and eventually an agreement was reached between the FBI and New York City Police Department calling for mutual cooperation in the handling of civil rights cases.

For the most part, the FBI has found local law enforcement officers willing to cooperate in civil rights investigations. Some police departments, such as that of Dallas, Texas, notify the FBI immediately whenever a civil rights complaint is made against an officer. An attitude has developed—and is growing—that if a police officer has treated a prisoner brutally and denied him his civil rights, then the officer deserves to be exposed, punished and fired for the good of the entire force and law enforcement generally. But if the charges are untrue, then the officer's innocence should be established beyond doubt.

While the FBI has worked for years establishing a program to bring about closer cooperation between special agents and local law enforcement officers, the Bureau cannot make investigations on the basis of whether or not the FBI's popularity will be affected. If that were the case then the FBI would never check into civil rights cases involving public officials. There probably would never have been any investigation into the powerful Pendergast political machine in Kansas City, Missouri.

Tom Pendergast ran Kansas City's politics and its underworld. His power was legendary and it seemed that he was untouchable, until the federal government cracked down on him and his political stooges who had corrupted the ballot boxes in the November, 1936, election.

A committee of citizens who had revolted against boss rule had watched the violations of election laws at some precincts and given their evidence to the United States Attorney. Federal Judge Albert L. Reeves ordered a grand jury investigation of the reported irregularities. On the face of it, something was wrong, because Kansas City had a population of less than 400,000, and there were some 270,000 registered voters. The FBI was called into the case.

Judge Reeves told the Grand Jury:

> . . . I can't sit quietly in my district here, charged with responsibility as I am, and allow my fellow countrymen who stand for the law, and the citizens who stand for the law, witness some man going with dripping

fingers to the ballot box. A corrupt vote is akin to a gun pointing at the very heart of America.

FBI agents piled up damning evidence of fraud, stuffed ballot boxes, intimidation and thievery of votes by the changing of markings from Republican candidates to Democratic candidates. One precinct captain was heard to say, "I've had a hard day. I've been in the basement and those damn Republicans certainly write heavy. It was a tough job erasing."

FBI Laboratory experts studied the ballots and found proof of erasures, with clear indications that cross marks had been made on different ballots by the same person. Latent fingerprints of defendants were found on ballots which they had had no right to handle. Indentations in the paper showed that ballots had been marked while lying one on top of the other.

The evidence was overwhelming, and 256 defendants were convicted. This was the beginning of the end for one of the most corrupt political machines in American history.

Another landmark case in FBI records, however, was an effort that failed because of a court interpretation of the law. The Mobile, Alabama, *Register* was crusading against vice and gambling in 1939 when one of its editors was lured into a compromising and intimidating situation and then badly beaten by an underworld gang determined to stop the paper's crusade.

The FBI pushed an investigation on the grounds that there had been a conspiracy to abridge freedom of the press. Five defendants were convicted but the United States Circuit Court of Appeals reversed the decision, holding that the Constitution and federal statutes did not protect the press from the actions of private citizens.

The FBI's oldest enemy in the field of civil liberties has been the Ku Klux Klan, which FBI agents have been fighting for more than thirty years—and which has been run to cover as an effective hate group. The fight against the Klan has forced the FBI at times to move against officers of the law who joined a mob or did nothing to halt mob action.

In one case at Hooker, Georgia, in 1949, a mob of fifty to seventy-five persons dressed in Klan robes and hoods burned a cross near the home of a Negro woman whom they accused of giving "wild parties." In her home at the time were six Negro men, ranging in age from nineteen to thirty, who had come by to see one of her sons. The mob rounded up the visitors and took them onto a hill, flogged them, and told them, "Get on over that hill and get out of here."

Among those watching the cross-burning at the woman's home were

Dade County Sheriff John William Lynch and Deputy Sheriff William H. Hartline. Hartline helped the mob load the Negroes into the automobiles and the sheriff stood by without uttering a word of protest or making a move to protect the Negroes.

A Federal Court jury in Rome, Georgia, found Sheriff Lynch and Deputy Hartline guilty of violating a federal civil rights statute by failure to protect the Negroes. They were each fined $1,000 and sentenced to a year in prison. Their convictions were affirmed by the United States Circuit Court of Appeals and the Supreme Court refused to review their case.

By far the most unusual part of the episode was the resolution adopted by the Federal Grand Jury at Rome, composed of local residents, which said:

> The members of the Federal Grand Jury . . . hereby resolve: That the following agents of the Federal Bureau of Investigation . . . by their great fidelity and singleness of purpose in developing the information in the Dade County, Georgia, conspiracy trial have gone far beyond the line of duty to aid, assist and protect the citizens of the United States and to further the cause of equity and justice in America.

It would be pleasant to report at this point that all these efforts had achieved harmony and understanding. But despite the progress made in the field of civil liberties over the years, the threat of violence still hung over the land.[6]

FBI agents began reporting mounting racial tensions soon after the Supreme Court decision calling for the integration of white and Negro students in the public schools. When the tensions were at their peak in the spring of 1956, Hoover said:

> This mounting tension has manifested itself in overt acts on the part of individuals, organized resistance in legislative bodies, and the creation of organizations on a widespread basis in the South to resist integration . . .
>
> If the bloodshed, which both the proponents and opponents of integration now discuss, is to be avoided, there needs to be real understanding and public education with regard to the factors contributing to the present situation which can boil over at any moment into acts of extreme violence . . .
>
> The law-abiding people of the South neither approve nor condone acts of brutality and the lawless taking of human lives. On the other hand, historic traditions and customs are a part of a heritage with which they will not part without a struggle . . . The mounting tension can be met only with understanding and a realization of the motivating forces . . . The area of danger lies in friction between extremists on both sides ready with violence.

The warning was timely.

The Cold War

29: *The Great Illusion*

AMONG the people who entered FBI Headquarters one warm June evening in 1950 was a middle-aged man whose calm, intelligent face gave no hint of the storm in his soul.

He stepped from an elevator on the fifth floor and walked down the marbled hall to an office where a special agent was waiting to keep their appointment.

The visitor—let's call him Mr. A.—explained that he was intensely interested in having more detailed information on the workings of the Federal Employees Loyalty Program, which had been launched by President Harry S. Truman. There were aspects of the program involving civil liberties that bothered Mr. A. and he wanted to talk the whole thing over with someone close to the problem.

The agent explained the workings of the Bureau in loyalty investigations, but as they talked he sensed that the conversation was mere shadowboxing and that Mr. A. had something on his mind other than the loyalty program. Gradually the talk turned to the underground operations of the Communists.

"I've never been able to understand," the agent said, "how it is that a man can live the life of deceit that a Communist must live, and then square this life with his own conscience and the trust placed in him by his friends and his government."

The comment hit the mark. Mr. A. launched into a denunciation of the double life which communism required of those who were dedicated Party members; and he deplored the stealth and deceit and disloyalty of Communists who had forced the government to screen its employees as a security precaution.

"You know a lot about those things, don't you?"

The visitor looked at the agent a long, long time. "Yes," said Mr. A. "I know a lot. I don't know how much you know about me—perhaps more than I think."

Then, as though talking to himself, Mr. A. said, "I debated a long time about what I should do . . ."

"You were in the Party?"

"Yes."

The word was a long sigh of relief. He told how he had gone on missions for the Party in the 1930's, his dedication to the cause, and his honest but tragic conviction that communism was liberalism with work-callused hands. When the Nazis and the Communists joined in their nonaggression pact, Mr. A. saw communism for what it was. He saw the Fascist and Communist imperialists with clasped hands and recognized them as twins.

The agent finally said, "You've carried this around with you a long time. Isn't it about time to help the government with your knowledge and information?"

Mr. A. nodded. "I'll be glad to give any information I can."

"What about your family?"

"I want to talk to my wife and let her make up her own mind."

Several days later, Mr. A. arranged for an agent to visit his home and talk to his wife. She, too, was disgusted with the shabby trick which communism had played—and was playing—on mankind. She had been even deeper into the Party than her husband, and had worked with the underground apparatus.

Between them, the two gave information [1] which supplied the missing parts in one puzzle here and another there. Their stories threw light on another hidden strand in the web spun by the Party and its successes in placing Party members in positions of trust in the government.

The story told by Mr. and Mrs. A. wasn't unusual. By the dozens, men and women came to the FBI with dramatic confessions of how they were duped by a kind of fascism which clothed itself in the raiments of liberalism. They wanted to clear their own conscience and set the record straight for the future. They had discovered that in the battle for men's minds, the Party wasn't interested in intellectual or personal freedom for the individual. The Party sought men's minds because those minds were the tools with which to conquer a world; and the more brilliant the mind, the more useful it was in the Party's hands. These people who came to the FBI were no longer willing for their minds to be a mere cell in the super-brain of a dictatorship which denied the freedoms it claimed to champion. They had the courage to admit their mistake in the intellectual nightmare in which the darkest reaction had seemed to them to be a liberal dream.

The fight against communism has been by all odds the strangest chapter in the history of the FBI—and the least understood. The FBI's role cannot be understood unless there is an understanding of the FBI approach to the problem under the leadership of J. Edgar Hoover and the men around him.

First, Hoover looked on communism as an international conspiracy from the time Lenin exulted in November, 1917, that at last the world revolution of communism had begun, and the Third International established the ground rules for those who played on the Party's team. The Party was no "fraternal society" espousing the ideals of liberalism and it was not a political party in the accepted sense. This was a dangerous mechanism organized on an interlocking world-wide basis to wreck the existing social system and in so doing to overthrow the government of the United States by force and violence after it had been weakened by subversion.[2]

Second, the men in command at the FBI had no illusion that the *Communist Manifesto* and the writings of Lenin and then Stalin and then Malenkov and then Khrushchev were intellectual exercises to be classified only as opinion. They saw in these writings what they saw in *Mein Kampf*—the battle plan for conquest. The tactics might change and shift, but the grand strategy of world conquest had never changed. The FBI leadership accepted the Soviet Red chiefs at their word.

Third, communism threatened to destroy the freedoms and the government which these men were sworn to defend. This threat had to be fought just as the gangster threat was fought in the early 1930's. Not with the same methods and weapons, of course, but by every legal means and just as relentlessly.[3]

Fourth, those who were members of the Communist Party, and those who followed the Party line consistently, willingly and knowingly, were nothing more than pawns of Soviet Russia. And being the willing tools of Russia they were a potential menace to the security of the United States. As guardians of the nation's internal security, it was the legal and moral duty of the FBI to combat this menace and checkmate it where possible.

This was the basic outlook toward communism which the FBI carried into the task of keeping a check on Communist activities as requested by President Roosevelt in 1936. The viewpoint remained unchanged over the years because the estimate made by Hoover of the menace of communism was as sound in 1956 as it had been in 1919,

when he wrote the lawyer's brief against the Communist Party. Time
had only confirmed the estimate.

And so it was that the FBI watched the unbelievable happening
in America—but unbelievable only because most Americans refused
to believe that such words as these by Lenin could be applied by
Americans against their own country:

> In all countries, even the freest, "legal and peaceful" in the sense that the
> class struggle is less acute in them, the time has fully matured when it is
> absolutely necessary for every Communist Party systematically to combine
> legal with illegal work, legal with illegal organization . . .
>
> The absolute necessity in principle of combining illegal with legal work
> is determined . . . also by the necessity of proving to the bourgeoisie
> that there is not, nor can there be, a sphere or field of work that cannot
> be won by the Communists.

But the Communists believed these words. They formed their underground in the United States as Lenin said they should. FBI special
agents and informants followed the "illegal" Party underground into
a weird half-world of deceit where men and women lived one part of
their lives in a normal way while secretly giving the remainder of their
lives to "The Cause." As for the morality involved in living a double
life, didn't Lenin say: ". . . Our morality is deduced from the class
struggle of the proletariat"? It was "moral," therefore, to lie, cheat, steal,
betray and even liquidate tens of thousands of people if "the facts and
needs of the class struggle" called for such tactics. And the hard-core
Communists understood this well.

The American Communists concentrated from the very beginning
on trying to win labor to their ranks, by boring from within and by
trying to get agreements with established labor leaders. They succeeded in gaining control of some unions by infiltration, but they
failed to win the sympathy of the rank-and-file or the top leadership.

By the time the FBI began its intelligence investigation for President Roosevelt in 1936, the country was coming out of the Depression
but millions were still jobless. Fascism was on the rise in Germany,
Italy and Japan, and fighting already had broken out in Spain and in
the Far East. The idea of collective security had suddenly become
appealing to the Soviets and in 1934 Russia had joined the League of
Nations. The Communists set themselves up as the champions of a
united front for peace.

At the Seventh Congress of the Communist International in 1935
—attended by a large delegation from the Communist Party in the
United States—Georgi Dimitrov told the comrades:

The first thing that must be done . . . is to form a united front, to establish unity of action of the workers in every factory, in every district, in every region, in every country, all over the world. Unity of action of the proletariat on a national and international scale is the mighty weapon which renders the working class capable . . . of successful counterattack against fascism . . .

"Unity" for the time being took precedence over revolution. Almost overnight the Communists in the United States became "progressives" and "liberals." Communist-front groups began to mushroom. Communism was heralded as "twentieth-century democracy." The Party's membership soared from 19,200 in 1933 to 70,000 in 1939. In numbers they were few among America's millions, but they used the now well-known technique of capturing key positions of authority from which to maneuver or influence others in "front" organizations, government agencies, labor unions, universities, social clubs and other groups.

The Communists had once operated on a narrow front concentrated on influencing organized labor; now they became self-proclaimed liberals and allied themselves with the New Deal whenever this maneuver was useful to the Party line. The cry of "Peace and Bread" has touched the hearts of men down through the centuries, and with a Depression at home and Fascist bandits rising to power abroad, the Communists found this cry useful in spreading their influence. The Party's official newspaper, the *Daily Worker,* dropped the symbolic hammer and sickle from its masthead and proclaimed itself "People's Champion of Liberty, Progress, Peace and Prosperity."

Some people joined the Communist Party without having the faintest notion of the fire they were playing with. Some honestly believed that communism was liberalism. Thousands of people were drawn into "front" organizations and permitted the use of their names in causes which the Communists found useful for the moment.

The hard-core Communists had no illusions. They knew that their strength was far greater than their numbers, and the long-time Communist William Z. Foster put it in words when he said in 1932:

. . . The actual strength of the Communist movement in the United States is not something that can be accurately stated in just so many figures. It has to be measured largely by the general mass influence of the Party and its program.

They knew the power that could be wielded by a dedicated minority willing to sacrifice all else to reach its final goal.

In mid-August of 1939 the Communists were outraged by rumors that Germany and Russia might sign a nonaggression pact. The *Daily Worker* took exception to such a report in the New York *Daily News* and said:

The Daily News published the filthy falsehood that the Soviet Union was considering an "agreement" with the most vicious enemy of the USSR and all democracies, the bestial Nazi regime . . .

The "filthy falsehood" came true on August 24, 1939, leaving Hitler free to make war in the West. The "bestial" Nazis were now the friendly neighbors of the Soviet Union. As for the Russian attack on Finland, William Z. Foster explained that nicely by saying: "The Red Army is cooperating with the toiling masses of the Finnish people . . ."

The Communists changed their "line" literally overnight after the pact was signed. The United States under the New Deal Administration was no longer "progressive"—it was an "imperialist warmonger," along with Britain and France. The new Communist theme was "Keep America Out of the Imperialist War" and "The Yanks Are *Not* Coming." The Party fought lend-lease to Britain and rallied against sending aid to France. The "anti-Fascist" united front became the "anti-imperialist" united front.

Comrade Earl Browder, the Communist Party's General Secretary, asked, "What reason is there to believe that an Allied victory will bring anything better to the world than a German victory?"

But when Germany turned on Russia it was another story. The Communists flipflopped back again. The war that was "unjust" on June 21, 1941, became a "just" war on June 22. The war of the "imperialist warmongers" became "a mighty people's crusade against fascism and oppression." The fronts organized to mobilize the people for peace melted away. The anti-imperialist leagues disappeared. In their place emerged the "fronts" for unity, for a second front, and for all-out aid to Great Britain, China and the Soviet Union.

The Party lost some 20,000 disillusioned members who saw in the flipflopping the Party's dedication to Soviet Russia and to communism rather than the American ideals of freedom. But with the old "united front" reestablished, and with the United States at war, the Party's membership climbed to an all-time high of 80,000 members by 1944.[4] The FBI estimated that almost 1,000,000 people knowingly or unknowingly had been drawn into Communist-front activity. The Communists themselves boasted that for every member of the Party there were ten others who willingly followed the Party "line."

Into and through the war years the FBI traced the twists and turns of the Communist Party and the fronts which changed their names as casually as a man changes a suit of clothes. When a front or a name had served its purpose, a fresh one was ready. For example, the Friends of Soviet Russia was organized in 1921. Through the years, to suit the condition, it became the Friends of the Soviet Union, the American Committee for Friendship with the Soviet Union, the American Council on Soviet Relations, and then the National Council of American-Soviet Friendship.

During the Soviet-Nazi amity, the most flagrant effort to damage the aid-to-Britain program came in June, 1941, when a Communist-inspired wildcat strike closed down the North American Aviation Corporation plant at Inglewood, California, a plant with some $200,000-000 worth of airplane contracts.

Ignoring their national CIO leadership, plant leaders led the workers on strike with support from the state CIO organization. President Roosevelt ordered the Army to seize the plant and declared that the strike was "not a bona fide labor dispute, but a form of alien sabotage, inspired and directed by Communist forces, interested not in the advancement of labor, but in the defeat and overthrow of the United States."

After the United States and Russia became allies in the war, the Communist Party went all out in favor of a no-strike pledge. Earl Browder advocated total aid to Russia and Britain and urged "not an idle man, not an idle machine, not an idle acre."[5]

In October, 1940, Congress had passed the Voorhis Act, which required all organizations subject to foreign control to register with the Attorney General, and a month later the Communist Party of the United States of America "formally" severed its relationship with the Communist International (Comintern). The home-grown Communists could boast there was now no open link between them and Moscow. Nevertheless, the FBI's reports on Communist activities showed that the Party was following the Moscow line as faithfully as ever.

But a crisis was building in the Communist Party in America. Stalin dissolved the Comintern in June, 1943, as an expedient to win closer ties with the Western Allies. And immediately after this decision the FBI noted feverish activity among the Communist leaders in New York and other cities. Word went out to confidential informants to find out what was happening.

The informants reported that the Party's National Committee had ordered a study of the possibility of dissolving the Party and reorganizing under another name. Browder and other leaders felt that it would be in line with Moscow's friendship front to drop the word "party" from their name. Under another name, they reasoned, there would be a better chance of winning broad support from labor and other groups throughout the country. And besides, the informants said, the dissolution had been ordered by the Comintern before it was dissolved.

This was the state of the Party when President Roosevelt, Prime Minister Winston Churchill and Premier Stalin met at Teheran in December, 1943, to pledge a united fight against the Axis to the end, and cooperation in the postwar reconstruction. Again the American Communist leaders went into huddles to interpret the meaning of this agreement in relation to their own program.

Browder concluded that the Teheran agreement meant there must be friendly coexistence between capitalism and communism in the postwar world, and that the idea of a socialist revolution in the United States should be abandoned. He declared, "If J. P. Morgan supports this coalition and goes down the line for it, I as a Communist am prepared to clasp his hand on that and join with him to realize it."

At a mass meeting in New York on January 10, 1944, Browder proposed that the Party's name be changed from the Communist Party of the United States of America to the American Communist Political Association. This Association would work within the two-party political system, lending support to candidates on the nonpartisan basis of issues and not party affiliation.[6]

But the Browder interpretation of Teheran wasn't the interpretation made by William Z. Foster, who wrote the National Committee that big business couldn't be trusted to cooperate with the workers. He also challenged the Browder concept of soft-pedaling socialism in the postwar world. Communist leaders out in the districts were demanding to know whether the Browder "line" meant that the no-strike pledge was to carry over into the postwar years.

Again the FBI noticed unusual excitement among the Party's leadership. An informant reported that a top-secret meeting of the National Committee's Political Bureau had been called to discuss the Teheran agreement and the Foster letter. The meeting was certain to be one of the most important held by the Party in several years.

Soon the agents learned that a woman, acting for the Party, had rented a room at a midtown New York studio for a meeting to be held from 10:00 A.M. until 10:00 P.M. on February 8. The woman didn't disclose to the management that she was the agent for the Communist Party.

The studio was one used by professional and amateur singers and musicians for making recordings. There were several rooms wired for recordings and two unwired practice rooms which sometimes were rented to discussion groups and societies. The Party had reserved Room 11, one of the practice studios.

Once they knew the meeting place, the FBI agents went to work. They reserved Room 11 from 8:00 A.M. to 10:00 A.M. on February 8 and arranged to rent the adjoining room, Studio 14, for the entire day. If anyone looked at the FBI reservations, it appeared that Studio 14 was to be used by various musical groups throughout the day and into the night.

Two hours before the Communist meeting, agents carrying musical instruments walked into Studio 11, and while some of them beat out a ragtime tune, others swiftly removed the acoustical drapes from the wall adjoining Studio 14 and began the installation of a microphone.

A hole was drilled into the wall deep enough to allow the microphone to fit flush with the wall surface, and the lead wire was passed through the wall into Studio 14, where other agents tied it into a recording machine. A thin layer of cheesecloth was wrapped around the front of the microphone and the rough edges of plaster were covered with plaster of paris. A slight layer of the plaster of paris was daubed on the cheesecloth. To anyone looking at the wall, it appeared that a steam pipe above the microphone had at one time gone through the wall at that point and the hole had since been patched over. The wall drapes were replaced as they were before—nailed to the ceiling and the floor. The "musicians" closed their instrument cases and left.

At 11:00 A.M. people began drifting into Studio 11. Among them were Browder and Foster and Eugene Dennis and Sam Darcy and Abram Flaxer and Robert Minor and James Ford and Ben Davis and Ella Reeve "Mother" Bloor and more than a score of others whose names were well known to those who followed the trail of communism.

The voice of Foster came through the microphone to agents in Studio 14:

> . . . it is not necessary for me to stand up here and recite to you the many splendid achievements or splendid contributions that Comrade Browder has made to the life of our Party . . . But I think Comrade Browder . . . is also subject to making a mistake . . .

Foster ripped into Browder's suggestion that capitalism and communism could collaborate in the postwar world. He derided the notion that capitalism could be "progressive" or that there could be collaboration between the classes.

"Let us have no illusions," Foster said, "that Teheran has abolished the class struggle in the United States." He ended his long argument by accusing Browder of painting a picture of "flourishing capitalism" made to flourish by the support of the Soviet Union.

"I just want to say," he added, ". . . that all the help that the capitalist system of the world will get from the Soviet Union you could put in your small tooth in the long run . . ."

Foster saw the future clearly. He well knew that Moscow had not abandoned the class struggle and never would. But among the thirty-five people in the room that day there was only one—Darcy—who supported Foster.

While the argument over Teheran dragged on through the day,

"musicians" were entering and leaving Studio 14 next door. Each time the door was opened there was the blare of a hot trumpet, the wail of a saxophone or the tinny sound of an old piano. Every agent in New York who could play a musical instrument had been drafted that day to act in the drama of Studio 14.

The meeting disclosed the split in the Communist leadership and alerted the FBI to watch for another flipflop in the Party line, now that they knew Browder and Foster were at odds.

The Browder "line" prevailed. The Party was dissolved in May, 1944, and its place was taken by the Communist Political Association, which proclaimed its willingness to cooperate with "progressive capitalism." This was the most popular front ever devised by the Communist leadership, as it publicly pledged cooperation with the Administration's domestic and foreign policies.

But even as the Communists were playing a theme of close harmony with capitalism and avoiding talk of the class struggle, the Soviet espionage apparatus was busily at work. Men like Klaus Fuchs and Harry Gold and Julius Rosenberg and the Washington subversive underground in government were passing secrets to Soviet agents and to Russian diplomats. The diplomats had complete freedom of movement throughout the United States, a privilege not granted American diplomats in Russia.

The wartime atmosphere of friendship with Russia opened the way for the Communists to pursue their activities with a freedom that many times bordered on arrogant disregard of United States laws. Some Russian diplomats were known by the FBI to be linked with the Soviet espionage apparatus. At times they were strong-arm bully-boys actually taking part in kidnapings.

One such kidnaping occurred in San Francisco in 1943. San Francisco police walking their water-front beat at dawn on October 7 saw four or five men beating a struggling captive as they dragged him aboard the Russian freighter *Leonid Krasin*. The captive was Alexander S. Egorov, a young Russian seaman who had jumped ship in 1942 and hidden on a chicken farm in Oregon. The Soviet Consulate had reported the escape and U. S. Immigration authorities had found Egorov. He told them he had fled to escape the Communist dictatorship which had shot his father and thrown his mother into a concentration camp. The Immigration authorities allowed him to leave San Francisco aboard a Norwegian ship, but when the vessel docked in Oregon, Egorov slipped away again.

This time the Russians themselves tracked down Egorov. They caught him in San Francisco and dragged him, struggling, aboard the freighter. The FBI began an investigation, but the State Department ruled that the Bureau did not have jurisdiction in the case. An officer of the Immigration Service boarded the freighter two days after Egorov was shanghaied. He found the youth who pointed to Yakov Lomakin, the Soviet Consul General,[7] as one of the men who had kidnaped and beaten him. The official report said of the shipboard meeting:

Egorov was brought to the room under guard to be interviewed. He was wearing trousers and an undershirt. His shoulders were badly bruised and his body bore other marks of severe manhandling. He was obviously frightened and in great fear of his life. Egorov said that he had been attacked two days before by four or five men, one of whom was Lomakin. He said that he had been dragged aboard the ship. He stated that he did not want to depart from the United States and that he feared for his life. He begged the United States officials to take him from the ship.

But Lomakin claimed that he, personally, already had signed the captive aboard as a "crew member." The freighter sailed the next day.

The report concluded: "Egorov broke down and sobbed when the United States authorities left the vessel . . . He is obviously sailing to certain death."

It was almost five years before the public heard of the Egorov kidnaping. This incident and the desertion of other Soviet seamen in United States ports during the war impelled Hoover to write Attorney General Biddle in November, 1944, and say:

I believe that these individuals who leave the service of the Soviet Union because of political reasons are bona fide political refugees, and to turn them back into the custody of the Soviets is to turn them back to certain death. Because of their status as bona fide refugees they deserve at least a temporary haven in the United States and an opportunity to leave this country to proceed to a permanent haven or refuge of their choice.

On the national scene, the Browder policy of collaboration began to wear thin during the United Nations Conference in San Francisco in April, 1945, when the United States and Communist delegations clashed over the seating of members.[8] At this time, also, the French Communist leader, Jacques Duclos, after a visit to Moscow, wrote an article for a French Communist journal in which he criticized Browder for leading the American Communists down a path of "revisionism." He explained to the comrades why Browder was wrong in dissolving the Party and organizing the Communist Political Association.

Duclos said:

Earl Browder drew from the [Teheran] Conference decisions erroneous conclusions in no wise flowing from a Marxist analysis of the situation. Earl Browder made himself the protagonist of a false concept of the ways of social evolution in general, and in the first place, the social evolution of the U. S. . . .

And he added:

. . . one is witnessing a notorious revision of Marxism on the part of Browder and his supporters, a revision which is expressed in the concept of a long term class peace in the United States, of the possibility of the suppression of the class struggle in the postwar period and of establishment of harmony between labor and capital.

The voice of Duclos was recognized by the American Communists as the voice of authority. The same men who had supported Browder in the meeting in Studio 11 now turned against him. Browder was voted out as General Secretary and Foster stepped into the Party leadership. The Communist Political Association was tossed aside and the Communist Party of the United States of America was reestablished in July, 1945. The Party was back in business at the old stand.

In gathering intelligence information on the Communists, the FBI was in a position to see how a few Party members could influence the actions of a great number of people merely by being in key positions. An example of this happened in 1943, when the CIO held its national convention in Philadelphia at the Bellevue-Stratford Hotel.

FBI agents discovered that the Communist Party had set up headquarters in the St. James Hotel, where a member of the Party's National Committee huddled with the Party faction leaders to determine their strategy and tactics and discuss the CIO's executive board decisions. After the convention's resolutions committee had approved the resolutions to be placed before the delegates, the only existing rough drafts were brought to the Communist Party's command post.

The rough drafts were read to the National Committeeman, who changed the phrasing of some and then gave instructions on the sequence in which the resolutions should be presented to the convention in order to get the emphasis desired by the Party. After the rough drafts were changed, they were sent to the printers.

The FBI was frequently attacked for making investigations into Communist activities and at times for making loyalty checks at the request of other agencies.

In one case, the story went the rounds in Washington that the FBI had been "caught" investigating Edith B. Helm, social secretary to Mrs. Franklin D. Roosevelt, and Malvina Thompson, Mrs. Roosevelt's personal secretary. And it was added that Mrs. Roosevelt had taken the FBI to task.

The facts in the case were that William H. McReynolds, Secretary

of the Advisory Commission to the Council of National Defense—
and a White House secretary—sent a letter to the Attorney General
on July 11, 1940, asking for a loyalty check on several persons.
Enclosing a list of names, McReynolds wrote:

> It is the President's desire, and that of the Commission, that a careful
> check be made with respect to each individual involved, but particularly
> those on the first section of the list, for the purpose of making sure that
> these persons are dependable and justify the trust placed in them . . .

Three months later another list of fifteen names was sent over by
McReynolds' assistant with a written request that the FBI "institute
an investigation." One of the names on the list was Edith B. Helm.
Since the request came from an office in the White House, the check
was made.

When the news of the investigation leaked out, criticism was heaped
on the FBI. Hoover wrote to Major General Edwin M. Watson, the
President's secretary, explaining how the inquiry had developed, and
he sent a similar letter to Mrs. Roosevelt. Mrs. Roosevelt replied that
she was surprised by the investigation of Mrs. Helm and that someone
had been making inquiries about the private affairs of Miss Thompson.
"This type of investigation seems to me to smack too much of the
Gestapo methods," Mrs. Roosevelt said, "[and] seems to me to show
inefficiency on the part of the person who ordered it."

Hoover wrote Mrs. Roosevelt there had been no investigation of
Miss Thompson by the FBI and that the FBI had nothing to do with
Mrs. Helm's name being on the list received from the White House.
He agreed the investigation of Mrs. Helm "indicated inefficiency upon
the part of the person who ordered it," but said that the order had
not originated with the FBI and the investigation had been handled
in routine fashion.

The Helm incident was only a flurry, but it was a small warning
of the difficulties and misunderstandings that would develop in the
government's investigations of its employees during the Cold War that
was to come.

30 : *The Awakening*

CRIME has many faces. But one of the greatest crimes against the people of the United States ever recorded by the FBI was the Communist crime of poisoning the trust which men placed in each other's loyalty to their country.

Until international communism succeeded in convincing some Americans that they owed their allegiance to the cause of Soviet Russia, a citizen's loyalty to the United States was conceded in the normal course of events. Loyalty was a quiet love of country and a pride in its ideals which all men were presumed to carry in their hearts. The government didn't question it.

But communism sowed the seeds of suspicion and distrust. The followers of communism, by their own disloyalty, by espionage and subversion and deception, created the doubts that should never have been injected into the stream of American political life.

At last the federal government had to face the hard facts of life. And the facts were that there had been some employees in government who were disloyal. There had been some employees who could not be trusted with the secrets of state. Among the 2,000,000 government workers there was an overwhelming majority whose loyalty and integrity were beyond the shadow of doubt. But there had been some who had betrayed their government's trust. They had spread the subtle poison of doubt and distrust in men's minds.

And so it was that because the relatively few had betrayed a trust, the federal government felt it was necessary to take a sharp look at everyone who drew a salary check from the United States Treasury. While each man was presumed loyal until there was information to the contrary, the very fact that loyalty investigations had to be made showed the enormity of the Communist crime. The realization grew that a Communist's loyalty to the United States could not be taken for granted.

As Soviet Russia turned free nations into slave states and the Cold War became a grim struggle in the postwar months, President Harry S. Truman in November, 1946, appointed a temporary commission to study the problem of employee loyalty and how best to bar the disloyal from the federal service. There was general agreement inside and outside the Administration that Communists and their kind should be weeded out of positions of trust, and that the job should be done as far as possible without injuring the reputations of others.

The Truman Commission studied the past efforts to deal with the problem, and then reported:

Although these efforts to prevent disloyal persons from either obtaining or retaining Government employment were well intended, they were ineffective in dealing with subversive activities which employ subterfuge, propaganda, infiltration and deception.

More than seven years earlier, on August 2, 1939, Congress had passed the Hatch Act, which, as amended on July 19, 1940, made it unlawful for a federal employee to be a member of any political party or organization advocating the overthrow of our constitutional form of government. There was no provision for prosecution. The penalty was dismissal.

Three days after amendment of the Act, the White House laid down the ground rules under which the FBI would make loyalty investigations. President Roosevelt's administrative assistant, William H. McReynolds, sent a memorandum to Attorney General Jackson advising him that any complaints about an employee's loyalty should be referred to the head of the agency in which the employee worked; and there was to be no investigation by the FBI unless and until the agency head requested it. Actually, the investigative policy outlined by McReynolds was no different from the one under which the FBI had been operating in loyalty cases. It meant, in effect, that even when the FBI received conclusive proof of a Hatch Act violation, FBI agents could not open an investigation until requested to do so by an agency head.

This investigative policy was in force until October, 1941, when Attorney General Biddle advised the various government agencies that whenever the FBI received information indicating a Hatch Act violation an investigation would be initiated without notice to the interested agency head. However, the agency head would receive the results of the investigation as soon as a check was completed.

No effort was made under the Hatch Act to investigate any federal employee unless a specific complaint was received. The Department of Justice ruled that Congress, in passing the Act, had not intended that all employees be investigated.

On May 18, 1942, the Chairman of the Interdepartmental Committee sent a memorandum to the top-ranking executives of departments, agencies and independent establishments in which he said in part:

> There can be no doubt that Congress regards the dismissal of Communists and Bundists from the Federal service as not only desirable but mandatory.[1]

Nevertheless, there were few dismissals resulting from investigations and it was clear that the screening program wasn't accomplishing its security purpose.[2]

In reviewing this period from 1940 to 1946, J. Edgar Hoover said:

In some cases the Bureau established that the employee was a member of the Communist Party and in some instances the employee admitted such membership. However, because the Bureau was unable to establish membership in the Communist Party at the time the case was being considered by the employing agency, no administrative action was taken against the employee.

The Truman Temporary Commission on Employee Loyalty recommended in its first rough-draft report that each department and agency be responsible for its own loyalty procedures. After a study of this report, the FBI suggested that there be a Loyalty Review Board which would act as an appeals board with the power to approve or overrule actions taken against employees by the department and agency heads and which would give directions and guidance to the program.

On March 21, 1947, President Truman issued Executive Order 9835 establishing the Federal Employees Loyalty Program. The primary responsibility for employee investigations was given to the Civil Service Commission, except in cases where agencies had their own investigative staffs. A Loyalty Review Board was established, and it was ordered that the investigative agencies could refuse to disclose the names of confidential informants.

The President's Order said:

The standard for refusal of employment or the removal from employment in an executive department or agency on the grounds relating to loyalty shall be that, on all the evidence, reasonable grounds exist for belief that the person involved is disloyal to the Government of the United States.

In 1951, Executive Order 10241 amended Executive Order 9835 to make the standard "reasonable doubt as to loyalty" rather than "reasonable grounds exist . . . that the person involved is disloyal. . . ."

In the determination of disloyalty, the President's Order, which applied only to the executive branch of the government, gave this list of forbidden activities:

1. Sabotage, espionage or associating with spies or subversives.

2. Treason or sedition.

3. Advocacy of revolution or force or violence to alter the constitutional form of government.

4. Intentional unauthorized disclosure of documents or information of a confidential character where the circumstances indicated disloyalty.

5. To serve the interests of another government in preference to the interests of the United States.

6. Membership in, affiliation with or sympathetic association with any foreign or domestic organization designated by the Attorney General as totalitarian, Fascist, Communist or subversive or advocating the overthrow of the government.

This was the beginning of the first broad-scale effort of the federal government to protect itself from subversion in the ranks of government workers. But as the months passed, the impression was lodged in the minds of many people that the FBI was investigating each employee in government and each job applicant; that the FBI was tapping employees' telephones and that surveillance was kept on thousands of employees.

Actually, the FBI had nothing to do with the great majority of the investigations of employees and applicants except to run a name check against the Bureau's files to determine whether the files reflected any background information indicating disloyalty—if that person's name happened to be in the files.[3] When no such indication was found, the loyalty form was stamped "No Disloyal Data FBI Files," and returned to the Civil Service Commission or the employing agency.[4]

The President's Order directed that the Civil Service Commission have each job applicant's background checked against the files of the FBI, the Civil Service Commission, the Armed Forces, other appropriate government investigative and intelligence agencies, the House Committee on Un-American Activities, and local law enforcement; and with schools and colleges attended, former employers and references. In addition, fingerprints of incumbents and appointees were checked against FBI fingerprint files.

The FBI's responsibility ended with the name check against its files unless somewhere along the line of checks the FBI or another agency received information or found something which raised a question of disloyalty. In all such cases, the FBI had the responsibility of making a full investigation and gathering the facts to be placed before the loyalty boards.

These FBI investigations came about as the result of: (1) processing loyalty forms and finding evidence of disloyalty in the FBI files; (2) complaints alleging disloyalty; (3) requests received from the Civil Service Commission or another government agency; and (4) information developed in the course of making other investigations.

The FBI's duty in the loyalty investigations was one of gathering as completely and accurately as possible facts to be presented to the various agencies where the power of decision rested. The FBI report never carried a recommendation for or against an employee or applicant. It is not the FBI's job to be investigator, judge and jury.

Frequently a phrase was heard that someone had been "cleared by the FBI." This, of course, was not true, because the FBI had not been given that authority, nor did it seek it. Nor did the FBI "make charges" against anyone. FBI agents were instructed to collect the facts which would prove or disprove an allegation of disloyalty.

From its inception, the Truman loyalty program came under heavy attack from left-wing and Communist groups. One of the first attacks was sponsored by the United Public Workers of America (CIO),[5] which hammered on the theme that the entire program was a "witch hunt." There were the usual mass meetings, petitions, fund-raising campaigns and efforts to discredit the program and the FBI. "Who'll Investigate the Man Who'll Investigate You?" was the bannerline on one pamphlet. Another one was entitled "$11,000,000 for Snoopers and Peepers to Harass Government Employees." The FBI was accused of conducting "a union busting drive under the guise of a loyalty investigation" because the loyalty forms asked employees and applicants to list the organizations to which they belonged.

UPWA President Abram Flaxer stated in a press release, "When the FBI is given such wide latitude to get trade union membership lists, we are no longer in danger of becoming a police state, we have already arrived."

After Chairman Seth Richardson of the Loyalty Review Board issued a statement outlining the rules and procedures to be followed in handling the reviews of loyalty cases, the UPWA put out a press release saying:

> A careful study of the 58 pages of directives and regulations . . . exposes the shocking fact that the Board is embarked on a course of serving as a window dressing for police state procedures. It is obvious that the Board has issued a façade of sham hearings and procedures to hide the real situation; that a police agency, the Federal Bureau of Investigation, now has sole and exclusive authority to render judgment on the Loyalty of Government employees . . .

And so it went. One woman employee refused to go before a loyalty board after being formally charged with Communist Party membership and activities. She wrote:

> I refuse to continue any employment that levels charges against me . . . I know that under the Presidential order a person is guilty unless he can prove to the board he is innocent. I know of nothing in the Constitution of the United States which allows such a procedure.

Over and over, the program was described by some as a planned assault on civil liberties. And there were honest men who were disturbed that any government program should deal with the depth of a man's love for his country or even raise the question of a person's loyalty until he was caught in an act of disloyalty.

In stating his views on this point, Hoover said:

> A government job is a matter of privilege and not a right. Misunderstanding of this point has led to much of the current nonsense voiced about the program. The late Justice Oliver Wendell Holmes put it very neatly in 1892 when he was a member of the Massachusetts Supreme Court. A New Bedford policeman, discharged for prohibited political activity, had petitioned for reinstatement. In turning down the application, Justice Holmes remarked that "the petitioner may have a constitutional right to talk politics, but he has no constitutional right to be a policeman."

Thus began the Great Debate over the issue of "Communists in Government," which stirred one of the bitterest political controversies in the nation's history. But the tumult from the right, the left and the middle didn't change the basic fact that subversion was abroad in the land. The degree might be argued, but no honest and responsible man in or out of government could truthfully deny its existence or the need to do something about it.

It was in this atmosphere that the Hiss case exploded, shocking the nation as no other case had before. Pudgy, rumpled Whittaker Chambers, a man with heavy jowls and heavy-lidded eyes, went before the House Committee on Un-American Activities in August, 1948, and confessed that he had been a member of the Communist Party from 1924 to 1937. He said he had been a member, also, of a Soviet espionage apparatus dealing in stolen United States Government documents. As one of his partners in this work he named Alger Hiss, a brilliant young diplomatic star in the Department of State before and during the war years.

The script was all wrong. The handsome young intellectual who had rubbed elbows with the nation's great men should have been pointing the finger of accusation at the unknown, secretive-looking Chambers. But this was type casting in the Hitchcock manner.

As a dramatic stage play unfolds with surprise following on surprise, so did the Hiss-Chambers story. There were the denials by Hiss; the "confrontation" of Hiss by Chambers; Hiss's insistence that he knew Chambers only as George Crosley, a free-lance writer; the filing of a $75,000 slander-libel action by Hiss against Chambers for publicly calling him a Communist; Chambers' producing the State Department documents which he claimed were handed over to him by Hiss to be given to Colonel Boris Bykov, a Soviet agent; Hiss's admission that four handwritten notes among the documents were in his own handwriting; and Chambers' uncovering of the "pumpkin papers," two strips of microfilm containing photographs of original State Department documents and three rolls of undeveloped film.

The FBI's part in this controversy was to investigate the accuracy of the charges by Chambers and of the denials made by Hiss. In all, 263 agents at one time or another worked on the investigation in forty-five of the FBI's fifty-two field divisions. Some of the damning evidence against Hiss went like this:

FBI agents established that documents in the Chambers collection had been written on a Woodstock typewriter which belonged to the Hisses in 1936 and 1937. This typewriter had been used by Mrs. Hiss to write a report for the Bryn Mawr Alumnae Association in 1937 and a letter to the University of Maryland in 1937. At the Landon School at Bethesda, Maryland, agents found a letter written in 1936 and signed by Hiss which had been written on the same typewriter.

Agents looked for someone who might have seen Chambers and Hiss together. The search seemed hopeless until Mrs. Chambers recalled that she had painted a portrait of a maid named Edith Murray, who might recall such a meeting. By using photographs of the portrait, the agents located Edith Murray. She identified both Hiss and his wife, recalling that she had seen them in the Chambers' home in Baltimore.

Chambers told of receiving about $1,000 from Bykov to buy gifts for his best four "sources"—Hiss, A. George Silverman, Harry Dexter White, and Henry Julian Wadleigh. Chambers said he arranged to have a Bokhara rug sent to Hiss. Hiss admitted receiving the gift, but he said Chambers had received the rug from a friend, and having no use for it himself, had passed it on to him.

Chambers said that late in 1937 he went to Hiss and asked for a loan of $400, which he needed in buying a new car. He said Hiss lent him the money. Hiss denied it. Agents found that on November 19, 1937, Hiss's bank account reflected a $400 withdrawal. They also found that on November 23, a Ford car was sold to Esther Chambers (Whittaker Chambers' wife) for a trade-in of a 1934 Ford sedan and $486.75 in cash.

Chambers said he had an arrangement with Hiss whereby Mrs. Hiss would type up copies or summaries of documents brought home by Hiss. Mrs. Hiss denied that she was proficient in typing. Agents found that in 1927 Mrs. Hiss had passed an examination in typewriting and in English at Columbia University.

Chambers said the documents given to him by Hiss were photographed by a photographer whose name he recalled only as "Felix." He did remember, however, that Felix had lived on Callow Avenue in Baltimore and had once worked at an electrical appliance store. Agents found that one Felix Inslerman had lived on Callow Avenue in 1937 and had been employed by an electrical appliance shop. They found him in Cambridge, New York, and Chambers identified him from a photograph. The agents found that Inslerman, before coming to Baltimore, had registered as a

member of the Communist Party with his local election board. Inslerman
denied knowing Chambers, but he admitted having a Leica camera which
had been given to him as a birthday present in 1937. In the FBI Laboratory, agents found that microscopic marks on the "pumpkin" film were
identical with the marks left by the edge of the mask of Inslerman's Leica
camera. Their conclusion was that the "pumpkin" microfilm had been
exposed in the Leica camera owned by Inslerman.[6]

The revelations by Chambers and other ex-Communists shocked the
people of the United States, just as the Canadian people had been
shocked after World War II by the news that trusted scientists and
government officials had been giving Canadian Government secrets to
the Soviet diplomats at the Russians' Ottawa Embassy.

But in the political uproar accompanying the revelations of subversion there were steady attacks on the FBI investigations as being
something mysterious and sinister—particularly the use of confidential
informants and the manner in which the FBI assembled its files of
information.

When President Truman issued Executive Order 9835 establishing
the Loyalty Program, he recognized the need for protecting the identity
of confidential informants in loyalty cases.[7] And as the program was
being formulated, Hoover told the Truman Loyalty Review Board,
which established the operating policies of the Loyalty Program, that
it was the policy of the FBI to protect the identity of informants. He
advised the Board it could take one of two courses in establishing its
policy on witnesses. In recalling his position later, Hoover said:

I appeared before the Loyalty Review Board and outlined the problems
involved. I stated that a basic operating policy of the FBI was not to make
charges against Government employees. Our responsibility is limited to
the securing of facts. I stated that the FBI was the investigator, not the
prosecutor, judge or jury. I informed the Board that we planned to make
our Special Agents available to testify to those matters of which they had
personal knowledge and that we would list the names and addresses of
those persons interviewed who did not object to their identities being
known. I stated that whenever an FBI Agent interviews a person who says
that he is giving information in strict confidence, his confidence must be respected. Likewise, I pointed out that we have highly confidential sources
of information which, if disclosed, would not only deprive the Government of valuable information bearing upon our internal security but
which also might result in physical injury to the informant.

I pointed out that as an alternative, we could explain our mission to each
person and explain that he might be called as a witness and be required
to testify in public and then report only such information as was furnished
without any restrictions as to source. I advised the Loyalty Review Board
that this was a matter of policy for the Board to determine.

In most cases the FBI gathered its information from bankers, doctors, lawyers, laborers, housewives, salesmen and anyone else who had known and associated with the person being investigated. In short, agents talked to everyone they could find who could help in establishing the truth or falsity of an accusation. The FBI's training for agents included classes on the interrogation of witnesses. Each agent was warned that he must obtain information without any color of accusation in his questions and that he must avoid any implication that a "charge" was being made. If any agent failed to carry out his interrogation in this fashion, then he had failed to carry out the instructions given by Hoover.

If, during an investigation, someone asked "Why are you investigating this person?" the agent was instructed to reply, "Under an Executive Order, Government employees and applicants are being checked as a part of the Loyalty Program. Mr. X is a Government employee [or applicant]. He is being checked under this program."

There were insinuations that the FBI was tapping telephones in loyalty investigations, watching employees' mail, and keeping a surveillance on activities throughout the entire government. In reply to these accusations, Hoover set forth Bureau policy in these words:

> As a matter of policy, technical surveillances [wire taps] were not used during these investigations. Likewise, other confidential techniques used in espionage and internal security cases were not utilized in these investigations, but information received from them where such techniques were utilized in other type investigations, was included in the loyalty reports where pertinent.

Just as a businessman might check every possible source for information as to the honesty and reliability of a prospective employee, so did the FBI check the backgrounds of employees and applicants when a question of loyalty was raised.

Those giving the information were asked if they would sign a statement and appear before a Loyalty Board as a witness. If they agreed, their names and addresses were given in the FBI's report. But the Bureau protected the confidences of those who requested it, and in these cases a symbol such as "T-199" was used instead of a name, since the Executive Order specifically provided, ". . . the investigative agency may refuse to disclose the names of confidential informants . . . ." But the Loyalty Board was not left without a basis for judgment as to the reliability of the information. Confidential sources were identified as being of "known reliability" or "who have furnished reliable information in the past" or "unknown reliability" or by setting forth descriptive data of the source—and the report where necessary and possible reflected the person's reputation and standing in the community in which he lived.

If for any reason an informant's reliability became questionable,[8] the informant was dropped by the FBI, and action was taken to see that this change was reflected in any past reports and that interested agencies were notified so that they could take remedial action if it was needed. Appropriate agencies were also advised when the need to conceal the identity of an informant ceased.

Despite all the precautions and safeguards, mistakes were made on occasion. In one loyalty case, an informant named a Voice of America applicant and members of his family as being members of the Communist Party. He identified A. B. as having attended various secret Party meetings and as having a desk in a Communist Party headquarters.

A. B. denied the allegations, and in checking further the FBI discovered that it was not A. B. who had been active in Communist affairs, but his brother. The strong family resemblance had caused the error in identification by the informant. The interested government agencies were notified by the FBI that the original accusation had been wrong, and the Loyalty Review Board then rated A. B. "eligible on loyalty."

The Eisenhower Administration—like the Truman Administration —approved the use of information from confidential sources and the protection of the informants' identities in loyalty cases in FBI reports and loyalty files. President Truman said in a 1948 Presidential directive:

> The efficient and just administration of the Employee Loyalty Program . . . requires that reports, records, and files relative to the program be preserved in strict confidence. This is necessary in the interest of our national security and welfare, to preserve the confidential character and sources of information furnished . . .

In all the controversy involving the Bureau and its operations, there was none which was worse, perhaps, than that which exploded in the government's espionage case against Judith Coplon in 1949.[9]

For twenty-five years, Hoover had jealously guarded the integrity of the FBI's investigative files to protect informants and to protect innocent persons from the embarrassment of unevaluated reports, complaints, and insinuations accumulated in the course of an investigation, or received in unsolicited letters and telephone calls.

But in the Coplon case, Attorney General Tom C. Clark overruled Hoover and permitted government attorneys to place in evidence documents from the "raw files" of the FBI to comply with a bench order by Federal Judge Albert L. Reeves. Only a small portion of the information in the file was relevant to the government's case against Coplon. Much of it, in the course of normal procedure, would have been tossed out as a matter of course. The FBI files were ridiculed as a storehouse of gossip and the trivia were given prominence above all else.

Editor J. R. Wiggins, writing in *The Washington Post,* said:

> The Federal Bureau of Investigation is just beginning to pick itself up after its worst legal smashup in 25 years . . .
>
> The bench order opening up the documents . . . dealt the FBI a triple blow.
>
> (1) It uncovered secret informants, destroying their usefulness and in some cases perhaps exposing them to mortal risks.
>
> (2) It damaged the reputations of many persons named only incidentally in unevaluated and incomplete files.
>
> (3) It has added to the reluctance of informants who hitherto were shielded by confidential status.
>
> . . . Oddly enough, the FBI itself is being blamed and criticized for the nature of Coplon disclosures that it tried its best to prevent . . .

In a letter to his executive assistants and to all special agents in charge at district offices, Hoover explained what had happened:

> When the issue arose on the introduction of Bureau investigative reports, I, of course, did not in any way wish to deprive the court or the defense of all the facts bearing upon the issue . . . There were certain reports that could be introduced in evidence without compromising sources of information, other investigations, or embarrassing innocent persons. We were willing for these to be admitted if necessary. I took a strong stand against making public other reports that would reveal the identities of confidential informants or embarrass innocent persons by the publication of unevaluated complaints and reports. I urged the Attorney General to seek a mistrial or a citation for contempt rather than produce these reports with consequent devastating harm to the FBI's responsibility for internal security, as well as the disclosure of as yet uncorroborated information in our files concerning individuals.
>
> The first knowledge I had that the reports had been introduced in evidence occurred after they had been presented in court. The reports introduced in evidence were selected by the Department and not by the Bureau . . .

The Coplon incident did more than anything else to create a misunderstanding as to how the FBI's "raw files" were assembled and how they were later developed into a factual report giving a rounded picture of a case.

A file begins for any number of reasons—for example, when someone makes a complaint, or a confidential informant supplies information indicating disloyalty or a violation of federal law.[10] At this stage the information might be a case of mistaken identity, an ill-formed suspicion, a line of scandal or a shocking charge of disloyalty backed by what purports to be documentary proof.

The next step is the investigation. Agents in perhaps a dozen cities send in bulky reports of their interrogations of witnesses. Information is supplied by confidential sources. Documents are assembled.

At this stage, the "raw file" may contain information that is false, trivial, or perhaps malicious. It also includes reports on administrative details in the investigation, the investigative techniques used, and the identity of informants. For the incomplete file to fall into anyone's hands at this stage would be damaging to innocent people and perhaps endanger the life of an informant. For these reasons, the FBI has refused access to such files to outsiders.[11]

The results of investigations are set forth in the agents' investigative reports. These are the reports containing the information which proves or disproves the allegations which brought about the investigation, and which are sent to other agencies of government. They are the refined product of the "raw files," supplying the information relevant to the prosecution of a case or for use in a loyalty hearing. A dozen or more of these investigative reports may be part of a single file—and it is necessary to view all of the investigative reports in a given case to know whether the weight of evidence will indicate guilt or innocence.[12]

Hoover gave his views on guarding the integrity of FBI files to a Senate Foreign Relations Subcommittee in 1950:

> . . . the files do not consist of proven information alone. The files must be viewed as a whole. One report may allege crimes of a most despicable type, and the truth or falsity of these charges may not emerge until several reports are studied, further investigation made and the wheat separated from the chaff.
>
> I, for one, would want no part of an investigative organization which had the power of discretion to decide what information would be reported and what would be omitted . . .
>
> Should a given file be disclosed, the issue would be a far broader one than concerns the subject of the investigation. Names of persons who by force of circumstance entered into the investigation might well be innocent of any wrong. To publicize their names without the explanation of the associations would be a grave injustice. Even though they were given an opportunity to later give their explanation, the fact remains that truth seldom, if ever, catches up with charges. I would not want to be a party to any action which would "smear" innocent individuals for the rest of their lives. We cannot disregard the fundamental principles of common decency and the application of basic American rights of fair play . . .
>
> FBI reports set forth all details secured from a witness. If those details were disclosed, they could become subject to misinterpretation, they

could be quoted out of context, or they could be used to thwart truth, distort half truths, and misrepresent facts. The raw material, the allegations, the details of associations and compilation of information in FBI files must be considered as a whole. They are of value to an investigator in the discharge of his duty. These files were never intended to be used in any other manner and the public interest would not be served by the disclosure of their contents . . .[13]

The tumult in the Coplon case was matched perhaps only by that which came when Hoover was called before the Senate Internal Security Subcommittee on November 17, 1953, to answer the question of whether he had been a party to an agreement made in 1946 to keep Harry Dexter White in a government position, even though White had been accused at that time of being a Soviet spy.

When Hoover flatly denied ever entering into such an agreement, he was accused bitterly of having "taken sides" with the Republicans against the Democrats, although he had established a twenty-nine-year-old record for nonpartisanship.

Hoover's extraordinary appearance before the Senate group came about in this fashion: On November 6, 1953, Attorney General Herbert Brownell, Jr., told the Executives Club of Chicago that Harry S. Truman had appointed White to the International Monetary Fund despite two FBI reports which had described White's "spying activities."

Brownell's speech created a political uproar. The Senate Internal Security Subcommittee began calling upon Hoover to testify. He refused twice.

Soon stories began to appear in the newspapers suggesting that President Truman had made this move so that "White could be better kept under surveillance in his job" by the FBI. The New York *Times* on November 14, 1953, headlined a story by Arthur Krock: "Aides Say Truman Appointed White with F.B.I. Consent." The story was attributed to "persons who were in a position to know" and said that "According to their account, J. Edgar Hoover suggested or at least agreed to the procedure recommended to and followed by President Truman."

Other stories reported that White's transfer from the Treasury to the International Monetary Fund had been made with Hoover's approval in a conference attended by Hoover, Tom C. Clark (then Attorney General) and Fred Vinson (then Secretary of the Treasury). After these stories appeared, Chief Counsel Robert Morris of the Internal Security Subcommittee notified the FBI that a formal request would be made for Hoover to testify. Morris was told he would have to take the matter up with the Attorney General.

The Subcommittee's formal request was then made to the Department of Justice and Attorney General Brownell told Hoover on November 16 that it would be proper for him to testify. Hoover in recalling the incident said: "I agreed to testify on the third request because I wished to avoid a subpoena and because the story which was going around reflected on me and the FBI."

When Hoover appeared before the Senate group on November 17, 1953, Chairman William Jenner made the point that Hoover, except in special cases, should not be called to testify before Congressional committees but that "there has been a widely publicized rumor that Harry Dexter White was allowed to stay in office pursuant to an agreement worked out with Mr. J. Edgar Hoover . . . it has been necessary for us . . . to ask him to give his account." In all the tumult at no time did former President Truman make the statement that Hoover had been a party to the agreement.

Hoover denied he had entered into any such agreement with Vinson and Clark. "I did not enter into any agreement to shift White from his position in the Treasury Department to the International Monetary Fund. This was not within my purview . . . At no time was the FBI a party to an agreement to promote Harry Dexter White and at no time did the FBI give its approval to such an agreement . . . The decision to retain White was made by a higher government authority . . ."

Hoover spoke with finality about his conversations with Clark and Vinson concerning White, because after each discussion he had dictated a memorandum for his files.

In a story on the Hoover testimony, the New York *Times* said in part:

> Several days ago, Mr. Truman's former aides here began "explaining" that, of course, there had been a reason for keeping Mr. White in the Government. The "reason," it was suggested, was that if he had been dismissed, the five-alarm bell would have sounded and all the Communists in the spy ring would either have lain low or slid down the pole.
>
> They went beyond this. They told of a "meeting" attended by Mr. Hoover and the implication was dropped that the FBI chief had been a party to the keep-White-and-trap-him plan . . . Mr. Hoover . . . was almost forced to testify in order to clear up this key point . . .

When President Eisenhower had been in office a little more than three months, he issued Executive Order 10450, which established a broader base in judging the suitability of a person to hold or obtain a job with the federal government.

The government's loyalty program became a security-risk program. And a security risk could be anyone who was a drunkard, a drug addict, a mental case or an untrustworthy individual. The Loyalty Review Board was abolished, and the decisions for hiring or firing were returned to agency heads.

As far as the FBI was concerned, the Bureau's responsibilities under the new program were roughly the same as they had been under the old loyalty program.

31 : *The Attack on Communism*

ON October 14, 1949, at 11:10 A.M., a whisper ran through the federal courtroom at Foley Square in New York City, "The jury is coming in! It's a verdict!"

Judge Harold Medina came from the judges' chambers in his black robes and mounted the bench. From his high-backed chair he looked down at the eleven defendants seated in the courtroom—the top commanders of the Communist Party of the United States of America, who had been tried on charges of teaching and advocating the overthrow of the United States Government by force and violence.

Their trial had lasted just two days short of nine months. It had been one of the longest criminal trials in federal court history. And there were some in the courtroom who believed the defense attorneys had deliberately tried to bring about a mistrial by the use of insolence, delaying tactics and a contemptuous disobedience of the Court's orders. Now they sat silently, watching the Judge.

"You may bring in the jury," Judge Medina said to the clerk of the court.

The jurors filed into the courtroom and walked to the jury box, where they sat in the red upholstered chairs from which they had followed the testimony for so many weeks.

"Shall I proceed, Your Honor?" the clerk asked.

"Yes."

The jurors' names were called and they answered present. And then the clerk turned to Mrs. Thelma Dial, Negro foreman of the jury, and said: "Madam Foreman, have you agreed on a verdict?"

"We have."

"How say you?"

"The jury finds each of the defendants guilty."

A murmur was heard through the room. That was all.

The clerk polled each juror separately, asking each of them: "You say you find the defendants Eugene Dennis, John B. Williamson, Jacob Stachel, Robert G. Thompson, Benjamin J. Davis, Jr., Henry Winston, John Gates, Irving Potash, Gilbert Green, Carl Winter and Gus Hall guilty as charged." [1]

All the replies were in the affirmative. Judge Medina thanked the jurors and praised them for their patience and the attention they had given to the case. Then the jury was dismissed.

"Now," said Judge Medina, "I turn to some unfinished business."

He called the names of the six members of the defense counsel, Harry Sacher and Eugene Dennis, of New York City; Abraham J. Isserman, of Newark, N. J.; Richard Gladstein, of San Francisco; George W. Crockett, Jr., of Detroit; and Louis F. McCabe, of Philadelphia. He asked them to rise.

". . . I find," said the Judge, "that the acts, statements and conduct of each of the defendants [counsel] constituted a deliberate and willful attack upon the administration of justice, an attempt to sabotage the functioning of the federal judicial system and misconduct of so grave a character as to make the mere imposition of a fine a futile gesture and a wholly insufficient punishment . . ."

He sentenced Sacher, Gladstein and Dennis to six months' imprisonment, Isserman and Crockett to four months' and McCabe to thirty days'.

A babble of protest arose from the six men, who shouted angrily at Judge Medina as they had shouted day after day and week after week with insinuations that the Court was guilty of racial prejudice, bias, corruption, partiality and connivance with the United States Attorney.

Judge Medina broke in to say: "Let these contempt adjudications be notice to you and all who may be tempted to follow your example that there is power in the judicial system of the United States under its Constitution and there are laws to protect and maintain the dignity of the Court and the orderly administration of justice."

Then Dennis delivered himself of his final insolence: ". . . I would say to Your Honor, as in Nazi Germany, in Mussolini Italy, men also sat in high tribunals, also wore black robes and also handed down pro-Fascist decisions; but I would remind the Court that the people reversed those verdicts and decisions just as our people will reverse the decisions and the verdict in this case, and the people's verdict will be for peace, for democracy and for social progress."

So ended the trial which claimed attention around the world.

This drama had begun more than ten years earlier, when the FBI began assembling evidence to prove that the leaders of the Communist Party were not advocating a peaceful political revolution within the framework of the United States Constitution, but were conspiring to bring about the violent overthrow of the United States Government.

During the "friendly" years of the 1930's, the FBI had watched the Communists' activities just as they watched the Bundists'. Both groups were regarded by J. Edgar Hoover and his men as dangerous to American security and potential agents of a foreign power. Informants planted in the Party and disillusioned ex-Communists helped in the long, secret investigation which went on night and day in city after city across the nation. Because it was dealing with a secret, conspiratorial group, the FBI had to use secret, clandestine methods to penetrate the Party's operations.

In 1940, Congress passed the Smith Act, which said in part: "It shall be unlawful for any person to knowingly or willfully advocate, abet, advise, or teach the duty, necessity, desirability, or propriety of overthrowing or destroying any government in the United States by force or violence . . ."

The first convictions under the Smith Act came in 1941, after FBI agents gathered evidence against members of the Socialist Workers Party, a Trotskyite organization, who were charged with a violation of the "unlawful conspiracy" section of the Act. Eighteen of the defendants were convicted. Six were sentenced to prison terms of a year and a day, while twelve received sentences of sixteen months. The U. S. Circuit Court upheld the convictions and the U. S. Supreme Court refused three times to review the case.

Some people felt the government had acted not too wisely, and perhaps unconstitutionally, in this case. But the Communists, while deploring passage of the Smith Act, applauded the use of the law against the Trotskyites. One Communist writer said: "To call their [the Trotskyites'] case a civil liberties case, is a mockery of the most elementary concept of democracy. It is the same as championing civil liberties for Fascists . . ." And others echoed the sentiment.

When the Communists turned against Earl Browder's "peaceful collaboration" policy in 1945, dissolved the Communist Political Association, and re-formed the Communist Party of the United States of America, then the FBI saw that the Party openly as well as secretly had rejected anything but the Marxist-Leninist line of a revolutionary class warfare that sought the violent destruction of all non-Communist systems of government.

In 1946–1947, the FBI assembled a 1,350-page legalistic brief, with 546 exhibits, which contained the evidence gathered over the years against the Party and its leaders. Two supplemental briefs added another 500 pages and 300 exhibits. These 1,850 pages and 846 exhibits were the product of untold hours and days of investigative work and they formed, perhaps, the most complete summary of the Communist Party's activities and aims in the United States ever put together. It was, in fact, a giant new edition of the brief which Hoover had drawn against the same Communist Party twenty-seven years earlier.

The brief was sent to Attorney General Tom C. Clark in February, 1948, and the Department of Justice decided to move against the twelve members of the Communist Party's National Board. After more than a quarter of a century, the government was aiming a massive blow at home-grown Communists.

A Federal Grand Jury in New York City returned a conspiracy indictment on July 20, 1948, charging the Party leadership with a conspiracy in violation of the Smith Act. The indictment said that they ". . . unlawfully, wilfully and knowingly, did conspire with each other . . . to organize as the Communist Party of the United States of America a society, group, and assembly of persons who teach and advocate the overthrow and destruction of the Government of the United States by force and violence . . ."

Federal Judge Vincent L. Leibell signed bench warrants for the arrest of the defendants and FBI agents began the roundup which the *Daily Worker* promptly labeled "a giant frameup."

Hoover recognized that it would be necessary to uncover some of the confidential informants whom the FBI had planted in the Party years before, and to make them available as witnesses for the government if prosecutions were to be started. From August, 1948, until January, 1949, FBI agents were busy arranging for some sixty interviews between U. S. Attorney John F. X. McGohey and the confidential informants and former Communists willing to testify.

The trial opened on January 17, 1949. Perhaps the greatest shock to the defendants and to their fellow Party members in the entire case was the dramatic appearance of young Herbert A. Philbrick as a government witness. It was shocking because Philbrick had become known in Boston as a trusted member of the Communist Party's inner circle; no one, not even his wife, had been aware that he was also an undercover agent for the FBI.

In 1940, at the age of twenty-five, Philbrick had helped organize a youth group in Boston and had become chairman, only to find the group was secretly controlled by young Communists. He discussed the

situation with the FBI and agreed to continue in the work to help uncover what he could about the Communists' operations. He worked his
way deeper and deeper into the Party. In this weird double life, Philbrick
played the role of a dedicated Communist while keeping the FBI informed on the Party's maneuvers, until the time came for him to testify
at Foley Square. He was one of six FBI confidential informants who
testified for the government.

Witness after witness spread before the jury the Communist teachings which were summed up concisely and accurately by Stalin's statement that a revolution in the United States was "impossible without
the violent destruction of the machinery of the bourgeois state." And
the defendants were linked in the testimony with a conspiracy to put
these words into action. The shadows of Marx and Lenin fell across
the courtroom and there were echoed the words of an ideology which
had drawn nation after nation into slavery.

The trial was a bitter struggle in which the defense claimed the
eleven men on trial had only been exercising their right of free speech
and freedom of thought.

The jury thought otherwise.

The verdict of guilty was upheld by Circuit Judge Learned Hand,
who said in part:

> We know of no country where they [the defendants] would have been
> allowed any approach to the license here accorded them; and none, ex-
> cept Great Britain, where they would have had so fair a hearing. Their
> only plausible complaint is that freedom of speech which they would be
> the first to destroy, has been denied them. We acknowledge that that
> freedom is not always easy to protect; and that there is no sharp line
> which marks its scope. We have tried to show that what these men taught
> and advocated is outside the zone . . .

The Smith Act was held to be constitutional by the U. S. Circuit
Court of Appeals in a unanimous decision. In referring to the government's use of testimony by the FBI informants, Judge Hand said:

> Courts have countenanced the use of informers from time immemorial;
> in cases of conspiracy or in other cases where the crime consists of pre-
> paring for another crime, it is usually necessary to rely upon informers
> or accomplices because the criminals will almost certainly proceed cov-
> ertly. Entrapment excluded, of which there was none here, decoys and
> other deception are always permissible.

On June 4, 1951, the United States Supreme Court also affirmed
the Communist leaders' conviction in upholding the constitutionality of
the Smith Act. The vote was six to two.

Chief Justice Fred Vinson wrote the majority opinion, which said,
in part: "Their conspiracy to organize . . . and advocate the over-

throw of the Government of the United States by force and violence created a 'clear and present danger' of an attempt to overthrow the Government by force and violence."

The Supreme Court's decision was the signal for four of the eleven convicted Communists to jump their $20,000 bail and go into hiding. Gus Hall, Robert Thompson, Henry Winston and Gilbert Green disappeared. FBI agents began the search for them.[2]

Hall, the Party's national secretary, slipped into Mexico over a Communist escape route with the help of the Party's underground. He dyed his blond hair, eyebrows and eyelashes dark brown. He shaved off his mustache and thinned himself down by forty pounds. But the disguise didn't work. Mexican police found Hall in a tourist court in the outskirts of Mexico City. His papers were not in order, and he was escorted to the border at Laredo, Texas, where FBI agents took him into custody on October 10, 1951.[3]

Robert Thompson eluded the FBI for more than two years. But he was tracked down to a cabin hideout high in the Sierra mountains some 120 miles east of San Francisco.[4] He had grown a mustache and his hair was dyed a strawberry blond. He had taken as his own the name of John Francis Brennan, who had fought with the Abraham Lincoln Brigade in the Spanish Civil War and then committed suicide in New York City in 1938.

Thompson carried a birth certificate, Pennsylvania and Illinois automobile driver's licenses, a social security card and other identification papers which bore the name of Brennan. He refused to talk to agents. But his silence posed no problem. He was identified beyond question at the cabin when his fingerprints were checked against a fingerprint record carried by the agents.

Thompson's arrest shocked the Communists, and the Party began a frenzied search for the "traitor" who had disclosed the hideout. But they never learned the FBI secret.

With the top command of the Party convicted, the FBI went after seventeen "second-string" Communists, again piecing together the evidence to prove that Marxism-Leninism was not merely a social theory, but a guide to revolutionary action in the Communist struggle to smash the United States Government, and that the seventeen defendants were part of a conspiracy to bring this revolution into being.[5]

Alexander Bittelman, one of the defendants, had underlined the absolute necessity for Communists to convert theory into action in these words: "In Leninism revolutionary theory has been raised to unprecedented heights. In the Communist Parties—the Marxist parties of a new type—revolutionary theory has become a decisive factor as a guide to action . . ."

In a trial lasting nine and a half months, thirteen of the seventeen defendants were convicted.[6]

The trials of the Communist leaders were part of a broad attack by the government against communism in the Cold War years that followed World War II. And when the Supreme Court upheld the constitutionality of the Smith Act, the Communists began to go underground.

An FBI study of the Communist underground made in 1952 said:

> The present Communist underground apparatus of the Communist Party, USA, is a real potential danger to the security of this country and therefore it is a hostile force which must be reckoned with in calculating our national defense plans. This danger proceeds from the Communist underground's capacity (a) to engage in espionage; (b) to conduct sabotage; and (c) to combine its efforts with the representatives of Communist nations in the event of warfare involving this nation.

The FBI had found over the years that in the development of the Communist movement in the United States—as elsewhere—the Party exposed only part of itself to public view. Part of it was open and above ground and its leaders made no effort to conceal their connection with the legal operations. But there was always a hidden part known to Communists themselves as "the illegal apparatus," working secretively and hiding the identities of its members. Some members worked only in the underground, some above ground, and others in both organizations. And where the one ended and the other began was not always clear, although the line between them was always there.

In a frank discussion of "legal" and "illegal" activities as demanded by the Third International, the official organ of the Communist Party of America said:

> . . . The center of gravity of our activities is not fixed. It is constantly shifting; sometimes in the direction of the legal organization, sometimes in the direction of the underground organization. This center of gravity is at all times determined by the ever-changing realities of the actual class struggle.

Late in 1946, as the "realities" of the class struggle began developing into the Cold War, the Communist Party shifted its center of gravity toward the underground. By October, 1947, the Party had completed arrangements for an effective underground organization, according to reports received by the FBI. And by late 1948, state groups had reached agreement on the use of certain "fronts" for their activities. Party members began disappearing from their old haunts and turning up in other cities under assumed names. Reports from all parts of the United States showed that the same precautionary measures were being taken.

When the Party's top leaders were convicted in the New York City trial, lesser leaders began arranging for hideouts and renting offices and residences as fronts for future meeting places. Members were canvassed for the names of "politically safe" sympathizers whose homes would provide a shelter. One Party chief sent his wife and child into hiding, stored his furniture, and then disappeared himself. When he came out of hiding he used an assumed name.

FBI agents discovered that in preparing for underground operations, the Party had adopted these security measures among others:

1. Elimination of membership cards.
2. The basic Party unit, the club, was limited to no more than five members and a group captain was named to control their activities. Members of one group should not know the identities of other groups.
3. Use of telephones was restricted to a minimum for Party operations and members were encouraged to use code words and double talk in their conversations.
4. Use of mails was restricted. Mail drops and confidential return addresses were used more and more.
5. The courier system was expanded.
6. Meetings were reduced in number and camouflaged as social meetings of small groups in the members' homes.
7. Party records were destroyed or hidden and it was forbidden to maintain membership records containing the names of individuals.
8. Duplicating machines and quantities of paper were bought and hidden in the homes of trusted members.
9. The National Committee set up its own "loyalty program" and committees were named to review personal histories, activities, employment records, social activities and associations of members. Detailed biographical questionnaires were issued delving into members' most personal affairs and habits. State committees were instructed to review these reports, analyze them, and then report to the National Committee. Anyone whose conduct or activities aroused suspicion was to be dropped on orders of the National Committee. Where doubt existed, the suspect was questioned at length.

In piecing together the story of the Party's underground, the FBI learned that in 1948 three Communist leaders had been chosen to expand the hidden apparatus. Each of the three was instructed to name three immediate subordinates, and this same system was to be extended down through the district, state, county, city and club units. Thus one layer in the underground would know only the next layer above and below; and penetration to the top by the FBI would be more difficult.

By mid-1956, the FBI estimated that the Communist Party, USA, was stripped down to a hard core of about 20,000 members, due to the prosecutions of the Party leaders and the gradual postwar realization throughout the country of the growing world threat of communism.

Congress moved in 1950 to put a tighter curb on subversive activities by passing, over the veto of President Truman, the Internal Security Act of 1950,[7] which required that all Communist-action organizations, their officers and members register with the Attorney General as agents of a foreign power. The Act also required the registration of Communist-front groups and their officers.

The Act provided for the establishment of the Subversive Activities Control Board to determine whether an organization was or was not a Communist-action or Communist-front group.

In October, 1950, the FBI sent to Attorney General Clark a 660-page report containing material supporting the Bureau's view that the Communist Party, USA, was a Communist-action organization. On the basis of this report, Clark filed a petition before the Subversive Activities Control Board asking for an order requiring the Party to register under the terms of the Act. The Board received arguments from both sides and on April 20, 1953, ruled that the Communist Party was a Communist-action organization "nurtured by the Soviet Union." The Party was ordered to register with the Attorney General.[8]

But the Party's National Committee promptly refused to comply with the order and counsel for the Party attacked the constitutionality of the Internal Security Act in an appeal to the U. S. Court of Appeals. The Appeals Court held the Act to be constitutional and affirmed the Subversive Activities Control Board order by a two-to-one decision. The decision was appealed by the Party to the U. S. Supreme Court, which after considering the case, remanded it to the Board for further proceedings on April 30, 1956 where the matter is still pending.

The next major blow aimed against the Party came when President Eisenhower signed the Communist Control Act of 1954, which, among other things, empowered the Attorney General to file a petition with the Subversive Activities Control Board asking for a finding whenever it was proved that a union was Communist-infiltrated. Under such a finding, a union would be barred from using the facilities of the National Labor Relations Board and it would lose the rights provided under the Labor Management Relations Act.

Through the fabric woven by the FBI's investigations of Communist activities ran one continuous and unbroken thread: the dedication of the Party to the interests of Soviet Russia and world communism. Whenever the interests of the United States and those of Russia clashed, the Party stood with the Soviet interests.

When the North Korean Communist Army invaded South Korea

on June 25, 1950, the United States' Communists accused their own government and "Wall Street" of being responsible for the war. The United Nations Security Council was assailed for blaming North Korea for the attack across the 38th Parallel, and the United Nations decision to give help to South Korea and block the aggression became the "United States' imperialistic intervention in Korea." But at the same time the Soviet Union's foreign policy was "a policy of defending the sovereign equality of small nations, of supporting the liberation struggle of colonial peoples."

With the nation on a partial wartime footing and tension growing between the United States and Soviet Russia, the FBI shouldered an increased burden of work in the security field. More agents were moved into the coverage of Communist activities, particularly in the underground.

Hoover ordered some of the old security measures which had been used successfully in World War II to be instituted again. These included specialized programs of cooperation with the American Legion and local law enforcement agencies and reestablishing security programs at defense plants.[9]

In those tense days, there was the recognition that the American Communists' loyalty was doubtful in case of war with Russia. It was for that reason that the FBI took extraordinary measures to keep a check on the Party's underground operations and to identify its members.

And this doubt was not to be dispelled after the war.

This first break in the pattern of the Communists' underground activity came in 1955, in the afterglow of the Geneva Conference, when the Russian leaders began to promote the idea of "friendly coexistence" between communism and capitalism, and to encourage the hope that the two systems could live at peace in the same world.

It was in this atmosphere that fugitive Communists suddenly began to come out of hiding and to surrender. Party members who had been missing for months reappeared to take up open Party activity again. FBI informants reported that many of the Communists themselves believed another "friendly" era was ahead and that the smiles of N. S. Khrushchev, First Secretary of the Central Committee, and N. A. Bulganin, Chairman of the Council of Ministers of the Soviet Union, meant an easing of tensions at home as well as abroad.

But then the FBI received information late in 1955 disclosing that Party leaders were discussing an analysis of Leninist action which they interpreted as meaning that there would be no "peaceful evolution" of socialism in the United States and the Party should make its future plans on that basis.

Informants said the analysis had thrown Party leaders into confusion. Some of them argued that peaceful coexistence still should be the "line." But the stern facts of life became clear when the Communists met in Moscow in February, 1956, for their Twentieth Congress. Khrushchev and other Party leaders talked of nonviolence and the peaceful evolution of communism throughout the world. But Khrushchev also told the Congress:

> In the countries where capitalism is still strong and has a huge military and police apparatus at its disposal, the reactionary forces will, of course, inevitably offer serious resistance. There the transition to socialism will be attended by a sharp class, revolutionary struggle . . .

A. I. Mikoyan, First Vice Chairman of the USSR Council of Ministers, said:

> . . . A peaceful revolution is possible, of course, only if the working class is strong, well-organized and class-conscious. In other cases, when the bourgeoisie possesses a strong military and police machine, it will undoubtedly force an armed struggle on the proletariat in order to maintain its domination. The proletariat must be prepared for this beforehand . . .

And M. A. Suslov, member of the Secretariat, Central Committee of the Communist Party of the Soviet Union, said:

> . . . in a number of capitalist countries, in those where the reactionary forces and the military and police machine are especially powerful, the transition to socialism will be attended by frenzied resistance from the exploiting classes, and, consequently, by sharp revolutionary struggle on the part of the working class . . .

> . . . the application of more peaceful or more violent methods depends not so much on the working class as on the degree and form of resistance offered by the exploiting class, which do not want voluntarily to relinquish their wealth, political power and other privileges.

The Party "line" was clear as far as the FBI was concerned. In countries where capitalism was strong and resisted communism, the Communists must prepare themselves for the struggle of violent revolution.

The Communist hierarchy's down-grading of Stalin in the Twentieth Congress, the bitter denunciations of the "cult of the individual," and the seeming relaxation of Moscow's stern authority over world communism were viewed by the FBI as just other tactical maneuvers in the Party's grand strategy.

If, as the Communist leaders said, they were returning to Leninism, then it was time to remember what Lenin taught:

> . . . we must . . . be ready for any and every sacrifice, and even if necessary, to practice trickery, to employ cunning, and to resort to illegal methods, to sometimes even overlook or conceal the truth . . .

32 : *The Scientist and the Stranger*

IT WAS December 3, 1943. The United States Fifth Army in Italy was slowly hacking a bloody path across the Nazi-held mountains toward Cassino. On the Russian front, the tide had turned against the Germans in the battle for Stalingrad . . .

From out of the Atlantic's icy mists, the British transport *Andes* steamed into the sheltered waters of Norfolk, Virginia, and dropped anchor. The long, hazardous voyage from England was over and the tension was draining out of the crew and the passengers. At the ship's rail a small group of British scientists laughed and joked as the lines were made fast and preparations completed for them to go ashore.

Tonight, New York City! A city that fairly sparkled with lights when compared with London, where people had stumbled through dreary blackouts for four long years . . . a city with no enemy planes droning overhead, no flames leaping up to silhouette jagged bomb scars . . . no crash of blockbusters or antiaircraft batteries and no wail of the sirens night after night to shatter sleep and edge the nerves. . . .

Beneath the excitement of arrival was another, greater excitement. This was generated by being a part of a war effort so secret that only a handful of people knew its real meaning—and even among their own select group they could only guess at what the future held.

None of these men of science could know that in the pooling of their knowledge with the Canadians and Americans they would harness the atom as a military weapon in the incredibly short time of nineteen months.[1] Not even the brilliant, sallow-faced young physicist, staring for the first time at the United States, could imagine such an achievement.

An older scientist leaned on the ship's rail beside the young man, whose eyes seemed large and round behind his thick-lensed glasses.

"There it is, Klaus," the older man said. "The colony we traded for a cargo of tea. And I'm bloody glad to be here."

Klaus Fuchs smiled. "I'm glad, too. I have never been in the United States before."

"Oh, you will find old friends . . ."

"No," Fuchs said. "I have only a sister in Cambridge, Massachusetts."

It was the truth. Fuchs knew no one well in America other than his sister. He had fled to England from Germany in 1933 after Hitler had risen to power in the Reich, just as many scientists had fled. When Germany and England went to war against each other, he had been interned briefly as an enemy alien, but the internment hadn't lasted long. He had gone to work for the British in nuclear research and now he had British citizenship. Already he had established a reputation as an extraordinarily brilliant physicist and mathematician. That's why he was a member of this mission.

No, Klaus Fuchs knew no one well in America other than his sister. But somewhere out there among the millions of people a stranger was waiting for him. Fuchs knew that one day he and this man would meet and each would recognize the other. In that meeting a bond would be formed, just as the bonds had been formed back in England with the Stranger. A faceless, formless, nameless shadow. Each time it was the same. He was out there at this moment, walking strange streets in a strange city, waiting for the day, the hour and the minute of their meeting.

A voice called, "Klaus!" The young scientist blinked. He turned from the rail and hurried with the others down the gangplank.

There was no bothersome red tape or checking by security officers. The Army had exclusive responsibility for guarding atomic security and for clearing personnel [2] assigned to the Manhattan Engineer District, which directed the atomic energy program. The British had assured the Army's Manhattan Engineer District that Fuchs had been screened and found to be trustworthy and loyal. These assurances were accepted.[3]

Within a short time the British group was en route to New York, to enjoy the city's glitter and then to plunge into the atomic unknown.

But one member of the group was not entirely engrossed with atomic problems. A few weeks after the arrival of the *Andes,* Klaus Fuchs strolled from the Barbizon Plaza Hotel on a windy Saturday afternoon. A few minutes later he stepped from the subway in New York City's Lower East Side.

Passers-by may have smiled faintly at the thin, sallow fellow, bundled in an overcoat, who carried a white tennis ball in his hand. But perhaps not. Even more uncommon sights go unnoticed on New York's streets.

And then Klaus Fuchs saw the Stranger. The scientist knew him instantly by the gloves in his hand and the book with the green binding. He was middle-aged, perhaps five feet, ten inches tall and solidly built. His face was round and impassive. The Stranger's eyes flicked to the tennis ball in Fuchs's hand. He spoke, and the two of them stepped into a cab.

When they were seated at a table in a restaurant on lower Third Avenue, the Stranger said, "I am Raymond." Never was he to let Fuchs know that his real name was Harry Gold.

A flicker of a smile twitched the scientist's lips. "I am Dr. Klaus Fuchs." The Stranger nodded.

Fuchs told his companion of the super-secret Manhattan Engineer District. He talked of the concentrated effort to solve the scientific and industrial puzzle of quantity production of fissionable uranium, and of the goal of harnessing the atom's energy to a military weapon. He promised specific details later, and after arranging a recognition signal for the next meeting, they parted.

In those few, fleeting minutes, Klaus Fuchs and the Stranger had unlocked an unguarded door leading to the most appalling crime in our time—the theft of atomic secrets for Soviet Russia.

This was early 1944.

In early September, 1949, the struggles on the battlefields of Europe and in the Pacific were a four-year-old memory. Communist Russia no longer was an ally. She was, in nondiplomatic language, the Cold War enemy of the Western World.

At his desk in the Department of Justice building on Pennsylvania Avenue, FBI Director J. Edgar Hoover studied a top-secret report— and his face flushed with shock and anger. Here was information, reliable beyond doubt, that agents of a foreign power had stolen the very heart out of the atomic bomb, stolen the secret of its construction and detonation.[4]

Hoover reached for the intercom telephone. He gave a series of orders to his key subordinates and soon the vast machinery of the FBI was in high gear. In essence, Hoover's orders were: "The secret of the atomic bomb has been stolen. Find the thieves!"

Hoover and the FBI, not the Army, were now responsible for atomic security. In the Atomic Energy Act of 1946, which tightened up on atomic security, Congress said:

> Except as authorized by the [Atomic Energy] Commission in case of emergency, no individual shall be employed by the Commission until the Federal Bureau of Investigation shall have made an investigation and report to the Commission on the character, associations, and loyalty of such individual . . . all violations of this Act shall be investigated by the Federal Bureau of Investigation . . .

This responsibility became effective January 1, 1947.

And here in Hoover's hands was information of a crime so shocking that it was to be called "the crime of the century."

Hoover's men swarmed into the Los Alamos atomic plant near Santa Fe, New Mexico, and other plants. They dug into records and personnel files of the Atomic Energy Commission, and interviewed hundreds of people who might have some clue. Within a few days, the FBI reached the conclusion that the key figure in the crime had very likely been a member of a foreign mission; a man with free access to all the work done on the uranium processing and bomb assembly; and, most likely, a physicist. The British were notified of these conclusions.

During this intense man-hunt, President Truman jolted the nation with his announcement that the government had "evidence that within recent weeks an atomic explosion occurred in the U.S.S.R." Now the world knew that the United States no longer had a monoply on the atomic bomb. It was clear, too, that somehow Russia had made seven-league strides in atomic development, drastically weakening the free world's power position in relation to the Communist world.

Near the end of September, the coil of evidence was tightening around Klaus Fuchs. On the known record, it seemed impossible. He was now the respected head of the Theoretical Physics Division of Britain's atomic energy establishment at Harwell, a man with a brilliant future. He seemed to have been a discreet fellow, totally absorbed in his work. The women who had known him remembered him as "a shy, sweet guy," with no apparent interest in politics. British security officials had vouched for his loyalty.

Then a small alarm bell sounded. An agent digging through old Nazi records seized by intelligence officers in Germany during World War II spotted an entry bearing the name of a Klaus Fuchs.

Translated, the entry said: "Klaus Fuchs, student of philosophy, December 29, 1911, Russelsheim, RSHA-IVA2, Gestapo Field Office, Kiel."

The agent noted that the Klaus Fuchs in the Gestapo file had the same birth date and birthplace as the German-born British physicist who had worked at Los Alamos. The initials RSHA stood for *Reichssicherheitshauptamt,* Central Office of Security Police. The Roman numeral IV was a department of the RSHA. The symbol A2 identified the special file into which the Gestapo dropped the names of those they listed as Communists. In the Communist file, also, was another name identified as that of a relative of this Klaus Fuchs.

By itself, the old Gestapo file was proof of nothing. The Nazis, for political and other reasons, undoubtedly had accused many innocent persons of being Communists. Still, the information couldn't be ignored.

Agents sifted through every record they could find that might produce any sort of lead. They turned to the file of the 1946 Canadian spy case in which Igor Gouzenko, the cipher clerk, had fled from the Russian Embassy at Ottawa to disclose the operation of an atomic spy ring. In this file was a photographic copy of an address book picked up by Canadian police. Among the names was the entry: "Klaus Fuchs, 84 George Lane, University of Edinburgh, Scotland."

The entry had held no special significance for the FBI in 1946, and neither had the name of Kristel Heineman, who, it later developed, was Fuchs's sister. When the notebook of names was received from the Canadians the FBI had been on the sidelines as far as atomic personnel security was concerned.

But now his name meant something. The bits and pieces of information, when joined together, all weighed against Fuchs. Hoover notified British Intelligence (MI5) of the new developments and suggested Klaus Fuchs as the man to watch. MI5 agents shadowed Fuchs. By the end of October the British themselves had decided he was the atomic spy—or at least one of them.

It was December, 1949, when William J. Skardon, Harwell security officer, tapped on Fuchs's door. Once inside, he told Fuchs he was suspected of passing information to the Russians.

Fuchs seemed surprised. "I don't think so," he blurted. Skardon persisted. He told Fuchs there was precise information that he had.

Fuchs repeated, "I do not think so."

"That's an ambiguous reply."

"I do not understand," Fuchs said. "Perhaps you will tell me what the evidence is. I have not done any such thing."

Fuchs continued to deny his guilt. But on January 24, 1950, he sent word to Skardon that he wished to see him.

Skardon came to Fuchs's rooms. "You asked to see me and here I am."

Fuchs said, "Yes, it is rather up to me now." It was plain that he was under strong emotional stress.

In rambling fashion, Fuchs reviewed for Skardon his life in Germany; his fight against Nazis; his early belief that communism held the cure for the world's ills; and his fear for his father, who was in the Red zone in Germany.

Skardon listened. Fuchs's ramblings, he knew, were providing the motive for his acts, but Fuchs still wasn't talking about the acts themselves.

Skardon suggested to Fuchs that he might as well unburden himself and clear his conscience by telling the full story.

"I will never be persuaded by you to talk," Fuchs exclaimed.

But after they had had lunch together, the confession came tumbling from Fuchs's lips. Yes, he had given the Russians atomic secrets from the time he began working on nuclear research in 1942 until a year ago. He had sought out the Russians himself and on his own initiative. Before he went to the United States, he was given the recognition signals and told where he would meet the Stranger. Yes, there had been an irregular but frequent passing of atomic information to the Russians. Shortly after he returned to England from the United States in 1946,

Fuchs continued, he had accepted £100 from the Russians as a "symbolic payment" which would signify his "subservience to the cause."

Was Fuchs ever bothered by doubts about such treachery?

Yes, he said, he had begun to suffer doubts. He still believed in communism, but not as it was being practiced in Russia. Now, too late, he saw communism as something to fight against.

A significant little scene took place when Skardon accompanied Fuchs to the War Office on January 27, 1950, where Fuchs was to make a formal statement. Skardon faced Fuchs, the man who had betrayed England, the United States, Canada, his associates, and men of freedom wherever they were.

The Briton said, "I ought to tell you that you are not obliged to make a statement, and you must not be induced to do so by any promise or threat which has been held out to you."

Fuchs looked at Skardon. Perhaps at that moment he understood for the first time in his twisted life the true protector of human dignity—government by law. He said, "I understand. Carry on."

Four days after Fuchs signed the statement, the British advised Hoover that they had "resolved" the case and that it was established that Fuchs had been spying continuously for the Russians from the end of 1941 until February, 1949.

The FBI Director notified the government's top echelon of the turn of affairs. On February 3, the British announced Fuchs's arrest.

Into FBI Headquarters came a message from Steve Early, former White House press secretary and then Deputy Secretary of Defense: "I'm glad to see Edgar is in it. I've been fighting a battle for a long time that he is the only one competent to handle this kind of matter and this will strengthen my arguments."

And Hoover cabled Sir Percy Sillitoe, who headed MI5: "Congratulations on a job well done. Your cooperation in this case is much appreciated. Regards."

The Joint Congressional Committee on Atomic Energy was to say: "It is hardly an exaggeration to say that Fuchs alone has influenced the safety of more people and accomplished greater damage than any other spy not only in the history of the United States but in the history of nations."

This Committee noted that Russia, through espionage agents, had been able, at a vast savings in time and money, to solve the broad problems of (1) quantity production of fissionable materials; and (2) the design and assembly of practical weapons. Fuchs had access to all these secrets at Los Alamos.

Klaus Fuchs was brought to trial in Old Bailey on March 1. He pleaded guilty to charges of giving "to persons unknown" information calculated to be useful to an enemy. Fuchs's chief defense counsel, Derek Curtis-Bennett, told the court that when Fuchs was given his citizenship in 1942 "he was a known Communist, and he had never pretended he was anything else."

The attorney said that Fuchs had mingled freely with British Communists, and he also said, "Anybody who had read anything about Marxist theory must know that a man who is a Communist, whether in Germany or Timbuctoo, will react in exactly the same way. When he gets information, he will automatically and unhappily put his allegiance to the Communist idea first."

Lord Chief Justice Goddard, after hearing the evidence, said to Fuchs: "You have betrayed the hospitality and protection given to you with the grossest treachery . . . The maximum sentence ordained is fourteen years. That is the sentence I pass upon you."

Fuchs was led away to Wormwood Scrubs Prison.

From the time Fuchs confessed, the FBI concentrated on getting the answer to one question: who was the Stranger, the mystery man to whom Fuchs slipped atomic information on at least ten occasions in New York; Santa Fe, New Mexico; and Cambridge?

The single clue on which to work was a vague description by Fuchs of a man in his middle years, say forty to forty-five. About five feet ten. Solidly built. Round face. Not a physicist. Probably not even an atomic employee. A man who knew something about chemistry. Perhaps a chemist. He called himself "Raymond," but obviously that wasn't his real name.

Beyond this shadowy image, Fuchs could give no further help.

This is a big, broad land. There are millions of middle-aged, solidly built, round-faced men who are not physicists and who are not atomic employees. Where to start? From the top, bottom or side of this haystack?

"Perhaps a chemist . . ."

Agents of the FBI called on Mrs. Kristel Heineman, Fuchs's sister, and her husband in Cambridge. The Heinemans recalled that in late January, 1945, a stranger had called at their home asking for Klaus, who hadn't yet arrived for his vacation with them. The man was middle-aged and solidly built. He left a telephone number in New York for Klaus to call, and he returned the following month. Klaus seemed to know him. The two of them talked for quite a while. The visitor appeared to be fond of children because he had promised their son a chemistry set. The Heinemans could recall no name.

The information wasn't much help except that the Heinemans' recollection of the Stranger tallied with Fuchs's description; and it was confirmation of Fuchs's statement that he had turned over atomic information to "Raymond" in Cambridge.

But there again was the reference to chemistry. The search narrowed. Now the FBI concentrated on finding a chemist who would fit the description they had. Through the days and weeks after Fuchs's confession, agents searched the ranks of chemists. They pored over files and records. The task was enormous. For example, in 1945, New York City alone had issued 75,000 licensing permits to chemical firms.

But by the slow process of elimination, the possibilities thinned to 1,500 . . . 1,000 . . . 100 . . . 20 . . . and then at last to Harry Gold.

Gold's name had come to the FBI's attention in May, 1947, during an investigation which grew out of information supplied by Miss Elizabeth T. Bentley, a self-confessed Communist courier. The file showed that Gold was a chemist.

A further check disclosed that Gold was now in charge of biological research at the Philadelphia General Hospital's heart station. On May 15, 1950—some six weeks after Fuchs's conviction—two FBI agents visited the Philadelphia hospital and asked Gold if he would give them an interview.

"Of course," Gold said. "But we are very busy at the moment. Would you come back this evening?"

The agents returned after dinner. Gold was waiting for them. He recalled he had been questioned by the FBI on another occasion, and he asked what it was they wanted to know this time. He was shown a picture of Klaus Fuchs and exclaimed, "This is a very unusual picture. He is that English spy!" Then he added that he didn't know Fuchs, of course, but he had recognized his face because of all the newspaper publicity.

No, he didn't know the Heinemans in Cambridge or anyone in Santa Fe, New Mexico. As a matter of fact, he had never been in New England or west of the Mississippi River. He answered questions willingly and even with an air of candor, as a man would with nothing to hide.

But the agents noted discrepancies in Gold's story. Small flaws. Nothing of any vital importance. Merely evasions and occasional denials of things which the agents knew to be true.

A week passed, during which Gold was questioned several times, and finally he said to the agents, "I've told you everything I know. I've got nothing to hide. If it will help, go ahead and search the place." He gave his written consent for the search of his home, a two-story row house at 6823 Kindred Street in Philadelphia.

At Gold's suggestion, the agents started their search in the bedroom, the room where he had most of his papers, books, journals and letters. Gold made himself comfortable in a chair. This would take time.

One of the agents looked behind a bookcase which obviously hadn't been touched in years. He picked up a yellow folder, one of those Chamber of Commerce maps for tourists. It was a map of "Santa Fe, The Capital City."

The agent spread the map open. "You said you had never been west of the Mississippi? Or have you?"

Harry Gold stared at the map. For a long minute no one spoke. The agents stood watching Gold, waiting. Then suddenly he seemed to crumple, like a man so bone-weary that he couldn't carry his burden another step.

Gold said, "I . . . I am the man to whom Klaus Fuchs gave his information."

Just as with Klaus Fuchs, once the words began they came in a steady flow. He told of meeting Fuchs in New York and Cambridge and Santa Fe, detailing how he picked up the information and gave it promptly to "John," whom he later identified as Anatoli A. Yakovlev, Russian Vice Consul in New York.

But why? Why? . . . Why was it men like these betrayed their own country in spying for a cause which had made a mockery of freedom for millions of people?

Gold's explanation was an old, familiar refrain: confused idealism leading to treachery. He said:

> I began the work of industrial spying for the Soviet Union in 1936, with the full realization of what I was doing. I thought I would be helping a nation whose final aims I approved, along the road to industrial strength.

His reaction to working with Fuchs: ". . . I felt that as an ally, I was only helping the Soviet Union obtain information that I thought it was entitled to."

Doubt had finally come to Gold, just as it had to Fuchs. He began to fear exposure. He worried that his family, who knew nothing of his actions, would be "completely and horribly disgraced."

But it was too late to turn back.

> . . . I got so involved, that even had I wanted to, it would have been extremely difficult to get out. However . . . I never once actually suggested it to any people with whom I worked . . .
>
> . . . the realization that I was turning over information to another power . . . was so frightening that the only thing I could do was to shove it away as far back in my mind as I could and simply not think on the matter at all . . . what I did . . . was to simply blot out of my mind as well as I could any thoughts whatever on the subject.[5]

33: *Worse Than Murder*

NINE months after J. Edgar Hoover flashed the warning that atomic secrets had been stolen by agents of a foreign power, the whole wretched story of espionage was known to the FBI.

FBI agents had followed the spy trail to Dr. Klaus Fuchs, and from Fuchs to the Philadelphia chemist, Harry Gold. From Gold, the path branched into a maze of treachery. Gold recalled for the FBI the paths he had trod for fourteen years as a Soviet agent. One of those paths led to a twenty-eight-year-old ex-Army sergeant, David Greenglass, who lived with his wife, Ruth, and their two children at Apartment No. 6, 265 Rivington Street, New York City.

Greenglass was in the kitchen preparing the baby's milk formula when two FBI agents knocked on the door. It was 1:46 P.M., June 15, 1950. Greenglass left the kitchen and opened the door.

"Mr. Greenglass? David Greenglass?"

"Yes."

"May we come in?"

Greenglass nodded and the two visitors stepped into the room.

"We're from the FBI," one of the agents said. They showed their identification. "We are trying to locate information on materials lost, misplaced or stolen at the Los Alamos project. You worked at Los Alamos, didn't you?"

"Yes," Greenglass said. "But I can't help you. I know nothing about it."

The agents continued to question the ex-sergeant. Would he have any objections if they looked around the apartment? He could refuse if he wished, of course.

"I have nothing to hide," Greenglass persisted. "Go ahead." He signed a waiver of search.

A few minutes later one of the agents left the apartment with twenty-four pictures of Greenglass and his wife, including a snapshot taken while Greenglass was in uniform during World War II.

The agent took the pictures to Harry Gold. The chemist studied them. At last he said: "This is the man I contacted at Albuquerque."

"When did you contact him?" the agent asked.

"In June, 1945."

"On whose instructions?"

"I was acting on instructions from my Soviet espionage superior, 'John.' The man in this picture gave me information about his work at Los Alamos—and I turned over the information to 'John.' "

"Will you sign a statement to that effect?"

Gold nodded.

For a time Greenglass protested his innocence. But then, like that of Fuchs and Gold, his part of the story finally spilled forth. Piece by piece, the parts fell into place. No one person had all the information, but when the FBI had gathered together the parts, there was the clear picture of espionage. In its essentials, here follows the story as it was given to the FBI and later revealed in testimony in federal court.

On November 29, 1944—three months after T/4 Sgt. David Greenglass's transfer to the secret Los Alamos atomic bomb project—Ruth Greenglass arrived in Albuquerque, New Mexico. David had managed to wangle five days' leave from his job as a machinist. He met Ruth at the Hotel Franciscan. This was their second wedding anniversary.

One day while walking along Highway 66, out beyond the city limits, Ruth told David about a talk she'd had with Julius and Ethel Rosenberg in New York. Ethel was David's sister.

Ruth said that Julius had told her he and Ethel had dropped their Communist Party activities; they didn't attend club meetings or subscribe to the *Daily Worker*.

David was surprised. "But why?"

"Because Julius said at last he's doing what he always wanted to do —giving information to the Soviet Union!"

Ruth said that Julius knew what David was doing, too. David was working on the atomic bomb, the deadliest weapon ever conceived by man. Julius and Ethel wanted David to give them information about his work which would be useful to Russia. They said Russia was an ally and she wasn't getting the information she deserved to have. If all nations had this atomic information—then, Julius said, one nation couldn't use the bomb as a threat against another nation.

David was scared. "I can't do it, Ruth," he said. But next day he saw things differently.[1] He agreed. Julius had been his hero for years. Julius and Ethel had persuaded him to join the Young Communist League when he was fourteen. His father and mother didn't like Julius because he was a Communist, and they didn't like Ethel's running around with him or marrying him for that matter. But David liked Julius. He didn't want to see Julius fail at anything he tried.

David gave Ruth a description of the Los Alamos layout, the approximate number of people working in the restricted area, and the names of scientists whose connection with the atomic project was supposed to be top-secret. He had picked up their names by overhearing talk at the plant. Ruth memorized all David told her and repeated it to Julius Rosenberg when she returned home.

Two months after this meeting David returned to New York on leave. At Julius' request he made a number of sketches of a flat-type lens mold being used in atomic experiments. He also gave Julius the names of people at Los Alamos who seemed to him to be sympathetic to communism and who might possibly be recruited to give information.[2]

A day or so later, the Greenglasses went to the Rosenbergs' apartment for dinner. Julius said to Ruth, "How would you like to go to Albuquerque to live?"

"I would be very happy," Ruth exclaimed.

"You are going to be there," Julius said. He told her not to worry about money. He would take care of the expenses. The money would be a gift—and it would come from the Russians.

Later the talk turned to finding a means by which David would be able to identify any stranger who might come to get information for Julius.

"Well," Julius said, "I'll give you something so that you will be able to identify the person who does come."

Ruth and the Rosenbergs went into the kitchen. Julius cut the side from an empty Jello box and then cut the piece of cardboard into two notched parts. He gave one half to Ruth Greenglass, and the three of them returned to the living room.

David Greenglass saw the two pieces of cardboard and how the notched edges would fit when joined together. "Oh," he said, "that is very clever."

Julius smiled. "The simplest things are the cleverest."

Ruth put one piece of cardboard into her wallet. Julius kept the other half.

Greenglass returned to Los Alamos late in January at the end of his leave. But Ruth arrived in Albuquerque in February and soon found an apartment at 209 North High Street, where David could come to her on his days off.

David and Ruth were at home in their combination living room–dining room–bedroom when a strange man knocked on their door, a man whose name they would later learn was Harry Gold.

Only a few days before, Harry Gold had met Soviet Vice Consul Anatoli Yakovlev in a little bar and restaurant at 42nd Street and Third Avenue in Manhattan. They had a drink, and then sat at a table where they could talk without being overheard.

The two men discussed the time and place of their next meeting. It would be after Gold's return from Santa Fe, where he was to pick up atomic information supplied by Dr. Klaus Fuchs. Then Yakovlev told Gold that after seeing Fuchs, he must go to Albuquerque on another extremely important mission.

Gold protested. The additional trip to Albuquerque might endanger the entire arrangement for getting the Fuchs information. But Yakovlev cut him short: "You go! That's an order!"

The Russian gave Gold a sheet of onionskin paper on which was written the name "Greenglass," and a High Street address. Below the name was a notation: "Recognition signal. I am from Julius."

Yakovlev next handed Gold a piece of cardboard cut from a Jello box, his identification, and an envelope containing $500 to be given to Greenglass.

Gold arrived in Santa Fe on June 2, 1945. He had time on his hands, so he wandered about town. He stopped at a newsstand and picked up a Chamber of Commerce map of the city—a yellow folder marked "Santa Fe, The Capital City." Absently, Gold tucked the map in his pocket. With that single careless act, Harry Gold made the mistake which almost five years later would shatter his composure when an FBI agent found the forgotten yellow folder behind a bookcase in Gold's bedroom in Philadelphia.

But Gold wasn't thinking of the FBI as he strolled through Santa Fe's streets toward his meeting with Fuchs. He saw the pale scientist driving toward him in an old car. The car stopped and he got in. Within a few minutes, Fuchs had given him a thick packet of information on atomic bomb secrets. He told Gold the bomb would be tested at Alamogordo, New Mexico, the next month.

With this part of his mission completed, Gold left Santa Fe by bus for Albuquerque. The Greenglasses were not at home that Saturday night. Gold found a place to sleep in the war-crowded town, a cot in the hallway of a boarding house. Next morning he registered at the Hotel Hilton. Then he set out for the address on High Street.

The Greenglasses had just finished breakfast when the stranger knocked. David opened the door.

"Are you Mr. Greenglass?"

"Yes."

Gold stepped into the living room. He said, "I come from Julius."

"Oh! You arrived sooner than I expected," Greenglass said. Then he picked up his wife's purse and fished out the piece of Jello box. Gold produced the other half. The pieces matched.

Gold said, "Have you any information for me?"

David said: "I have some but I will have to write it up. If you come back later I'll give it to you." He introduced Gold to his wife.

The stranger left and Greenglass went to work. He drew sketches of the lens mold [3] on which he had been working, and described in writing how the lens was used as a triggering device in atomic experiments. Again he listed names of people he regarded as possible espionage recruits.

Gold came back in midafternoon. He took the information from Greenglass and left behind the envelope containing $500.

Greenglass was back in New York on another furlough in September, 1945. The atomic bombs had been dropped on Hiroshima and Nagasaki. Japan had surrendered. The war was over.

This time David gave Julius a sketch of a cross-section of the Nagasaki type bomb as he visualized it from knowledge of his own work on the triggering device and from the discussions he had heard between scientists and others. Besides the sketches, he gave Rosenberg a handwritten report on the work at Los Alamos.

Julius was pleased. "This is very good," he said. They set up a card table in the Rosenberg living room and brought out a typewriter. Ethel Rosenberg typed the information Greenglass had written, while Julius and Ruth corrected the grammar. Rosenberg told Greenglass he had stolen a proximity fuse while working at Emerson Radio.

And later he boasted that he had information from his contacts about research into atomic-powered airplanes, in addition to research information about a "sky platform."

At one time Julius urged Greenglass to enter a college where he could study engineering and cultivate friendships with students of physics and nuclear science; the Russians would furnish whatever money he needed beyond the G.I. Bill of Rights aid, as they did for other students he had recruited.

But then the British announced Fuchs's arrest on February 3, 1950. Julius Rosenberg came to the Greenglass apartment and asked David to go for a walk. They walked to Hamilton Fish Park, and Julius told David about Fuchs's arrest.

"You remember the man who came to see you in Albuquerque?" Julius said. "Well, Fuchs was also one of his contacts." He figured that Gold would be caught next, and that Greenglass had better leave the country.

After Gold's arrest, Julius urged David to leave as soon as possible by way of Mexico, Sweden or Switzerland and Czechoslovakia; he gave David traveling instructions and a total of $5,000 in cash.[4]

But Greenglass didn't go.

Julius and Ethel Rosenberg, Morton Sobell and David Greenglass were indicted by a Federal Grand Jury on charges of conspiracy to commit espionage, a violation of the Federal Espionage Act of 1917, specifically, Subsection A, Section 32, Title 50, of the United States Code. Greenglass pleaded guilty. The Rosenbergs pleaded not guilty.

The Rosenberg-Greenglass trial opened on March 6, 1951, in the United States Court House in Foley Square, New York. The trial judge was Irving Robert Kaufman, who, at forty, was the youngest federal jurist in the United States. He was assigned the case by Chief Judge John Knox.[5]

Judge Kaufman made it clear from the first that he was aware of the profound implications in the case—the chances that prejudices, religious or political, might color a juror's thinking either for or against the defendants. He questioned prospective jurors closely. Where he noted the slightest doubt of objectivity or any reluctance to serve, the prospect was excused by the Judge himself and thus the prosecution and the defense were saved a challenge.

Judge Kaufman gave defense attorneys a total of thirty juror challenges, ten more than they were entitled to. The defense saw fit to use only twenty-nine before accepting the jury. During the trial and in his charge to the jury, Judge Kaufman emphasized that membership in the Communist Party was relevant solely as it might show intent to aid the Soviet Union; otherwise it was not to be considered in reaching a decision.

The jury found the Rosenbergs and Sobell guilty of violating the Espionage Statute, which provided that those found guilty "shall be punished by death or by imprisonment for not more than thirty years." The courtroom was hushed on the day Judge Kaufman was to pass sentence—April 5, 1951. The lawyers had made their final statements and now they were watching the black-robed Judge, whose attention was centered on Julius and Ethel Rosenberg.

"Is there anything defendants wish to say?"

Julius Rosenberg said, "No, sir."

The Judge looked at Ethel Rosenberg. "Do you care to say anything?"

"No, sir."

Judge Kaufman began speaking. His words were those of a man who had reached a decision only after searching the law for long, weary hours; only after probing deep into his own heart.

> . . . Espionage, as viewed here today, . . . is rather a sordid, dirty work —however idealistic are the rationalizations of the persons who engaged in it—with but one paramount theme, the betrayal of one's own country . . .
>
> I consider your crime worse than murder. Plain deliberate contemplated murder is dwarfed in magnitude by comparison with the crime you have committed. In committing the act of murder, the criminal kills only his victim . . . But in your case, I believe your conduct in putting into the hands of the Russians the A-bomb, years before our best scientists predicted Russia would perfect the bomb, has already caused, in my opinion, the Communist aggression in Korea, with the resultant casualties exceeding 50,000 and who knows but that millions more of innocent people

may pay the price of your treason. Indeed, by your betrayal you undoubtedly have altered the course of history to the disadvantage of our country . . .

What I am about to say is not easy for me. I have deliberated for hours, days and nights. I have carefully weighed the evidence. Every nerve, every fibre of my body has been taxed . . . I have searched the records—I have searched my conscience—to find some reason for mercy—for it is only human to be merciful and it is natural to try to spare lives. I am convinced, however, that I would violate the solemn and sacred trust that the people of this land have placed in my hands were I to show leniency to the defendants Rosenberg.

It is not in my power, Julius and Ethel Rosenberg, to forgive you. Only the Lord can find mercy for what you have done . . . you are hereby sentenced to the punishment of death . . .

Judge Kaufman also sentenced Sobell to thirty years. Sobell had previously fled to Mexico with his wife but he was expelled and taken into custody by the FBI. Greenglass received a fifteen-year prison term.

But before the Rosenbergs died as traitors in Sing Sing Prison's electric chair, their case was to be given one of the most careful and thorough reviews of any case in American criminal history. It was reviewed sixteen different times, on various points, by the United States District Court. There were seven appeals to the United States Circuit Court of Appeals; seven petitions for review to the United States Supreme Court; and two applications to the President of the United States for executive clemency.[6]

Judge Kaufman's decision stood.

Before the jury returned its verdict, Julius Rosenberg's attorney, E. H. Bloch, seemed to be satisfied that Judge Kaufman had conducted a fair and just trial.

Bloch told the Court and the jury: ". . . I would like to say to the Court on behalf of all defense counsel that we feel that you have treated us with the utmost courtesy, that you have extended to us the privileges that we expect as lawyers, . . . we feel that the trial has been conducted . . . with that dignity and that decorum that befits an American trial."

And Bloch was also to say: ". . . I know that the Court conducted itself as an American judge."

But two years later Bloch appeared to have forgotten those words. At the funeral service for the Rosenbergs he stormed: ". . . this was an act of cold, deliberate murder . . . I place the murder of the Rosenbergs at the door of President Eisenhower, Attorney General Brownell and J. Edgar Hoover . . . These sweet, tender, cultured people have been killed . . . Insanity, irrationality, barbarism and murder seem to be part of the feeling of those who rule us."

What had happened between the day in 1951 when Bloch praised the conduct of the trial and that June day in 1953 when he shouted at the Rosenbergs' funeral, "This was an act of cold, deliberate murder"?

The Communist press had been silent throughout the entire Rosenberg trial. There was only a bare mention of their conviction.

The FBI detected in mid-August of 1951 the first small warning of what was to come when the left-wing *National Guardian,* unofficial weekly publication of the Progressive Party, began a series of articles on the Rosenberg case. The *National Guardian* said, in part, ". . . there are strong grounds for suspecting the Rosenbergs are victims of an out-and-out political frameup."

Five months later, the Communist-organized National Committee to Secure Justice in the Rosenberg Case opened headquarters in New York City. And then began a shameful campaign to depict the Rosenbergs as innocent victims of anti-Semitism, trapped by a deliberate plot involving Judge Kaufman, the FBI and the government.

The Committee's first press release, on January 3, 1952, said: "It is significant that none of the jurors was Jewish"; and then the release added that the Rosenberg sentence had "raised fears in the leading Jewish press . . . that the Rosenbergs were 'victims of religious bigotry.' "

Actually, Kaufman and two of the federal attorneys, Irving Saypol and Roy M. Cohn, were Jews. Lucy S. Dawidowicz, in the July, 1952, issue of *Commentary* reported: "A check of 156 names impaneled . . . reveals that fifteen names were obviously Jewish. Of these, ten were excused by the Court for personal reasons, four were challenged by the defense and one was challenged by the government. There were probably other Jews on this panel, but only these fifteen names were clearly Jewish."

Having set up the straw man of anti-Semitism, the Communists ripped into it. The Communist *Daily Worker* joined the campaign with: "The Rosenberg case is a ghastly political frameup. It was arranged to provide blood victims to the witch-hunters, to open the door to new violence, anti-Semitism, and court lynchings of peace advocates and Marxists as 'spies.' "

The Communist-front Civil Rights Congress chimed in: "The lynching of these two innocent American Jews, unless stopped by the American people, will serve as a signal for a wave of Hitler-like genocidal attacks against the Jewish people throughout the United States. . . ."

Now the "Save the Rosenbergs" drive was in high gear. There were mass rallies, parades, and picketing at the White House. Thousands of signatures were obtained on clemency petitions with many signers not even aware of what they had signed. The two Rosenberg children were used as pawns in the game.

Responsible Jewish organizations tried to stem the tide of Communist propaganda. The *Bulletin* of the Anti-Defamation League of B'nai B'rith said bluntly: "The Communists aren't interested in the Rosenbergs as Jews. They are not concerned with the welfare of the Jewish community. They're yelling anti-Semitism for their own, partisan purpose."

The American Civil Liberties Union, while neither approving nor disapproving the death sentences, announced that civil liberties were not an issue in the Rosenberg case.[7]

The campaign achieved such emotional intensity that many honest men and women throughout the free world were disturbed; the line became blurred between appeals for clemency and protests against the trial itself as a "frameup." There was encouragement for the attitude that, after all, the betrayal of American secrets wasn't so bad because the Russians probably would have discovered everything, anyway.

Many Americans accepted the Rosenbergs' guilt without question— but considered the penalty too severe. Some abhorred capital punishment for any crime whatever. Some were fearful that the Rosenbergs would be made "martyrs" to serve the Communist cause in the Cold War. Some parents were swayed by sympathy for the two Rosenberg children. And there were others, doubtless, who wondered why there had not been similar outbursts of emotion over the death sentences given to the kidnapers of little Bobby Greenlease and the Nazi saboteurs of World War II.

The man on whose shoulders these pressures fell most fearfully was Judge Kaufman. But he would not bend. In denying an application for reduction of the death sentence, Judge Kaufman said: "I recognize that some forces are attempting to use this case to fan anti-American fires . . . I still feel that their crime was worse than murder . . . this court has been subjected to a mounting, organized campaign of vilification, abuse and pressure. This court, however, is not subject to such an organized campaign . . . nor does it require such tactics to make it cognizant of the human tragedy involved . . ."

And neither would President Eisenhower relent. The President said: ". . . The execution of two human beings is a grave matter, but even graver is the thought of the millions of dead whose death may be directly attributable to what these spies have done . . . I will not intervene in this matter."

Julius Rosenberg was executed at Sing Sing Prison at 8:05 P.M., June 19, 1953. Ethel Rosenberg was executed ten minutes later.

The path of treason had led to Klaus Fuchs . . . to Harry Gold . . . to David Greenglass . . . to Julius and Ethel Rosenberg . . . and then to the death house at Sing Sing.

That was the end of the trail.

A Look at the Record

34: *The Sum Up*

WHEN President Theodore Roosevelt ordered an investigative force organized in the Department of Justice in 1908 to combat the land thieves, the "trusts" and other federal law violators, there were dark warnings that the move was leading to political espionage and the suppression of civil liberties.

And almost half a century later the question was being heard at times: "Is it true there is danger the FBI will become a Gestapo?"

Sometimes this question was asked for political purposes. Often it was asked by Communists and their sympathizers with the deliberate intent to create suspicion and fear and to undermine the FBI's position. But there can be no doubt that in some instances the question was asked because the American people, abhorring the idea of a "spy system" directed against the private affairs of the people themselves, knew little about the "mystery" organization called the FBI.

The Gestapo was Hitler's secret police system which had the power to make arrests, hold prisoners incommunicado, make searches without warrants, execute without trial, and persecute anyone whose political thinking and racial background didn't conform to the Nazi ideology. It was the twin of the secret police system of Soviet Russia and her satellites.

To compare the FBI with these foreign police systems is as absurd as to compare the independent judiciary of the United States with the courts of the Soviet Union.

No one who studies the FBI operation from the inside—reading the orders from J. Edgar Hoover to his agents, leafing through the policy directives, and watching the transformation of a politically corrupt agency into a force struggling to achieve an ideal—can come to any other conclusion but this:

The FBI cannot become a repressive arm of government or of a clique as long as—

—the President of the United States is a man who rejects the idea of a secret political espionage system.

—the FBI is manned and directed by men of integrity who respect the spirit of the law as well as the words.

—establishing innocence is as important as establishing guilt in agents' investigations.

—Congress watches the FBI's spending and operating policies with a critical eye and the Budget Bureau continues to keep a close check on how and why the FBI spends its money.

—the judicial branch of the government remains free to question investigative procedures in all criminal proceedings, to review the evidence gathered by agents, and to protect the rights of the accused by due process of law.

—the nation's press has the freedom and courage to expose wrongdoing.

—the Bureau is kept free of politics.

But there is one condition under which the FBI could become a "Gestapo." This could happen if the traditional checks and restraints were corrupted or eliminated by a dictatorial government, and the FBI was then used as a political tool.

This same condition, of course, applies to other government investigative agencies. While the FBI has become the most widely known investigative unit within the government, few people realize that it is only one among eighteen federal agencies having investigative staffs with specific responsibilities for enforcement of federal laws and national security. But it is inconceivable that all these restraints could be corrupted or eliminated.

The FBI is not a robot of efficiency. It is a human organization like all others, subject to mistakes in judgment and procedures in making investigations.

In every case of error—and they are a minute fraction of a percentage in the total of FBI investigations—the failure has been one of mechanics and not the result of intent. Over and over, Hoover has drilled into agents the absolute necessity for making such complete inquiries that there "can be no margin for error" and that even though there was no intent to do injury, it was wrong when an injury was done. This attitude represents the wide difference between the FBI and the police of a totalitarian state.

In each failure, the FBI has held a "fire drill" to tighten up its procedures to insure against the same thing happening again.

It isn't difficult to pick out the flaws and mistakes in almost half a century of Bureau operations, particularly those in the early years of its development. But the important fact is that the FBI has moved forward in the protection of civil rights just as the nation has made progress in this direction.

Federal Judge Jerome N. Frank, of the U. S. Court of Appeals for the Second District, has pointed out this progress in the United States by noting that in the year in which the Constitution was adopted, only three states gave Catholics the right to vote. New Jersey didn't allow Catholics or Jews to hold public office until another fifty-five years had passed. The Negro was held in slavery until the Civil War settled that issue. And New Hampshire didn't give Catholics and Jews the right to hold public office until 1867.

Much less than a half century ago, little if anything had been done on a national scale to bring law enforcement into repute as an honorable career, although officers of the law held tremendous power to protect or destroy civil liberties. The idea was strongly planted that "it takes a thief to catch a thief," which of course was absurd.

The history of the FBI, in reality, is the story of America itself and the struggle for an ideal. It isn't perfect, but it has made progress in giant strides, and it's incomparably better than it was thirty years ago.

There is nothing magical about the way the FBI operates or the methods used to unravel mysteries in which agents have only the scrap of a clue as a point of departure.

The facts are that the most baffling crimes are solved by hard grinding hours of labor and that the FBI "never closes" a case until it is solved. These are the keys to the FBI's brilliant achievements, such as the solution of the kidnaping of thirty-three-day-old Peter Weinberger who was stolen from his carriage on July 4, 1956, at Westbury, Long Island. When Mrs. Morris Weinberger went out on the patio to check on her child, she found to her horror that he was gone. In the empty carriage was a ransom note demanding that $2,000 be left in a brown envelope next to the signpost on a corner near the Weinberger home.

The Nassau County police were notified. The search for the kidnaper and child began. The FBI learned of the kidnaping at 8:40 P.M. that evening when a citizen who had learned of the abduction reported it to the supervisor on duty in the FBI's New York office. Agents were dispatched to the scene to obtain the facts. At this stage there was no evidence that the child had been carried across a state line or that interstate communications had been used by the kidnaper, and so the matter was left to the local police. The ransom note demands were met and the money was left at the signpost but the kidnaper didn't pick it up.

Six days after the kidnaping, the mother received a call from the kidnaper and negotiations were started anew. Again the kidnaper did not make any apparent effort to pick up the ransom money, although he left a second note, written on the back of a window products company order blank. Seven days after the kidnaping, the FBI entered the case under the Lindbergh Kidnaping Act, passed in 1934, which provided that unless the victim were released within seven days after the abduction, a presumption was created that the victim had been carried across state lines.

Among the meager clues, the two handwritten extortion notes offered the best opportunity to identify the kidnaper. A special squad of agents established headquarters at Mineola, Long Island, and handwriting experts were dispatched from the Washington headquarters of the Bureau to start the wearying task of checking the handwriting of hundreds of thousands of people; in fact, the handwriting of everyone that could be secured.

The agents began their screening of the handwriting with fingerprint cards and police files in Long Island. They checked for handwriting specimens in post office files, civil service files, hospital records, automobile registration records, job applications, business firms, and every other conceivable record on which there was handwriting. At times more than a hundred agents were working on the Weinberger case. Whenever a signature or a piece of writing even remotely resembled the writing on the extortion notes, it was sent to the special headquarters at Mineola for examination by the FBI's handwriting experts.

On Wednesday afternoon, August 22, an agent checking through the records of the Federal Court for the Eastern District of New York picked up the file of Angelo John LaMarca, who had been arrested in 1954 in a raid on an unregistered still. LaMarca had been sentenced on July 28, 1955, to ninety days in jail. The sentence had been suspended and he had been placed on probation for a year. The agent looked closely at LaMarca's handwriting. It was suspiciously like that on the kidnaper's notes. LaMarca's file was rushed to Mineola. Handwriting experts compared the handwritten reports of the defendant and made a positive identification. The handwriting was the same.

After sifting through two million specimens of handwriting, the FBI had found its man. A few hours later he confessed. Agents found a pad of order blanks in the garage where LaMarca worked as a mechanic. The blanks bore the name of the same window products company whose name was on the second ransom note. A microscopic examination of the pad and the note showed that the same cutting knife had been used to trim the pads and had left its tell-tale microscopic markings on the edges of the paper.

The body of little Peter Weinberger was found the following day and the FBI withdrew from the case when it was established that the child had not been carried across the state line. As an aftermath of this case, Congress changed the kidnap law to give the FBI authority to enter kidnap cases within twenty-four hours after an abduction—rather than waiting seven days.

Another spectacular case into which the FBI plunged and worked on for weeks was the acid attack made on labor columnist Victor Riesel, who had been crusading against racketeers among New York's labor unions.

Victor Riesel and his secretary, Betty Nevins, stepped out of Lindy's Restaurant in the early morning hours of April 5, 1956. They turned from Broadway onto 51st Street. A man suddenly stepped from the shadows. His hand darted toward Riesel's face and hot, searing acid splashed into his eyes to eat away the sight forever.

In an agony of pain, Riesel's first words to Miss Nevins were: "Call the FBI. They'll know what to do."

It was 3:25 A.M., about five minutes after the attack, when Miss Nevins telephoned the FBI. Her report was relayed to the top command.

The United States Attorney for the Southern District of New York held that the attack on Riesel was a clear case of obstructing justice— because Riesel was to be used as a witness in a federal investigation of labor racketeering in New York City. So FBI agents began seeking those who were responsible for the crime.

Across the nation, agents began checking on the movements of "hoodlums" who might have been involved. They looked for someone missing from old haunts or whose actions suddenly had aroused the interest of informants. At last they identified the acid thrower. He was Abraham Telvi who had been found lying in the street on the Lower East Side of New York City with a bullet hole in the back of his skull. He was dead.

Less than five months after the attack on Riesel, the Department of Justice announced that FBI agents had arrested the culprits responsible for the blinding of the New York columnist. Riesel wrote Director Hoover: "The only emotion that is not difficult to express is my deep and warm feelings of thanks to you and your colleagues who have done so truly a tremendous job in solving the mystery of the attack upon me."

Under Hoover's direction, the FBI has become known as an organization that is efficient and incorruptible. He has operated it on the private corporation principle of delegating administrative authority and responsibility. And no other agency in government, perhaps, keeps a closer check on its employees and the quality of their work.

During seven of the worst years of the Prohibition era, when the Prohibition Bureau, local law enforcement agencies, and politicians were being corrupted by the bootleg millions, only one FBI agent was known to have "gone bad." He accepted $350 in a bankruptcy case, was caught by the FBI and was promptly prosecuted.

One of the strengths of the FBI has been in the continuity of its leadership, which has meant a continuity of policy. The basic policies established by Hoover under the direction of Harlan Fiske Stone in 1924 have remained unchanged.

In most agencies and departments of government, a new head has arrived every few years to establish new policies and new operating procedures. They have come and gone with the changes in the national administration. But Hoover has remained at the helm of the FBI through and into the administrations of five Presidents and eleven Attorneys General.[1]

In looking back over the years, one interesting strand of the story has been the FBI's relationship with some of the liberals and intellectuals during the Bureau's fight against communism. By all logic, every liberal intellectual should have stood shoulder to shoulder with the FBI in its fight to expose communism as the most reactionary and imperialistic movement the world has ever known. The stakes in this fight were far too great for diversions by politics or demagoguery. If some people used communism as a political football, this didn't change the evil of communism itself.

Many of the liberal intellectuals did stand by the FBI. They spoke out to suggest that there was nothing contrary to liberalism in supporting the FBI as the professional agency equipped to deal with espionage, sabotage and subversion. But among others there was antagonism against the FBI, as though the FBI were invading a realm of political sophistication which was outside the understanding of law enforcement officers. One myth which was planted by the Communists was that an attack on communism was an attack on freedom of thought. The suspicion gained headway in some quarters that the FBI was an agency of reaction and a symbol of intolerance.

Along this line, Judge Frank wrote in the *Bulletin* of the Anti-Defamation League of B'nai B'rith in 1953:

One fact must be recognized if we are to capture the historical import of those eras of intolerance that have marred American democracy. That fact is: in each of those periods there was some objective justification for the fear which prompted the wave of persecution. There were persons who deserved not persecution, but prosecution and conviction after a fair trial.

So, in our revulsion against despicable, fear-stimulated conduct, we cannot lose sight of the frightening dangers that warrant some real apprehensions, and of the fact that the totalitarian regime which deems us the enemy does have active, secret agents in our midst . . .

Today the fashion in pseudo-liberal circles dictates severe criticism of the FBI. But here is a force, held by a chief to the best police standards, abjuring the third degree and trained to respect civil liberties . . .

The record suggests that the articulate "pseudo-liberal," as Judge Frank called them, has not been willing to face up to the cold truth, which is this: Communism is the brain child of the intellectuals—Marx, Engels and Lenin—and not of the toiling masses. Communism didn't spring from the workers as a liberal movement for personal and intellectual freedom. Communism is a brilliantly thought out plan to destroy the old world and build a new one in which "The Party" will be the central, all-powerful brain ruling the world's millions. It is a dictatorship by the "scientific" mind, which uses the workers as a means to an end. Marx and Lenin and those who followed them understood this well.

The top command of the FBI have no illusions that communism can be destroyed in the United States by the investigation, prosecution and conviction of Communist Party leaders who conspire to overthrow the government by force and violence. That is merely one phase of the job to be done in a world-wide struggle.

The FBI knows that the bigger job lies with the free world's intellectuals—the philosophers, the thinkers wherever they may be, the professors and scientists and scholars and students. These people who think, the intellectuals if you please, are the ones who can and must convince men that communism is evil. The world's intellectuals themselves must see that communism is the deadliest enemy that intellectualism and liberalism ever had. They must be as willing to dedicate themselves to this cause as the Communists have been to dedicate themselves to their cause.

Those intellectuals in the free world who assume a neutral role in the struggle and stand by merely as uncommitted observers are jeopardizing the cause of freedom.

America's top labor leaders have never had any illusions about communism. They have fought the Communists in their ranks for years and with few exceptions have succeeded in kicking them out of places of influence. These leaders know that wherever communism has taken over a country, the "toiling masses" have lost their rights and whatever chance they had for personal dignity.

In a 1956 address to the FBI National Academy graduating class, President George Meany of the American Federation of Labor and Congress of Industrial Organizations said:

> Any system of government in which a party is the government—particularly when there is only one party with absolute power over every walk of life—cannot be government by law. And without government by law there can be no freedom . . . Where *the* Party is the State and has all power, there tyranny is unbridled. Tyranny cannot be reformed. It must be abolished . . .

The record seems crystal clear. Communism was conceived by reactionaries and communism must be destroyed by true liberals who have the intellectual capacity to reach the minds of men with a counter-logic to communism, which strengthens man's faith in himself, his free institutions and the ideal that personal freedom and government by law shall not perish from this earth.

In the whole struggle, the FBI represents the people's effort to achieve government by law. It is an agency of justice. And the FBI in the future will be as strong or as weak as the people demand it to be. No more. No less.

Notes

1: THE FBI IN ACTION

[1] FBI agents have secured degrees from approximately 750 colleges and universities. They have had experience in 150 professions, businesses and trades, and in 36 fields of science. Out of 8,623 male employees, 4,924, or 57 percent, are veterans. In addition, 405 were on active military duty in mid 1956.

2: THE STORY BEGINS

[1] Riding horseback through Rock Creek Park one day in 1901, President Theodore Roosevelt turned to the Negro mounted policeman accompanying him and said: "Have you got a boy you would like to go to work?" Policeman Joseph F. Amos nodded. "I've got one I can't control," he said. The President replied: "That is the one I want." And so it was that James E. Amos became Roosevelt's bodyguard, aide and friend. He alone was beside Roosevelt the night he died in 1919. Jim Amos became an FBI Special Agent in 1921, and something of a legend in the organization. He was eligible for retirement in 1941, but at Director J. Edgar Hoover's request, he remained on active duty until October, 1953. He died at age 74—two months after his retirement.

[2] Correct name not used.

[3] The Dufaurs forfeited bonds of $25,000 and fled, apparently back to France.

[4] Justice McKenna read the court's decision on Feb. 24, 1913, and said in part: "There is unquestionably a control in the states over the morals of their citizens, and, it may be admitted, it extends to making prostitution a crime. It is a control, however, which can be exercised only within the jurisdiction of the states, but there is a domain which the states cannot reach and over which Congress alone has power . . . Its exertion does not encroach upon the jurisdiction of the states." Hoke v. U. S., 227 U. S. 308.

[5] U. S. v. Holte, 236 U. S. 140.

[6] FBI investigations have led to more than 15,000 convictions on White Slave Traffic charges in federal courts since the passage of the Act in 1910. Greed, avarice, brutality and corruption have been disclosed by investigations into interstate ramifications of vice. Notorious criminals engaged in one of the most degrading of the vice rackets have been brought to justice. A traffic in human flesh that has netted vice overlords millions of dollars has been curtailed.

The big vice rings which once existed cannot be organized as frequently today as a result of the FBI's vigilance and action in making arrests before they can become entrenched.

[7] In 1912 the principal FBI investigative responsibilities consisted of the following: antitrust, white slavery, neutrality statutes, illegal interstate shipment of intoxicating liquors, bankruptcy, impersonation and locating of fugitives.

[8] In a "Preliminary Report of the Select Committee to Investigate the Executive Agencies of the Government" (U. S. Senate, 1937), it was stated that "in 1908, when the Bureau had its real beginning, it was the intention of Congress that general law enforcement work should be centered in the Department of Justice; and that other Federal law enforcement agencies should be kept within the jurisdictional boundaries of their respective departments."

3: ESPIONAGE AND SABOTAGE, UNLIMITED

[1] Von Papen was later to help Adolf Hitler to power and become an important Nazi diplomat. From 1936 to 1938 he served as Ambassador to Austria and during World War II as Ambassador to Turkey. He was tried after the war by the Allies as a war criminal, but freed.

[2] The German-American Mixed Claims Commission, after lengthy litigation, finally placed the legal responsibility on the German Government. Final awards were not made until June, 1939, on the Black Tom Case and the Kingsland, N. J., explosion when $50,000,000 in damages was set.

[3] During August, 1915, von Rintelen, who had been recalled to Germany, was taken off a ship and interned in London. In April, 1917, he was returned to the United States and tried in federal court on a charge of conspiracy in restraint of trade in foreign commerce. He was convicted and sentenced to a prison term in May, 1917. During November of the same year, von Rintelen entered a plea of guilty on a charge of perjury arising from his efforts to obtain a United States passport. He was sentenced to twenty months in the United States Penitentiary at Atlanta, Georgia. In February, 1918, he received an additional sentence of eighteen months and a fine of $2,000 for the unlawful delivery of bombs on board a ship. He was pardoned in 1920 on condition he leave the country.

4: THE VIGILANTES

[1] Hoover was born in Washington, D. C., January 1, 1895. He attended the public schools and was graduated from The George Washington University Law School in 1916, where the following year he received his master's degree in law. He was admitted to the District of Columbia Bar. He entered government service October 13, 1913, in the Library of Congress, and started work in the Department of Justice in 1917 at a starting salary of $990 a year.

5: THE NEW ENEMY—COMMUNISM

[1] Among intended victims of the bombs were: Senator Lee S. Overman, Chairman of the Senate Committee which investigated bolshevism in Eu-

rope and the U. S.; Senator William King, a member of the Overman Committee; Congressman John Burnett, Chairman of the House Committee on Immigration; U. S. Judge Kenesaw M. Landis of Chicago (later to become baseball commissioner); Justice Oliver Wendell Holmes; Mayor John F. Hylan of New York City; Postmaster General Albert S. Burleson; and Secretary of Labor William B. Wilson.

[2] Hoover's principal assistant in this study was George F. Ruch, who had entered the Bureau's service in 1918 and was detailed to the Departmental assignment. He left the Department in 1923 and became an official of the H. C. Frick Coal Company. Ruch and Hoover had become acquainted at The George Washington Law School, and until his death in 1938 Ruch was one of Hoover's closest friends.

[3] Twelve days after the GID was organized, Director Flynn notified his Special Agents: "The Bureau requires a vigorous and comprehensive investigation of anarchistic and similar classes, Bolshevism, and kindred agitations advocating change in the present form of government by force or violence, the promotion of sedition and revolution, bomb throwing, and similar activities." Flynn's order centered particular attention on aliens whose activities, if illegal, would make them subject to deportation by the Department of Labor's Bureau of Immigration.

[4] In analyzing these differences later, William Z. Foster, as head of the Communist Party in America, said that the two Communist groups developed "a basically correct" Marxist-Leninist position but "failed in applying" these principles "to the concrete American situation."

6: PALMER'S "RED RAIDS"

[1] Sec. 2, Chap. 186, 40 Stat. 1012, Act of October 16, 1918.

[2] Anthony Caminetti, Commissioner of Immigration, cooperated closely with the Department of Justice in initiating deportation proceedings. These cases brought him and Hoover together almost daily in working out legal problems. Caminetti, who had been District Attorney at Jackson, California, was the first native of his state elected to Congress (1891–1895). He died in 1923. The man who suggested using the Immigration laws as a curb against alien anarchists was Assistant Attorney General Francis P. Garvan. Garvan was one of the first men in the Department to take an interest in young Hoover and push him forward.

[3] Statements made by Leon Czolgosz, after his arrest for the assassination of President McKinley, were used in the proceedings against Emma Goldman. Czolgosz said he had been influenced to kill by hearing Emma Goldman speak and by reading her writings. He had a copy of a Goldman speech in his pocket when arrested. While he was in prison, Goldman wrote him saying: "My heart goes out to you in deep sympathy and to all those victims of a system of inequality."

[4] Goldman and Berkman became disillusioned with Russia. They soon realized that the land of the Soviets was not the great hope of mankind they had thought. Goldman wrote: ". . . I had erred grievously when I had de-

fended Lenin and his party as the true champions of the Revolution." In 1921 they left Russia and wandered from country to country. Goldman lived in Germany and England and finally came to Canada. In 1934 she obtained permission for a ninety-day visit to the United States, where she delivered a series of lectures. In New York City she met George Sokolsky, nationally syndicated columnist, who was giving a speech in an adjoining room. She told Sokolsky she wanted to die in the United States. She returned to Canada, where she died in 1940. Berkman committed suicide in 1936 at Nice, France.

⁵ Arthur Adams, who was later to be denounced in Congress as a Soviet atom spy after he presumably fled to Russia, first came to the attention of the FBI when he was employed on Martens' staff.

⁶ Colyer *et al.* v. Skeffington, 265 F. 17 (1920).

⁷ U. S. *ex rel.* Abern v. Wallis, Commissioner of Immigration, 268 F. 413 (1920).

7: A NATIONAL DISGRACE

¹ It was a common practice in the Department in those early days to detach individual agents on special assignments where they were separated from the routine checks of the Bureau. Those in the Bureau simply had no means of knowing where they were or what they were doing. The Wheeler case brought to a head the issue of central control and supervision of Bureau agents. Hoover previously had complained of the practice of having agents assigned to either U. S. attorneys or Department officials. He outlined his views on the misuse of agents in the Wheeler case in a memorandum to Colonel William J. Donovan, then Assistant Attorney General, on April 8, 1928. He said, "When I assumed the duties of Director . . . I found that the Accountants and Agents upon the case had been . . . detached from the Bureau . . . and had been assigned to Special Assistant to the Attorney General Pratt. I didn't know even where the Accountants or Special Agents were. And it was only after several months that I was able to have orders issued which would at least enable me to know where these men were . . . I did not even then assume direction of their investigative work nor see any of their reports nor know what they were doing." Hoover gradually was able to establish the principle that agents on the Bureau's payroll were responsible to the Director.

8: HOOVER'S HOUSECLEANING

¹ The Bureau's first Inspector in the new regime was James S. Egan, who helped Hoover establish new administrative procedures and clean out the

political appointees. A strict disciplinarian, Egan was a force in establishing the Bureau's new policies. He later had charge of all the Bureau's accounting work and retired in 1952 after thirty years of service.

[2] Harold Nathan was Hoover's first Assistant Director. He headed the Bureau's Investigative Division until 1937, and then its Identification, Administrative and Training Divisions. He retired in 1945 after twenty-eight years of service. Now seventy-five, he lives in San Francisco and reports in at FBI offices on his travels around the country.

10: THE GANGSTERS RISE TO POWER

[1] Durkin entered the Illinois State Prison on November 9, 1926, and was discharged on August 8, 1945. He was then taken into custody by the U.S. Marshal and sent to Leavenworth Federal Prison. He was fifty-three when he was released from Leavenworth on July 28, 1954, upon expiration of his sentence.

[2] Special Agent James G. Findlay was born in Eldon, Missouri, on May 20, 1882. He entered on duty as a special agent on August 29, 1911, and is the oldest agent in the FBI in years of service. For the past several years, he has been assigned to the Los Angeles office; during his career he has worked in Kansas City, San Francisco and Birmingham in addition to Los Angeles. A lawyer, Findlay graduated from Knox College, Galesburg, Illinois, in 1906. In 1955, he was presented with the Knox Alumni Achievement Award in recognition of his long and distinguished career in government service.

Special Agent Arthur A. Hopkins entered on duty with the Bureau of Investigation as a special agent on July 19, 1919. He voluntarily resigned on October 3, 1927. He died on January 18, 1944, in Los Angeles, California, at the age of sixty-seven.

[3] In his memoirs, former President Herbert Hoover recalled: ". . . I had been somewhat responsible for the appointment of J. Edgar Hoover to head the Federal Bureau of Investigation through my recommendation to Attorney General Stone. J. Edgar Hoover was a lawyer of uncommon ability and character. He served throughout my administration and assisted greatly in building up the Bureau . . ."

11: REBELLION AGAINST CRIME

[1] In the blast of gunfire from Richetti, Floyd and Miller, Special Agent Raymond J. Caffrey was instantly killed along with officers W. J. Grooms and Frank Hermanson of the Kansas City, Missouri, Police Department, and Otto Reed, Chief of Police, McAlester, Oklahoma. Reed E. Vetterli, then Special Agent in Charge of the FBI's Kansas City office, suffered an arm wound. Special Agent F. J. Lackey of the FBI's Kansas City office was badly wounded. Two forty-five-caliber slugs lodged in his spine, while a third lodged near his pelvic bone. These wounds kept him confined for more than

two months and finally forced him to retire. Special Agent Frank Smith of the Kansas City FBI office, now retired, was uninjured.

[2] During the FBI's hunt for Vernon Miller, his bullet-riddled body was found on the outskirts of Detroit, Michigan, on the morning of November 29, 1933. Apparently he was the victim of a gangland murder. Adam Richetti was caught by local police near Wellsville, Ohio, on October 21, 1934. He was tried and convicted of murder in the first degree and was executed in the lethal gas chamber of the Missouri State Penitentiary at Jefferson City, Missouri, on October 7, 1938. On October 22, 1934, "Pretty Boy" Floyd was located by special agents of the FBI and officers of the East Liverpool, Ohio, Police Department, on a farm between Sprucevale and Clarkson, Ohio. Floyd elected to shoot it out with FBI agents and the police officers, and was mortally wounded.

[3] In the Urschel kidnaping case the FBI applied a clean-sweep policy against kidnapers, harborers, crooked lawyers and money changers involved in this case. Twenty-one persons were convicted. Of these, the following received life sentences: Robert G. Shannon; his wife, Ora Lillian Shannon; his daughter, Kathryn Thorne Kelly; George "Machine Gun" Kelly; Albert L. Bates; and Harvey J. Bailey. The remaining persons convicted received sentences ranging from fourteen months to ten years in prison. George Kelly and Bates are now dead. Robert G. Shannon's sentence was commuted to thirty years.

12: THE ROUNDUP

[1] In May, 1933, Dillinger had been paroled from the Indiana State Prison after serving over eight and a half years on joint sentences of two to fourteen years and ten to twenty years for assault and battery with intent to rob and conspiracy to commit a felony.

[2] In April, 1934, the Dillinger gang was found at Little Bohemia Lodge, a summer resort some fifty miles north of Rhinelander, Wisconsin. Warned by barking dogs of the approach of an FBI raiding party, Dillinger and his buddies escaped. A short distance from the lodge, Lester Gillis, alias "Baby Face" Nelson, a member of the Dillinger gang, killed Special Agent W. Carter Baum, and wounded another agent and a local officer. Previously, in March, Dillinger had escaped in St. Paul, Minnesota, after a gun battle.

[3] Cowley received his Dillinger assignment while serving as assistant to Harold Nathan, Assistant Director in charge of investigations. Cowley's Headquarters assignment was filled by Edward A. Tamm, who had been the Special Agent in Charge at Pittsburgh. Tamm was Assistant to the Director when he was appointed a Federal District Judge in Washington, D. C., in 1948.

[4] Inspector Cowley paid Ana Cumpanas $5,000 from the $10,000 in reward money which the federal government had placed on Dillinger's head. The two East Chicago policemen each received $2,500. Melvin Purvis did what he could to help Ana Cumpanas in her deportation case. But a federal judge ruled that even had Cowley and Purvis promised that the deportation proceedings would be dropped, as the woman's attorney claimed, such a

promise was not within the jurisdiction of an officer outside the Department of Labor. When Ana Cumpanas was put aboard a ship to be deported in 1936, New York reporters asked if she felt she had been "double-crossed by the Government in the deportation proceedings." She replied, "I have never felt that way." She died of a liver ailment in 1947 in the little Romanian town of Timisoara.

[5] Gillis' criminal career began in 1922. He was arrested in Chicago for auto theft and sent to a home for boys, being paroled in April, 1924. He was returned the following September as a parole violator, but in July, 1925, was granted a second parole. He was again returned to the home in October, 1925, and again paroled—for the third time—in July, 1926.

Later Gillis was sentenced to serve one year to life in the Illinois State Penitentiary on a charge of bank robbery. However, in 1932 he escaped from a prison guard while being returned to the penitentiary from Wheaton, Illinois, where he was removed to stand trial on another charge of bank robbery. While an escapee, he killed three agents of the FBI.

[6] After Cowley's death, Earl J. Connelley, then Special Agent in Charge, Cincinnati, Ohio, took charge of the Special Squad in Chicago. He helped run down the gang members in the Dillinger, Barker-Karpis, Kansas City Massacre and other major cases. He entered the Bureau in 1920, became an Inspector in 1936 and then served as a field Assistant Director from 1940 until his retirement in 1954—a career span of thirty-four years.

[7] The Dillinger gang was completely broken up. Frechette was sentenced to serve two years and pay a fine for conspiracy to harbor Dillinger; Homer Van Meter was killed by officers of the St. Paul Police Department on August 23, 1934, while resisting arrest; John Paul Chase was captured in California and sentenced to a life term; John Hamilton died from wounds received in the Little Bohemia gun battle. His body was later found by FBI agents buried near a gravel pit not far from Oswego, Illinois.

[8] "Ma" Barker, born in Missouri Ozark country, raised her four sons to become criminals. She taught them marksmanship by setting tin cans on fence posts and encouraging target practice. She dominated their every move, becoming the "brains" of the gang. She and Fred died in the 1935 battle with FBI agents; Arthur, sentenced to a life term after his capture by the FBI in Chicago, was killed in 1939 while trying to escape from Alcatraz; Herman, the eldest, committed suicide in 1927 rather than submit to arrest on murder charges; Lloyd was prevented from becoming a member of the gang because he had been sent to Leavenworth Penitentiary in 1932 on a twenty-five-year mail robbery sentence. After his release from prison, he was employed as the assistant manager of a grill in Colorado. He was killed by his wife in 1949.

[9] Senator McKellar's sniping at Hoover has been widely advertised over the years, but few ever knew the rest of the story. Jack Carley, Associate Editor of the Memphis *Commercial Appeal* and a lecturer before the FBI National Academy, brought the Senator to an Academy graduation exercise on April 10, 1943. Hoover introduced the Senator, who arose, unexpectedly, and launched into a speech during which he said: ". . . let us stand for . . . this great instrument of law and order that has been built up

by the grand man who is your Director. He believes in the Constitution, he believes in the enforcement of law in this country, let us stand by him." Hoover told a friend: "I was so surprised I looked around to be sure he was talking about me." As Chairman of the Senate Appropriations Committee, McKellar became a strong supporter of the FBI in the years that followed.

[10] Among the first Hollywood producers to popularize the work of the FBI and de-emphasize gangster glorification were Harry Warner and his brothers who produced "G-Men," starring James Cagney. Another film in which the FBI cooperated was Universal's "You Can't Get Away with It" which won an award for the best short subject in 1937.

[11] Wattawa said in his letter: "I am a nephew of the late Senator Walsh, and was closely associated with him. Shortly before he was to assume the post of Attorney General, he told his brother, Mr. John Walsh, and me, that after careful consideration he had decided to retain Mr. J. Edgar Hoover in the position of Director of the Bureau of Investigation."

13: MURDER BY PROXY

[1] Hale was released from prison on parole in July, 1947.

14: THE ANONYMOUS NINE

[1] Tolson, fifty-six, born in Laredo, Missouri, came to Washington, at eighteen, from Cedar Rapids, Iowa, to work as a clerk in the War Department. At nineteen, he was handling routine correspondence for Secretary of War Newton D. Baker. Tolson thought Baker was one of the most brilliant men he ever knew. He once told a friend; "If Baker had been two inches taller, I believe he would have been President of the United States." Baker thought so highly of Tolson he made him his confidential secretary, and for eight years Tolson worked also as confidential secretary to Secretaries of War John Weeks and Dwight Davis. During this time he attended night school at The George Washington University, getting an A.B. degree in 1925 and a law degree in 1927.

[2] Nichols, fifty, joined the FBI in 1934 as a Special Agent. He attended Kalamazoo College, Michigan, and got his LL.B. degree in 1934 at The George Washington University. He is a native of Decatur, Illinois. Boardman, forty-seven, entered the service as a Special Agent in 1934. He was graduated from the University of Minnesota in 1929 with an A.B. degree and in 1934 with an LL.B. degree.

[3] These six men, with their birthplaces and dates of entrance into FBI service, are: *Identification:* C. Lester Trotter (b. 11/13/15), Charles County, Maryland, 1934. *Training and Inspection:* Quinn Tamm (b. 8/10/10), Seattle, Washington, 1934. *Administrative:* John P. Mohr (b. 4/20/10), West New York, New Jersey, 1939. *Domestic Intelligence:* Alan H. Belmont (b. 1/22/07), New York City, 1936. *Investigative:* Alex Rosen (b. 9/14/05), New York City, 1933. *Laboratory:* Donald J. Parsons (b. 5/21/09), Washington, D. C., 1934.

[4] Since March 25, 1918, Helen W. Gandy has been Hoover's secretary and in 1939 she was designated as Executive Assistant to the Director. Awarding Miss Gandy a scroll at the end of thirty-five years of service, Hoover called her "the truly indispensable person in the FBI."

[5] Out of every hundred applicants for the position of special agent, seven are appointed.

[6] Director Hoover credits the accomplishments of the FBI largely to the selection and training of agents. Through the years the brunt of the training has been assigned to such FBI officials as:

Inspector John M. Keith, a man with wide field experience, was one of the best investigators in the service. He was in charge of the Washington Field Division and handled the bulk of the lectures to new agents in the early thirties. He resigned December 1, 1936, to enter private industry and died in 1938.

T. Frank Baughman pioneered in firearms training for new agents and in the development of highly specialized firearms instructions. Baughman entered the Bureau in 1919 and was one of Hoover's close associates. He became chief of the Physics and Chemistry Section of the FBI Technical Laboratory and was regarded as one of the foremost experts in firearms examinations until his retirement in 1948.

Hugh H. Clegg, who entered the Bureau's service on August 31, 1926, served as a field agent, a Special Agent in Charge, and on the headquarters staff as Inspector. Late in 1932, he was named Assistant Director and later was placed in charge of the FBI's Training and Inspection Division, the position he held until his retirement on January 31, 1954.

W. H. Drane Lester, a Rhodes scholar, joined the Bureau in 1932. Within a year he was assigned to training duties, and within three years was promoted to Inspector. Lester left the Bureau on September 3, 1940, to enter private business. He died as a result of an automobile accident on June 4, 1941.

Rolf T. Harbo joined the FBI in March, 1932. In November of that year he joined the headquarters staff. He served as an Inspector, and prior to heading the Training and Inspection Division with the rank of Assistant Director, he was in charge of the FBI Laboratory. Harbo retired on September 30, 1955.

[7] In addition to these voluntary donations of time and money, in 1953 the FBI instituted an Employees Consolidated Charity Fund wherein one campaign a year is conducted rather than a series of individual charity drives. The last campaign brought in a total of $98,315.91. In view of its proven success, a modified version of the "one-package" charity drive has recently been adopted for Government-wide use.

[8] In February, 1956, SAMBA was opened for FBI clerical employees. They have the same benefits as agents, except in life insurance, with agents being insured for $5,000 and clerks $1,000. Cost: Agents, with dependents, $11.50 a month, without dependents $6.00; clerks, $9.50 and $4.00.

[9] A fund created by the widow of Charles S. Ross, who was killed by kidnaper John Henry Seadlund. Seadlund was caught by the FBI. He was

later convicted and executed for his crime. Mrs. Ross wanted to show her gratitude by creating this fund to go to families of agents killed in line of duty.

[10] The maximum allowable is 75 percent of Agent M.'s current salary (not to exceed $525 per month). Of this amount, 40 percent is awarded to the agent's widow and the remaining 35 percent is alloted to his three children. The award terminates on her death or remarriage. The awards to the children end upon death, marriage or attainment of age eighteen. All the above awards are tax free.

15: FINGERPRINTS

[1] From 1933 to mid 1956, experts from the Latent Fingerprint Section testified at 642 trials which resulted in 31 death sentences, 41 life sentences, 2,494 years of imprisonment and fines of about $100,000.

[2] A pamphlet compiled by Maxwell Lehman for distribution by the American Civil Liberties Union.

16: THE FBI LABORATORY

[1] Official examinations in the FBI Laboratory were begun in August, 1933. In its first eleven months of active operation, ending June 30, 1934, a total of 963 examinations were made. During the fiscal year 1956, the Laboratory made more than 140,000 examinations of evidence submitted by agents and by local law enforcement agencies.

[2] Agent Charles A. Appel, Jr., now retired, was the first pioneer on the Laboratory staff. He was soon joined by Donald J. Parsons, now Assistant Director in charge of the FBI Laboratory; Edmund P. Coffey, who left the Bureau in 1945; T. Frank Baughman, retired; Walter G. Blackburn, retired; Ivan W. Conrad; Fred M. Miller; George W. Dingle; Edwin R. Donaldson; Richard L. Millen; Ted D. Beach; and Robert F. Pfafman. These men hold at least one degree and some are Ph.D.'s in chemistry, physics, electrical engineering, biology and other physical or biological sciences. The staff has grown to more than seventy special agents and about ninety other employees.

[3] The FBI Laboratory facilities are available to all federal agencies, U. S. attorneys, military tribunals, etc., in both civil and criminal matters, and to all official state, county and municipal law enforcement agencies throughout the United States. There is no charge for the Laboratory's services, including the testimony of its experts when they are used as witnesses in criminal cases.

[4] The Laboratory scientists must hold at least one degree from a college or a university. They must meet the same physical standards as other agents and their backgrounds are investigated just as thoroughly. They take the regular FBI course of agent training and then work in the field to gain first-hand experience with investigative problems. After assignment to the Laboratory, they are given intensive training in specialized subjects.

[5] Beginning in 1947, the Associated Press, United Press and International News Service began distributing feature stories at intervals on the "most important" criminals sought by the FBI. In 1950, the INS popularized this

program as the "Ten Most Wanted Fugitives" and the FBI began issuing a continuing list for use by newspapers, magazines, radio and television. As one criminal was caught, his name was replaced by another. Of the 98 criminals on this list, 88 have been captured.

17: THE WEST POINT OF LAW ENFORCEMENT

[1] The First Session of the National Academy: Those still active: Ralph W. Alvis, Warden, Ohio State Penitentiary, Columbus, Ohio; Matthew J. Donohue, Chief, Bergen County Police Department, Hackensack, N. J.; Earl J. Henry, Colonel, Commissioner, Pennsylvania State Police, Harrisburg, Pa.; Camille Marcel, Captain, Pittsfield, Mass., Police Department; Harry T. Riddell, Captain, Dallas, Texas, Police Department; Clarence Smith, Lieutenant, Stamford, Conn., Police Department. Retired: William Adams, Assistant Chief of Police, Cincinnati, Ohio, Police Department; Claude Broom, Inspector, Detroit, Mich., Police Department; Francis X. Latulipe, Director, Bureau of Criminology, San Francisco, Calif., Police Department; Fred J. Manning, Inspector, Miami, Fla., Police Department; Leo J. Mulcahy, Captain, State Police, Hartford, Conn.; C. W. Ray, Captain, W. Va., State Police, Charleston, W. Va.; James B. Nolan, Sixth Deputy Police Commissioner, New York, N. Y., Police Department. No longer in law enforcement: Charles R. Blake, Lieutenant, R. I. State Police, Providence, R. I.; L. E. Goodrich, Special Investigator for Governor of Florida, Tallahassee, Fla.; Morgan J. Naught, Detective, Elizabeth, N. J., Police Department; Norman R. Purnell, Superintendent, Del. State Police, Wilmington, Del.; Edwin W. Savory, Superintendent of Police, Radford, Va., Police Department; Ellis J. Wyatt, Supervisor, Ariz. Highway Department of Motor Carriers, Phoenix, Ariz. Deceased: James C. Downs, Captain, Baltimore, Md., Police Department; Nelson Hughes, Chief of Police, Tamaqua, Pa., Police Department; Michael P. Naughton, Supervising Captain, Chicago, Ill., Police Department; James T. Sheehan, Deputy Superintendent, Boston, Mass., Police Department.

18: THE ENEMY WITHIN

[1] May 15, 1936, Chap. 405, Title II, 49 Stat. 1322. This says: ". . . for such other investigations regarding official matters under the control of the Department of Justice and the Department of State as may be directed by the Attorney General. . . ." Also Sec. 299, Title 5, U. S. C., authorizes the Department of Justice to make investigations for the Department of State.

[2] The FBI conducts two types of security investigations—one to uncover admissible evidence to be used in the prosecution of an individual or group in federal court, the other for intelligence purposes only. The intelligence investigation is intended to identify and determine the activities of individuals who are potentially dangerous to the nation's security, thereby supplying information on which to base preventive or counterespionage action. Often

clandestine methods are necessary to uncover clandestine operations, as for example, obtaining an espionage agent's diary or secret papers. The evidence in the diary may be inadmissible in federal court, but it may contain information which would enable the United States to protect itself at a later date. This is in contrast to a case where legal evidence, admissible in court, has to be obtained to convict the espionage agent of violating the laws of the United States.

[3] The Communists are known to have made numerous efforts to penetrate the FBI, but there is no evidence that they ever succeeded.

[4] Officials attending this conference expressed the opinion that the only federal law which would be applicable was the Immigration Law. The President decided that the Commissioner of Immigration and Naturalization would confer with the Chief of the Secret Service and with the Director of the FBI for the purpose of working out details of an investigation of Nazi activities.

[5] On December 2, 1938, Johanna Hofmann was sentenced to four years; Otto Voss, to six years; and Erich Glaser and Rumrich each to two years.

[6] Duquesne was born in 1877 in South Africa, educated in the Belgium Military Academy at Brussels and, according to his own statements, served as a spy with the Boer Army. He came to the United States in 1902 and later became a naturalized citizen. Duquesne was actively pro-German during World War I. A federal warrant was issued for Duquesne in 1918 based on a complaint filed by the British Consul General in New York City asking for the extradition of Duquesne to England on charges of murder and attempting to sink and destroy the British SS *Tennyson*. Duquesne, aged seventy-eight, died in May, 1956, in a New York welfare hospital.

19: FDR SIGNALS "THUMBS DOWN"

[1] The indictments returned by the Federal Grand Jury on February 3, 1940, charged sixteen people with conspiracy (Section 88, Title 18, U. S. C.) to violate the statute against enlisting persons in the United States to fight in foreign conflicts. (Section 22, Title 18, U. S. C.)

[2] Gurnea, a native of San Francisco, was appointed a Special Agent in 1934. After serving in the field and on the headquarters staff, he was made an Inspector in 1938. Gurnea drowned in the Potomac River on August 19, 1950. Bugas, a native of Wyoming and a graduate of the University of Wyoming Law School, was appointed a Special Agent in March, 1935. He served as Special Agent in Charge of FBI offices in Alaska, Birmingham and Detroit. He resigned from the Bureau on January 15, 1944, to go with the Ford Motor Company, where he is now Vice President in Charge of Industrial Relations. A December 22, 1955, Boston *Globe* headline said, "FBI Paid Bugas $6,500, Ford Salary $183,785."

[3] In the fiscal year ending June 30, 1924, Bureau personnel totaled 657, of which 441 were agents and 216 were clerks. By the end of the next fiscal year, the personnel had dropped to 501, of whom 402 were agents and 99 were clerks. In a request for appropriations for fiscal 1941, the records later

disclosed that the agents' force was increased to 4,272—representing a 137 percent increase over fiscal 1938, while appropriations increased 134 percent and the work load increased 327.7 percent in the same period.

[4] The FBI found support among members of both Houses of Congress, editorial writers, newspaper columnists, radio commentators and private citizens. The dean of Washington commentators, Earl Godwin, summed up the general feeling of those supporting the FBI in his NBC broadcast of March 13, 1940, when he said, "In the meantime—I believe much of the attack on Hoover is not well intentioned—but is the result of a maudlin idea that civil liberties are at stake—wherever the G-man invades civil liberty he is wrong. . . . But wherever the enemies of this country gain the ear of well-known liberals to plead a cause which this morning has come closer to our shores through the ravaging of Finland, then I say it's time we awoke. In many cases an attack on Hoover is an attack on the President of the United States—and what's more, an attack on the safety of the government."

[5] At this time Henry Schweinhaut was a Special Assistant to the Attorney General in charge of Civil Rights matters. On January 10, 1945, he was appointed to the Bench of the Federal District Court in the District of Columbia.

[6] The old charge was revived that the Bureau in 1920 under William J. Flynn had helped the State District Attorney at Boston "frame" the anarchists Nicola Sacco and Bartolomeo Vanzetti on a charge of murder, and that evidence had been suppressed which would have proved their innocence. In 1927, Attorney General John G. Sargent, Assistant Attorney General Oscar Luhring, and, later, Acting Attorney General George R. Farnum reviewed old Bureau files with Director Hoover. They found nothing in them reflecting on either the guilt or innocence of Sacco and Vanzetti, and that the Bureau's only role had been in the investigation of the Communists' influence in a world-wide propaganda drive to have the condemned men freed. An advisory Committee appointed by Governor Alvan T. Fuller of Massachusetts—consisting of President A. Lawrence Lowell of Harvard, President Samuel W. Stratton of M.I.T. and Judge Robert Grant—had previously upheld the decision of the trial judge. The appeals by Sacco and Vanzetti to the Supreme Court and to President Coolidge were denied. The men were executed on August 22, 1927.

[7] It is an interesting fact that some who publicly opposed wire tapping practiced it privately. One newspaper which condemned wire tapping editorially scored a beat on the outbreak of World War II by intercepting phone calls with the help of a telephone girl. The paper had a special reporter who, according to his own words, "persuaded the telephone operator here to either plug me in, or if that isn't possible, to listen in and report to me on all telephone calls . . ." to a Cabinet officer. The reporter got the details of a telephone call from FDR to the Cabinet officer "at four A.M., fifteen minutes after . . ." FDR called advising that Poland was at war with Germany. In the same manner, the paper had another scoop on England's declaration of war one hour before the late Prime Minister Neville Chamberlain's

speech was broadcast. How is this known? The reporter wrote his boss and the letter was picked out of a wastepaper basket by one who thought it wasn't cricket to listen in on the President's conversations with a Cabinet member. He took the letter to the FBI, which blocked further interception of calls.

[8] The existence of a wire tap was disclosed by which telephone conversations of the Mayor of Pawtucket, Rhode Island, were being intercepted by his political foes. J. Howard McGrath, then a United States Attorney and later to become a United States Senator and Attorney General, pushed an FBI investigation requested by the Federal Communications Commission. When the Department of Justice declined prosecution, a Senate investigation of the incident was made. But those who had done the wire tapping then denounced the FBI investigation as a "secret police" action.

[9] The new regulations for carrying out FDR's order, based upon Hoover's recommendations, required a specific justification for each wire tap be made in writing to the Attorney General. The Attorney General would personally approve or disapprove, except that in his absence, the Deputy Attorney General could grant such authorization to the FBI. The Director of the FBI is the only head of a federal intelligence or investigative agency who does not install wire taps on his own authority.

[10] The late Secretary of Interior Harold L. Ickes later denounced the FBI's action in tapping a telephone in an espionage case as ". . . 'Peeping Tomism' and door crack listening in order to pick up envious or malicious gossip to be used against Government employees and others who are denied their constitutional right to defend themselves." A few years earlier Louis R. Glavis, who once headed the Interior Department's investigative staff, testified before the Senate Public Lands Committee that wire tapping of Interior Department telephones was started after he discussed with Secretary Ickes leaks of confidential information. Ickes testified at these same hearings, however, that when he heard of the tappings, he stopped them.

20: THE FBI GOES TO WAR

[1] The Pearl Harbor attack resulted in 3,435 casualties of Armed Service personnel. Eight battleships, three light cruisers, three destroyers and four miscellaneous vessels were lost or severely damaged. In addition, 188 American planes were destroyed. Japanese losses were twenty-nine planes and five midget submarines.

[2] Robert L. Shivers entered on duty as a Special Agent on April 23, 1920, and voluntarily resigned on June 30, 1944. In addition to heading the Honolulu office, he had served as Special Agent in Charge at Little Rock, Pittsburgh, Buffalo and Miami. The strain of his work during and after the Japanese attack was believed to have caused a heart attack in 1942. After his resignation, Shivers was named Collector of Customs in Hawaii and served in that position until his death on June 28, 1950.

[3] There were 16,062 enemy aliens arrested during World War II. Of this number, 7,043 were German aliens, among whom 1,225 were interned;

2,449 were paroled; 2,589 were released; 691 were repatriated; and 47 died. Dispositions were unresolved in 42 of the cases. The Japanese aliens arrested totaled 5,428. Of these, 1,532 were interned; 2,423 were paroled; 955 were released; 415 were repatriated; and 88 died. In 15 of these cases the dispositions were unresolved. The number of Italian aliens arrested was 3,567. Of this number, 367 were interned; 861 were paroled; 2,237 were released; 87 were repatriated; and 14 died. There was one case in which the disposition was unresolved. These figures include 802 German seamen and 1,271 Italian seamen who were apprehended before the United States entered the war. In addition, 24 Hungarian, Bulgarian and Rumanian alien enemies were apprehended. Of these, 8 were paroled and 15 were released. The disposition in one case was unresolved.

There were 25,881 searches of enemy-alien premises, where 3,127 shortwave radios; 2,240 sticks of dynamite; 4,626 firearms; 306,247 rounds of ammunition; and other items of contraband were seized.

⁴ The Office of Censorship was closed and the operation ended on August 15, 1945.

⁵ The Secretaries of War and Navy wrote letters to all Bureau agents and officials holding reserve commissions, including Lieutenant Colonel Hoover and Commander Tolson, asking them to resign their commissions "in the interest . . . of utilizing every man in the capacity in which he can contribute the most to the national defense effort . . ." Draft deferments were requested only for those Bureau personnel whose services were deemed vital to the FBI.

⁶ On January 23, 1942, the commission headed by Associate Supreme Court Justice Owen J. Roberts reported to President Roosevelt about its hearings on the Pearl Harbor attack. The report said, "Efforts were made by the Bureau to uncover espionage activities in Hawaii . . ."; however, ". . . restrictions imposed prevented resort to certain methods of obtaining the content of messages transmitted by telephone or radio telegraph over the commercial lines operating between Oahu and Japan." The report said that the Bureau and the Army and Navy intelligence services were unable to obtain significant data on Japanese war plans prior to December 7, 1941.

⁷ The FBI has never doubted its legal position on wire tapping in view of the legal authorities who have ruled that the President has the authority to direct the FBI to utilize wire taps. Among the legal authorities who approved such action were the late Supreme Court Justices Frank Murphy and Robert H. Jackson; former Circuit Court of Appeals Judge Francis Biddle; Circuit Judge Charles Fahey; Supreme Court Justice Tom C. Clark; former Solicitor General, Senator and Attorney General J. Howard McGrath; and former Federal Judge James P. McGranery. These rulings on wire tapping have all been concurred in by Attorney General Herbert Brownell, Jr.

21: ESPIONAGE, LIMITED

¹ In the Pearl Harbor investigations, Chairman Fly explained the FCC's position in a memorandum which said: "The United States was at peace

with Japan prior to the attack on Pearl Harbor on December 7, 1941, and the Communications Act of 1934, under which the Federal Communications Commission was organized and from which it derives its powers, prohibited the tapping of wires or other interception of messages transmitted between points in the United States, including its territories, and a foreign country. Since that prohibition upon the Commission had not been in any way superseded, the Commission did not intercept any messages over the radio-telegraph, cable telegraph or radiotelephone circuits between the United States (including Hawaii) and Japan prior to December 7, 1941." In court cases wherein the issue of wire tapping has been raised no court as yet has ruled that the original wire-tapping authority issued by FDR was illegal. The FCC Act penalized the interception and divulgence of messages and legal experts have ruled that there is no divulgence within the meaning of the law when FBI agents report information intercepted from a wire tap only to their superiors and appropriate authorities of the executive branch of the government.

[2] Special Agent in Charge Shivers, of the FBI Honolulu office, told the Roberts Commission in the first Pearl Harbor inquiry: "If we had been able to get the messages that were sent to Japan by the Japanese Consul, we would have known, or we could have reasonably assumed, that the attack would come, somewhere, on December 7; because, if you recall, this system of signals that was devised by Otto Kuehn for the Japanese Consul General simply included the period from December 1 to December 6."

[3] Kuehn served at Leavenworth Penitentiary from December 1, 1942, until June 6, 1946, when his sentence was commuted in order to deport him to Germany. He was confined at Ellis Island, New York, until his parole was ordered on July 29, 1948. He voluntarily departed from the United States to Buenos Aires, Argentina, on December 3, 1948.

[4] On March 13, 1942, Ludwig and his eight confederates were sentenced in the United States District Court in New York City. Ludwig received a sentence of twenty years, as did Borchardt and René C. Froehlich. Fifteen-year sentences were given to Helen Pauline Mayer, Karl Victor Mueller and Hans Helmut Pagel. Frederick Edward Schlosser was given a twelve-year sentence, while Carl Herman Schroetter received a ten-year sentence. Lucy Rita Boehmler received a five-year sentence.

[5] One of the dots brought by the Balkan agent bore the message: "There is reason to believe that the scientific works for the utilization of atomic-kernel energy are being driven forward into a certain direction in the United States partly by use of helium. Continuous information about the tests made on this subject are required and particularly: 1. What process is practiced in the United States for transporting heavy uranium? 2. Where are being made tests with uranium? (Universities, industrial laboratories, etc.) 3. Which other raw materials are being used in these tests? Entrust only best experts with this."

[6] The Abwehr was the intelligence department of the Nazi General Staff. It had the responsibility for handling assignments of espionage, sabotage and subversion, counterespionage and security. It was headed by Admiral Wil-

helm Canaris until he was dismissed by Hitler in February, 1944. The Abwehr was then transferred to the National Police organization under Heinrich Himmler.

[7] The first Long Island radio installation was established on December 4, 1941, and until the final radio contact with Germany was received on May 8, 1945, a total of 2,829 messages were transmitted to Germany in connection with the several double-agent cases involving these installations. The Germans sent 824 messages.

[8] The Nazis sent money, diamond rings, diamonds, expensive watches and other valuables to the United States to finance their espionage. The wife of one agent tried to smuggle in $10,000 hidden in her girdle. A seaman courier hid a large bill in his bridgework. All such valuables seized by the FBI were turned over to W. R. Glavin, then Assistant Director of the FBI's Administrative Division, whose final accounting showed that $366,125 in cash and valuables had been seized from German Intelligence agents and turned over to the Treasury Department. Glavin retired in 1954 after twenty-three years of service.

[9] During the war years, espionage, sabotage and internal security cases were handled by the Domestic Intelligence Division headed by D. M. Ladd, who entered the FBI after his graduation from The George Washington Law School in 1928. Ladd became an Assistant to the Director in 1949 and retired in 1954 after some twenty-six years with the FBI. He was a son of the late Senator Ladd of North Dakota. When Ladd was placed in charge of the Domestic Intelligence Division, Stanley J. Tracy succeeded him as Assistant Director of the Identification Division. Tracy joined the FBI in 1933 and retired in 1954.

[10] In 1945, President Spyros Skouras of Twentieth-Century Fox backed Producer Louis deRochemont in making a feature-length documentary film called *The House on 92nd Street,* which used the Long Island radio operation as the theme to portray the FBI's experiences in combating espionage in World War II.

22: WHY THE SABOTEURS FAILED

[1] The FBI learned the full story of the German High Command's worry over the breakdown of its intelligence system in the United States, and the plan to send the saboteurs across the Atlantic by submarine, after the war, from Hermann Goering, Lieutenant Commander Heinrich Dietrich Wilhelm Ahlrichs, an Abwehr officer, and other German officers. These interviews supplied the parts of the story not told by the saboteurs themselves.

² The conversation on the beach between Dasch and Cullen is taken from the stories which these men gave to FBI agents who interviewed them.

³ The question frequently is raised as to why the FBI does not destroy its files when an investigation is completed. The case of the Nazi saboteurs and similar cases during World War II illustrate the value of holding such files indefinitely. A file jacket may not be opened for ten or twenty years, but it often happens that the file is suddenly found to be valuable in solving a crime or in security investigations. In some respects, the FBI's files are similar to the libraries on which newspapers depend for background information on individuals and events.

⁴ The trial of the saboteurs was held in a classroom in the Justice Department Building, the same classroom used by the FBI for many years for training its special agents. The military tribunal hearing the case was headed by Major General Frank R. McCoy. Other members were Major Generals Walter S. Grant, Blanton Winship and Lorenzo D. Gasser; and Brigadier Generals Guy V. Henry, John T. Lewis and John T. Kennedy. The prosecution was conducted by Attorney General Francis Biddle and Judge Advocate General Myron C. Cramer. The defense was handled by Colonels Cassius M. Dowell and Kenneth Royall. The tribunal and the defense counsels were appointed by President Roosevelt. The eight saboteurs were found guilty and sentenced to death. However, Hoover and Biddle recommended to the President that Dasch and Burger be shown leniency and as a result Dasch received a sentence of thirty years while Burger was sentenced to life imprisonment.

In 1948, President Truman commuted the prison terms of Dasch and Burger and they were immediately deported to Germany.

⁵ Doenitz's anger was reported by Lieutenant Commander Ahlrichs in a postwar interview.

⁶ After being turned over to military authorities upon instructions of the Attorney General, William Curtis Colepaugh and Erich Gimpel were tried by a Military Commission at Governor's Island, New York. On February 14, 1945, they were found guilty of violating the 82nd Article of War. Their sentence to death by hanging was subsequently commuted by the President to life imprisonment. Colepaugh was sent to the U. S. Penitentiary at Leavenworth, Kansas. Gimpel was paroled from prison and deported to Germany in August, 1955.

23: THE PERILOUS FIGHT SOUTH OF
THE BORDER

¹ Four agents were killed in carrying out their missions, all in airplane crashes. They were Assistant Director Percy J. Foxworth and Special Agent Harold D. Haberfeld (in Dutch Guiana); Special Agent J. Cordes Delworth (Argentina) and Special Agent Quenton H. Plunkett (Colombia).

² Fuhrmann and twelve other leaders of the German plot were arrested by Uruguayan authorities. He was given a sentence of thirteen years and

five of his associates received prison terms ranging from five to twelve years. The others were released.

[3] An SIS school, to train agents for foreign assignment, was set up by the FBI. Agents were given instruction in the history and customs of the country to which they were being sent. They were briefed on Nazi espionage and sabotage techniques and given technical training in codes, ciphers and laboratory methods. At first efforts were made to enlist agents who could speak Spanish or Portuguese, but eventually, as the volume of agents sent increased, special language schools were opened. Here agents were given an intensive course in conversational Spanish or Portuguese.

[4] Probably British ship *Eskdalegate*.

[5] Immediately after these arrests the Berlin radio began to attack Brazil and to threaten reprisals. Soon five Brazilian ships had been sunk by German submarines. On August 22, 1942, Brazil declared war on the Axis powers.

[6] An example of the unpreparedness of South American countries to cope with espionage and sabotage problems is found in the case of Chile's prosecution of a spy ring known as the PYL organization. The only statute under which subversive activities could be prosecuted was the Electrical Services Law, which prohibited the clandestine installation of a radio transmitter. The person who installed a secret station was guilty of a law violation —but those who used the station for espionage were not breaking the law.

24: OUTSMARTING THE ENEMY

[1] It is used in the breaker points in ignition systems, in the production of explosives and in electrical equipment. It is also an essential element in keeping ignition and electrical systems for airplanes, tanks, trucks, automobiles and other motor-driven vehicles operating at top efficiency.

[2] The National Intelligence Authority at the outset in 1946 was composed of Dean Acheson, Acting Secretary of State; John L. Sullivan, Acting Secretary of the Navy; Robert P. Patterson, Secretary of War; and Admiral William D. Leahy, personal representative of the President.

[3] The final accounting of the FBI's operations in Central and South America revealed that from July 1, 1940, until March 31, 1947:

A total of 887 espionage agents were identified, of whom 389 were arrested and 105 convicted; 281 propaganda agents were identified and 60 arrested; 30 sabotage agents were identified and 20 arrested. A total of 222 smugglers of war materials were identified, 75 arrested and 11 convicted. A total of 7,064 enemy aliens were moved from strategic areas; 2,172 were either interned or sent to a secure locale; 5,893 were either deported or expelled. Firms or persons placed on the list of blocked nationals totaled 1,545.

A total of twenty-four clandestine radio stations were located, and thirty radio transmitters were confiscated by local authorities. In addition, contraband materials seized by local authorities, ranging from diamonds, code books, mercury and other precious metals to pharmaceutical supplies, reached a staggering total.

25: THE PRINCESS WAS NO PAUPER

[1] Like many of the intrigues of World War II, nothing came of the peace plans hatched in San Francisco; however, the FBI sent reports on the "peace talks" to the President, as well as to the State and Treasury Departments, on November 29 and 30, 1940.

[2] The Princess gave a twenty-four-page statement to the Immigration and Naturalization Service on July 31, 1941. This statement referred to her early years; her work for Lord Rothermere; her contacts with the Nazis; and her efforts as an intermediary between Fritz Wiedemann and Sir John. This statement was made available to the Attorney General and the FBI.

26: A CONTRAST IN WARS

[1] This policy was effective. By September 1, 1945, the FBI had handled 277,589 cases which resulted in 190,178 men complying with the Act. A total of 12,674 evaders were prosecuted and convicted in Federal Courts. In the remaining cases, it was established that there was no violation; the person involved had been prosecuted on other grounds, or was deceased or insane.

[2] At the request of the Armed Services, the FBI undertook to locate those men who were designated as deserters by the Army, Navy and Air Force. From the time the program started in February, 1945, until June 30, 1956, the FBI received 123,615 cases. All but 1,920 were located by the FBI, local police and military authorities. Some returned voluntarily. It was a common occurrence for agents to find that a so-called deserter was actually in some other outfit, had joined another branch of the service, was already in custody or had just overstayed his leave.

[3] The FBI's jurisdiction is based upon Section 286, Title 18, U.S. Code, which carries penalties of ten years' imprisonment or a $10,000 fine, or both, following conviction for conspiring to defraud the government. From the beginning of the 1941 fiscal year through fiscal 1946, FBI investigations resulted in 1,002 convictions on charges of conspiracy to defraud the government. These convictions resulted in sentences of 1,395 years, six months and seventeen days, while fines totaling $1,219,351 were imposed. Savings and recoveries in these cases totaled $12,447,338.

[4] Amerigo Antonelli was sentenced to serve two years and fined $5,000. As for his associates, John and Joseph DeRitis were both given two-year terms, while Bennie Piteo, Dominick Barbollo and Frank Bianchi each received eighteen-month sentences. The sentences of Piteo and Bianchi were suspended and each was placed on probation for one year. The Antonelli Fireworks Company was fined $10,000.

[5] On May 3, 1944, five officials and employees of the Collyer Insulated Wire Company entered pleas of guilty to charges of fraud against the government. Joseph Lovell, Frederick A. McManus and Frederick L. Lawton were given fines of $5,000. Clarence Vigeant and Adolf P. Czerniawski were fined $2,500. A fine of $10,000 was assessed against the corporation. The

government went to court seeking a recovery of funds from the company because of 105 false claims. On October 9, 1950, the Federal District Court at Providence, Rhode Island, awarded a judgment to the government of $210,412.

[6] In the postwar era from fiscal 1946 through 1956, the investigation by the FBI of the renegotiation of war contracts resulted in claims being adjusted in favor of the government totaling $323,121,491. During the same period, FBI investigations in Court of Claims cases, in which the government is the defendant in civil suits, often resulted in uncovering discrepancies in the plaintiffs' claims which brought about savings and recoveries to the government totaling $171,198,211.

[7] The first prisoner of war escape in the United States in World War II was reported to the FBI on May 19, 1943. The last escape in the United States occurred on November 7, 1946. Between these dates, a total of 2,803 POW's escaped in this country. Of these, all except Kurt Rossmeisl, Georg Gaertner and Curt Westphal have been located. With the exception of exchanged sick and wounded POW's, the principal repatriation of German and Italian prisoners began in August, 1945.

27: POSTWAR CRIME

[1] During the war years Hoover frequently pointed to a breakdown in the standards of moral conduct and attributed this to the wartime philosophy which developed an attitude of impermanence. He feared a return of gangs and a regrouping of old alliances between rackets, the underworld and politicians. His predictions were borne out by the revelations of the Senate Committee investigating crime headed by Senator Estes Kefauver. This Committee also highlighted the breakdown of law and order in some communities and the fact that criminals had moved into legitimate business enterprises from which they operated on a "white collar" basis.

[2] In 1950, there was a hue and cry for federal intervention in many cases. Hoover opposed extending federal crime laws, as he saw in the clamor an attempt by some local officials to alibi for their own failure to act and an effort to shift responsibility from the local to the national level. He emphasized in an address to a Boys' Club meeting in Washington, D. C., on May 18, 1950, that there was no need for a national police force and that law enforcement was primarily the job of the local community. He added: "There is not a city, town, or hamlet in the nation which could not strike a telling blow against the forces of lawlessness within 48 hours if its people had the will and determination to eradicate the breeding places of crime."

28: TO SECURE THESE RIGHTS

[1] Now Section 242, Title 18, U. S. Code.
[2] Screws, *et al.*, v. U. S., 140 F. 2nd 662 (1944); 325 United States 91 (1945).
[3] U. S. v. Harris, 106 U. S. 629 (1882).

[4] The FBI has made a major contribution in protecting civil rights through its FBI National Academy and the 23,419 police training schools operated on the local level since 1945. With the growing racial tensions, the FBI experimented with a specialized Civil Rights School for police in late 1955 and then launched a country-wide program of Civil Rights Training Schools early in 1956, when 420 schools were held in the first six months. These schools have been well received and supported by local, county and state authorities, and as this is being written, the FBI reports that among the 21,980 officers attending the schools, not one of them has been involved in a civil rights accusation.

[5] At the time the Shivers complaint was made, the FBI notified the heads of agencies and institutions that an inquiry was being made. Since May of 1954 the heads of agencies and institutions are notified and the governor of the state is also given notice, to avoid any misunderstanding about what the FBI is doing and why.

[6] During the fiscal year 1956, the FBI handled 1,231 allegations of civil rights violations. This was a decline of 44 cases over the previous year.

In the 17 years which the FBI has been investigating civil rights violations growing out of acts of violence, a total of 39 lynchings have occurred as contrasted to 317 lynchings in the 17 year period preceding FBI investigations. In the last four years, not a single lynching has been reported.

29: THE GREAT ILLUSION

[1] This information was given and accepted by the FBI in the strictest confidence. Mr. A's membership in the Party wasn't disclosed until he voluntarily disclosed it himself.

[2] The State Department was called upon late in 1923 by a Subcommittee of the Senate Foreign Relations Committee to present its position on the recognition of Soviet Russia. Secretary of State Charles Evans Hughes requested J. Edgar Hoover, then Assistant Director of the Bureau, to prepare the brief for his use on Communist activities in the United States. Young Hoover's brief, supported by original documents, traced the interlocking relationship and control of Soviet Russia over the Third International and Communist leaders in the United States in the preparation and advocacy of the use of force and violence to obtain Communist ends. Hoover sat with Secretary Hughes at the witness table, and their presentation was neither controverted nor denied by Communist leaders in the United States or abroad. The Senate Foreign Relations Subcommittee refrained from acting favorably on the Senate resolution to recognize Soviet Russia.

[3] In a 1938 address Hoover pointed out, "Both communism and fascism are the anti-theses of American belief in liberty and democracy . . . There can be no room in this country for these destructive anarchic or despotic cults. Fascism has always grown in the slimy wastes of communism. . . . Our Nation cannot exist half American and half alien in spirit."

[4] Reliable figures now show that at the time of the November Revolution

there were only 80,000 members of the Communist Party in the Soviet Union and that this represented a 100 percent increase in eight months. The population of Russia when the Communists overthrew the government was about 142,000,000.

⁵ On October 23, 1939, Browder was arrested for a passport violation and on the following day was released on bail. While free, he carried on an active campaign as the Communist Party candidate in the 1940 Presidential elections. He was subsequently convicted in federal court and sentenced to serve a prison term of four years and pay $2,000 in fines. This conviction was upheld by the Supreme Court, and on March 27, 1941, he began serving his term at the Atlanta Penitentiary. On May 16, 1942, President Roosevelt commuted Browder's sentence.

⁶ From its inception in 1919 to the present time, the Communist Party, USA, has changed its name ten times.

⁷ In August, 1948, Mrs. Oksana Kosenkina leaped from the third floor of the Soviet Consulate in New York City in a desperate escape attempt. She was rescued and removed from the scene over the protests of Lomakin, then Soviet Consul General in New York. As a result of his actions in this case, Lomakin was declared persona non grata by the State Department for his "highly improper conduct."

⁸ The United Nations Conference, in San Francisco, which began on April 25, 1945, brought the first major public clash between the Soviet Union and the United States. The basis of the clash was the seating of the Argentine delegation and the refusal to seat the Lublin Provisional Government delegation as the representative of Poland. The leaders of the Communist Political Association promptly attacked the American UN delegation.

30: THE AWAKENING

¹ The first list of organizations declared subversive by the Department of Justice was sent to all FBI field offices in a directive dated September 15, 1941. The 8 organizations on the original list were: the Communist Party, USA; the German-American Bund; the American Peace Mobilization; the Washington Committee for Democratic Action; the Michigan Federation for Constitutional Liberties; the National Federation for Constitutional Liberties; the American Youth Congress; and the National Negro Congress.

² From 1940 until the start of the Loyalty Program on March 21, 1947, 6,296 cases were considered under the Hatch Act. The cases were disposed of in the following manner: employees discharged, 114; action other than dismissal, 78; resigned during investigation, 46; no longer in government, 1,963; no action, 2,818; complaint disproven, 1,144; no dispositions received, 90. Forty-three were later handled under the Loyalty Program.

³ The FBI was required in the postwar period to make applicant investigations for the Atomic Energy Commission; the Office of Civil Defense, District of Columbia; Foreign Aid Programs; the National Security Resources Board; the Voice of America; and others. Upon recommendation of the FBI, the Attorney General, on August 23, 1951, requested Congress to

relieve the FBI of making applicant-type investigations, and Congress enacted Public Law 298, 82nd Congress, which transferred to the Civil Service Commission the bulk of such investigations. This law became effective October 2, 1952. The FBI is still required to make investigations involving highly sensitive positions in the AEC, and others such as federal judges, U. S. attorneys, Department of Justice employees, presidential appointees and others as requested by higher authority in the executive branch of the government.

[4] Applicant investigations are made by the investigative divisions of various government agencies, such as the Civil Service Commission, Naval Intelligence, the Office of Special Investigations of the Air Force, the State Department, the CIA, G-2, the Treasury and the Post Office Department.

[5] On February 26, 1950, the CIO expelled the UPWA on the ground that its policies and activities ". . . are consistently directed toward the achievement of the program and the purposes of the Communist Party . . ."

[6] On December 15, 1948, a Federal Grand Jury in New York City indicted Alger Hiss for perjury. His first trial, which began the following May, resulted in a hung jury, but in the second trial, held in November, 1949, Hiss was convicted and sentenced to serve five years on each of two counts. In November, 1954, Hiss was released from prison.

Whittaker Chambers, summing up the Hiss case in his book *Witness* (Random House, 1952), states: "Those were the forces—Thomas Murphy [now Federal District Judge], Richard Nixon [now Vice President], the men of the F.B.I.—who, together with the two grand juries and Tom Donegan and the two trial juries, finally won the Hiss Case for the nation."

[7] From March 21, 1947, through May 27, 1953, under the Loyalty Program the FBI processed 4,660,122 sets of fingerprints, 8.5 percent of which were identified with previous records in Identification files; 4,756,705 loyalty forms were checked and 99.4 percent were returned marked "No Disloyal Data"; 26,236 full field investigations were conducted; and 26,833 preliminary inquiries were made to make certain that information received by the FBI referred to a government employee and not someone else with the same name. The Civil Service Commission reported that the 26,236 full field investigations were disposed of in the following manner: persons removed or denied federal employment, 560; resigned or applications withdrawn, 6,828; considered under Security Legislation by Army, 569; cleared by favorable decision as to loyalty, 16,503; subsequently processed under Federal Employees Security Program, 1,776.

[8] Perhaps the heaviest attack on the informant system involved Harvey M. Matusow, a former Communist Party member who supplied information to the FBI from June to December, 1950, when he was dropped. He later testified before committees of Congress and in several court trials as a government witness. Then in January, 1955, he announced publicly that he had given false testimony in two Communist trials and in several Congressional hearings. The Senate Internal Security Subcommittee in a report on the Matusow case disclosed that 90 percent of the persons Matusow identified as Communists to the Department of Justice were also so identified by other

evidence and that the Department found no information to disprove the identification of the remaining 10 percent.

Of the Matusow case, Attorney General Herbert Brownell, Jr. said, "The Matusow case is unique. It is part of the concerted drive to discredit Government witnesses, the security program, and ultimately our system of justice."

[9] On January 4, 1949, a full field loyalty investigation was opened on Judith Coplon. This was converted to an espionage investigation on January 16, 1949, after FBI agents observed a clandestine meeting between the Department of Justice employee and Valentine A. Gubitchev, who was attached to the Soviet U.N. Mission. Another clandestine meeting was covered by FBI agents on March 4, 1949, from 7:57 P.M. until 9:36 P.M., despite their efforts to use "evasive tactics" and avoid being watched. The two were arrested by FBI agents on orders of Attorney General Tom C. Clark. They were both indicted in New York City and Coplon was also indicted in Washington, D. C., on espionage charges. Coplon was convicted in Federal Court at both places and Gubitchev was returned to Russia.

The New York conviction was reversed on the grounds that Coplon was arrested without a warrant and the likelihood of escape was not established, and that the trial judge had erred in not giving the defense access to all records containing intercepted communications and had failed to allow the defense an opportunity to develop information to determine whether the original informant was a wire tap. Congress promptly amended the statute, giving the FBI authority to make arrests in such cases in the future. In the District of Columbia case the Court of Appeals remanded the conviction for a hearing to determine if the conversations of Coplon and the attorney were intercepted, which would be grounds for a new trial.

[10] A survey on June 26, 1956, disclosed that in the thirty-eight years since 1918, the FBI has opened a total of 4,742,000 individual files. These included 522,000 old files on German and related matters in World War I; 414,000 Selective Service files; 425,785 applicant-type investigations for the Atomic Energy Commission; 498,000 Bureau and Departmental applicant files; 126,000 files dealing with Armed Forces desertions; 211,000 cases involving Interstate Transportation of Stolen Motor Vehicles; 427,000 Internal Security files; and 104,465 files on cases dealing with government administration. The remaining 2,013,750 files cover investigations opened under 148 different categories, including general correspondence and housekeeping files.

[11] The necessity for the FBI and other investigative agencies to accept information regardless of its source was pointed out by Rex Collier of the Washington *Evening Star,* who said:

> If the FBI were to be restricted on the sort of information it could accept and enter in its records, its efficiency as the Nation's chief bulwark against foreign espionage would be greatly impaired. And if such restrictions were proper for the FBI, they would be proper also for the Central Intelligence Agency and the naval and military intelligence branches. The effect would be to hamstring our security forces in a most dangerous way.

[12] The FBI does not evaluate the results of its investigations and Hoover has resisted moves to place the responsibility upon the FBI to draw conclu-

sions. In 1950 the House of Representatives was about to amend the National Science Foundation Bill by requiring the FBI to certify to the loyalty of each person investigated. Hoover's protest through the Attorney General was honored by Congress.

[13] In answer to insinuations that FBI files were being "leaked" to favored members of Congress, Hoover said: "I can say unequivocally that is an absolute lie . . . People like to throw the name of the FBI around. They wave a report and say 'this is from the FBI'—but the report was not furnished by the FBI."

31: THE ATTACK ON COMMUNISM

[1] National Chairman William Z. Foster was indicted also but was not tried because of illness.

[2] The Communist Party later recognized in their private conferences that a tactical mistake was made in permitting their top leaders to become fugitives from justice.

[3] As a result of his flight, Gus Hall was found guilty of contempt of court and was sentenced to three years' imprisonment, in addition to his five-year sentence for violation of the Smith Act.

[4] Arrested with Robert Thompson were Sidney Steinberg, Carl Rasi, Samuel Coleman and Mrs. Shirley Kremen. Steinberg had been indicted for violation of the Smith Act in June, 1951.

Thompson was sentenced to four years for contempt of court. Steinberg, Rasi, Coleman and Kremen were indicted on charges of acting as accessories after the fact to prevent Thompson's arrest and Rasi, Coleman and Kremen were also charged with harboring Steinberg. Steinberg and Coleman were sentenced to three years' imprisonment, Rasi to two years' and Kremen to one year's imprisonment.

[5] The Smith Act trials held throughout the country have resulted in 145 indictments and arrests; 108 convictions; 5 severances; and 10 acquittals. Two individuals were granted new trials after being convicted. Sentences in Smith Act cases total 418 years and one day, while fines in the amount of $435,500 have been imposed.

[6] The trial of seventeen Communist leaders began in New York City on April 15, 1952, and ended on January 21, 1953, with thirteen Communists found guilty. Alexander Bittelman, Elizabeth Gurley Flynn, V. J. Jerome, Arnold Johnson, Pettis Perry, Alexander Trachtenberg, and Louis Weinstock were each sentenced to three years' imprisonment and fined $6,000. George Blake Charney, Betty Gannett, Albert Lannon, Jacob Mindel and William Weinstone were each sentenced to two years and were fined $4,000. Claudia Jones was sentenced to one year and one day and fined $2,000.

Isidore Begun and Simon W. Gerson were acquitted by directed verdict. Israel Amter and Marion Bachrach were severed from trial due to illness. Amter later died, and Marion Bachrach was acquitted on June 18, 1956. Trachtenberg and Charney were granted new trials because of the alleged perjured testimony of government witness Harvey Matusow, although on

July 31, 1956, following a retrial in Federal Court they were again found guilty.

[7] Also known as McCarran Act because of the sponsorship of Senator Pat McCarran of Nevada, now deceased.

[8] The Internal Security Act of 1950, which was passed on September 23, 1950, specifically required registration with the Attorney General of all Communist-action and Communist-front organizations, as well as their officers. If the Communist-action organizations did not register within the specified time, each individual member was required to register with the Attorney General.

[9] In addition to the FBI, many other federal agencies have internal security responsibilities. The Immigration and Naturalization Service protects our borders from illegal entries and administers the immigration and naturalization laws; the Bureau of Customs has the responsibility of detecting smuggling activities and administering customs and navigation laws; the Commerce Department controls exports; the State Department handles passport control and entrance visas; the Federal Communications Commission detects clandestine radio transmitters; the Atomic Energy Commission handles the physical security of atomic energy installations; the Army, Navy, Air Force and Marines have responsibility for the security of their own installations and personnel, as well as industrial security of plants handling Armed Service contracts; the Central Intelligence Agency has the responsibility for coverage of intelligence matters outside the United States; the Civil Service Commission and the various individual agencies handle the adjudication of security and disloyalty charges involving federal employees; and the National Security Council has the responsibility of establishing overall security policies and has chartered numerous committees to handle specialized matters.

32: THE SCIENTIST AND THE STRANGER

[1] The FBI first became aware of the development of the atomic bomb, not through official government channels, but through its surveillance of West Coast Communist Party leaders in 1943. Comments were heard with increasing frequency by informants in Party circles concerning a new and powerful weapon, the use of uranium and the application of atomic theory to the development of the new weapon. The information was known to be leaking from a secret project at the University of California, where Party members had friendly contacts with some of the scientists. The FBI passed this information on to the Army. But on March 18, 1943, Major General George V. Strong, head of Military Intelligence, requested the FBI to discontinue its investigation of one of the scientists working at the University of California project. The Bureau's first official knowledge of the atomic project came on April 5, 1943, when General Strong confided to E. A. Tamm, then an Assistant to the Director, the Army's plans for protecting the top-secret development of the new weapon under the Manhattan Engineer District.

[2] The Delimitations Agreement which was signed on February 9, 1942, by the heads of Military Intelligence, Naval Intelligence and the FBI, provided that the War Department would be responsible for investigation of all of its civilian employees, as well as civilians on military reservations or under military control. The Manhattan Engineer District was under jurisdiction of the War Department. In a conference between representatives of G-2 and the FBI, on April 5, 1943, G-2 stated that it took complete responsibility for protective activities in connection with the MED project. This agreement was in effect until the Atomic Energy Commission, under the Atomic Energy Act of 1946, took over the MED project on January 1, 1947.

[3] Under the terms of the 1943 Quebec Conference, the United States, Britain and Canada agreed to collaborate as partners in the atomic field. Each was responsible for the security of its own personnel.

[4] Under the Atomic Energy Act of 1954, it is a criminal offense to disclose data concerning the design, manufacture or utilization of atomic weapons.

[5] Harry Gold was indicted by a Brooklyn grand jury on June 9, 1950, on a charge of conspiracy to violate the Espionage Act of 1917. He pleaded guilty in Philadelphia on July 20, 1950, and was sentenced by Federal Judge James P. McGranery on December 9, 1950, to thirty years' imprisonment. Alfred Dean Slack, a chemist from Syracuse, New York, pleaded guilty in Greeneville, Tennessee, on September 18, 1950, to a charge of espionage. As a member of a Soviet espionage ring in 1943–1944, he was accused of passing secrets of a high explosive to Harry Gold. He was sentenced on September 22, 1950, to fifteen years' imprisonment.

33: WORSE THAN MURDER

[1] Julius Rosenberg first requested Ruth to enlist David's help in securing information for the Soviets. She refused and then Ethel Rosenberg urged Ruth to relay their request to David and let him decide.

[2] While in New York, Rosenberg arranged for his Soviet contact to question Greenglass on the development of the atom bomb.

[3] During the trial of the Rosenbergs, Dr. Walter S. Koski, a nuclear chemist who worked at Los Alamos from 1944 to 1947, testified that he recalled seeing Greenglass in a machine shop where he, Koski, brought sketches of the flat-type lens in order to have molds made. He said the sketches of the lens made by Greenglass were reasonably accurate copies of those he had prepared; and these copies could have been of value to a foreign power in revealing to any expert what was going on at Los Alamos and the relation of the flat-type lens to the atom bomb.

[4] Greenglass testified that his wife used $1,000 of the money to pay household bills. Then he gave $4,000, wrapped in a brown-paper bag, to a brother-in-law to keep for him. He said this $4,000 was the money he sent to his lawyer after his arrest.

[5] The Government's prosecuting counsel were U. S. Attorney Irving H. Saypol and Assistant U. S. Attorneys Roy M. Cohn, Myles J. Lane, John M.

Foley, James B. Kilsheimer, III, and James E. Brannigan, Jr. Emanuel H. Bloch and his father, Alexander Bloch, represented the Rosenbergs. O. John Rogge was attorney for Greenglass. Harold M. Phillips and Edward Kuntz were counsel for Sobell.

[6] During the time that defense committees and propaganda campaigns were being organized for the convicted atom spies and appeals were being taken to the President and to the Supreme Court, Communist Party Secretary Khrushchev indicated that a directive was in effect in Russia which ordered:

I. Investigative agencies are directed to speed up the cases of those accused of the preparation or execution of acts of terror.

II. Judicial organs are directed not to hold up the execution of death sentences pertaining to crimes of this category in order to consider the possibility of pardon, because the Presidium of the Central Executive Committee USSR does not consider as possible the receiving of petitions of this sort.

III. The organs of the Commissariat of Internal Affairs are directed to execute the death sentences against criminals of the above-mentioned category immediately after the passage of sentences.

[7] In denying one of the many motions filed in this case, Federal Judge Sylvester Ryan observed, ". . . that full and complete enjoyment of the Constitutional rights of petitioners has been extended them and has in no way been denied or infringed." This ruling was upheld by the Circuit Court of Appeals (22 F. 2nd 666), and the U. S. Supreme Court upheld Judge Ryan by refusing to consider his ruling on two occasions (345 U. S. 965 and 1003).

34: THE SUM UP

[1] Since 1924, when Hoover was appointed Director, the cost of operating the FBI has totaled $983,179,844 while fines, savings and recoveries have totaled $1,390,093,138. In other words, the FBI balance sheet shows a net profit of $406,913,294. In addition, a total of 157,110 fugitives have been arrested and 226,087 convictions have been recorded in cases investigated by the FBI.

INDEX